Writing Windows™ Device Drivers

DANIEL A. NORTON

Addison-Wesley Publishing Company, Inc.

Reading, Massachusetts Menlo Park, California New York
Don Mills, Ontario Wokingham, England Amsterdam Bonn
Sydney Singapore Tokyo Madrid San Juan
Paris Seoul Milan Mexico City Taipei

Many of the designations used by manufacturers and sellers to distinguish their products are claimed as trademarks. Where those designations appear in this book, and Addison-Wesley was aware of a trademark claim, the designations have been printed in initial capital letters or all capital letters.

The author and publisher have taken care in preparation of this book, but make no expressed or implied warranty of any kind and assume no responsibility for errors or omissions. No liability is assumed for incidental or consequential damages in connection with or arising out of the use of the information or programs contained herein.

Library of Congress Cataloging-in-Publication Data

Norton, Daniel A.
    Writing Windows device drivers / Daniel A. Norton.
        p. cm.
    Includes index.
    ISBN 0-201-57795-X
    1. Microsoft Windows (Computer program) 2. DOS device drivers
(Computer programs) I. Title.
    QA76.76.W56N66 1992
    005.4′3—dc20   91-37279
                                                                  CIP

Cover design by Ned Williams
Set in 11-pt Century Schoolbook by Carol Woolverton, Lexington, Mass.

Sponsoring Editor: Julie Stillman
Project Editor: Elizabeth G. Rogalin
Production Coordinator: Kathy Traynor

6 7 8 9 10-MA-97969594
Sixth printing, May 1994

For Charles & Julian

CONTENTS

ACKNOWLEDGMENTS

Although only one name appears on the cover of this book, many people are responsible for making it possible.

I am very grateful to my publisher, to the staff at Addison-Wesley, and Gary Ferguson, my technical editor. I am a software developer by trade, and they have shown endless patience and understanding to this newcomer to the book publishing business.

I would like to thank all of the developers in the CompuServe forums who asked questions of me and encouraged me to find the answers. I am also deeply grateful to those who answered questions for me, when solutions to my own technical problems seemed impossible. I have found electronic correspondence to be the best method of expanding on my own limited experience; it allows me to share my experience with others and to review others' experiences which otherwise I would not have considered. The support provided by my peers in the various forums has proven many times more valuable and accurate than any paid support service.

Joel Diamond, of WUGNET, has proven to be an invaluable associate in assisting me in getting this book to you. Not only did he help me find a publisher for this book, but has consistently known who in the industry to send me to for any amount of third-party driver background information that I might need.

Terry Reed was very gracious in offering to prepare the figures for this book. His true artistic talent, however, is severely masked by my technical requirements for the figures.

I want to particularly thank a number of people who have provided a level of support and encouragement that previously I did not know was available. These people prefer to remain anonymous, but they know who they are.

Despite all of the assistance provided by others, the responsibility for any deficiencies is entirely mine.

CHAPTER

1

Introduction

Microsoft Windows Version 3 has become the environment of choice for running multiple applications on a personal computer. While many of the old DOS TSR programs remain, most users prefer the easy-to-use and consistent interface provided by Windows. Since its introduction, the number of products written for Windows has risen dramatically. With the removal of real mode and the improved performance and reliability of version 3.1, it is now clear that Windows has won the operating system wars.

Part of the reason for Windows' success lies in two key architectural strategies: standardization and encapsulation. With standardized programming interfaces, programs can take advantage of the sophisticated features offered by Windows. Although DOS has a certain level of standardization with its INT 21h interface, it is not totally effective for many DOS programs. In DOS, for example, there are no standards for drawing figures on the screen in graphics modes, accessing the keyboard scan codes, or for reading from and writing to the COM port. By standardizing the interfaces at higher levels, Windows provides a consistent and complete program interface.

A natural result of this standardization is encapsulation or, more specifically, hardware isolation. With a standardized interface to hardware, the application program no longer needs to be concerned with the type of hardware installed on a machine in which it is running. The application program is isolated from the hardware and does not need to be written with any specific hardware in mind. This applies not only to video display hardware but also to printers and serial communications ports.

A **device driver** is a distinct program module that is integrated with an operating system to provide a standard interface between an application program and an external device. Under the terms of this definition, DOS does offer a device driver interface—but it is much too simplified for today's complex applications and graphical program interfaces. Windows device drivers, in contrast, provide a much more sophisticated level of support and serve to isolate applications programs and device drivers more effectively from one another.

Application Programming

In DOS, there is often no distinction between application programming and device programming: DOS application programmers must be familiar with hardware issues in order to write product-quality software. In Windows, however, programmers can write applications without such low-level knowledge and thus avoid hardware issues.

Application programmers appreciate the Windows environment especially because it simplifies the task of the user interface. Now we can develop programs without being concerned about many of the hardware aspects that plagued us under DOS. The Windows environment offers us a standard interface by isolating application programmers from the details of the hardware.

With Windows, device programming can now be isolated from application programming. For most programmers, this means that a large portion of code that was formerly required to support certain video displays, printers, and so forth, can be discarded in favor of a standard programming interface. We can write user-interface code to the standard interface and the application will work with any device that is supported under Windows. Most Windows programs, for example, are written without regard to the type of video adapter used. Instead, the programs are written to the Windows interface, and the video device driver takes care of actually writing to the video adapter memory. Such programs will run equally well on EGA and VGA adapters. A spreadsheet programmer no longer needs to be concerned with how the video graphics hardware works.

Device Programming

All of this is not to say that the hardware-dependent code has somehow magically disappeared. Those of us who program at the lowest levels of the computer still have work to do; it is just isolated from the application program using a standard interface. Now we can write code to support a particular device, without having any idea how the user application works. The video device drivers for Windows work with any Windows program, but the developers at Microsoft certainly did not have to understand the details of all application programs that need video display.

Instead, Microsoft provides a standard interface for the application developer. Similarly, the device driver has a standard interface for working with Windows. By going through this standard interface, the device driver writer is isolated from application programs, just as the application programmer is isolated from device drivers. By adhering to the standard interface, the device driver programmer provides access to any application that also follows its own programming interface. Not only does this allow the application programmer to focus on application programming issues; it also allows the device programmer to focus on device interface issues.

The Windows device programmer now has a bigger responsibility. Since under DOS the application program and the device support program are often tightly integrated and interspersed, it is easy to change the device interface to the application program. Under Windows, this is no longer practical, since the same device driver may ultimately support thousands of different applications.

A Review of DOS Device Drivers

In DOS, there are two basic types of device drivers: block mode and character mode. Block mode device drivers handle the interface between DOS and devices that store files in the DOS file system format: hard disks and tapes, for example. Character mode device drivers include all other types of drivers: COM, LPT, keyboard, and so forth.

With both types, DOS always calls the device driver in order to read from or write data to the device. Device drivers can support DMA and/or interrupts, but no data is transferred to DOS unless DOS specifically calls the device driver to obtain the data. For example, when a program needs a keystroke, the keystroke is read only when the program specifically asks the device driver to read a keystroke. If the user presses a key when the program has not asked for one, the keystroke is saved until the program specifically requests it.

For applications under DOS, this type of interface is fine. In fact, Windows still uses this same interface to access block devices, such as when a file is opened or accessed. For some character devices under Windows, however, this type of interface is inappropriate. For example, if you have programmed a Windows application, then you know that keystrokes may be posted to the application as soon as the user presses any key on the keyboard. A Windows program does not specifically request a keystroke. The DOS approach to device drivers is clearly inappropriate for certain Windows devices.

Windows Device Drivers

Windows device drivers must support a more sophisticated, more complex interface in order to work properly with Windows programs. Since the interface to Windows is at such a high level, each device interfaces to Windows in a different way. For example, even though both the COM port and the keyboard can send data to a program, programs use these devices in very different ways. Programs typically accept data from the keyboard one keystroke at a time, but data from the COM port is often received a block at a time. Consequently, the two device drivers are written to interface with Windows in entirely different ways.

The Windows device driver architecture comes close to an object-oriented architecture with its standardization and isolation, but falls short due to the many different forms that device drivers can take. It is this variety of different device types that makes it difficult to discuss Windows device drivers in a general way. Figure 1-1 lists the different device types in Windows. Unlike the simple distinction between character and block mode DOS device drivers, the distinction among these drivers is at a much higher level.

The communication driver, for example, is responsible for both serial and parallel ports. This is because, at the application program level, the serial and parallel ports look very similar: They are used to transfer device data in 8-bit bytes, often a block at a time. The printer drivers are also defined at a higher level. They are written without concern for the physical interface to the printer—whether serial or parallel. Instead of getting a command to transfer a byte, a printer driver may be handed a bitmap, which the driver is responsible for taking and converting to the printer commands appropriate to the printer.

In this book, I have divided the types of drivers into four classes: system drivers, printer drivers, virtual device drivers, and nonstandard drivers.

Driver Type	Examples
Display driver	CGA EGA
Printer driver	HP/PCL Epson Fx ProPrinter
Network driver	NETBIOS IPX
Keyboard driver	XT AT Enhanced
Mouse device driver	Bus Serial
Communication driver	COM: 8250 COM: 8530 LPT: 8255
Sound driver	8254
Virtual device drivers	Virtual COM Virtual LPT Virtual Interrupt

FIGURE 1-1 Device Driver Types

System Drivers

The **system drivers** are the device drivers that are fully integrated into the Windows system. These drivers include those for the display, the network, the keyboard, the COM and LPT ports, the mouse, and sound. These drivers are distinguished from, say, printer drivers, in that they are directly associated with attached system hardware. System drivers run at privileged levels within Windows and are actually linked into Windows when Windows is first loaded. The hardware that they support is found in almost all systems, and they offer little room for customization.

Printer Drivers

Printer drivers are written at a higher level within the Windows environment. Instead of communicating with printer port hardware directly, they depend on a system driver to perform hardware I/O instructions. Printer drivers convert bitmap and font data to a form appropriate to the attached printer and are more concerned with the actual type of printer attached to the system. For example, the commands sent to an HP LaserJet III are quite different from the commands sent to an Epson FX-85. Therefore, different drivers are provided to support the two different types of printers. Both printers can be connected to a standard parallel port, so the printer drivers do not include code for programming the parallel port hardware.

A large number of printer drivers are provided with Windows, and quite a few more are available from third parties. If you are interested in writing a printer driver, you may wish to check with the printer manufacturer to see if one is already available.

Virtual Device Drivers

Virtual device drivers (VxDs) are probably different from any type of device driver that you may have encountered. They are treated separately from other device drivers within Windows and by this book. They should probably be called device emulation drivers, since they actually emulate hardware rather than provide a software interface to hardware. For a proper understanding of virtual device drivers, it is necessary to understand the virtual 8086 mode of the 80386 processor, which is discussed in detail in the next chapter.

For now, it is important to know that virtual device drivers are used only in the 386 enhanced mode of Windows running on an 80386 CPU.

Although only one physical instance of a type of hardware (for example, a COM port) exists on a machine, virtual device drivers allow all DOS boxes to access the hardware (although not necessarily all at the same time).

Nonstandard Drivers

Microsoft's Windows Device Development Kit (DDK) describes how to write drivers only for the types of devices shown in Figure 1-1. Often, such drivers are of interest only to the actual hardware manufacturers developing the hardware. You may, however, want to write an interface for some custom hardware or for hardware that does not properly provide support using the old DOS device driver model.

Chapter 10 describes a method of interfacing such devices to Windows, taking full advantage of the Windows programming environment. In particular, it is possible to create a nonstandard device driver that will send messages to a Windows program rather than require the program to poll the device for input.

Summary

Whether you are writing a standard or nonstandard device driver, you will need to have a thorough understanding not only of Windows programming, but also of the internal aspects of Windows and the various protection modes of the Intel 80x86 processors.

CHAPTER

2

Windows Operating Modes

If you have programmed for Windows, you probably know that the Windows environment can be run in one of two operating modes: standard or 386 enhanced. Prior to version 3.0, Windows had a third mode—real mode. The three modes reflect the history of Windows as well as its future, since Windows can be run on older hardware and on the very latest 486 machines. When Windows starts, it selects the most advanced mode possible on the machine it is running under. On a system with 640K of memory, real mode is selected. If the system has more memory with an 80286 CPU, standard mode is selected. With an 80386 CPU and sufficient memory, enhanced 386 mode is selected.

In order to develop device drivers that will run in the various modes, you will need to have a good understanding of each mode, both in terms of hardware and in the way Windows uses memory in each mode.

Intel CPU Modes

The various modes of Windows reflect the various modes of the Intel CPUs. From the 8086 on up through the 80486, each processor is capable of simulating the modes of the less capable processors. All processors, for example, are able to run in **real mode**, behaving like the 8086 CPU. The 80286 adds **protected mode**, which offers memory protection and access to more than 1MB of memory, but still supports 8086 real mode. The 80386 adds several major features including larger memory segments, memory paging, and virtual 8086 mode. The 80386 still supports 80286 protected mode and 8086 real mode.

All processors are capable of converting memory addresses to refer to physical memory. The 8086 is capable of addressing up to 1024K of physical memory. With most PC compatibles, the upper 384K of this space is reserved for the ROM BIOS, video, and other hardware, leaving 640K of this address space available for read/write memory. The CPU addresses the memory in the ROM BIOS above the 640K boundary in the same way that it address RAM below the 640K boundary and sees one large block of memory of one megabyte.

This memory space is often referred to as the **physical memory space** of the processor and indicates the amount of physically installed

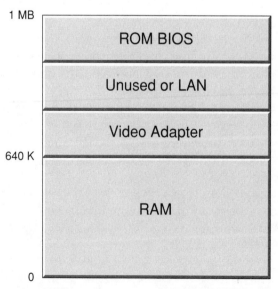

FIGURE 2-1 Typical 8086 Physical Memory Layout

memory that the CPU can access. Figure 2-1 illustrates typical 8086 physical memory organization (depending on the actual system, the layout of the memory above 640K may vary). To generate 1024K bytes of physical addresses, 20 address bits are required, and the 8086 CPU has 20 pins on its package, named A0 through A19. The 80286 can access 16M bytes of physical memory, and thus requires 24 address bits; it has additional pins on its package, named A20 through A23. The 80386 can access 4 gigabytes of physical memory and has 32 memory address pins named A0 through A31.

Another way of looking at the addressing modes of the various processors is to consider how they convert the addresses used by applications into the addresses used by hardware.

Real Mode Addressing

If you have programmed at the device level, you are probably quite familiar with the way memory segments and offsets work and the capabilities and limitations of 8086 real mode addressing. But to lay down the groundwork and terminology for understanding the other processor modes, let's review real mode addressing.

In real mode, memory is referred to using a 16-bit **segment** and a 16-bit **offset**. Although these are often combined in a 32-bit memory address structure, the processor always treats them separately when calculating the physical memory address. In fact, there are no memory access instructions in the 8086 and 80286 processors in which the full 32-bit logical address can be specified. The segment must always be loaded into a segment register in a separate instruction.

All CPUs, when running in real mode, are capable of accessing only one megabyte of memory. (The non-8086 processors can actually access 1024K + 64K – 17 bytes in real mode in a manner explained in the next few pages.) This means that the segment and offset need to be converted into a 20-bit physical address.

This is accomplished by treating the segment portion of the address as a base pointer and adding the offset. Instead of simply adding the numbers, however, the segment portion is first multiplied by 16 and then added to the offset. Since multiplying by 16 is the same as shifting left by 4, the calculation is easily illustrated as shown in Figure 2-2.

For example, if the segment portion of the address is 0xA000 and the offset portion is 0x00A0 (often referred to jointly as A000:00A0), then the physical address is the segment shifted left by 4 (0xA0000) plus the offset, or 0xA00A0. The relationship between logical addresses and physical

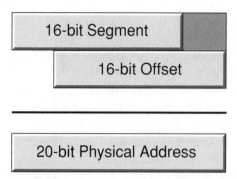

FIGURE 2-2 Real Mode Address Calculation

addresses is not one-to-one. The logical addresses A00A:0000, A009:0010 and 9800:80A0 all refer to the same physical address of 0xA00A0.

What happens if this calculation overflows, as in the case of the logical address FFFF:0010? (See Figure 2-3.) We are no longer looking at a 20-bit result, but instead end up with the 21-bit physical address of 0x100000. The answer is that it depends on the type of processor. With the 8086 processor, there are only 20 address lines (A0–A19); as a result, the bit carried out of the calculation is lost, and the physical address appears as 0x00000. Note how the address appears to "wrap around" from the end of memory back to the beginning. With the other processors, however, the result is not so simple.

The 80286 and later processors have at least 24 address lines. The calculation yields a full 21 significant address bits in address lines A0 through A20, so this example can indeed refer to the address 0x100000. This results in an incompatibility between the 8086 and later processors running in real mode. One wonders why a programmer would program in this

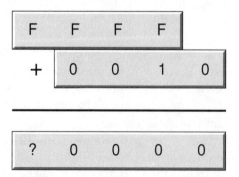

FIGURE 2-3 Real Mode Address Calculation Overflow

cryptic fashion, but many do. To provide backward compatibility, PC compatibles have a hardware modification to set what is called **address line 20** or **A20 mode**.

When the A20 mode is set for compatibility, hardware external to the CPU forces this address line always to report a zero. As a result, any calculations in real mode that would overflow wrap around to the beginning of memory instead, just as they would with an 8086 CPU.

When the A20 line is set for full memory access, the A20 line is passed unmodified from the CPU. In this way, a limited amount of memory above the 1MB boundary can be accessed from real mode with non-8086 processors. The highest memory address that can be accessed in this fashion is FFFF:FFFF, or 1MB + 64K − 17, or the physical address 0x10FFEF. The region of memory from 0x100000 to 0x10FFEF is sometimes referred to as the **high memory area** or the HMA. The range of memory above physical address 0x100000, including the HMA, is called **extended memory**. The 8086 processor has only 20 address bits and is incapable of accessing extended memory. Extended memory is often confused with expanded memory (described later in this chapter). Expanded memory can be used with any processor.

Windows real mode corresponded to the processor's real mode or the native 8086/8088 execution mode. Note that in this mode extended memory was not accessible and was not used by Windows, but that expanded memory was used when available.

Protected Mode Addressing

In real mode, none of the processors can access extended memory (with the exception of the HMA). The processors can access extended memory only when they are running in protected mode. Logical addresses, however, still consist of two 16-bit fields—just as they do in real mode. The offset field remains the same except that a **selector** replaces the segment as a base.

Figure 2-4 illustrates how the processor uses the selector and offset to calculate a physical address from a protected mode logical address. Instead of the physical address calculated from the base, a selector value contains an index into a table that describes the physical memory base address. The processor then adds the base to the offset to compute the actual 24-bit physical memory address. The table that the selector points to is called a **descriptor table**. A descriptor table is a processor-defined table in memory that describes the beginning of a memory region, or segment, the length of the segment, and certain privileged information.

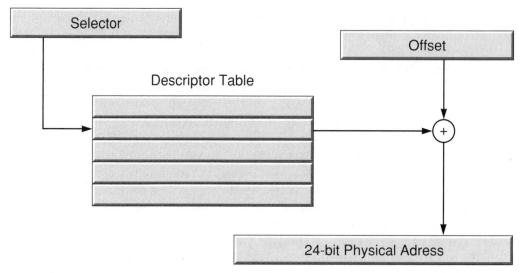

FIGURE 2-4 Protected Mode Addressing

As with real mode, there are no 80286 instructions in protected mode that specify a full 32-bit logical address for an assembly instruction operand. Instead, a program must first load a segment register with a selector value and then use an instruction that has the offset encoded in the instruction or in a CPU register. In real mode, it is possible to calculate the physical memory address from the segment and offset each time that memory is referenced. If this were the case in protected mode, however, the memory reference would also require a lookup in the descriptor table. Clearly, this would yield unacceptable performance if it was required for each memory access.

Instead, a small cache within the CPU holds the segment information for each segment register (CS, DS, SS, ES, FS, GS). Whenever a program loads a segment register, the CPU automatically loads the corresponding descriptor table entry into the CPU segment cache for that segment register. That way, each memory reference requires only that the offset be added to the segment base to determine the physical memory address.

This means, however, that the CPU makes a memory reference whenever a program in protected mode loads a segment register. Even if the source operand is a register, as in MOV ES,AX the descriptor table entry must still be read from memory in order to determine the base physical memory address. Consequently, an instruction that changes a segment register generally takes significantly longer in protected mode than in real mode.

This means that, for the best performance, programmers should write programs that minimize segment register changes. For example, a near call (or near return) is faster than a far call (or far return). References to a segment already identified by DS or ES will be faster than references that require loading a segment register. If you are writing for an 80386 processor in assembly language, you might be able to improve performance further by using the FS and GS registers.

Benefits of Protected Mode

At this point you may be wondering what the benefit of protected mode is. One of the biggest benefits is that protected mode allows access to much more memory than real mode does. Figure 2-5 shows the bit fields within a selector. Note that the index is only 13 bits wide, allowing for up to 8192 descriptor table entries. Since each index can refer to a separate segment, and each segment can be as large as 64K, this addressing scheme can refer to as many as 2^{29}, or 512M bytes of logical memory. The 80286 processor, of course, can address only 16M bytes of memory, but you can see how this method can easily map the entire physical address space. Since most segments are much smaller than 64K, the large number of entries allowed seems more practical. As the name protected mode implies, there are other important benefits, too.

The RPL field in the selector indicates the **requested privilege level** of the selector. Programs under Windows may run at one of two privilege levels: 0 or 3. When running at privilege level 0, a program is sometimes said to be running in **supervisor mode**. The level 3 mode is sometimes referred to as **user mode** or **application mode**. The RPL field in the selector indicates the mode of the selector. If the selector is for level 0, then the selector may not be loaded into a segment register when a program is running at levels 1, 2, or 3. An application segment, however, may be accessed from supervisor mode. If a program attempts to violate this protection mechanism, the CPU traps the program and Windows displays an appropriate dialog box indicating that the program was aborted.

In this way, protected mode not only allows access to more memory; it also provides protection to the operating system from errant applications.

FIGURE 2-5 Fields in a Selector

In other words, an application program cannot—either accidentally or deliberately—write over system data.

The T field in the selector indicates which one of two descriptor tables to select: the **global descriptor table** (GDT) or the **local descriptor table** (LDT). Some operating systems, such as OS/2, keep a single GDT available to all programs running in the operating system and reserve a separate LDT for each program. At any instant, only one LDT can be active. In standard or enhanced mode, Windows currently uses a single LDT for all applications.

Because Windows has only a single LDT, Windows programs are not protected from errant (or deliberate) memory accesses by other programs: One Windows program can overwrite the data of another Windows program. Furthermore, an errant Windows program can overwrite Windows memory and crash the Windows environment. If an application loads an invalid selector value or attempts to access beyond the range of a segment, the CPU will catch the violation and stop the program. Even though Windows can run the processor in protected mode, it does not allow protection to a program other than protecting a program from itself.

I mentioned that the descriptor table has entries that describe the physical base address of the segment. A descriptor table entry has other fields, too. Figure 2-6 shows the layout of a segment descriptor table entry as it is used by Windows. The base fields specify the physical base address of the segment. Although the base address can be set to any byte in memory, Windows positions segments that begin only on physical paragraph boundaries. In other words, the base address is always a multiple of 16.

The DPL field indicates the **data privilege level**. Just as the RPL specifies the privilege level of the selector, the DPL specifies the privilege level of the segment. The protection mechanism not only protects against

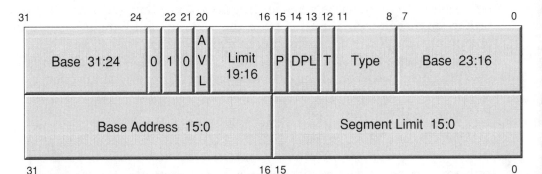

FIGURE 2-6 Segment Descriptor Table Entry

accessing supervisor data while in application mode; it also protects against accessing supervisor data using an application selector, even when using the selector in supervisor mode.

For example, in application mode a supervisor selector may not be loaded because the requested privilege level (0) is lower than the current mode, or **current privilege level** (CPL) (3, in the case of Windows). On the other hand, an application selector may be loaded in supervisor mode, since the CPL (0) is lower than the RPL (3).

Applications can (and often do) pass data pointers to the operating system. An errant application might pass a pointer with the correct RPL in the selector, but the index might point to a descriptor with a DPL set for supervisor mode. If a program running in supervisor mode attempts to use such a selector, the CPU will trap the attempt and generate a fault.

The descriptor also contains a **limit field**. The limit field indicates the size of the segment. Unlike offsets in real mode, which can be up to 64K, offsets in protected mode are limited to the size of the segment specified by the selector. If an attempt is made to specify an offset beyond the end of the segment, it is treated the same way an attempt to access an invalid selector is treated: the CPU traps the attempt and generates a fault.

The **type field** indicates if the segment is for code or data. A segment whose descriptor is marked as a code segment may not be written to. A segment whose descriptor is marked as a data segment may not be executed. A data segment may be marked read-only or read/write.

Note that two descriptors can point to the same physical memory segment. In this way, a segment may be accessed as both a code segment and a data segment, depending on the selector used to access it. Selectors used in this way are called **aliases**.

The description of the other fields in the descriptor are beyond the scope of this book. Unfortunately, many books on 80286 or 80386 assembly language programming do not describe the protected mode features of these processors. Appendix H lists some of the newer books that do describe the descriptor format in more detail.

Protected Mode Interrupts

In protected mode, interrupts are processed differently from the way they are treated in real mode. In real mode, a table in low memory, the **interrupt vector table** (IVT), contains the real mode addresses of the routines that process interrupts. When an interrupt occurs (or an INT instruction is executed), the processor disables interrupts, saves the flags on the stack,

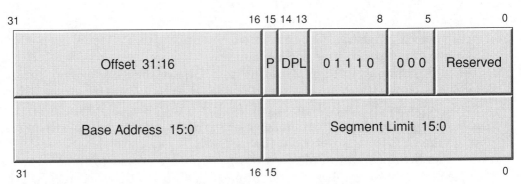

FIGURE 2-7 Interrupt Descriptor Table Entry

saves the return address on the stack, and passes control to the **interrupt service routine** (ISR) for the indicated interrupt.

In protect mode, however, there is no IVT. There is instead an **interrupt descriptor table** (IDT). An interrupt descriptor, shown in Figure 2-7, is different from a data or code descriptor. Instead of a base and limit, an interrupt descriptor has a selector and an offset. The DPL is always zero with Windows and indicates that the interrupt may be processed while the processor is in either application or supervisor mode.

This means that when you are programming with Windows in protect mode, the method of simply overwriting the IVT will not work: The documented INT 21h function calls (35h and 25h) must be used to establish an ISR.

Accessing I/O Ports from Protected Mode

Intel processors can be set up in such a way that input and output instructions cannot be used in application mode. This is done by setting the **I/O privilege level** (IOPL) to supervisor mode (zero). When the IOPL is set to zero (referred to as IOPL0 in the Microsoft documentation), as with Windows only specified I/O ports may be accessed in application mode. These ports are specified via the **I/O permission bitmap** (IOPM).

Why set the IOPL to zero when the IOPM just re-enables access? The reason is that the IOPL also affects the operation of the interrupt flag. In real mode and when IOPL is 3, the interrupt flag is treated like any other flag. The flag is set or cleared whenever the flag's register is loaded, as with a POPF instruction. In Windows, however, the IOPL is 0, and the interrupt flag is not affected by POPF.

Also, the CLI and STI instructions are not allowed by the processor in application mode under Windows; their execution generates an instruction

Normal Method	Windows Method
| ```
PUSHF
CLI
.
. ; critical code
.
POPF
``` | ```
PUSHF
CLI
.
. ; critical code
.
POP AX
TEST AH,00000010b
JZ   short lbl
STI
lbl: ...
``` |

FIGURE 2-8 PUSHF/POPF Method for Windows

fault. Windows, however, ignores the fault on these instructions and changes the interrupt flag accordingly.

What this means for the programmer is that old device driver code that used PUSHF/POPF pairs to save and restore the interrupt flag will not work under Windows. Only CLI and STI will properly set the interrupt flag. PUSHF/POPF pairs are frequently used in a critical section of code that must insure that interrupts are disabled when the code is executed. In such a case the code does not care about the entry state of the interrupt flag but restores it to its original value. Figure 2-8 illustrates the normal and Windows methods for saving and restoring the state of the interrupt flag around a critical section of code.

If you have code that accounts for a very obscure bug in older 80286 microprocessors, with regard to interrupts and POPF, you can ignore it for Windows when you are running in standard application mode, since POPF does not affect the interrupt flag in this case, anyway.

Memory Paging

The 80386 processor adds another dimension to protected mode programming through its **memory paging** mechanism. Basically, the segments, selectors, and descriptors are still used with paging, but instead of providing physical memory addresses, the addresses are referred to as **linear addresses**. These linear addresses are provided as input to the onboard paging hardware of the 386 processor, which determines the actual physical addresses. In a sense, the paging mechanism, through the linear address space, adds another level of indirection between logical addresses and physical addresses.

Figure 2-9 illustrates the transformation from linear to physical addresses. Just as descriptor tables provide the mapping from logical addresses to physical addresses by specifying the base address of segments, **page tables** provide the mapping from linear addresses to physical addresses by specifying the base address of pages.

Unlike segments, however, pages are fixed in size. Each page is exactly 4096 bytes long. A page table entry, therefore, does not have a limit field. Instead of a DPL, a page table entry simply has a bit that indicates if the page is for supervisor or application access. The page table entry also indicates if the page can be written to or if it is read-only.

As with segment violations or invalid accesses to a segment or selector, page violation attempts are trapped by the processor, providing another level of protection. Note that the paging mechanism is not independent of the segment mechanism: It is another integral step in the translation of logical addresses to physical addresses.

Several important concepts of linear-to-physical address mapping are illustrated in Figure 2-10. First, the order of the linear pages does not need

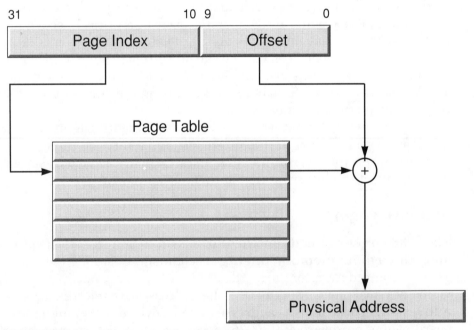

FIGURE 2-9 Linear to Physical Address Mapping

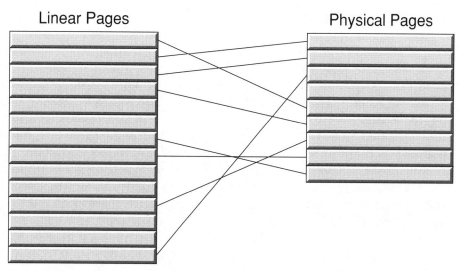

FIGURE 2-10 Memory Map View of Linear-to-Physical Mapping

to match or even resemble the order of their corresponding physical pages. Second, it is not necessary for the linear pages to be mapped to any physical pages. A reference to an unmapped page will cause a **page fault** causing the processor to trap the instruction that caused the fault. Note that most DMA hardware makes transfers to and from *physical* memory space. The device driver developer must keep this in mind when calculating DMA addresses. Note also that the number of linear pages may greatly exceed the number of physical pages.

Large Segments and 32-bit Offsets

So far, I have mentioned only that the offset portion of a memory pointer may be 16 bits. This is a restriction of the 286 processor; the 386 processor may have offsets of 32-bits, and consequently segments may be as large as 4 gigabytes. The 286 processor can address up to 512MB of logical memory, assuming each segment is 64K bytes, but the 286 can physically access only 16M bytes. In the same way, using 4 gigabyte segments, the 386 processor can theoretically address up to 2^{45} bytes, or 32768 gigabytes. Its physical address space, however, is limited to "only" 4 gigabytes.

Note that, with 32-bit offsets, a single segment may map the entire physical address space. Also a single 32-bit segment is large enough to map all of the data and code of a program, paving the way to getting rid of segments altogether. Windows is not at this point yet, but it does provide some primitive support for creating and using 32-bit segments.

Virtual 8086 Mode

Although the 80286 and 80386 provide full 8086 compatibility when they are running in real mode, it has proved difficult and clumsy to provide a computing environment that supports both real mode and protected mode. Windows standard mode and 16-bit versions of OS/2 both provide support for DOS programs by switching processor modes from protected mode to real mode and back. Although switching to protected mode is relatively painless (tables are set up, and a special mode bit is set), switching back to real mode on the 286 is achieved by effectively resetting the processor.

What's more, the memory in real mode is restricted to the lower 640K region, and this region must be initialized before the switch back to real mode is made. This means reserving the lower 640K for real mode, or swapping the memory in and out from disk whenever modes are changed. The **virtual 8086 mode** of the 386 processor, however, allows real mode programs to run without some of these problems.

The memory paging feature of the 386 processor may be enabled only when the processor is running in protected mode. In that case, addresses are interpreted as a selector and an offset. In virtual 8086 mode addresses are treated in the same way they are treated in real mode: as a segment base and offset. The paging mechanism, however, is still enabled, and the addresses formed in virtual 8086 mode are linear addresses. These addresses can then be translated to any (or no) physical address in the 4G physical address space. In this way, programs written for the real mode of the processor can run in virtual 8086 mode, but do not depend on reserving the lower 640K of physical memory.

Within the protection scheme, virtual 8086 programs under Windows run at the application level. At this level, I/O instructions are permitted only for those ports specified in the IOPM. Some ports are enabled in the IOPM; other ports are disabled and will cause instruction faults if they are accessed. As with other application level modes, `CLI` and `STI` are disallowed.

While most processing in virtual 8086 mode is handled as in real mode, interrupts are still handled in protected mode. If an interrupt occurs or even if an INT instruction or instruction trap occurs, virtual 8086 mode is disabled, and the processor transfers control to the selector and offset address specified in the IDT.

Later in this chapter, I describe the relationship between virtual 8086 mode and the Windows virtual DOS machine and how device drivers can support that environment.

Expanded Memory

Expanded memory, or EMS, provides yet another twist to the many different ways that memory can be addressed. EMS is not supported by the 80x86 processors, but is instead supported by external hardware and software or, in some implementations, solely in software.

Figure 2-1 illustrates the layout of memory that is accessible in real mode. The unused area can be mapped by external hardware. Often, EMS hardware is installed to fill this gap. This area of the lower 1MB of memory can be thought of as a porthole to a particular area of expanded memory. Although the 80x86 processor only "sees" a few kilobytes of real mode memory at a single time, calls can be made to the EMS interface, using INT 67h, to change this porthole to map a different area of EMS memory. In this way, EMS can provide many megabytes of additional memory without requiring the protected mode of the processor.

The porthole is referred to as a **page** (not to be confused with a 386 CPU memory page) and has a fixed size of 16K bytes. An EMS implementation can support several pages. Pages that are contiguous in memory are referred to as **frames**. With most EMS hardware, Windows uses the expanded memory in what is referred to as **small-frame mode**. If an expanded memory emulator, such as EMM386.SYS is installed, Windows can work in **large-frame mode**. Depending on the mode used, Windows will store various program and system structures in expanded memory.

For device driver developers, it is important to be aware that most EMS hardware does not allow DMA transfers to be made directly into a page frame. Instead, a DMA transfer may first need to be made into a device driver buffer and subsequently copied into a page frame.

Windows Operating Modes

Windows Real Mode

When Windows 3.0 runs in **real mode**, it runs the same way that version 2.x runs, using the real mode of the processor. Although it is not normally recommended, Windows can run in real mode on an 8086 processor. If expanded memory is present, Windows will also use that memory. Although Windows 3.1 does not support real mode, it provides background to understanding the other modes.

Figure 2-11 shows the way memory is organized when Windows runs in real mode. In this mode, Windows is much like any other DOS application: Calls can still be made to the BIOS and to DOS, by way of INT 21h. Memory is accessed as a segment and an offset, and all memory is directly addressable. Note that although Figure 2-11 shows discardable segments in the high end of memory, such segments are often stored in the EMS frame and swapped in and out using EMS.

Although I am assuming that you are familiar with Windows memory segments and the `GlobalAlloc` and `GlobalLock` functions, a quick review of the basic Windows memory functions is in order. In many respects, the way Windows manages memory in real mode is similar to the way the 80x86 processors manage memory in protected mode. Instead of a selector to a memory segment, Windows maintains a handle to a memory segment. This handle is a table that describes the size and location of the segment. This table is called the `BURGERMASTER`, and it functions in much the same way as an 80x86 protected mode descriptor table.

All memory in Windows real mode is allocated from the **global heap**. This region of memory consists of the three areas shown in Figure 2-11 separated by the heavy lines plus the EMS frame. Within this heap, there are three fundamental types of memory segments: fixed, discardable, and non-discardable. Fixed memory segments are assigned a physical memory address that never changes. In real mode, fixed memory segments do not need a handle, since all references to the segment may be made directly. Although you may not have run into this type of segment when programming conventional Windows applications, fixed memory segments play an important role in device drivers, particularly for interrupt service routines.

Windows can manage hundreds—perhaps thousands—of memory segments. Often, only a small subset of the segments may actually be in use by the programs running at any particular moment. From time to time, the system may allocate a new memory segment, for example, as a result of a program being loaded or due to a call to `GlobalAlloc`. When a system is properly configured with sufficient memory, such allocations usually are satisfied by allocating memory from the heap, assigning a handle to the memory, and updating `BURGERMASTER`.

One of the big advantages of working in the Windows environment, even in real mode, is the possibility of running multiple applications that, although each may use only several hundred kilobytes of memory, when combined require more memory than may be physically available to the system. Windows tries to satisfy memory allocations by reorganizing memory and by throwing away segments that are not needed in physical memory.

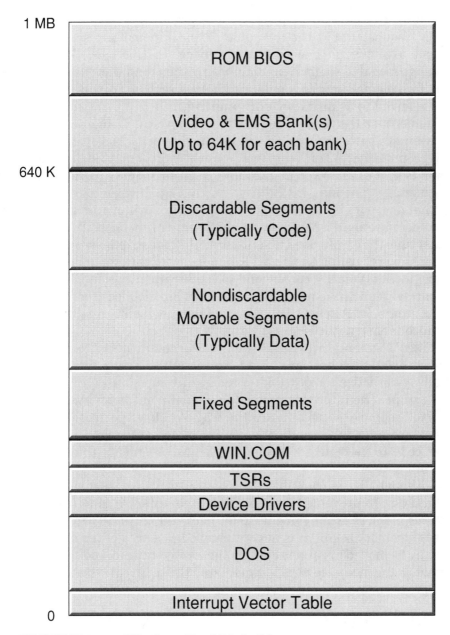

FIGURE 2-11 Windows Real Mode Memory

Often, the amount of physical memory available is more than the amount requested, but the available physical memory is scattered about and not available in one contiguous piece. In this case, Windows can rearrange movable segments, compressing them and thereby collecting all of the free memory into a single, contiguous region. This process is sometimes referred to as **memory compaction**.

Sometimes the request requires more physical memory than is available even after it is compacted. When this happens, the system is said to be overcommitted. When Windows becomes overcommitted, it looks for the segments that are marked discardable. Such segments are those that Windows manages but may not be currently using, for example, segments of code that are required to initialize a program or parts of a program that are accessed infrequently. Windows ranks them chronologically according to the last time they were used and discards the oldest, or least-recently used, segments by returning their physical memory to the global heap. Discardable segments typically correspond to code segments from EXE files, so if a discarded segment is needed again, it can be reloaded from the EXE file that contains it. Alternatively, discardable segments may be stored in expanded memory, if it is available.

Fixed segments are those that must remain in a fixed location in memory. Fixed segments are used for interrupt service routines, since it is not always practical or possible to reorganize memory in order to service an interrupt. The interrupt vector table must point to a physical address, and fixed memory segments are the way Windows permanently assigns physical memory to an application. It is not necessary for all of the device driver code to be in fixed segments: just the segments that process the interrupt.

Although it is possible to use a movable segment and call `GlobalLock` to prevent it from being moved, this will tend to undermine Windows memory management. Refer back to Figure 2-11 to see why. If a movable memory segment is never unlocked, the area of the heap that can normally be moved around is split by the "wall" of the locked segment. This fragments the heap; several segments of this sort can thwart Windows' attempts at memory compaction.

Expanded Memory Usage

In real mode with small-frame EMS, any EMS banks are used for discardable segments only. Thus, if there is sufficient expanded memory available, the system will copy code segments to expanded memory instead of discarding them. Even if the system has 2M bytes of expanded memory, however, all data segments must fit entirely within the lower 640K. Only code segments are stored in expanded memory. This means that, although the programs can be much bigger with EMS, the size of data objects is still quite limited with Windows in real mode. Furthermore, the code of a single application must fit within the combined lower 640K and the visible EMS banks. If an application is larger than this, an overcommit will result in Windows discarding the segment rather than swapping it to expanded memory.

With large-frame expanded memory, the restriction on data segments is relaxed to allow program data segments to be included in the memory that may be stored in the page frame.

Disk swapping is not supported at all under Windows real mode. Segment discarding and reloading relieves some of the problems of memory overcommitment, but the memory constraint of 640K still remains for read/write program data.

The End of an Era

Windows real mode is provided primarily for compatibility with existing applications that are capable of running only in real mode. Unfortunately, these old systems are too slow to provide acceptable performance for running Windows. The value of Windows is seen in faster and more capable systems, particularly in the newer modes provided by Windows Version 3.

Windows Standard Mode

Windows **standard mode** takes full advantage of the protected mode capabilities of the 286 processor. Since the 386 and 486 processors are fully compatible, Windows standard mode runs equally well on these. Standard mode runs Windows applications in the protected mode of the 286 processor. All of the memory access and protection benefits described earlier in this chapter are realized when Windows programs are run in standard mode.

DOS applications can also be run, but Windows switches the processor back to real mode to run them. In fact, Windows frequently switches between the processor's protected mode and real mode as it processes requests (which is costly in terms of performance).

In protected mode, the processor descriptor tables play the role that the BURGERMASTER segment plays in real mode. Remember that in Windows real mode a handle to a memory segment is just an index into BURGERMASTER. In protected mode, the Windows memory handle is actually a selector (with the RPL field invalidated) to the memory segment. In real mode, it is necessary to call `GlobalLock` to convert the handle to a pointer. In protected mode, however, since the handle is actually the selector, the pointer can be constructed from the selector after adjusting the RPL field to user mode.

One of the most frustrating aspects of Windows programming is having constantly to call `GlobalLock` and `GlobalUnlock`. In protected mode, the selector value never changes. Once the segment is allocated, the resultant pointer also never changes, and `GlobalLock` never needs to be called again. Rather than manipulating the handle directly, you just call `GlobalLock` once after calling `GlobalAlloc` and only refer to the segment using the pointer. Since the pointer contains the selector, and the hardware automatically converts the selector and offset to a physical address, the actual physical address can change frequently. When Windows moves the segment around in physical memory, it needs to change only the descriptor table entry.

What happens when the system is overcommitted? As with BURGERMASTER, Windows can indicate in the descriptor table that a discardable segment has been discarded. When a program attempts to access such a segment, the 80x86 hardware triggers a segment fault. A segment fault is treated much like an INT instruction. Windows processes the interrupt, recognizes that the selector is valid, reads in the discardable segment from the EXE file (or DLL), corrects the descriptor, and resumes the program at the point that the segment fault occurred.

Device driver developers have to watch out for another big difference between pointers in real and protected mode. In protected mode, a segment locked by `GlobalLock` is free to be moved around in physical memory. In order to guarantee that a segment remains fixed in physical memory, either you must allocate it with the fixed attribute or an additional call, `GlobalFix`, must be made. Windows memory management is compromised by a call to `GlobalFix` in much the same way that `GlobalLock` affects memory management in real mode. This call should be used sparingly. If you need to fix a segment in memory, such as for an interrupt service routine, it is usually best to allocate the code segment as fixed, instead of using `GlobalFix`. Alternatively, you can use `GlobalWire` first. This moves the segment into the fixed allocation area without fragmenting the movable area of memory.

Figure 2-12 illustrates the typical organization of memory in Windows standard mode. Essentially, the Windows heap extends above the 640K boundary. Although the figure shows discardable segments in extended memory, there is no restriction on the boundary between

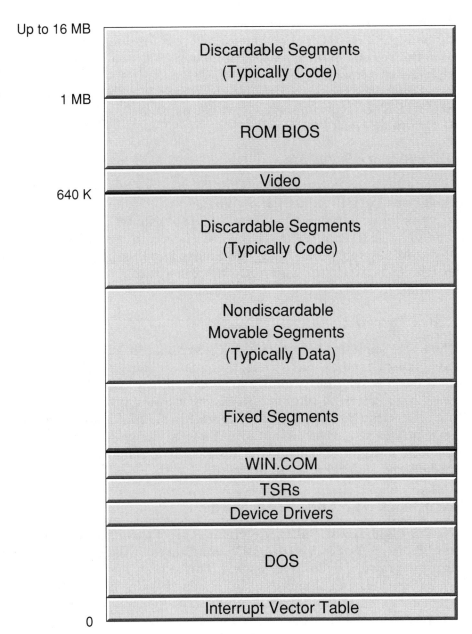

FIGURE 2-12 Windows Protected Mode Memory

discardable and nondiscardable segments. Note, however, that the organization is similar to that of real mode, and that fixed segments are allocated from the low end of memory. Discardable segments are allocated from the high end of memory.

Expanded memory is not directly used in Windows standard mode. If SMARTDRV.SYS is running, it may use expanded memory, but only indirectly through disk I/O.

Huge Memory Segments

Despite the physical limitation of 64K bytes per segment, huge memory allocations are still supported by Windows in standard mode. A reference to a pointer declared in C with the _huge attribute will cause the correct code to be generated, whether the code is run in real mode or protected mode. In assembler, the ahincr global variable provides the selector increment between the segments that constitute a huge memory object. Appendix C describes this in more detail.

A Step Forward

The 640K boundary for data segments is removed, since data can be allocated in extended memory. Thus, the greatest benefit of Windows in standard mode is seen in its ability to access all available extended memory. Does it get better? If you have an 80386 or 80486 processor, it might, but not necessarily. As in real mode, Windows in standard mode does not swap segments to disk. Overcommit situations, although less likely with more memory, are still possible. This restriction is removed in the Windows mode designed for the 80386 processor.

Windows 386 Enhanced Mode

Windows **386 enhanced mode** provides all of the features found in standard mode, but adds **virtual DOS machines** (VDMs) plus the benefits that are provided by memory paging. This is best seen when the system is overcommitted. In enhanced mode, Windows will successfully manage an overcommit situation of nondiscardable segments. Instead of quitting when physical memory is exhausted, Windows selects certain 4K pages that have not been accessed recently and writes them to disk. If these pages are needed again later, they can be read back from disk. This reading and writing of pages between memory and disk is referred to as paging (although it is often mistakenly referred to as swapping).

Remember the difference between linear addresses and physical addresses? Linear addresses are the input to the paging hardware; physical addresses are the output. Whenever the system approaches the over-committed state, Windows first attempts to reorganize memory through memory compaction. When there are many large segments, this can be a lengthy process. Windows in enhanced mode can speed this up tremendously. Instead of the segments actually being moved around in physical memory, the paging logic can be utilized to move the segments around in logical memory, without moving the physical data.

This is done by changing the page tables to reflect the moved data. Changing the page tables for large segments is much faster than moving the actual data, since many fewer bytes need to be accessed.

Virtual DOS Mode

To many, the most important benefit of Windows 386 enhanced mode is the support of VDMs. Windows takes advantage of the virtual 8086 mode of the 80386 processor to emulate a DOS environment. Thanks to the paging mechanism that translates the linear addresses to physical addresses, several VDMs can be active within Windows at the same time.

Normally, when a DOS box from Windows is running in real or standard mode, other Windows programs are suspended. Likewise, when Windows is active, any background DOS boxes are suspended. In 386 enhanced mode, however, the DOS boxes are allowed to continue processing, even when minimized. Furthermore, the programs are allowed to run in a Window. In addition to all of this, the DOS boxes can be provided with access to expanded memory, even if the system hardware does not include expanded memory hardware.

Normally, the biggest problem of running a DOS box concurrently with Windows programs is video access. Many DOS programs expect to access the video display buffers directly. For this reason, DOS programs are suspended when they are in the background in Windows standard mode. In 386 enhanced mode, however, background applications are allowed to access the video hardware directly. This is made possible, in part, by changing the linear-to-physical mapping for the DOS box to point to nonvideo memory. In text mode, the mapping can be simply to a normal memory buffer. In graphics modes, however, the access to the memory can cause a trap to a special portion of the video device driver responsible for managing access to the video while in a DOS box. This part of the device driver is called a **virtual display driver** (VDD). It is so named, because it manages a "virtual" display for the DOS box, rather than the actual display. It must be closely coupled with the normal display driver.

There are other virtual drivers for the other standard devices, too. For example, there is a virtual device driver that supports access to the COM communication ports. Rather than trapping memory accesses, this driver traps accesses to the I/O ports normally assigned to the COM hardware. In this way, the virtual device driver for the COM port can arbitrate access to the COM ports.

What Next?

Windows 386 enhanced mode takes advantage of almost every feature of the 80386 processor. The most notable exception is the use of large segments. Windows normally allocates segments whose sizes are limited to 64K bytes. The 80386 processor, however, allows segments with sizes over 4 gigabytes.

There is currently support in Windows for these large segments, via some special system calls contained in the WINMEM32 dynamic link library. These calls, however, are clumsy, and there is little direct support for the segments from high-level programming languages. The next step for Windows, then, is to provide full support for 32-bit segments. Taken further, once a segment is so large, there is less need for multiple segments. All data and code can be located within the same segment, effectively removing the concept of segments from the domain of the programmer. This model is akin to the DOS "tiny" model, in which all code and data are found within the same segment. The difference, of course, is that the segment can be as large as 4 gigabytes. In Windows (and OS/2), this memory model is referred to as the **flat memory model**, since the memory space is one-dimensional, not qualified by segments.

Summary

Windows memory models have evolved over time, but there is still room for improvement even without changing the underlying hardware architecture. Perhaps before too long, the programming environments of the various windowing systems—Windows, Presentation Manager, and X-Windows—will become similar enough to make porting between systems easier. The device driver developer, however, may never have it so easy.

CHAPTER

3

GDI—The Graphics Device Interface

The **graphics device interface**, or GDI, enables an application program to describe graphical information and commands without reference to the specifics of the underlying hardware. This provides the encapsulation mentioned in Chapter 1 that keeps the details of printer and video characteristics away from the application programmer. As device driver writers, we must be concerned with these details while keeping the application program isolated from them. It is up to us to use and cooperate with the GDI in order to maintain this encapsulation.

The GDI is used for both video display and printer drivers. In this chapter, I describe the GDI and its structures without going into the specifics of video or printer drivers. These are covered in Chapters 4 and 5.

To the application developer, the GDI consists of the functions that create or obtain a device context and the functions that operate on a device context. You might want to review the SDK reference for some of the GDI calls that Windows provides to application programs before continuing. `CreateDC` creates a device context for a particular device and configuration.

The device context describes a particular configuration of a device. The *lpInitData* parameter can specify a particular device configuration as the device context is created. When an application calls `CreateDC`, Windows calls the device driver to initialize parameters for the device context.

Other calls to the device require the handle to the created device context. When an application makes a call to the device, Windows converts the call to calls to the device driver, making appropriate transformations. The device driver typically receives only commands that affect the physical appearance of the display or hardcopy. Because Windows translates the calls from applications, the calls to the device driver are usually for low-level graphics operations.

As a Windows programmer, you have probably used some features of the Windows GDI—looking "down" into the GDI from the application. Ideally the GDI provides an interface that is powerful and at a sufficiently high level, but that allows some application control over some of the lower-level functions. For example, one application may be interested in the simple task of drawing a circle on any type of display. Another application may be willing to sacrifice high-level interface for performance and so may prefer to transfer bit images directly to the device. The GDI provides both types of interfaces.

GDI drivers are not restricted to raster- or pixel-oriented surfaces; they may also be vector oriented. While we usually think of vector-oriented devices as pen plotters, it is possible to write a printer driver that drives a vector-oriented CRT. Even though a display driver must have some raster capabilities, a display driver can drive a hybrid raster/vector CRT.

When first enabled, the device driver returns two structures to the Windows GDI: the `PDEVICE` structure, which is driver specific, and the `GDIINFO` structure, which is defined by the GDI.

The GDIINFO Data Structure

In order for Windows to translate the GDI calls to the device driver, it needs to have certain information about the device driver on hand. Most of this information is contained in a data structure named `GDIINFO`, which describes the general physical characteristics of the graphics device. The device driver initializes this data structure when an application calls the `CreateDC` function or when Windows creates the initial device context for display devices. Application programs can access the fields in this structure by calling `GetDeviceCaps`. Each field in `GDIINFO` is a 16-bit word.

Appendix A summarizes the fields in `GDIINFO`, but let's look at them in detail to understand their specific nature.

`dpVersion`	The version of Windows that the driver is compatible with. For Windows 3.1, this value is 030Ah, but future versions of Windows may have different values. Windows examines this value when the driver is loaded to insure that the driver understands how it is being called. This way, if some of the interfaces change between Windows and the device driver, Windows will know what to expect from a back-level device driver.
`dpTechnology`	The general class of the device. Although Windows does not use it directly, an application may be interested in this information. The field can be set to one of the following values:

Value **Description**

Value	Description
0	vector plotter
1	raster display (e.g., CGA / VGA / EGA / 8514)
2	raster printer (e.g., laser printer)
3	raster camera
4	character stream
5	metafile
6	display file

`dpHorzSize,` `dpVertSize`	The physical width and height of the display area, measured in millimeters. Windows uses these values when in a metric physical mapping mode, such as `MM_LOMETRIC` or `MM_HIMETRIC`.
`dpHorzRes,` `dpVertRes`	The physical width and height of the display, measured in the smallest discrete unit supported by the device in the configured mode. This definition accommodates a plotter device, which does not deal with pixels. For raster devices these values represent the number of pixels in the X-direction and the number of scan lines, respectively. For example, for a typical 300 dpi laser printer with a `dpHorzSize` of 203 (8

inches) and `dpVertSize` of 254, `dpHorzRes` is 2400 and `dpVertRes` is 3000. For a standard VGA video display, `dpHorzRes` is 640 and `dpVertRes` is 480.

`dpBitsPixel`

The number of bits per pixel in a single plane (see the `dpPlanes` field). Windows uses this value to determine how bits are packed into memory when it passes data to the device. For a VGA display, for example, this value is 1. For a typical black-on-white printer, this value is also 1. For an 8514-compatible display, this value is 8. (See `dpPlanes` for a complete description of `dpBitsPixel` and `dpPlanes`.)

`dpPlanes`

The number of planes. Windows uses this value along with `dpBitsPixel` to pass multiplane data to a device. For an EGA display, for example, this value is 3. For a typical black-on-white printer, this value is 1. For an 8514-compatible display, this value is also 1.

To understand how `dpBitsPixel` and `dpPlanes` relate, consider an EGA-compatible display in which each color (red, green, and blue) is stored in a different memory plane. Each display pixel is represented by a bit in each plane; 1000 pixels on the screen require 3000 bits of memory. Instead of taking up 375 bytes (3000 bits) of memory address space, the pixels take only 125 bytes. The mode of the device determines which plane is accessed. When Windows passes 1000 pixels of color data to this device, it passes 125 bytes of red, followed by 125 bytes of green, followed by 125 bytes of blue. It knows to pass the data this way, since `dpPlanes` is 3, and `dpBitsPixel` is 1.

For single-plane devices (`dpPlanes` = 1), Windows packs the bits according to `dpBitsPixel`. For a typical black-on-white printer, with `dpBitsPixel` equal to 1, Windows packs 8 pixels to a byte. For an 8514-compatible display, with `dpBitsPixel` equal to 8, Windows packs 1 pixel per byte.

`dpNumBrushes`

The number of pattern brushes supported by the device. With most hardware this value is zero; Windows must issue other device commands to the device driver to achieve different brush styles. Post-Script printers and more advanced video displays support more brushes.

dpNumPens
The number of line-pattern pens supported by the device. As with brushes, many devices do not provide pens and this value is zero. Windows issues other commands to simulate different pen styles. Drivers for plotters and more advanced video controllers often have a nonzero value here when they are capable of generating different pen styles in hardware.

dpNumFonts
The number of fonts supported by hardware. For typical PC display adapters this value is zero. For printers this value is at least 1, and often greater.

dpNumColors
The number of colors supported by this device. For black-on-white printers, this value is 1. For plotters, this value represents the number of pens available.

dpDEVICEsize
The size, in bytes, of the PDEVICE data structure for this device. The common fields of the PDEVICE data structure are described later in this chapter.

dpCurves
This bitmapped value indicates whether the device can create various curved figures. A set bit (1) indicates that the device is capable of creating the figure itself. A reset bit (0) indicates that the device is not capable of creating such a figure. Bits 8 through 15 must be zero. The other bits indicate the device capabilities:

Bit	Figure
0	circles
1	pie wedges
2	chord arcs
3	ellipses
4	wide-line borders
5	styled-line borders
6	combination wide- and styled-line borders
7	brushed interiors

| `dpLines` | This bitmapped value indicates whether the device can create various combined lines. Bits 0, 2, 3 and 8 through 15 must be zero. The other bits indicate the device capabilities: |

Bit	**Figure**
1	polylines
4	wide-line borders
5	styled-line borders
6	combination wide- and styled-line borders
7	brushed interiors

| `dpPolygonals` | This bitmapped value indicates whether the device can create various line figures. Bits 8 through 15 must be zero. The other bits indicate the device capabilities: |

Bit	**Figure**
0	alternate-fill polygons
1	rectangles
2	winding-number-fill polygons
3	scanlines
4	wide-line borders
5	styled-line borders
6	combination wide- and styled-line borders
7	brushed interiors

| `dpText` | This bitmapped value indicates the various text-drawing capabilities of the device. Unlike the other bitmapped values, some of these bits indicate a certain level of capability. If the device has a certain capability, Windows assumes that the device has all lesser capabilities. If bits 1 through 12 are all zero, the device driver may safely ignore all font attributes when drawing text. Bit 15 must be zero. The other bits indicate the device capabilities: |

Bit(s)　Capability

0–1　　These bits indicate how closely Windows will match an actual font to a requested font. If neither bit is set, STRING precision is assumed and the device may optionally ignore the height, width, escapement, and orientation text attributes. If bit 0 is set, CHARACTER precision is requested and the device must respect the escapement text attribute. For STRING and CHARACTER precision, if the device does not support the requested font size, the size used will be either the size of the next smallest font requested or the smallest font supported by the device. If bit 1 is set, bit 0 must also be set and STROKE precision is requested. The device must respect the height, width, escapement, orientation, and size text attributes. *A console device driver must set both of these bits for Windows to operate properly.*

2　　　This bit indicates if the device is capable of clipping or displaying a character that lies on the boundary of a clipped area. If the bit is set, a partial character that lies partially within the clipping region can be drawn. Otherwise such a character is omitted from output.

3–4　　These bits indicate if the device is capable of rotating a character. If neither bit is set, the device can only draw text along the X axis (if it has text capabilities at all). If bit 3 is set, the device can rotate the character by 90, 180, or 270 degrees. If bit 4 is set, bit 3 must also be set, and it indicates that the device can rotate a character any number of degrees.

5　　　This bit indicates if the device is capable of scaling in the X direction independently of scaling in the Y direction.

Bit(s)	Capability
6–8	These bits indicate the degree of scaling supported by the device. If none of these bits is set, the device is not capable of scaling. If bit 6 is set, the device can double the size of a character. If bit 7 is set, bit 6 must also be set, and it indicates that the device can increase the character size by any integer multiple. If bit 8 is set, then bits 6 and 7 must also be set, and it indicates that the device can scale a character to any degree.
9	This bit indicates if the driver `StrBlt` function (described in Appendix B) is capable of doubling the weight of characters drawn (typically by shifting the character one pixel to the right and overstriking).
10	This bit indicates if the driver `StrBlt` function is capable of skewing characters.
11	This bit indicates if the driver `StrBlt` function is capable of underlining characters.
12	This bit indicates if the driver `StrBlt` function is capable of striking out (or drawing a line through) characters.
13	This bit indicates if the device is capable of using raster format fonts.
14	This bit indicates if the device is capable of using vector format fonts.

`dpClip`   This value indicates if the device is capable of clipping output within a specified clipping rectangle.

`dpRaster`   This bitmapped value indicates various raster-device capabilities. Bits 14 and 15 must be zero. The other bits indicate the device capabilities:

Bit	Capability
0	The driver supports the `BitBlt` function. This bit must be set for display drivers.
1	The device requires Windows to provide banding support (printer drivers only).

Bit	Capability
2	The device requires Windows to provide scaling support.
3	The device can accept bitmaps larger than 64K bytes.
4	The device supports one of the `ExtTextOut`, `FastBorder`, or `GetCharWidth` functions. If the device does not provide support for all of these functions, it may return –1 as the result for the functions that it does not support.
5	The driver supports state block (printers only).
6	The device can save bitmaps internally for fast recall for display or printing.
7	The device can do `GetDIB` and `SetDIB` and RLE to and from memory for device-independent bitmaps (DIBs) in 1, 4, 8, and 24 bits per pixel.
8	The device supports color palette management.
9	The driver supports the `SetDIBitsToDevice` function.
10	The device supports Windows 3.x fonts larger than 64K.
11	The driver supports the `StretchBlt` function.
12	The driver supports the `FloodFill` function.
13	The driver supports the `StretchDIBits` function.

`dpAspectX,`
`dpAspectY,`
`dpAspectXY`

The aspect ratio of the device. Specifically for raster devices, `dpAspectY`/`dpAspectX` describes the aspect ratio of a pixel. The `dpAspectXY` value is the relative distance across the diagonal of a pixel. As an example, a CGA driver might provide values of 5, 12, and 13, respectively, for these fields. A typical 300-

dpi laser printer driver might have values of 500, 500, and 707. Note that dpAspectXY is the square-root (rounded) of the sum of the squares of dpAspectX and dpAspectY. Because other fields in GDIINFO are based on these units, and because Windows multiplies these values by other scaling factors, they should remain below 1000 to avoid overflow.

dpStyleLen   The minimum length, in pixels times dpAspectX, of a line generated by a styled pen. If you use the laser-printer example in the dpAspectX description, a minimum length of 3 pixels is specified by a dpStyleLen value of 1500 (500 × 3). For printer drivers, this value is typically 2 × dpAspectXY.

dpMLoWin,   The width and height of the window and viewport in
dpMLoVpt   MM_LOMETRIC mapping mode. See the Mapping Modes section later in this chapter for an explanation.

dpMHiWin,   The width and height of the window and viewport in
dpMHiVpt   MM_HIMETRIC mapping mode.

dpELoWin,   The width and height of the window and viewport in
dpELoVpt   MM_LOENGLISH mapping mode.

dpEHiWin,   The width and height of the window and viewport in
dpEHiVpt   MM_HIENGLISH mapping mode.

dpTwpWin,   The width and height of the window and viewport in
dpTwpVpt   MM_TWIPS mapping mode.

dpLogPixelsX,   The number of pixels per inch in the horizontal and
dpLogPixelsY   vertical directions, respectively. Windows uses these values to match fonts to the device. For display devices, these values can correspond to logical inches, which may be larger than physical inches to accommodate relatively low display resolution. For printer drivers, these values are the actual values. For a 300-dpi printer, for example, both these values are 300.

dpDCManage   This bitmapped value specifies how multiple device contexts (DCs) for the same device are treated. This field is specific to printer drivers, which are discussed in Chapter 4. This field should contain 0x0004 for display drivers.

dpPalColors   The number of entries in the Windows 3.x system palette. It is meaningful only if bit 8 in the `dpRaster` field is set. Drivers that do not support palettes may ignore this value. This field is for display drivers only.

dpPalReserved   The number of reserved entries in the Windows 3.x system palette. Drivers that do not support palettes may ignore this value. This field is for display drivers only.

dpPalResolution   The actual simultaneous-color resolution of the device, in bits per pixel. For example, the value for an EGA-compatible device is 3 and the value for an 8514-compatible device is 8. This field is for display drivers only.

Common GDI Driver Features

For the most part, the Windows GDI supports both display and printer drivers transparently to the application programmer. The GDI translates the application calls to calls to the device driver. Sometimes, there are direct correlations between GDI calls and driver calls. Usually, however, the Windows GDI simplifies the operations and makes lower-level calls to the drivers. While most calls apply to both display and printer drivers, there are a few that apply only to display drivers and others that apply only to printer drivers. This section discusses the calls that Windows makes to both display and printer drivers. Chapters 4 and 5 describe the driver-specific calls. All GDI device entry points are documented in Appendix B.

Enable and Disable

The `Enable` and `Disable` functions bracket access to a GDI driver. The `Enable` function returns the information in the `GDIINFO` and `PDEVICE` structures to the Windows GDI. Since it is up to you to define the `PDEVICE` structure, the GDI does not know the size of your `PDEVICE` structure. To resolve this, the GDI calls `Enable` twice: the first time to obtain the

GDIINFO structure and the second time to obtain the PDEVICE structure. Since the GDIINFO structure contains the size of the PDEVICE structure, the GDI can specify a buffer of the appropriate size in the second call to Enable. During this second call, the driver performs its initialization. The GDI calls the driver's Disable function to return the hardware to its original state. (See Chapters 4 and 5 for details on how the GDI calls this function.)

Mapping Modes

The GDIINFO structure contains fields that describe the various coordinate mapping modes. These mapping modes correspond to the same mapping modes that can be specified by the Windows API SetMapMode function.

The MM_TEXT mode is the most direct. It simply provides a direct mapping between dimensions of the application and the physical device. In the MM_LOENGLISH and MM_HIENGLISH modes, an application expresses coordinates and sizes in 100ths and 1000ths of an inch, respectively. In the MM_LOMETRIC and MM_HIMETRIC modes, an application expresses coordinates and sizes in 10ths and 100ths of a millimeter (or units of 100μ and 10μ), respectively. The MM_TWIPS mapping mode is used for typography applications. Its units are specified in 1,440ths of an inch.

When transforming coordinates and sizes among the various modes, the GDI refers to the GDIINFO fields that describe the viewport and the window for the mapping mode. The fields are declared as POINT structures, although they do not actually relate to a point on the surface. Instead, they provide a closest approximation ratio in order to map from the desired coordinate system to the physical coordinate system.

Consider the MM_TWIPS mapping mode, for example, with a display that has a resolution of 1024 pixels wide by 768 pixels high. For an average 14-inch monitor, this resolution yields dimensions of approximately 280mm × 210mm. Looking at the horizontal values first, the linear resolution is 3.657 pixels per millimeter or 92.89 pixels per inch. The linear resolution of a TWIP (twentieth of a point) is 72×20 or 1,440. The ratio of TWIPS to pixels is $1,440 \div 92.89 = 15.50$. Since we need to store the information as a ratio between two integers (the numbers must range between −32768 and +32767), we can store 1,550 in dpTwpWin.x and 100 in dpTwpVpt.x. Unfortunately, this does not give us satisfactory results, due to rounding. We can multiply each number by 10, carrying in another digit, but there is another method that yields more accurate results.

Let's look at the numbers again to find an exact ratio. If we multiply

280mm by 1440 TWIPS per inch, we get 403,200 mm-TWIPS/inch. We need to multiply the linear horizontal resolution, 1024 pixels, by some number to get a value in units of pixel-mm/inch. If we multiply 1024 pixels by 25.4 mm/inch we get 26009.6 pixel-mm/inch. This ratio of the two values yields 403,200/26,009.6 TWIPS/pixel. Multiplying by 10 to convert to integers, we get 4,032,000/260,096 TWIPS/pixel. This ratio is exact, but the numbers are not expressed as 16-bit signed quantities.

By simple factorization, we can reduce the two numbers by dividing out their greatest common divisor, 512. The final ratio is (4,032,000 ÷ 512) / (260,096 ÷ 512) = 7875 / 508. Unlike the previous approximation, this number is exact. Similar calculations using the vertical components yield the same ratio, since the aspect ratio of the pixels is one-to-one. If the aspect ratio were not one-to-one, the vertical ratio would have been different.

Putting the results of this example back into GDIINFO, the value for dpTwpWin is (7875, 7875), and the value for dpTwpVpt is (508, –508). If we had used a 300-dpi printer as our example, the calculation would have been trivial, yielding (1440, 1440) for dpTwpWin and (300, –300) for dpTwpVpt.

Objects and Drawing

Before most operations can be performed, the GDI needs to create certain objects that allow it to draw on the device surface. These objects are similar to the objects used by application programs: brushes, pens, fonts, and so on. Instead of using structures defined by the GDI, the device driver is responsible for creating and maintaining structures in its own native format. This allows you to define the structures so that drawing functions operate with optimal speed and efficiency.

In addition to the normal objects visible to application programs, the GDI also allows the device driver to define physical formats for other objects—namely colors and bitmaps. There are, however, some limits to the concept of device-dependent structures. The physical color structure PCOLOR, for example, must be exactly 4 bytes long. You can get around this limitation, however, by designating this structure as a pointer; you are then free to have it refer to a larger structure if you want. The physical bitmap structure is an extension of the standard BITMAP structure, with some added fields. Since this structure has a pointer to the data, which are in any format you choose, you can add anything you like here. Similarly, the physical font descriptor is based on the font file FONTINFO structure, with some changes.

Once the driver is initialized and at least one object is created, the GDI can call the driver to draw on the device's surface. The typical driver functions that the GDI calls include a PDEVICE parameter and one or more physical object parameters. Even the most primitive of functions (although not the easiest to implement), BitBlt, requires a physical brush structure for some of its raster operations.

Object Boundaries

You must be careful when you refer to rectangle or line sizes with the output functions. The limits of rectangles and lines are *noninclusive*—that is, the upper bounds are not included. For example, a clipping rectangle specifies upper left and lower right points for the rectangle. If the upper left point is (1,1) and the lower right point is (14,13), then the clipped region is a rectangle that is actually 12 pixels wide by 11 pixels high, for a total of 132 pixels.

BitBlt—Transfer Bitmap

The BitBlt (bit block transfer) function is one of the most fundamental of the raster driver functions but perhaps the most difficult to implement in software. If you are writing a typical monochrome printer driver, however, your job might be easy. Windows provides an entry point into the display driver that the printer driver can use: dmBitBlt (the dm stands for dot matrix). The only restrictions for using dmBitBlt are that the source and the destination must both be memory bitmaps, and the bitmaps must be monochrome. See the GDI Driver Support Functions section later in this chapter for more information. If you are writing a display driver or a printer driver that requires color, or if you cannot use memory BitBlt operations, then you will need to write your own version of BitBlt.

Most of the parameters for BitBlt are straightforward except the *lRop3* parameter. This 32-bit parameter is the **ternary operation code**. The upper 16 bits of this parameter make up the **raster operation index** and the lower 16 bits make up the **raster operation code**. Microsoft provides the operation index for drivers that control a device that can perform BitBlt in hardware. Drivers that perform BitBlt in software use the raster operation code to determine the operation that is to be performed. Both fields require some explanation.

The Raster Operation Index

The 256 raster operation (ROP) indexes are listed in an appendix of the Windows SDK reference. The index is constructed by performing the operation on permutations of the input operands: the source bitmap (S), the destination bitmap (D), and the brush (P). The best way to explain how Windows constructs the operation index is by a few examples. Refer to Table 3-1 in the following discussion.

The simple SRCCOPY operation has an index value of 0xCC. In binary, this value is 11001100. The high bit (bit 7) contains the resultant value if the SRCCOPY operation is performed when P, S, and D all have the value 1. Specifically, the result is 1 since S is 1. This corresponds to the top line of Table 3-1. The next bit (bit 6) contains the resultant value if the SRCCOPY operation is performed when P and S are 1, and D is zero. Again, the result is 1 since S is 1. Bit 5 is zero, since S is zero. Note that for this operation the values of D and P do not affect the resultant value, which is what we would expect for a simple copy operation.

Some operations are unusual and do not have common names like that of the SRCCOPY function. These operations are referred to by their reverse Polish notation (RPN). If you have ever used a Hewlett-Packard calculator you are already familiar with this notation. With the BitBlt operation codes, however, we have only four possible operands (P, S, and D) and only three possible operations, all Boolean: AND (a), NOT (n), OR (o), and exclusive-OR (x).

TABLE 3-1 Raster Operation Code Index Construction

Bit	P	S	D	SRCCOPY	SDPSnoax
7	1	1	1	1	0
6	1	1	0	1	1
5	1	0	1	0	1
4	1	0	0	0	0
3	0	1	1	1	1
2	0	1	0	1	1
1	0	0	1	0	1
0	0	0	0	0	0

One operation code, for example, has the RPN notation SDPSnoax. Decomposing this yields a number of operations in a specific order, each of which leaves the result in the accumulator:

1. Perform a NOT operation on S.
2. Perform an OR operation with the accumulator and P.
3. Perform an AND operation with the accumulator and D.
4. Perform an exclusive-OR operation with the accumulator and S.

The final result is in the accumulator. To determine the value of bit 7 of the operation index for this operation, let P, S, and D all have the value 1 (as in the first row of Table 3-1). Step 1 leaves a zero in the accumulator. Step 2 performs an OR with zero and 1, leaving 1. Step 3 performs an AND with 1 and 1, leaving 1. Step 4 performs an exclusive-OR with 1 and 1, leaving zero. Bit 7 of the operation code, therefore, is zero. Bit 6 is determined by letting P and S have the value 1, and letting D have the value zero. These steps yield a value of 1. Continuing through the remaining 6 bits and listing them from left to right yields 01101110 binary, or 6E hex. This corresponds to the index for the operation code SDPSnoax. The same technique is used to construct all 256 operation indexes.

Although hardware BLTers can make the best use of the index, a device driver may also use the index for operation tables. If you do this in your driver, note that the ROP codes 80h up through FFh are the same as ROP codes 7Fh down through 00h (note the change in direction), the final result being ones complemented (NOT). For example, operation index F6h has the RPN PDSxo. The RPN for operation index 09h (FFh-F6h) is PDSxon. While the complement of operation index B7h is SDPxann, the two NOTs cancel one another, yielding SDPxa, which corresponds to operation index 48h (FFh-B7h). Therefore, if you use a table based on this index, you need only the entries for the first 128 operations, with simple logic to account for the symmetry.

The Raster Operation Code

The raster operation code, like the index, is also encoded. Unlike the index, however, the operation code does not completely describe the raster operation. Although it is possible to decode the index to determine the operation to be performed, the raster operation code makes it easier for drivers to perform Blt'ing in software. If you are implementing BitBlt in software, you should take advantage of both the index and the code.

The operation code uses eight lexical strings, each composed of a permutation of the three S, P, and D operands, and the push (+) and pop (−) operators, as shown in Figure 3-1. The operation code specifies the lexical string and the way the various logical operations are applied to the string. Again, the operation code can best be explained by a few examples. Previously, I showed how the RPN operation code SDPSnoax yields the operation index 6E hex. Let's look at how Windows creates the operation code value for this operation.

The RPN for all operations usually consists of a number of operands followed by a number of operators. The sequence of operands can be described by one of the strings listed in Figure 3-1 along with a bias to indicate which operand in the string is first. For example, the sequence PDS is represented by string 1 with a bias of 1, since PDS begins with the second character of this string. The sequence DSP also is represented by string 1, but with bias of 2. Looking back at our earlier example SDPSnoax, the operand string is represented by string 2 with a bias of zero. Although I have shown you where a sequence begins in a string, you still need to know the length of the sequence.

Looking next at the operators in the example, we have NOT, OR, AND, and exclusive-OR. In this operator sequence, there is one unary operator (NOT) and three binary operators (OR, AND, and exclusive-OR). The number of binary operators also tells us how many operands we have. Using the strings listed in Figure 3-1 and the operators, we can describe all raster operations.

Figure 3-2 illustrates how the 16-bit operation code packs all of the

Index	String
0	SPDDDDDD
1	SPDSPDSP
2	SDPSDPSD
3	DDDDDDDD
4	DDDDDDDD
5	S−SP+DSS
6	S−SP+PDS
7	S−SD+PDS

FIGURE 3-1 Raster Operation
(ROP) Code Lexical Strings

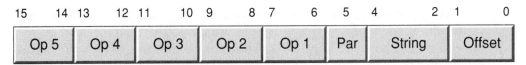

| 15 | 14 | 13 | 12 | 11 | 10 | 9 | 8 | 7 | 6 | 5 | 4 | 2 | 1 | 0 |

| Op 5 | Op 4 | Op 3 | Op 2 | Op 1 | Par | String | Offset |

FIGURE 3-2 Raster Operation Code Packing

necessary information. I described the bias and string fields already. The operator fields indicate the order and the operations that are performed on the operands. Each of the operator fields can be a number from zero to 3. A value of zero indicates a NOT operation, 1 indicates exclusive-OR, 2 indicates OR, and 3 indicates AND. There are five fields, but there is nothing that directly indicates how many operators are used. What if, as in our example, there are less than five operands?

Let's encode the operation code for our example and leave the undefined fields as zero for now. We end up with the binary value 00/01/11/10/00/0/010/00. Decoding this value results in the RPN string SDPSnoaxn. This is almost what we started with, but we have an extra NOT on the end of this one. How do we account for this? The solution lies in the P field.

The P field, or the parity, can also be treated as an optional sixth operator. If it is set, we are meant to append another NOT to the raster operation. By setting this bit, we end up with the binary value 00/01/11/10/00/1/010/00, or 1E28 hex. This literally results in the RPN string SDPSnoaxnn, but if we remember that two adjacent NOTs cancel each other, we can simplify this string to end up with the string that we started with, namely SDPSnoax. If we had started with a raster operation that had fewer operators, we would always fill the remaining operators with zeros (NOTs) and set the parity bit to account for the final desired result.

When interpreting the operand string and the operators in a device driver, we really treat the operation code as if it is in **postfix** notation. In other words, we take each operand from the string (moving from right to left) and apply the given operator to it. The result is the first operand for the next operator. Using the same example, we take the operand S and apply the unary NOT operator to it. The next operator is binary, so we take the P operand and apply the binary OR operator. AND is a binary operator, so we apply AND to the previous result and the D operand. Finally, we apply the XOR operator to that result and S, leaving the final result. Note that conceptually, we need only an accumulator and the next operand.

Referring again to Figure 3-1, let's look at the last strings in the figure: 5, 6, and 7. Unlike the other strings, these strings have the push (+)

and pop (–) operators in them. While almost all the raster operations can be described using the other strings, sixteen raster operations require the push and pop operators in combination with everything else we have seen.

To understand how push and pop are used, consider the raster operation `SSDxPDxaxn`. Note that unlike the RPN for most other operations the RPN for this operation has a binary operator between two operands. In terms of postfix evaluation, we need another conceptual variable to store an intermediate result. If, when retrieving the operands from right to left, we see a push operator we must save the accumulator for later recall. If we include push and pop as normal operators, another way to write this operation code in RPN is `SSDPDx+x-axn`.

One other difference with the push and pop operators is that instead of adding one, we add two to the number of binary operators to determine the length of the operand string. This accounts for the additional push and the pop tokens in the string.

The Output Function

Like the `BitBlt` function, the efficient implementation of the `Output` function in software requires a thorough understanding of primitive graphics operations, the details of which are beyond the scope of this book. The parameters of the `Output` function consist of: the number of a function code (or output style), endpoints, a pen, a brush, a clipping rectangle, and various mode options. As a minimum, the GDI requires that a driver implement the `OS_POLYLINES` and `OS_SCANLINES` styles.

The `OS_POLYLINES` style consists of two or more points specifying the endpoints to lines that the driver must draw. The line is drawn using the specified pen object. The `OS_SCANLINES` style consists of pairs of endpoints that are joined using the specified brush object or the specified pen object if the brush object is nil. Appendix A describes these and the remaining styles in more detail.

Text Drawing Functions

In addition to graphics, the GDI will request the device driver to draw text in a wide variety of typefaces, styles, and sizes. Unlike the `Output` function, however, the text drawing functions are entirely optional: If not supported by the driver, the GDI will use the `BitBlt` or `Output` functions to draw the characters on the physical surface. If you have a display driver whose aspect ratio does not match that of one of the default system fonts, however, you must include fonts with your driver. Furthermore, if you expect to use the supplied fonts with your display driver, then the values in the dpLogPixelsX and dpLogPixelsY fields of GDIINFO must match those of one of the standard CGA, EGA, VGA, or 8514 drivers.

The Control Function

The Control function provides a way to extend the number of functions a device driver can provide. Application programs access this function through the Windows API Escape function. Although the Windows GDI generally passes calls to the Escape function directly to Control, the GDI does manage some Escape function calls itself.

The Control function interface is generic. It accepts a PDEVICE parameter, a function code (also referred to as an **escape**), a pointer to input parameters, and a pointer to output parameters. All GDI drivers must support the QUERYESCSUPPORT function, which indicates whether or not a specific escape is supported by the driver. Depending on the type of driver, the GDI may require the support of other escapes.

In its most familiar use to application programmers, a program calls this function, using Escape, to manage printing and print banding. Another, less common use allows application programs to take special advantage of hardware-specific features of attached hardware. For example, the Windows 3.0 API does not support Bezier curves. If the hardware allows it, a device driver writer can choose to support the SET_POLY_MODE escape. An application can draw a Bezier curve by approximating (a slow process), or it can allow the hardware to draw the curve if the SET_POLY_MODE escape is available. Other escapes provide other functions, including allowing applications to specify high-quality color-separation printing options.

Some of the escapes listed in the SDK are included for their compatibility with older versions of Windows. For example, the GETSETPAPERMETRICS escape has been replaced with the GetDeviceCapabilities and ExtDeviceMode functions. Future versions of Windows will probably make some existing escapes obsolete, particularly those that perform advanced graphics operations.

Device-Independent Bitmaps

GDI drivers can provide a method of converting a device-independent bitmap (DIB) so that it can be displayed on the driver's output device. Although the GDI will perform this conversion into a monochrome bitmap, having the driver do this conversion allows it to take advantage of its knowledge of the capabilities and limitations of its hardware when it converts such bitmaps. Most of the conversion problems are related to color output devices, so if you are developing a driver for a monochrome device, you don't need to implement the DIB functions in your driver.

The `SetDIBits` function copies a DIB to a memory or device destination. The `SetDIBitsToDevice` function is similar, but allows transfer directly to the output device only. `GetDIBits` is the inverse of `SetDIBits` and copies a device or memory bitmap to a DIB. `StretchDIBits` is similar to the `StretchBlt` function, except that the source bitmap is a DIB. Windows 3.0 calls `StretchDIBits` only to transfer from a DIB; it never calls it to transfer a bitmap to a DIB. This restricted use, however, may change in a future release of Windows. In addition to these functions, a driver that supports DIBs must also support the `CreateDIBitmap` function as a dummy stub, since it is not used in the current version of Windows.

Font Format

Windows defines two versions of a structure that contains the fonts that are passed to the driver's `RealizeObject` function: the Windows 2.x version and the Windows 3.x version. In addition to these two versions passed in memory, there are two more formats that describe the fonts as they are stored in a file, again for Windows 2.x and Windows 3.x. These four formats have the same structure name: `FONTINFO`. This confusion of formats with a single name may partially explain why version 3.x fonts were not fully supported in Windows 3.0.

The essential difference between the font formats of version 2.x and 3.x is that the 3.x format allows a font file that is larger than 64K. Windows will pass such a font only to a driver that has bit 10 (0x0400) of the `GDIINFO dpRaster` field set.

Unlike the memory format of `FONTINFO`, the file format contains a version ID field and a copyright text field. Instead of memory pointers, the corresponding file format fields contain file offsets relative to the beginning of the file.

GDI Driver Support Functions

Unlike DOS device drivers, a Windows device driver is able to call most Windows functions, including memory allocation, disk input/output, and even dialog box functions. Since Windows rarely calls GDI drivers except as a result of a Windows API call, GDI drivers have even fewer restrictions on them than other device drivers. Functions in the kernel library may be called directly, either by linking with `LIBW.LIB` or by specifying the function in the `IMPORT` section of the driver's linker DEF file.

Functions in the USER library, however, may not be called directly. If you accidentally import a function from the USER directory into your driver, Windows 3.0 will not load. Instead, to call a function in the USER library, you must call the `GetModule` and `GetProcAddr` functions to get the entry point of the desired function.

The rest of this section discusses some of the functions that a device driver may call for driver-specific services. The detailed interfaces of these functions are in Appendix C.

Memory Access Functions

The interface to many devices—such as the standard display devices—is provided through system memory. Video memory, for example, can start at physical address 0xA0000. In real mode, access to this type of device is trivial and direct. The physical address is calculated simply as A000:0000. When the processor is running in protected mode, however, access is not so direct.

If you need to access the memory between 640K and 1M, the Windows kernel exports a few selectors as assembler `ABS` values that your device driver can access. So to load the ES and BX registers in order to access the memory starting at physical location 0xA0000, you can write:

```
pVideo LABEL DWORD
    DW              0
    DW              __A000h
    .
    .
    .
    LES           BX,pVideo
```

If you have a routine written in C, you can write:

```
extern _near _A000h ;
WORD FAR *pVideo ;
pVideo = (WORD FAR *)MAKELONG(0,(WORD)(&_A000h)) ;
```

Other symbols are exported by the kernel to access other portions of memory in a similar fashion. Their names reveal their corresponding physical memory addresses: `__0000h`, `__0040h`, `__B000h`, `__B800h`,

__C000h, __D000h, __E000h, and __F000h. Each of these symbols gives you access to physical memory in the first megabyte.

To access physical locations higher in memory, you need to be careful. Windows expects to have exclusive access to all memory provided by HIMEM.SYS. If your device is memory mapped, then it generally must be mapped above the highest physical memory address. This will prevent the BIOS from interpreting it as system memory. If the memory does not conflict with the conventional memory map, then all you need is a selector that maps the specified memory. You can create the selector using AllocSelector and set its linear base and size using SetSelectorBase and SetSelectorLimit.

Remember, when 386 enhanced mode is running, the linear address is not necessarily the same as the physical address. If you need access to such an object in 386 enhanced mode, you will need to write a virtual device driver and call the MapPhysToLinear function to obtain an appropriate offset into linear memory.

Display Versus Printer Drivers

So far, I have restricted the discussion of GDI drivers to the areas that display drivers and printer drivers have in common. Although the two are the same in most fundamental respects, there are substantial differences between the two that make them more like cousins than siblings.

Windows allows only one display driver to be defined. Zero, one, or many printer drivers, on the other hand, can be configured and active. A display driver typically has direct access to hardware, either through I/O ports or through memory-mapped hardware. A printer driver typically makes API calls to the GDI to perform output, and never directly controls hardware. Certain functions required for display drivers, such as BitBlt, can be stubbed to make calls to GDI brute force functions.

Summary

In this chapter I discussed the basic structure of GDI drivers in general. As you can see, much about this type of driver can be said without getting too specific about the presentation medium. There are, however, important differences between display drivers and hardcopy drivers; the next two chapters describe these differences.

CHAPTER

4

Printer And Plotter Drivers

Unlike all other types of drivers, printer and plotter drivers typically do not access or control the hardware they drive. Instead, they rely primarily on GDI interfaces and functions in order to do their work. If you are writing a printer or plotter driver, then your work may be relatively easy in terms of Windows programming.

If the driver is viewed as a black box, then the inputs to the driver come from the GDI through the driver's entry points, and the output is forwarded or echoed back to the GDI through the GDI spooler calls. In a very real sense, then, you can regard a printer driver as a filter (or a protocol converter if your background is in data communications). The GDI protocol is converted to a protocol that the printer understands. A printer device driver need not be informed whether the print spooler is installed. The GDI spooler calls will relay I/O directly to a serial port if the printer is not installed.

The complexity of this conversion depends to a great extent on how closely your printer's commands match the driver's entry point functions.

If your printer is "dumb," then you may have quite a bit of work to do in implementing many of the functions. If your printer is "intelligent," then the driver may need to do little more than relay calls from the GDI format to the printer's format.

For the typical black-on-white bitmap printer, the GDI provides a number of shortcuts that can ease the development process. For many of the driver's entry points, the GDI provides similarly named functions that operate on memory bitmaps. Instead of redeveloping all of the bitmap routines for your printer's format, you need only call the appropriate GDI function to create the bitmap in memory.

For example, for your driver's `BitBlt` entry point, you can translate the call into the GDI entry point `dmBitBlt` to perform the operation in memory and then transfer the bitmap to your printer, as required. The *dm* stands for dot matrix, although the functions are appropriate for any type of monochrome raster printer. The Microsoft documentation sometimes refers to the `dm` functions as the **brute** or **brute force** functions.

If your printer is monochrome raster, then you do not need to implement memory bitmap support in your functions. Instead, you can simply return an error code (–1) from such functions and the GDI will perform the operation for you.

Some printer devices may not provide a conventional serial interface, that is by way of RS-232 or parallel connections. If your printer does not, then you may need to control the interface hardware yourself. If you do this in the printer device driver, then the GDI has no way of spooling your printer output. If your "printer" is actually a secondary display monitor, this may be of little consequence, but for hardcopy printers it may be unacceptable.

If your printer has (from Windows' point of view) a nonstandard interface, then consider modifying the existing serial driver that comes with the DDK in order to support your device. Although the standard names are LPT1, LPT2, COM1, COM2, and so forth, your replacement driver need not access the same type of hardware, as long as the serial driver interface is the same. If you write such a driver, then your printer driver can call the standard GDI spooler functions and the Windows Print Manager will be able to spool your printer's output. (Chapter 6 discusses the serial driver in more detail.)

The GDIINFO Structure

While most of the fields in the `GDIINFO` structure have similar meanings for both display and printer drivers, some of the fields have special significance for printers. For most of the capabilities fields, a raster monochrome printer driver can list itself as "incapable," forcing the GDI to perform most of the work and calling the driver's `BitBlt` function to perform an `SRCCOPY` of the final resultant bitmap.

The other `GDIINFO` fields that apply specifically to printers are as follows.

`dpDCManage` Unlike display drivers, the GDI may open multiple instances of a printer. These instances can be separate spooler files or simultaneous activities to separate printers on separate serial ports. In other words, a single printer driver can drive more than one printer at a time.

The `dpDCManage` field tells the GDI how the device driver will treat multiple instances of a printer or, more specifically, how the driver will respond to multiple calls to `Enable` (without corresponding calls to `Disable`). Three bits in the `dpDCManage` field indicate the method.

If bit 2 (0x0004) is set, then the driver essentially ignores subsequent calls to `Enable`. (This value is used by display drivers, because Windows does not support multiple display instances.)

If bit 1 (0x0002) is set, then the driver treats each call to `Enable` as a separate instance only if the device name and port name combination is different from that of all other existing instances. In this case, the printer has only one mode active for all instances at any given time. In other words, the information returned in `GDIINFO` does not change for each instance, once set by the first instance, even if the information in `PDEVICE` does change.

If bit 0 (0x0001) is set, then the driver creates separate instances for each call to `Enable`. The information in `GDIINFO` and `PDEVICE` can be different for each instance.

`dpPlanes` Although Windows provides the brute functions primarily for monochrome printers, a color printer driver may take advantage of these functions if the colors can be represented as separate planes, each considered a separate bitmap by the brute functions.

dpPalColors,   Although Windows provides these fields primarily
dpPalReserved,   for display drivers, they may also be used with
dpPalResolution   color printer drivers.

The Printer Device Mode

Printers under Windows can usually be configured in a variety of ways. Some of the printer configuration information is maintained in the Windows initialization file, WIN.INI. This includes device-independent information such as what serial port the device is connected to and what the default printer is, and device-dependent information such as what subtype of printer the driver is to emulate.

Other device-specific information relating to printer configuration is kept in the device's DEVMODE structure. This structure contains a number of fields that are defined by the Windows GDI API, but the data inserted in the space remaining in the structure is entirely up to the device driver. In general, DEVMODE contains information that can be set by the user using the driver's configuration dialog box. You can see this dialog box by selecting Configure from the Printers dialog in the Windows Control Panel.

Your own driver must have code that supports a similar dialog box. Your driver supports this by exporting the ExtDeviceMode function. Unlike other functions, this one is not called by the GDI; instead it is called directly from an application (typically by the Control Panel, but any application may call it). The DeviceMode function is an obsolete version of ExtDeviceMode, but you must provide it too, for compatibility with older application programs.

The GDI can query the current device mode by using the GetEnvironment function or set it by using the SetEnvironment function. The ExtDeviceMode function will generally call the SetEnvironment function to set the environment as selected in the dialog box by the user.

The GDI may also set the device mode when it creates a printer instance with Enable. The last parameter to Enable contains a pointer to the DEVMODE structure for the new instance. By calling the ExtDeviceMode function to create a device mode for a particular printer, an application can open the printer later, by calling CreateDC and specifying all of the parameters that the user previously entered.

Printer Escapes

An application passes printer escapes using the Windows API `Escape` function. Your device driver receives the escapes through its `Control` function entry point. For the most part, the escapes are passed through to the device driver without modification. A few of the escapes are managed entirely by the GDI and others are modified when they are passed to the driver. For example, your driver does not need to support the `EXTTEXTOUT` escape, because the GDI translates this call to your driver's `ExtTextOut` function. You should review all of the escapes that are defined in the SDK or the DDK before beginning the design of your driver.

`SETABORTPROC` is an example of an escape that is modified by the GDI. The input parameter to Escape, `lpAbortFunc`, is managed by the GDI. Instead of this parameter, the GDI passes the handle to the device context as the input parameter to `Control`.

There are a few inconsistencies in some of the escapes. For example, the `CLIP_TO_PATH` has different parameters between the `Escape` and `Control` functions. The `SET_MIRROR_MODE` escape is missing from the Windows 3.0 SDK documentation, so not many applications will be using this escape.

If you expect your driver to be used in Japan, then you need to consider some additional escapes that are not documented in the U.S. version of the SDK. Appendix G documents these escapes.

The Print Manager

A printer device driver typically sends its output to the Windows Print Manager, rather than using the serial communication functions or accessing hardware directly. Even though the driver uses the Print Manager calls, the Print Manager need not be installed. When it is not installed, the GDI forwards the output directly to the specified serial port, without spooling.

A print session, or job, begins when an application calls the GDI `Escape` function, specifying the `STARTDOC` escape. If an application wants to provide an abort procedure, it issues the `ABORTDOC` escape. These two escapes provide the parameters necessary to call the `OpenJob` function, which begins a Print Manager print job.

A print job is composed of one or more pages, which correspond to separate temporary disk files that are created during spooling. A device driver begins output to a page after calling the `StartSpoolPage` function; it ends a page by calling `EndSpoolPage`. These print job pages pages do not relate directly to physical printer pages. A printed page may consist of one or more spooler pages, or a spooler page may consist of one or more printer pages—the driver decides how to break up a print job into logical pages. This means the printer can begin printing one logical page as soon as the driver has released it. If the output were not divided up this way, printing would not begin until the application completes the entire print job.

After calling `StartSpoolPage`, a device driver may write data to the Print Manager by calling the `WriteSpool` function. This function simply writes the specified raw data to the device.

With the Print Manager, it is possible to suspend the spooler and run an application that writes to the printer. The application can then be terminated, unloading it and the printer device from memory. As long as the Print Manager remains, the job can be printed at any time.

When operator intervention is necessary—as when a plotter pen needs changing or a sheet of paper needs to be loaded manually—the `WriteDialog` function allows a print driver to insert a message with a pause directly into the output stream. The `WriteDialog` function is similar to the `MessageBox` function in that it displays a message box with an OK button. Unlike `MessageBox`, though, the `WriteDialog` function is not executed immediately; it is executed when the job is actually printed. Also unlike `MessageBox`, `WriteDialog` allows only an OK button, which simply resumes the print job; there is no provision for any other operator response. The `WriteDialog` interface does not allow for very complex error recovery and the device driver cannot receive any feedback from the device. However, the mechanism does provide the necessary basic support.

Once the device driver has printed the last page and has called the `EndSpoolPage` function, the driver ends the job in one of two ways: with `CloseJob` or `DeleteJob`. The `CloseJob` function ends the job normally. The driver calls the `DeleteJob` function to abort a job. Typically, the driver will call `CloseJob` in response to an ENDDOC escape and `DeleteJob` in response to an ABORTDOC escape.

The interfaces to the spooling functions are detailed in Appendix C.

Print Banding

Most printer drivers will implement print banding. Basically, banding relieves the device driver from maintaining a full bitmapped image while an application prints to a page. Usually little benefit results from banding a vector device. On a typical 300-dpi raster printer, however, a full page image can easily consume a megabyte or more of storage.

To avoid tying up so much storage, either the GDI or the application can restrict a page's output to a single band at a time. A **band** is a rectangular region of the page to which output is restricted. When a band is being output, output to other bands is ignored. In this way, the printer driver needs to keep track of the pixels within a single band at a time, resulting in less memory overhead.

Banding is slightly more complicated when there is text output. The bands are generally thought of as raster regions, and a printer driver typically sends text from `ExtTextOut` directly to the printer, without converting it to graphics. To resolve this, a text band is processed first. This text band comprises the entire printer page. After it processes the text band, the device driver processes each graphics band. When the text band is being processed, graphics calls are ignored; when the graphics band is being processed, text calls are ignored.

An application is not required to provide banding escapes. When it does not, the GDI bands the output for the application and sends the appropriate escapes to the device driver. In either case, the device driver does not need to be aware of the source of the escapes, since they are treated the same.

The following steps outline the GDI's banding process.

1. The GDI issues the NEXTBAND escape to begin the page.

2. The GDI issues the BANDINFO escape to determine the type of the band. The device driver replies, indicating a text band taking up the entire page.

3. The GDI issues all of the output operations for the page. The device driver ignores graphics operations and only processes the `ExtTextOut` (and `StrBlt`) calls.

4. The GDI issues the NEXTBAND escape.

5. The GDI issues the BANDINFO escape to determine the type of the band. The device driver replies, indicating a graphics band within a part of the page.

6. The GDI issues all of the output operations for the page, clipping the output to the specified band. The driver ignores all text output and all the graphics output that does not fall within the band.

7. Steps 4, 5, and 6 are repeated until the entire page is drawn.

8. The GDI issues the NEXTBAND escape.

9. The GDI issues the BANDINFO escape to determine the type of the band. The device driver replies, indicating a band rectangle of (0,0,0,0). This indicates to the GDI that the page is complete.

Note that when the input BANDINFO structure in step 2 indicates there is either no text or no graphics, then the driver skips the empty bands. Also note that the final NEXTBAND escape causes the paper to be released from the printer. A NEWFRAME escape is not necessary here and, if issued, causes a blank page to be ejected. In other words, an application issues either a NEWFRAME or NEXTBAND escape, but not both.

An application is not required to issue the BANDINFO escape, even if it issues the NEXTBAND escape. But by using the BANDINFO escape it can suppress text or graphics output at the application level—output that the device driver would otherwise need to ignore. This can improve printer performance for complex images. If the application does not issue the BANDINFO escape, the device driver processes the data in the same way, but the application sends output to the band, regardless of whether it is appropriate. The resulting output is the same, but will generally take longer.

Although Windows does not require that your printer or plotter driver support the BANDINFO and NEXTBAND escapes, you can easily support them by always providing one band per page for text and graphics output. If you are developing a driver for a vector output device or for a plotter that can maintain a full page image entirely in memory, you might consider implementing banding support in this way. If the device can draw its own fonts, then two bands can be used, each a full page with one for graphics and one for text output. If you don't support banding, an application will still be able to issue the NEXTBAND and BANDINFO escapes, but the GDI will simulate the functions by returning a single graphics and text band for the entire page.

Brute Functions

If your printer is a monochrome raster printer, such as a 300-dpi laser printer, then you may be interested in the brute bitmap functions, sometimes called the dot-matrix functions (which does not mean that the device has to be for a dot-matrix printer). The brute functions provided by the GDI are:

dmBitBlt	dmPixel
dmColorInfo	dmRealizeObject
dmEnumDFonts	dmScanLR
dmEnumObj	dmStrBlt
dmOutput	dmTranspose

These functions support the basic output operations on monochrome bitmaps and correspond directly to, and have the same parameters as, the GDI driver entry points of the same names (less the dm). In fact, the GDI simply forwards calls to these functions to the display driver. This is partly why the display driver is responsible for supporting monochrome bitmaps. The dmTranspose function is the single exception; it is actually implemented within the GDI.

If you have a color raster printer that supports colors in different planes and if you are willing to do a small amount of work, you can still use the brute functions. You have to call the functions for each plane. The DDK does contain source code for color versions of the brute functions, but you must integrate them into your code to use them.

If you have a monochrome printer, you will probably still need to perform some kind of coordinate transformation, when working on a particular band of an output page, before calling the brute output functions. For example, if you are working with an arbitrary band on the printed page, you will need to transform the coordinates to treat the upper left corner of the band as (0,0) within the bitmap that you pass to one of the brute functions.

Even if you are able to take full advantage of these functions, you may decide to implement them on your own. Microsoft has put a lot of work into the existing display drivers, but some developers have found that there is room for improvement. If you want to try to enhance the existing support for these functions, you can, of course, borrow some of the display driver source code from the DDK, making the changes you desire, and then integrate the modified code with your print driver. It is not practical to rewrite these functions from scratch unless you have a deep understanding of the theory and application of raster graphics operations.

Priority Queues

The Windows GDI forwards output to your driver in the order in which it is received from the application. Depending on your hardware or your driver implementation, you may determine that the given order is inappropriate. For example, when printing text, the application may provide the text in the order that it appears down the page with lines of text from a variety of fonts. You may find, however, that you can print faster if you work with one font at a time, printing all of the data on the page in a single font, then changing the font and printing all of the data in the next font. You might proceed this way through all of the fonts that are represented on the page.

In order to implement this type of approach, you need to save text output commands for processing when your driver receives a NEWFRAME escape or the last NEXTBAND escape on a page. When you process the commands, you do so with one font at a time.

The GDI Priority Queue functions help you manage these output commands in queues. You can assign an arbitrary priority, or key, with each entry in the queue. When you are ready to process the commands, you remove entries from the queue in order, according to the originally assigned priority.

Appendix C fully documents the GDI Priority Queue functions, which are summarized here in Figure 4-1.

Function	Description
CreatePQ	Create a priority queue.
DeletePQ	Delete a priority queue.
InsertPQ	Add an entry into a priority queue.
SizePQ	Set the size (maximum number of elements) of a priority queue.
ExtractPQ	Remove the highest-priority entry from a priority queue.
MinPQ	Query the highest-priority entry in a priority queue.

FIGURE 4-1 GDI Priority Queue Functions

Summary

Figure 4-2 lists the functions that are exported from your printer driver. Appendix B contains the interfaces and export ordinals. If you implement `DeviceMode` or `ExtDeviceMode`, then you also export the dialog procedure for the user dialog.

```
BitBlt              GetCharWidth*
ColorInfo           GetDIBits
Control             Output
CreateDIBitmap*     Pixel
DeviceBitmap        RealizeObject
DeviceMode          ScanLR
Disable             SetAttribute
Enable              SetDIBits
EnumDFonts          SetDIBitsToDevice*
EnumObj             StretchBlt*
ExtDeviceMode*      StretchDIBits
ExtTextOut          WEP
            *Optional
```

FIGURE 4-2 Printer Driver Exports

CHAPTER

5

Display Drivers

The display driver is Windows' principal device driver. Windows calls this display driver more frequently and depends on its performance more than any other driver. If you plan on implementing a display driver, you have as great a challenge as any Windows device driver developer.

The display driver is the most frequently called driver and is often the focal point of Windows performance. Windows calls the driver at least once (often several times) each time an application calls a GDI function. Windows also calls the display driver many times for most non-GDI function calls. Windows (or an interrupt routine) calls the driver whenever the mouse moves. Even when the system is otherwise silent, Windows may call the driver every half second or so in order to blink a text caret in an edit control.

Clearly, the display driver's performance is critical to the overall performance of Windows. Even though the performance of a printer driver is important, users have found ways of working around slow printer drivers: printing during lunch, or overnight. Clearly such solutions are not practical for display drivers. In fact, most printer drivers call a few of the routines provided in the display driver almost directly. The performance of the display driver thus directly affects printing performance.

For display drivers to achieve this level of performance, they are usually best implemented in assembly language, where every scrap of CPU power can be extracted. Not only do you need to be very familiar with raster graphic operations and your target video hardware to write a display driver; you should also be very familiar with the Intel CPUs. You might even find it worthwhile to take advantage of the CPU in use, using 80286 or even 80386 and 80486 instructions in situations where the CPU is available.

Display drivers are difficult even in the context of assembly language programs; they often take advantage of every trick in the book in order to improve performance. One commonly used technique is illustrated by the Microsoft DDK programming. The driver actually generates machine code on the fly, placing the code in an array on the stack and transferring control to code in stack memory. Even modification of the existing sample drivers in the DDK is a task for only the most experienced Intel assembly language programmers.

To some of you the prospect of display driver programming may be daunting. The purpose of this chapter is to least enhance your understanding of the interfaces and conventions that Windows expects of your display driver. Although the basic structure shared by printer drivers and display drivers is fundamentally the same, display drivers have a few interfaces that more specifically reflect the interactive nature of the display device, and that also reflect the increased performance expected from display drivers.

Unlike printer drivers, display drivers access hardware directly, through I/O ports and memory-mapped adapters. If you have advanced hardware capable of generating the various images that the GDI requests of the driver, then the implementation will be simpler. If, however, the hardware is not capable of performing the requested operations on main memory bitmaps, then you need to implement the functions in software. Although printer drivers can call dm functions to modify memory bitmaps, display drivers cannot call these functions, because the GDI depends on the display driver to do the actual work of the dm functions.

Because display drivers access hardware, developing a driver to run in 386 enhanced mode requires special treatment. In this chapter, I describe the real- and standard-mode interfaces. In Chapter 7, I discuss the issues related to implementing a display driver for 386 enhanced mode. Before you begin to develop a driver that will work in 386 enhanced mode, you need to understand all of the issues in this chapter and develop a driver for real and standard modes.

There are sample drivers that come with the Microsoft DDK for the common display adapters: CGA, EGA, VGA, and 8514/A. If your hardware is similar to one of these adapters, then a conversion may be somewhat less difficult. Even if your hardware is different, you may be able at least to copy the various dm functions to provide main-memory bitmap support.

The GDIINFO Structure

Many fields in the GDIINFO structure have special significance for display drivers. Some of the capabilities fields must indicate that the display driver has the associated capabilities, and the driver must provide corresponding support. Although Chapter 3 describes all of the fields in GDIINFO, let's look again at the fields that are display-driver specific.

dpDCManage
: This value is always 4, to indicate that all device contexts (DCs) share the same PDEVICE structure.

dpLines
: With most capabilities fields you can indicate capability even if it is limited and simply fail a requested operation if it exceeds the limits. With line styles, however, you must set the corresponding bit only if your driver is capable of generating the various line styles to both the display and to a memory bitmap.

dpText
: Bits 0 through 3 and 9 through 13 must be set in this field, indicating that the driver provides the corresponding text capabilities. (This field is fully described in Chapter 3.)

dpRaster
: The raster field must at least indicate that the display driver can accept bitmaps larger than 64K and that the driver exports the BitBlt, ExtTextOut, FastBorder, and GetCharWidth functions. You are not required to implement these functions fully, however. You can return an error code if your driver is requested to perform a function that it cannot provide. If you choose, you do not have to implement FastBorder at all; you can always return an error code from this call.

dpLogPixelsX, dpLogPixelsY
: Although these fields suggest that they record the horizontal and vertical pixel densities, the GDI actually uses these fields to match fonts to the display. If you expect to use the display fonts that are

dpLogPixelsX	dpLogPixelsY	Fonts
96	48	COURA, HELVA, TMSRA, SYMBOLA, CGASYS, CGAFIX (for CGA adapters)
96	72	COURB, HELVB, TMSRB, SYMBOLB, EGASYS, EGAFIX (for EGA adapters)
96	96	COURE, HELVE, TMSRE, SYMBOLE, VGASYS, VGAFIX (for VGA adapters)
120	120	COURF, HELVF, TMSRF, SYMBOLF, 8514SYS, 8514FIX (for 8514/A adapters)

FIGURE 5-1 Display Fonts Provided with the DDK

provided in the DDK, then these values must be set to match the provided fonts. Figure 5-1 lists the choices for `dpLogPixelsX` and `dpLogPixelsY`, and the corresponding fonts. You can specify other values for these fields, but if you do, you will not be able to use the provided fonts.

Display Escapes

Although not normally done, it is possible for an application to send escapes to the display driver in much the same way that escapes are sent to printer drivers. The two escapes that apply to display drivers are `QUERYESCSUPPORT` and `GETCOLORTABLE`. (A third escape, `SETCOLORTABLE`, is obsolete, due to the new color-palette functions. If you want to support custom applications that take special advantage of your hardware, however, you are free to implement the other escapes as documented in the SDK.

Driver Resources

As regular Windows programs and any Windows DLL do, the display driver can have resources bound in with the executable file. The display driver can use resources in much the same way that any Windows program uses resources. In addition, Windows expects certain resources to be pre-defined within the display driver. Instead of asking the driver for such resources, Windows loads the resources directly, using its `LoadResource` function to load the information from the DLL. The six resource types that must be predefined in the display driver DLL are as follows.

1. Thirty bitmap resources that illustrate the various visual components of Windows, such as the various buttons on a window title bar or on scrollbars.

2. Eleven cursor resources that illustrate the various standard Windows cursors.

3. Five icon resources that illustrate the various standard Windows icons.

4. A raw data resource that contains default configuration information about the display. Windows presents some of this information to applications through the `GetSystemMetrics` function.

5. A raw data resource that contains information about the color table used by the Control Panel.

6. A raw data resource that contains information about the stock fonts that the driver supports.

The bitmaps, cursors, and icons that must be included in the display driver are documented in the Windows SDK. The thirty bitmaps are described along with `LoadBitmap`; the eleven cursors are described along with `LoadCursor`, and the five icons are described along with `LoadIcon`.

The remaining resources are raw data resources. If you have never created a raw data resource before, you will find it is relatively easy. First, you need to create a file that contains the binary image of the resource in assembler. This is similar to creating a .COM file; the only difference is that there is no `ORG` statement and no instructions, just data statements. The assembler file may contain only one segment and it needs no external references or references to the segment name. After assembling the file, you link it and run it through the EXE2BIN utility to remove the EXE header information. The resulting file typically has .BIN as the file extension. In the RC file, you reference the .BIN file using the OEMBIN statement. The syntax for this statement is the same as that for similar resource statements: *nameID* OEMBIN [*load-option*] [*mem-option*] *filename*.

nameID	The resource ID or string name
load-option	PRELOAD or LOADONCALL
mem-option	MOVABLE, FIXED, or DISCARDABLE
filename	The name of the raw data file

The configuration resource contains basic information about the display configuration. Its resource ID is 1. The first 18 bytes of this raw data resource contain the information listed in Figure 5-2. The rest of this resource contains the nineteen default system colors for the device, in red-green-blue (RGB) format. These colors are described in the SDK under the SetSysColors function. The colors are stored 4 bytes per color, in ascending order by color index.

Note that some of the color values are included for backward compatibility with older Windows applications. The color of pushbuttons, for example, is not used with the standard Windows 3 controls, which use bitmaps instead. These values are still required, however, for older applications that can create their own controls.

The color table resource contains the list of colors that are to appear as the basic colors in the Control Panel's color dialog box. The ID for this resource is 2. The table may contain up to forty-eight colors, each in RGB format. The first word of the resource contains the number of colors provided. The remainder of the resource contains the color values for the basic colors. The list is not restricted to pure colors; it may also contain some dithered colors—it should, however, contain the most common pure colors supported by the device and the more attractive dithered colors.

The font information resource describes the three required standard fonts supplied with the device. The resource ID for this resource is the manifest constant FONTS. The first font is the OEM font. It has character codes that match those of DOS (typically IBM PC-8). The face name is Terminal. The second font is a monospace font in ANSI code order (typically the Courier font). The third font is a proportionally spaced font in ANSI code order (typically a sans-serif font). All three fonts must appear in this order as LOGFONT structures, except that the last field of each structure (the face name) must contain only one NUL byte, immediately followed by the first byte of the following structure. Thus, the size of each structure may vary, depending on the name of the corresponding face. It follows that the offset of the third structure can vary, depending on the name of the second face.

Offset	Size	Description
0	2	Width, in device units, of the thumb button for a vertical scrollbar.
2	2	Width, in device units, of thumb button for a horizontal scrollbar.
4	2	The factor by which the icon width is reduced before displaying an icon.
6	2	The factor by which the icon height is reduced before displaying an icon.
8	2	The factor by which the cursor width is reduced before displaying a cursor.
10	2	The factor by which the cursor height is reduced before displaying an cursor.
12	2	Kanji window height (set to zero for U.S. version); corresponds to the `SM_CYKANJIWINDOW` value returned by `GetSystemMetrics`.
14	2	The width, in device units, of vertical lines; corresponds to the `SM_CXBORDER` value returned by `GetSystemMetrics`.
16	2	The width, in device units, of horizontal lines; corresponds to the `SM_CYBORDER` value returned by `GetSystemMetrics`.

FIGURE 5-2 Configuration Resource Contents

Color Palettes

If your driver supports more than 255 colors from a single palette, it should provide color palette support. This support is straightforward; it consists of interfaces that allow Windows to query and change the hardware palette and to query and change the driver's logical palette translate table. The entry points are: `GetPalette`, `SetPalTrans`, `GetPalTrans`, `UpdateColors`, and `SetPalette`. These entry points are described in Appendix B.

There are two parts to the color palette: the static portion and the nonstatic portion. You define the number of static colors in the `GDIINDO dpPalReserved` field. Half of the colors are stored in the lowest entries of the hardware palette, and the other half are stored in the highest entries. Thus, the number of entries specified in `dpPalReserved` must be even. In addition, you must define at least twenty colors that are reserved by Windows. Windows reserves the first ten and the last ten palette entries.

Using the `RGB` macro defined in windows.h (your table will probably be defined in assembler), the first ten entries must be predefined as:

```
RGB(  0,  0,  0)
RGB(128,  0,  0)
RGB(  0,128,  0)
RGB(128,128,  0)
RGB(  0,  0,128)
RGB(128,  0,128)
RGB(  0,128,128)
RGB(192,192,192)
RGB(192,220,192)
RGB(166,202,240)
```

The last ten must be predefined as:

```
RGB(255,251,240)
RGB(160,160,164)
RGB(128,128,128)
RGB(255,  0,  0)
RGB(  0,255,  0)
RGB(255,255,  0)
RGB(  0,  0,255)
RGB(255,  0,255)
RGB(  0,255,255)
RGB(255,255,255)
```

The Color Translate Table

When Windows sends output to your display driver, the colors that it specifies are logical colors. When performing output to a memory context, your driver maintains these logical colors. When performing output to the hardware, however, it must translate the logical colors to physical colors (unless the source of a copy is the hardware).

The translation may come either from the logical palette, where Windows specifies the color in palette format (0xFF00*iiii*), or from colors specified in reverse RGB form (0x00RRGGBB).

Windows will call your driver's GetPalTrans function to query the current color translate table and will call SetPalTrans to set the color translate table. Immediately after Windows calls SetPalTrans, it can call your driver's UpdateColors function to update a portion of the screen.

DOS Sessions

Windows' DOS mode allows DOS applications to run under Windows. The display driver has to coordinate with Windows and DOS applications to provide proper screen display and repainting when it switches between DOS and Windows applications. In addition, when Windows is running in the DOS compatibility box under OS/2, the display driver must cooperate with OS/2 when the user switches in and out of the DOS box.

When the user leaves a DOS box and returns to the Windows display, the device driver is responsible for restoring the Windows screen to its previous state. One way to handle this is to save the screen image in memory or on disk, which requires substantial storage. Instead, Windows provides a special function, `UserRepaint`, that tells Windows to call the display driver to redraw the entire screen. Essentially, this function sends the `WM_PAINT` message to all the windows on the display.

In addition to providing the code that handles the redisplay of the Windows screen, you must also write the code that handles the redisplay of a real-mode DOS box screen when it is restored. You do this with a special module called a display grabber. You must provide two types of display grabbers with your driver: one for a real- and standard-mode driver and one for a 386 enhanced mode driver. Later in this chapter I will describe the real- and standard-mode grabber. I will talk about the 386 enhanced mode grabber in Chapter 7.

Interrupt 2Fh

Hardware interrupt vector 2Fh is the catchall vector in DOS for expanding non-DOS interfaces. OS/2 uses INT 2Fh to allow it to cooperate with DOS applications. Since Windows also runs in the OS/2 compatibility box, Windows and OS/2 use INT 2Fh to coordinate access to video. The Windows virtual display driver (VDD) may also issue these INT 2Fh functions to coordinate activity with the nonvirtual display driver.

The Windows display driver must hook interrupt vector 2Fh during initialization (in the call to `Enable`) in order to monitor calls from DOS applications. Since `Enable` may be called in standard mode, be sure to use the standard INT 21h functions 35h and 25h instead of modifying the interrupt vector table directly. The display driver must also relinquish the hook to INT 2Fh when Windows disables the display driver with a call to the display driver's `Disable` function.

OS/2 or the Windows VDD will call interrupt vector 2Fh with one of the following function codes in the AX register whenever the video display ownership changes:

4001h   OS/2 calls this function when OS/2 switches the DOS compatibility box into the background. The driver should save any video hardware information that may be necessary in order to restore the video hardware state. You may not need to save anything at all here, if your display driver simply reinitializes the video hardware when the display is restored.

4002h   OS/2 calls this function when OS/2 switches the DOS compatibility box into the foreground. This driver should restore any video hardware information that may have been changed by OS/2. Typically, you will restore (or initialize) the video hardware mode.

4005h   The Windows VDD calls this function to tell the display driver to save the video hardware state. This function is similar to function 4001h.

4006h   The Windows VDD calls this function to tell the display driver to restore the video state that was saved by the last call to function 4005h. This function is similar to function 4002h.

The display driver not only monitors calls to INT 2Fh, but may also issue requests to other system components by calling INT 2Fh itself. This is significant for the display driver in 386 enhanced mode, because it allows the driver to communicate with the VDD. The VDD of OS/2 version 2.x might also use this mechanism to improve video performance. The related INT 2Fh functions that the display driver (or any DOS application) may call are:

4000h   The display driver calls this function to determine how much work the VDD will do when it switches Windows between the foreground and the background. This call also tells the VDD to give the display driver direct access to the hardware registers. If the VDD is able to cooperate, it will return one of the following values in AL:

              001h   The VDD does not virtualize video access.

              002h   The VDD virtualizes the video when in text mode.

003h   The VDD virtualizes the video when in text mode or when in single-plane graphics modes.

004h   The VDD virtualizes text, single-plane, and VGA multiplane modes.

0FFh   The VDD provides full video hardware virtualization.

If the VDD does not provide certain capabilities, such as full graphics virtualization, it can depend on the display driver to properly restore the state of the video hardware when it switches Windows to the foreground via functions 4005h and 4006h, described previously.

By calling this function, the display driver also tells the VDD that it may call INT 2Fh functions 4005h and 4006h to have the display driver save and restore the video hardware state. Function 4007h, described shortly, reverses this effect.

4003h   The display driver calls this function to tell the VDD that it is currently in a video hardware critical section and is unable to process a call to save the state of the video hardware via INT 2Fh, function 4005h. The display driver must exit the critical section (see function 4004h) within one second after issuing this function.

4004h   The display driver calls this function to exit a critical section that was entered using function 4003h.

4007h   The display driver calls this function to tell the VDD that the display driver is finished accessing the video hardware and that the VDD may re-enable trapping of video register access. The VDD will not issue functions 4005h and 4006h until the display driver reissues function 4000h. Function 4007h reverses the effect of function 4000h.

Although the VDD no longer calls the display driver via functions 4005h and 4006h after the display driver issues function 4007h, the VDD (and OS/2) can still continue to issue calls to the display driver via functions 4001h and 4002h.

The Real- and Standard-mode Display Grabber

When you are writing a display driver, you will also need to write a **display grabber**. The display grabber's purpose is slightly different from that of the display driver. It assists in switching to and from a DOS session in Windows real or standard mode. Instead of saving and restoring the video mode for the Windows session, the display grabber is responsible for saving and restoring the video mode of the DOS session.

You need one display grabber that supports Windows in both real and standard modes. In addition, you need to write a display grabber for 386 enhanced mode (described in Chapter 9). Whenever I refer to the grabber in this section, I mean the real- and standard-mode version of the grabber. Likewise, whenever I refer to Windows here, I mean Windows running in real or standard mode.

Unlike every other device driver component in Windows, the display grabber is not implemented as a DLL. Instead, it is an absolute-image file, like a .COM file, with a single segment. It must be written in assembler. The grabber never runs in protected mode, only in real mode.

Windows calls the grabber by loading parameters into CPU registers and passing control to one of eleven grabber functions:

DisableSave	GetVersion	SaveScreen
EnableSave	InitScreen	SetSwapDrive
GetBlock	InquireGrab	RestoreScreen
GetInfo	InquireSave	

During initialization, Windows loads the grabber into memory. Since the grabber has no loader relocation fixups, Windows can load it anywhere in memory. The first 24 bytes of the grabber file contain an array of eight jmp instructions:

```
GRABBER SEGMENT WORD PUBLIC 'CODE'
    ASSUME CS:GRABBER,DS:GRABBER
    org  0
JumpTable label near
    jmp  InquireGrab
    jmp  Error              ; obsolete
    jmp  Error              ; obsolete
    jmp  Error              ; obsolete
    jmp  InquireSave
    jmp  SaveScreen
    jmp  RestoreScreen
    jmp  InitScreen
    .
    .
    .
```

Function	AX
GetBlock	0FFF8h
GetVersion	0FFFAh
DisableSave	0FFFBh
EnableSave	0FFFCh
SetSwapDrive	0FFFDh
GetInfo	0FFFEh

FIGURE 5-3 Grabber Functions Accessed by `InquireGrab`

As this code fragment implies, the CS and DS registers both refer to the grabber's segment on entry. The references to the `Error` routine reflect entries in the jump table that were used in previous versions of Windows, but are now obsolete. This table contains only five of the eleven functions. Windows accesses the remaining functions through the `InquireGrab` function. If Windows calls `InquireGrab` with a value between 0FFF4h and 0FFFFh, it is requesting access to the remaining entry points, listed in Figure 5-3. Note that some values of AX within this range are invalid and should result in a call to the `Error` routine.

Although the grabber is like a .COM file, all of its entry functions must exit with a far return (`RETF`) instruction. All of the entry points are documented in Appendix D. Beyond these interface requirements, the way you implement the grabber is up to you. The DDK contains sample code for various standard display adapters, and you may follow the model provided in these samples.

Summary

Figure 5-4 lists the functions that can be exported from your printer driver. Appendix B contains the interfaces and export ordinals.

Developing a display driver from scratch can take many developer-years. If you intend to implement such a driver, you will probably save yourself a lot of effort if you can modify one of the existing drivers provided in the DDK to suit your needs.

There are many topics relating to graphical display drivers that have not been touched on here. I have tried to explain how Windows expects to

```
BitBlt              Inquire
ColorInfo*          Output
Control             Pixel
CreateBitmap*       RealizeObject
CreateDIBitmap      SaveScreenBitmap
DeviceBitmap        ScanLR
DeviceBitmapBits    SetAttribute
Disable             SetCursor
Enable              SetDIBits*
EnumDFonts*         SetDIBitsToDevice*
EnumObj             SetPalette*
ExtTextOut          SetPalTrans*
FastBorder          StretchBlt*
GetCharWidth        StretchDIBits*
GetPalette*         UpdateColors*
GetPalTrans*        UserRepaintDisable
                 *Optional
```

FIGURE 5-4 Display Driver Exports

communicate with a display driver, but I have omitted many other topics that are beyond the scope of this book, including such major topics as the various algorithms relating to line drawing and pattern fill, and the various hardware "blitters" and less obvious topics such as the relationship between video screen appearance and font design. Appendix I lists some books that may help you in your search for more related information.

CHAPTER

6

System Drivers

The Windows system drivers provide the interface between Windows and the keyboard, the mouse, the COM and LPT ports, sound devices (including the standard PC speaker), and local area networks. As mentioned in Chapter 1, each of these driver types has its own unique interface into Windows. This makes it difficult to discuss a Windows device driver in general, but it allows the drivers to interface to applications at a much higher level.

In DOS, for example, both the keyboard and the COM device drivers have the same interface. An application can open both in the same way and read from both using the same INT 21h function calls. In contrast, the keyboard and COM drivers in Windows have dramatically different interfaces. The COM driver allows an application to read a block of data with a single Windows API call. The keyboard, on the other hand, presents keystrokes to the application one at a time through Windows messages. These interfaces reflect typical use of these devices by applications, rather than providing a bare-bones interface as do their DOS counterparts.

In this chapter I describe the device drivers as they are implemented for Windows running in real and standard modes. For the most part, the same drivers are used in 386 enhanced mode, but generally in conjunction with a virtual device driver (VxD), which manages hardware contingency and access for the various virtual sessions (including the session that manages Windows applications). I will describe VxDs in more detail in the next chapter.

The DOS Protected Mode Interface

The DOS protected mode interface (DPMI) provides a method of coordinating the activities of DOS programs and extended memory programs. Windows provides support for DPMI in standard and 386 enhanced modes. For detailed information on DPMI, see the Intel documentation listed in Appendix H.

The subset of DPMI provided for Windows applications and drivers is extremely limited, but at least offers some of the basic support required for handling interrupts that are received when it is running in either real or protected modes of the processor. The most fundamental restriction imposed is that the DPMI functions may be called only from protected mode. In addition, the INT 2F functions are not supported in real mode. Only the following functions may be called from a standard mode program or driver by loading the appropriate value in AX and executing an INT 31h instruction:

Function (AX)	Name
0x0200	Get Real Mode Interrupt Vector
0x0201	Set Real Mode Interrupt Vector
0x0300	Simulate Real Mode Interrupt
0x0301	Call Real Mode Procedure With Far Return Frame
0x0302	Call Real Mode Procedure With IRET Frame
0x0303	Allocate Real Mode Callback Address
0x0304	Free Real Mode Callback Address

You might find that you can use some of the other DPMI functions from standard mode, but since the other functions are available through Windows kernel calls, they are superfluous.

One use of these functions is to allow a device driver to process interrupts when a DOS session is active. When called from a standard mode Windows program or DLL, the DOS INT 21 function 25 sets the protected mode interrupt descriptor table and not the real mode interrupt vector table. When Windows standard mode runs a DOS session, the interrupt descriptor table is disabled, and the interrupt vector table is enabled. Functions 0x200, 0x201, 0x303, and 0x304 allow you to hook (and restore) the real mode interrupt vector table so that your driver does not lose interrupts when a standard mode DOS session is active.

Another use of these functions is to allow a protected mode program to call real mode code, such as a TSR. For many of the INT calls, Windows performs all the translation necessary; all you need to do is execute the INT instruction in the processor's real mode. If this does not work for your TSR, then you may need to use function 0x300, 0x301, or 0x302 to call real mode. Chapter 10 contains some examples of how these functions can be used in standard mode.

The Keyboard Driver

The Windows keyboard driver serves two distinct purposes. First, it provides the interface between Windows and the keyboard. Second, it converts text characters between the hardware or OEM character set (typically the default IBM PC character set) and the Windows (or ANSI) character set. While there is little reason to have a single device driver serve both purposes, the fact of the matter is that the keyboard device driver must be critically aware of internationalization issues and character sets, so it is likely that the person writing the keyboard device driver will be familiar with the internationalization issues and characters sets used by Windows.

If you need to write a keyboard driver for relatively standard keyboard hardware, you will appreciate the driver that is already provided in the Microsoft DDK. This source code is probably the most flexible of all the code in the DDK in terms of its configurability. Throughout this book, I have focused more on the driver interfaces than on the code provided with the DDK. With the keyboard driver, however, the changes you will most likely need will be some of the translation table entries—adding new keys or rearranging some of the key assignments. Even if you are writing a keyboard driver that has an unconventional interface, you will find much of the key translation code in the DDK very helpful.

Dead Key and Alternate Graphic Processing

This section is for readers who may never have heard the terms **dead key** or Alt-Gr key. If you are familiar with these keys, you may want to skip this section.

A dead key is a key on a keyboard that causes no action, but instead qualifies the next keystroke entered. It is somewhat like a shift key in this way, but, like the Caps Lock key, it does not need to be held down to affect the next keystroke. Unlike the Caps Lock key, however, a dead key affects the following keystroke only—subsequent keystrokes are unaffected.

An example of a dead key is the accent character key found on the keyboards for Spain and other countries. When this key is pressed, no character appears. If a vowel key (*a, e, i, o, u*) is pressed immediately following, however, the corresponding accented character is entered. For example, when the accent key is pressed followed by the *e* key, an *é* (note the accent) is entered. A similar sequence is followed for many other characters that have diacritics associated with them.

Before computers, dead keys were (and still are) used on non-U.S. typewriters. The way they work on a typewriter is similar to the way they typically work on computers. When a dead key is pressed on a typewriter, the character is typed, but the typewriter carriage does not advance. Thus, pressing the dead key for an acute accent followed by the letter *e* first shows the accent on the paper and, since the carriage has not advanced, the letter *e* is typed in the same position, producing *é*.

The U.S. version of Microsoft Windows includes support for keyboards for a variety of different countries; it even includes support for a Dvorak keyboard layout. Using the Control Panel, you can easily change to a Spanish configuration, for example, and see how this support works. Many of the key caps will not match, but you can get the general idea. To test it out, select the Spanish keyboard layout from the Control Panel. Then press the single-quote key in a text field or in the NOTEPAD utility. You will find that the Spanish keyboard layout treats the single-quote key as a dead key for producing an acute accent. If you next press the *e* key, you will see the accented *é*.

By the way, if you press a dead key followed by the spacebar, the diacritical mark appears by itself. This is logical following the model of the non-U.S. typewriter. However, the similarity ends here, because although a real typewriter allows any key to follow the press of a dead key, the keyboard driver allows only key sequences that produce characters in the currently selected character set. Thus the Spanish keyboard layout will not allow an accented *n*.

In addition to dead keys, most non-U.S. keyboards have an alternate graphics key, labeled Alt-Gr. This key replaces the Alt key to the right of the spacebar. The Alt-Gr key works in much the same way the regular shift key does: it provides another character for certain keys. U.S. keyboards are limited to two graphics per key, lower- and upper-case letters typically.

Many non-U.S. keyboard layouts allow four graphics on some keys, accessed by combining the Shift and Alt-Gr keys with the graphic key.

In the driver code, the Alt-Gr is treated as if Ctrl+Alt is pressed. The driver will behave in the same way, in fact, if Ctrl+Alt *is* pressed instead of Alt-Gr. Reflecting this identity, the driver translation tables for the Alt-Gr keys have `CtlAlt` in the table names.

Keyboard Events

In DOS the application is responsible for asking for a keystroke from the keyboard. In Windows, however, the keyboard driver sends a keystroke to Windows, which in turn forwards the keystroke to the application in the form of a `WM_KEYDOWN` message. For many keystrokes the `WM_KEYDOWN` message causes Windows also to send a `WM_CHAR` message to the focused application Window. The application can tell when a key is released through the `WM_KEYUP` message.

In order to implement the event-driven messages, Windows passes the address of an **event procedure** to the keyboard driver using the driver's `Enable` function (described in Appendix E). The driver passes parameters to the event procedure for each virtual key code received from the keyboard hardware. Although the driver is responsible for converting the scan code into a virtual key code, the driver passes both the virtual key code and the hardware scan code.

Because applications have access to this scan code via the `WM_KEYDOWN` and `WM_KEYUP` messages, some applications may be hardware dependent and rely on these scan codes to be compatible with the IBM PC. For this reason, if your hardware does not generate IBM PC scan codes, you may wish to translate your hardware scan codes to those matching the IBM PC keyboard in order to insure application compatibility.

Translation Table Libraries

Since there is only one driver for each type of keyboard hardware, there must be a way to configure the driver for the keyboard layout for each nation. Windows does this by using a dynamic link library (DLL) for each keyboard layout. These libraries contain all of the information that the driver requires in order to translate key-depression activity into keyboard events.

The libraries contain a number of tables that direct the driver during key translation. These tables are duplicated in the driver, which contains the tables for the default U.S. keyboard. If a nondefault keyboard is selected, the driver tables can be overwritten or redirected to the DLL tables. Most of these tables are used by the driver `ToAscii` function (which is itself called by the Windows `TranslateMessage` function). The various tables are:

Table	Description
`keyTrTab`	Translates hardware scan codes into virtual key codes. The driver uses this table to determine the virtual key code that is sent to the Windows keyboard event procedure.
`AscTran`	Translates unshifted and shifted nonalphabetic virtual key codes to Microsoft ANSI characters.
`AscControl`	Translates control-shifted nonalphabetic virtual key codes to Microsoft ANSI characters.
`AscCtlAlt`	Translates Alt-Gr virtual key codes to Microsoft ANSI characters.
`AscShCtlAlt`	Translates shifted Alt-Gr virtual key codes to Microsoft ANSI characters.
`CapitalTable`	Lists nonalphabetic keys that translate differently when shift-lock is active.
`SGTrans`	The Swiss-German keyboard differentiates between shift and shift-lock on certain keys. This table enumerates those keys.
`Morto, MortoCode`	These tables contain keyboard scan codes that correspond to dead keys.
`DeadKeyCode, DeadChar`	These tables map dead key sequences to the resultant diacriticized character code.

Keyboard Driver Entry Points

Since the keyboard truly serves two distinct purposes, the driver's entry points reflect the distinction. Figure 6-1 lists the entry points related to the keyboard interface. Notice that many of these functions have the same name as some of the Windows API functions: `VkKeyScan` and `MapVirtualKey`, for example. In fact, these keyboard functions are exactly those named in the Windows API; the keyboard driver directly supports these functions.

Disable	*Initialize*	SetSpeed
Enable	Inquire	ToAscii
EnableKBSysReq	MapVirtualKey	VkKeyScan
GetKeyboardType	NewTable	WEP
GetKeyNameText	OemKeyScan	
GetTableSeg	ScreenSwitchEnable	

FIGURE 6-1 Keyboard Driver Entry Points

The remaining functions are provided as the private interface between Windows and the keyboard driver. The *Initialize* function is not really an exported function, but is actually the entry point into the driver. Since the keyboard driver is really a dynamic link library, this entry point is the library initialization function. The `Disable` and `Enable` functions enable and disable the driver for switching between the Windows session and DOS sessions in real and standard modes. `EnableKBSysReq` enables and disables the Ctrl+Alt+Sysrq key sequence used with the CodeView debugger. `GetKeyboardType` returns the keyboard type and subtype codes. `GetKeyNameText` translates a virtual key code into an ASCII string. `Inquire` returns the `KBINFO` structure. `NewTable` loads a translation DLL. `OEMKeyScan` converts an OEM code to a keyboard scan code. `ScreenSwitchEnable` enables and disables OS/2 screen switches. `SetSpeed` sets the keyboard repeat rate. `ToAscii` performs key translation functions for the Windows `TranslateMessage` API. `VkKeyScan` translates a Microsoft ANSI code to a virtual key code and shift state. `WEP` is the normal Windows DLL exit procedure. All of these functions are described in more detail in Appendix E.

Figure 6-2 lists the entry points related to character set translation. These translate functions correspond directly to the Windows API functions of the same names. If you are considering writing your own keyboard driver from scratch, remember that all of these functions are already available in the Device Development Kit. You might consider using at least this portion of code from the DDK and write the hardware interface code separately. None of these functions is really related to the keyboard driver except that Microsoft decided to include these functions in the same library as the keyboard driver.

```
AnsiToOem
AnsiToOemBuff
GetKBCodePage
OemToAnsi
OemToAnsiBuff
```

FIGURE 6-2 Keyboard Driver
Character Translate Functions

Keyboard SYSTEM.INI Fields

The system initialization (SYSTEM.INI) file has several fields that are
used by the standard keyboard driver and the Control Panel utility. These
fields are in the [keyboard] section of SYSTEM.INI:

Field	Description
type	The keyboard type. If this field is omitted, the keyboard driver will examine the hardware to determine the keyboard type. Otherwise, the driver currently uses the following values: 1 for an XT keyboard, 3 for AT, and 4 for enhanced.
subtype	The keyboard subtype. This field is used internally for the Olivetti keyboard driver. You may use this field for your own driver if you wish.
keyboard.dll	The translation table library. If this field is omitted, the U.S. translation is used. Otherwise, this field specifies the name of the translation table library. For the German keyboard layout, for example, KBDGR.DLL is specified.
oemansi.bin	Code page translation. This field specifies an absolute-image file that contains translation tables that translate from the Microsoft ANSI table to the current code page. This field is blank for the default code page (437).

The [boot] section of the driver specifies the name of the keyboard driver
itself in the keyboard.drv field. The driver file must reside in the Windows system directory.

The Mouse Driver

After the keyboard driver, the mouse driver is perhaps the driver least likely to be written for Windows. The reason is that the DOS INT 33h interface provides all of the functionality required for the Windows mouse driver. The mouse driver provided with Windows will use the INT 33h interface if it does not detect a hardware mouse, so if you have a non-Microsoft-compatible mouse, it is likely that the existing Windows driver will work fine simply by installing the DOS version of your driver before starting Windows.

There are some situations in which you might want to change the mouse driver. One case might be that you want to provide a direct interface to your mouse hardware. In standard mode on an 80286 processor, this would avoid switching between real and standard modes for every mouse event. Another case might be to work around a conflict imposed by the existing mouse driver. The existing mouse driver, for example, does not use the communication driver for a mouse that is attached to a serial port. Instead, it accesses the hardware directly. The method that it uses to avoid contingency with the serial driver is nonstandard, obscure, and the source of many problems encountered by end-users. If you are developing a serial driver that replaces the existing driver, you may want to modify the mouse driver to call your serial driver so that a serial mouse can be connected to your serial hardware. Whatever your reason, the architecture of the mouse device driver is relatively simple. Appendix E describes each entry point into the mouse device driver (see also Figure 6-3).

The initialization function, while not a true exported entry point, is the first function that Windows calls during Windows initialization. The standard mouse driver, which supports a variety of mouse types, uses this opportunity to determine the type of mouse hardware installed.

The `Inquire` and `MouseGetIntVect` functions return information about the configuration and characteristics of the mouse. Although there are fields that indicate the number of mouse buttons available in the mouse, Windows currently uses only three buttons.

Initialization	`Inquire`
`Disable`	`MouseGetIntVect`
`Enable`	`WEP`

FIGURE 6-3 Mouse Driver Entry Points

Windows calls the `Enable` function when Windows is ready to receive information about mouse movement and button activity. Windows passes the address of an event procedure to the `Enable` function. The mouse device driver then calls the event procedure whenever the mouse moves or the state of one of its buttons changes (a button is pressed or released). This means that Windows is notified the moment the mouse status changes and does not need to query the mouse device driver about its state. In fact, there is no mouse driver function that returns the state of the mouse. This corresponds to the fact that there is no Windows API function to query the state of the mouse.

Windows calls the `Disable` function to temporarily suspend calls to its event procedure. This allows windows to disable such calls when a DOS box is created, allowing the DOS box to receive such messages.

The Windows exit procedure, `WEP`, is the standard exit procedure available to all DLLs. Since the mouse driver is always resident, Windows calls this function only when the Windows session is ending.

The Comm Driver

Although the hardware interfaces to an RS-232 device and a Centronics-compatible device are very different, the software interfaces are very much alike: data is transferred as a sequential series of bytes from an application to an external device. There are some differences (the RS-232 interface provides for application control of handshaking lines and RS-232 allows bidirectional data flow), but for the most part, the underlying application interface is the same.

The logical interface is close enough so that Windows provides the same API functions for both types of devices. Furthermore, a single device driver is responsible for managing both types of devices. Appendix D documents the entry points into the comm device driver, listed in Figure 6-4.

Although I do not want to waste time criticizing the architecture of the comm driver, there are some critical weaknesses that you should be aware of if you have certain expectations based on your experience with device drivers in other operating systems. First, the fact that the comm driver supports two different types of hardware means that the parallel port hardware and the comm driver hardware are interlocked. In other words, if you are developing a driver for a special set of comm hardware, you must also include the code for the driver for the parallel hardware. Similarly, if you are developing a driver for a special set of parallel

CCLRBRK	REACTIVATEOPENCOMMPORTS
CEVT	RECCOM
CEVTGET	SUSPENDOPENCOMMPORTS
CEXTFCN	SETCOM
CFLUSH	SETQUE
CSETBRK	SNDCOM
CTX	STACOM
GETDCB	TRMCOM
INICOM	WEP

FIGURE 6-4 Comm Driver Entry Points

hardware, you must also include the code for the driver for the comm hardware. What about a user who has custom parallel and comm hardware from different manufacturers? Since the custom comm driver will likely support standard parallel ports and the custom parallel driver will likely support only standard comm ports, the user must exclude one driver in favor of the other.

Another weakness of the comm driver is the way Windows maps the device name from the application to the actual device type and unit number in the driver. When an application calls the Windows API OpenComm function, it passes the device name as the first parameter. Unfortunately, the device driver never sees this name. Instead, the Windows kernel translates the name into a unit number (CID), which it passes to the device driver. What is worse, the kernel restricts the names to a limited subset of possible device names: LPT1 through LPT3, and COM1 through COM9. Although 16-port comm cards are readily available for the PC, Windows version 3.0 prevents a standard interface to such a board.

A third weakness lies in the way data is passed from the Windows kernel to the device driver. Although an application can write data to a comm port a block at a time, the kernel can only write to the device driver one byte at a time. This means that, for fast applications and external devices, the throughput bottleneck lies between the Windows kernel and the comm device driver. For external hardware that transfers data a block at a time, this bottleneck is unacceptable.

These weaknesses occur in version 3.0; let's hope they will be corrected in a later version of Windows.

The 386 Enhanced Mode Driver

I am deferring discussion of the 386 enhanced mode version of the comm driver for a later chapter (see Chapter 9), but you should be aware that virtual access to the hardware can slow things down substantially. Instead of having your standard driver poke at virtual I/O ports, you may wish to give your driver direct access to the ports in enhanced mode. Alternatively, you may wish to have a virtual device driver control direct access to the hardware, handling device interrupts and buffering directly. This way your standard mode driver is not bogged down with virtual I/O access.

Installing a New Comm Driver

Once you have written a replacement comm driver, you will need to tell Windows about it so that Windows loads it instead of the standard comm driver. First, you must place your device driver in the SYSTEM subdirectory off of the Windows directory. Second, you must change the SYSTEM.INI file (in the Windows directory) to point to your driver. You can do this by simply changing the `comm.drv` field in the `[boot]` section to specify the name of your driver. Although you could name your driver COMM.DRV, it is probably best to give it a different name to avoid ambiguity.

Music and Sound Effects

The music and sound driver API is one of the least used in Windows, with the possible exception of the Windows operator warning beep. This is due to the fact that many of the functions relating to multiple voices and even some of the single voice functions are not supported in the default driver. One reason for this deficiency is related to standard PC hardware. Another reason is that some serious bugs in the version 3.0 driver render even some of the primitive functions useless. There is probably little reason for using any code for the existing driver unless you intend to fix some of these bugs. More likely, you will be writing a driver for advanced sound hardware. Ironically, much of the architecture for the standard driver was directly related to the PC Junior architecture and was later disabled when that platform was clearly destined for the hall closet.

The Sound Driver Interface

The Microsoft Windows SDK documentation omits any discussion of the Windows sound functions. With the exception of the individual function descriptions, less than a page is given to explaining the sixteen sound functions and how they relate. This seems to be the device that Microsoft "forgot."

Only one application at a time may access the sound generator. An application opens the sound generator by calling `OpenSound` and relinquishes access by calling `CloseSound`. The API does not even return a handle from the call, so it is not possible to share a handle with the sound device between applications.

Although the standard IBM hardware can typically generate only a single sound at a time, the IBM PC Junior was able to generate four separate sounds simultaneously. In other words, the IBM PC Junior was able to generate the sounds for a musical quartet. In computer-generated-sound terminology, the PC Junior is said to have been capable of four-voice sound generation. The `OpenSound` function returns the number of voices supported by the driver; it is 1 for the standard driver that comes with Windows 3.0.

The sound driver stores a sequence of sounds in a queue, much like a communications stream transmission queue. Instead of storing bytes to be transmitted, the sound generation queue contains instructions for the sound hardware. Much like bars of music in a musical score, the entries in the queue contain instructions on what sounds the sound generator is to produce. An application places entries in the queue using the various sound API functions. Since the queue is limited in size and since a Windows application is not able to wait for events, but must either poll a device or be notified by a message, there are functions that help an application keep sound information in the queue so that there is no lapse in the sound that an application produces. The driver must maintain a queue for each voice that it supports. An application can specify the size of a voice queue by calling `SetVoiceQueueSize`.

The queue is circular, with an "in" pointer and an "out" pointer. The queue is never emptied and can actually be replayed without requiring the application to regenerate all of the queue messages. On the other hand, the queue can overflow. The distance between the out and the in pointers indicates the amount of space that is available in each queue.

The functions related to keeping track of the available queue space are `GetThresholdEvent`, `GetThresholdStatus`, `SetVoiceThreshold`, `CountVoiceNotes`, and `WaitSoundState`. These functions do not modify the size of the queues; instead they help an application keep track of how much room is available in each queue. Note that `WaitSoundState` is not a particularly safe call to make from a Windows program, since it will lock up Windows and prevent it from processing messages until the function returns.

An application puts normal musical sounds in a voice queue with the `SetVoiceNote` function. Various noises can be generated with the `SetSoundNoise` function. Oddly enough, this function is not related to a queue and is intended for setting background noise. Since there is no way to specify which channel the noise is transmitted on, there is no way to synchronize this noise with the tones that are placed in the voice queues.

Besides the basic sound events that are stored in the sound voice queues, the sound driver also maintains current information about the characteristics of each voice. Put in musical terms, this information specifies the quality of the voice (that is, the instrument), the speed at which the queue is "played" (the tempo), the volume (pianissimo to fortissimo), and the type of note (legato or staccato). Applications specify this type of information with the `SetVoiceEnvelope` and `SetSoundAccent` functions.

The remaining functions allow an application to synchronize with the sound generator. Although the other sound functions place sound information in the voice queues, the sound generator does not actually begin emitting sound until the application calls `StartSound`. The sound is emitted until all sounds in the queue have been played or until the application calls `StopSound`. The `SyncAllVoices` function places a synchronization mark in each voice queue, allowing the various voices to regain synchronization when such a mark is encountered in a queue.

If you are attempting to experiment with the standard sound driver for Windows 3.0 to get a feel for the API, beware that the `SetVoiceAccent`, `SetVoiceEnvelope`, and `SetSoundNoise` functions are not implemented. Of course, since the PC hardware is single-voiced, the `SyncAllVoices` function is meaningless. In addition, various bugs in the driver prevent half or whole notes from generating the proper sound, and the *nCdots* parameter in the `SetVoiceNote` function is ignored.

Figure 6-5 lists the exported sound driver entry points. Note that

CloseSound	SetSoundNoise	SetVoiceThreshold
CountVoiceNotes	SetVoiceAccent	StartSound
DoBeep	SetVoiceEnvelope	StopSound
GetThresholdEvent	SetVoiceNote	SyncAllVoices
GetThresholdStatus	SetVoiceQueueSize	WaitSoundState
OpenSound	SetVoiceSound	

FIGURE 6-5 Sound Driver Entry Points

almost all of these entry points correspond directly to the Windows API sound functions. `DoBeep` is the sole exception. Windows calls this function as a result of a call to the Windows `MessageBeep` function. By having this function in the sound driver, the same sound hardware can perform the beep function while managing other sounds emitted from the sound device.

Local Area Network

The skills required to implement properly a local area network (LAN) driver for Windows include practically every aspect of Windows device driver programming. Much of the work required to get a LAN driver working with Windows 3.0 involves understanding the 386 enhanced mode virtual environment, discussed in the next chapter. Nevertheless, support in real and standard modes also requires a thorough understanding of the Windows systems concepts, expanded memory usage, extended memory usage, and general memory management described in Chapter 2.

At the lowest level, the LAN driver software provided for DOS is what Windows relies on to gain access to the network. Since Windows relies on DOS to access disk drives and files, and since DOS relies on the LAN driver to access remote drives and files, much of the original LAN software used for DOS remains unchanged for Windows. There is a limit to this compatibility, but if your DOS network driver supports the MSNet and NETBIOS interfaces, Windows already does most of the work required for compatibility.

To programmers not used to Windows, an external event interrupting a program and a message being sent to a program may be foreign concepts. To those who program network applications, however, these concepts are basic. For applications that use the NETBIOS interface, **post routines** are commonly used. For Novell IPX applications, programmers are very familiar with **event service routines** (ESRs). In both these cases, the real mode address of a **callback** routine is passed in the call to the network service. At a later time, after timing out or when some specified event occurs, the network driver passes control to the specified routine by making a FAR call to it. This is fine in real mode when the routine is in conventional memory.

What happens if the network needs to call such a routine when the system is running in protected mode? For standard NETBIOS drivers, Windows standard mode handles the simpler cases. The standard mode WINOLDAP module takes care to prevent the operator from switching to the Windows session from a DOS session that is awaiting a response from a network driver to a post routine.

What about standard mode Windows applications that want to make calls to the network? Like the INT 21h calls, the network driver is responsible for mapping the buffer and control block addresses from protected to real mode and, if necessary, copying such structures into real mode memory.

A similar problem exists for Windows applications that want to have callbacks.

API Support

Some Windows utilities, including the Control Panel, the File Manager and the Print Manager, require a set of standard network support functions from the Windows kernel. In turn, the Windows kernel expects the network software to provide a driver DLL to support these functions. Figure 6-6 lists these functions.

The Windows kernel looks for the Network Support API functions in the library specified by the `network.drv` item in the `[boot.description]` section of SYSTEM.INI. In addition to the functions listed in Figure 6-6, the network driver must also provide an initialization entry point and return FALSE if the lower-level network driver support is not installed. Windows calls this initialization entry point when Windows starts up. If the driver returns FALSE, the driver is not loaded. The driver must also export a Windows exit procedure (WEP).

The various entry points fall into six classifications: initialization and termination, maintenance, connection management, print job queueing, print job monitoring, and print job control.

In addition to the initialization function just mentioned, the driver must also provide an `Enable` function. Windows calls this function when

WNetAbortJob	WNetGetCaps	WNetOpenJob
WNetAddConnect	WNetGetConnection	WNetReleaseJob
WNetBrowseDialog	WNetGetError	WNetSetJobCopies
WNetCancelConnection	WNetGetErrorText	WNetUnlockQueueData
WNetCancelJob	WNetGetUser	WNetUnwatchQueue
WNetCloseJobe	WNetHoldJob	WNetWatchQueue
WNetDeviceMode	WNetLockQueueData	

FIGURE 6-6 Network Driver Entry Points

Windows first begins and whenever the Windows session is reloaded after leaving a DOS session when running Windows in real or standard mode. Windows calls the `Disable` function when entering a real or standard mode DOS session. These two functions allow the driver to disable itself and re-enable itself when entering and exiting a DOS session.

One of the maintenance functions, `WNetGetCaps`, indicates which of the other functions are supported by the driver. This function returns a bit-mapped value indicating which functions are supported. Note that even if the driver does not support one of the functions listed in Figure 6-3, it must still be exported by name and replaced with a stub that always returns an error. The `WNetGetUser` function returns the current user name, if applicable. The purpose of the `WNetDeviceMode` function is up to the network driver developer. It can be invoked by the user from the Control Panel and allows the user to set up various driver-specific parameters. The `WNetGetError` function returns the last error reported by any network function. This function is probably not necessary since most functions return an error code, anyway. This function of the sample network driver in the DDK is disabled as is the `WNetGetErrorText` function. This last function might make sense for drivers that return error codes outside of the standard range, but could present problems for the non-English reader.

The connection management functions allow an application (typically the Control Panel) to create and destroy logical connections between the system and the server. The logical connections can be either logical drives (A: through Z:) or logical printers (LPT1: through LPT4:). `WNetAddConnection` creates, `WNetCancelConnection` destroys, and `WNetGetConnection` returns the status of a logical drive or printer connection. The `WNetBrowseDialog` function prompts the user with a dialog box to select a remote drive or printer. A Windows application can use the result of this function to create a new connection via `WNetAddConnection`.

When Windows applications direct output to a network queue, the Windows Print Manager calls the print queue functions to create and manage jobs. The Print Manager calls `WNetOpenJob` to start a new print job and, under normal circumstances, calls `WNetCloseJob` to end the job. To cancel a job in progress, the Print Manager calls `WNetAbortJob`. Note the similarity of these functions to the Print Manager `OpenJob`, `CloseJob`, and `DeleteJob` functions as described in Chapter 4.

The Print Manager also takes care of managing print jobs that have been completely submitted. The network driver provides functions to allow the Print Manager to do so. The Print Manager calls `WNetWatchQueue` to receive periodic notification from the network about the change in print queue status. The network driver provides this notification by posting (not sending) a message to a specified window. The Print Manager may periodically query the status of a queue (possibly as a result of a message from the driver) by calling `WNetLockQueueData` to get the address of an in-memory structure describing the status of the queue. This call insures that the driver will not modify the structure until `WNetUnlockQueueData` is called. Once the Print Manager is no longer interested in receiving messages about print queue changes, it calls `WNetUnwatchQueue`.

The Print Manager can also control and modify print jobs in the queue. It calls `WNetHoldJob` to suspend a specified job until it calls `WNetReleaseJob`. It can call `WNetCancelJob` to cancel a job that is already in the queue. `WNetSetJobCopies` allows the Print Manager to change the number of requested copies of a job that has already been submitted.

The network driver DLL provides API support into the network. While it is possible that this DLL can provide direct access to the network hardware, a typical implementation for real and standard mode Windows is to have the network driver DLL simply translate the API function calls into lower-level network calls. In standard mode, the DOS Extender (DOSX) takes care of the address and parameter mapping for the network calls supported through INT 21 and INT 5B. If your DOS network driver uses unconventional methods, you may have to implement all of your driver code in the network driver DLL, or prepare a special version of DOSX to properly implement your driver. If this is the case, you will need to make special arrangements with Microsoft to provide a special version of DOSX with your driver, since DOSX is not provided in the DDK.

On the other hand, if you are using INT 21h, INT 5C, and INT 2A only to access your driver, it may be that the MSNET.DRV driver provided with Windows will work without modification.

Summary

This chapter focused on the APIs for the various drivers that provide the function-call interface between Windows and various devices. For the most part, these drivers are required for all Windows operating modes, real, standard, and 386 enhanced. Given the widespread use of 386 enhanced mode, however, it is clear that your work cannot end here if you intend to allow your driver to be used in typical Windows systems. In today's market, support for 386 enhanced mode is a must. In the next chapter, I will go into detail describing the specifics for providing driver support in that mode.

CHAPTER

7

Virtual Device Drivers

Windows 386 enhanced mode provides two primary benefits over standard mode. The first is that DOS sessions can be allowed to execute in the background. Windows applications still multitask cooperatively as in standard mode, so DOS applications are the real winners in this regard. The second benefit of 386 enhanced mode is the access to large amounts of virtual memory. Real and standard modes only virtualize code segments: The size of program data in these modes is limited to the amount of physical memory. 386 enhanced mode, however, offers applications and end-users much more program data—limited only by the amount of disk space available. This second benefit is offered to both Windows and DOS applications alike: to Windows applications that use a lot of memory and to multiple DOS sessions that are active at the same time.

These benefits complicate the internal workings of Windows. When running in 386 enhanced mode, Windows 3.0 includes a system file (WIN386.EXE) that is more than one-half megabyte in size. Much of this file includes the base virtual device drivers (VxDs), which reflects the fact that much of the burden of providing support for virtual mode is placed on the VxDs. If you are writing your own device driver for Windows 386 enhanced mode, expect that your driver will be required to carry much of this burden and will be correspondingly complex.

If you have ever spoken to anyone about the implementation of VxDs under Windows, you may have heard about the large amount of work required to get such a driver working. Some of the basic concepts of a virtual driver are difficult to understand but even if you have a very good understanding of how Windows is *supposed* to behave, Windows 3.0 contains quite a large number of anomalies that make practice and experience invaluable for developers of drivers in 386 enhanced mode. The best way to face this type of problem is to discuss it with other developers through CompuServe forums or various developer bulletin boards. In the next few chapters, I hope to explain the necessary basics to get you started developing your own VxDs, but you should expect to need to call on others for help with specific problems.

If you are going to develop a virtual device driver for Windows, then you must have a license for the Device Development Kit. The virtual mode drivers are not in the normal DOS or Windows executable format but instead are in a format for loading into a FLAT memory model (more on the FLAT memory model later in this chapter). In addition to sample VxDs, the DDK also contains special versions of MASM and LINK that you must use to create a virtual driver.

Virtual Machines

As I described in Chapter 2, Windows 386 enhanced mode takes advantage of the virtual 8086 mode of the Intel 80386 processor. This mode allows Windows to set up a memory space where a copy of DOS can run as if it were running in real mode. Combined with the use of the memory paging logic of the 386 processor, the memory space can be made virtual; that is, the memory seen by the DOS program may actually be anywhere in physical memory. Since the location of the physical memory is no longer restricted to the lower one megabyte, multiple DOS sessions may be active in the system at a single time, each running in different areas of physical memory. Each one of these DOS sessions runs in its own **virtual machine (VM)**.

Windows is not a full operating system and relies heavily on DOS to perform many system functions, especially to provide access to disk files through the DOS INT 21 interface. Thus, whenever Windows is running, DOS must also be running in order to be able to service Windows' file access calls. In standard mode Windows must switch to real mode whenever an INT 21 function is required. 386 enhanced mode works a little differently.

The System Virtual Machine

Since 386 enhanced mode is capable of running virtual machines, it can easily create a virtual machine for running a copy of DOS that is dedicated to handling files that are used by Windows. Windows actually does reserve a special VM just for servicing requests from Windows applications. Other VMs may be created to support multiple DOS applications, but a special VM is reserved especially for supporting Windows applications. This virtual machine is referred to as the **system virtual machine**, or system VM.

When Windows starts it saves a copy of the initial DOS environment. (Note that in the rest of this chapter I will be referring to Windows in 386 enhanced mode unless otherwise indicated.) This copy is then used whenever Windows creates a new VM. When a new VM is created, this original copy of DOS is copied into the new VM. When a user loads a program into a new VM (also called a DOS session), the copy of the program is loaded into this new VM, and does not affect the memory used by other existing VMs or those created later. The program can even be a TSR. For example, a user can have two VMs loaded in the system with one TSR in the first VM, and a different TSR loaded in the second. A third VM could then be created without any TSRs.

Note that if a TSR is loaded into DOS memory before Windows is started and then Windows is started, Windows uses the copy of DOS with the TSR just loaded to create all new VMs. Thus, when each new VM is created, each will contain its own copy of the original TSR.

What if you want to have a TSR loaded in the system VM that will provide services only to Windows applications? You could load the TSR before you start Windows, but this would cause the TSR to be loaded in all VMs. It may be that you are not interested in having this TSR available to DOS applications and you do not want to waste the memory used by the TSR in all VMs. To solve this problem, Windows provides a mechanism whereby DOS programs can be loaded into the DOS area of the system VM. You can do this by putting the commands that you want to execute into a special batch file, WINSTART.BAT. Windows runs this batch file in the system VM before running any Windows applications. In this way, the system VM can be customized with DOS TSRs before Windows is loaded. You

can find more information about this batch file in the Microsoft Windows
User's Guide.

The Protected Mode Virtual Machine

So far, when talking about a VM, I have been referring to its virtual 8086
mode aspects. Virtual 8086 mode, however, is only one aspect of a Windows
VM. Through the support of the DOS protected mode interface (DPMI),
Windows removes the restriction of addressing in the lower one megabyte
of memory. A DOS application can switch to protected mode by calling the
DPMI Real to Protected Mode Switch entry point. After switching to protected mode, the DOS application is no longer restricted to segment:offset
addressing. In either real or protected mode, however, the VM is still
restricted to the hardware I/O ports that it can access.

Thus, the VM consists of virtual DOS memory, expanded memory, and
possibly protected mode memory, too. In any case, Windows treats the
entire VM as a single unit. This is significant from the point of view of the
VxDs and from the way Windows multitasks DOS applications. A DOS
application running in protected mode still has the same priority and is
scheduled in the same way as the same application running in real mode.
The difference is that the program operates in the protected mode of the
processor and addresses are formed by combining a selector and an offset,
rather than a segment and an offset. In addition, when a protected mode
program performs an INT instruction, the protected mode copy of the
interrupt vector table (the IDT) is used to resolve the interrupt address
first. If no program has registered for the interrupt, then the interrupt is
passed to real mode.

Figure 7-1 illustrates the similarity between the system VM and a
regular DOS VM. Both types of VMs contain a virtual 8086 mode portion
and a protected mode portion. The protected mode portion of the system
VM contains Windows applications. For DOS VMs, there is usually no protected mode portion unless a DPMI client is active in the VM.

Figure 7-2 illustrates the way the 80x86 privilege levels, or **privilege
rings**, are used by Windows in 386 enhanced mode. Ring 0 code has direct
access to the hardware. The Windows kernel runs at this level. Virtual
device drivers also run at this level. Note that at this level,VxDs have no
restrictions on their access to hardware or to any CPU functions. Windows
applications and protected mode DOS applications run at ring 1 (this may
change in a future version of Windows). Since these applications run at
ring 1, their access to I/O ports is restricted. Also, they are unable to access
any segments that have a data privilege level (DPL) of zero. The least

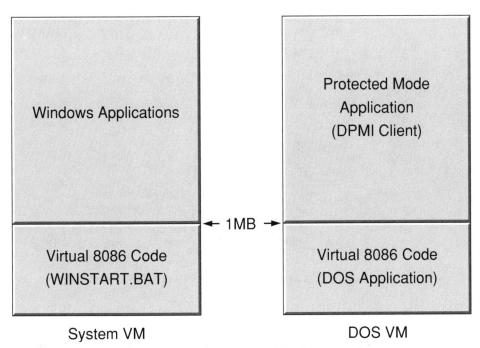

FIGURE 7-1 System and DOS Virtual Machines

trusted applications, the DOS applications, run at ring 3, as do virtual 8086 mode programs, which are required to by the 80386 CPU.

Virtual Machine Scheduling

The Windows virtual machine scheduler is actually divided into two components: the **primary scheduler** and the **time slicer**. The time slicer is the user-visible portion of the scheduler. Whenever a virtual machine is allowed to run, that is, **dispatched**, the time slicer determines how long the VM may run unhindered. Each VM is assigned a time slice priority value from 1 to 10000. This value is the same as that specified by the Windows PIFEDIT utility. The utility specifies two separate time slice priority values for each VM, one for when the VM is in the foreground (that is, has the focus) and one for when the VM is in the background. Alternatively, these values can be set by the user during VM execution.

The time slicer also maintains miscellaneous flags related to scheduling. The Exclusive flag indicates whether a VM will have exclusive control of the CPU when it is in the foreground. The Background flag indicates whether the VM will be scheduled at all if it is in the background. These

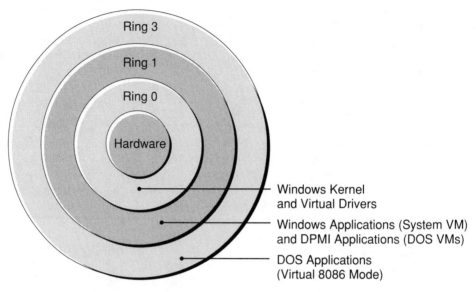

FIGURE 7-2 Privilege Rings

flags are visible to the user via the PIFEDIT utility or from the system menu of a VM. One flag not visible to the user, the High Priority Background flag, insures that a background VM with this flag set will receive time slices even if the foreground VM is Exclusive.

Like all VMs, the system VM has foreground and background priorities and an Exclusive flag, too. These values may be adjusted by the user using the Windows Control Panel "386 enhanced" dialog. The Windows *User's Guide* expands on these concepts and utilities.

The primary scheduler is not visible to the user. Instead of determining how much CPU time a VM will receive, the primary scheduler determines if a VM will receive any time at all. If the primary scheduler determines that a particular VM will not receive any time, the time slicer will not even consider it in its time slice calculations. The priority value used by the primary scheduler is called the **execution priority**. At any instant, the primary scheduler maintains a "highest execution priority" level. Any VMs at this level will be scheduled by the time slicer. Any VMs below this level will not be scheduled at all. VMs and virtual drivers use this type of scheduling to provide exclusive or properly restricted access to certain structures.

Note that the VM with the highest time slice priority still allows other VMs to run. If a single VM has the highest *execution* priority level, however, no other VM will run at all until the executing VM reduces its own execution priority.

Normally, a VM can be stopped by the time slicer and control can be passed to another VM at any time. The exception to this is when the VM is running at ring 0, such as when it is running in the Windows kernel or in a VxD. When at ring 0, control will be passed to another VM only in one of the following cases:

- The VxD calls the scheduler, changing the VxD's execution priority relative to another's.
- The VxD accesses page-demand memory, causing a page fault.
- The VxD allows the VM to run temporarily (in either protected or V86 mode).

Virtual Driver Organization

Windows VxDs are written entirely in assembly language. If you are not already intimately familiar with the Intel 80x86 family of processors, then becoming proficient with their architecture and instruction sets should be your first task. Not only is this important for writing in MASM, but much of the VM virtualization requires an understanding of processor instructions, flags, operation codes, and other specific behavior. In other words, even if it will someday be possible to write VxDs in a higher level language, such as C++, many virtual drivers still require an understanding of the various 80x86 instruction semantics in order to provide proper VM virtualization.

80386 Assembler

By now, you are probably quite familiar with the various 80826 instructions that are not available on the 8088/86. Since VxDs must be written in 80386 assembler, the development of a VxD offers you the opportunity to take advantage of additional instructions offered by the 80386. In addition, as you review the sample VxD code in the DDK, you are likely to encounter many of these instructions. In this section, I will summarize the more interesting aspects of programming in 80386 assembler.

Register Extensions

The most accessible addition to 80386 assembler is the additional 16-bit word in most of the CPU registers. The AX, BX, CX, DX, SI, DI, BP, and SP registers are extended to 32 bits and are given new names: EAX, EBX, ECX, EDX, ESI, EDI, EBP, and ESP. The 16-bit versions of these registers are available as before with their old names. The new 32-bit registers over-lay the 16-bit registers so that the lower 16 bits of the 32-bit registers correspond to the 16-bit registers. Figure 7-3 illustrates this with the AX and EAX registers. Note in this figure how the relationship between EAX and AX is similar to that between AX and AL. In other words, AX is to EAX as AL is to AX. These 32-bit registers are available in all modes of the 80386, but in VxDs we are guaranteed to have at least a 386 CPU and we can take unconditional advantage of them.

The instructions generated by the assembler for these 32-bit registers are usually the same codes as for their 16-bit counterparts. How does the processor know which type of register is desired? When running in real mode or in a 16-bit protected mode code segment, the processor assumes that the operands to an instruction are 16 bits. The 386 processor provides for 32-bit code segments in addition to the traditional 16-bit code segments. When it executes instructions in a 32-bit segment the processor assumes 32-bit operands. The processor provides a special instruction prefix (akin to a segment override) that tells the processor to assume an operand size opposite to what it would for the current code segment. In other words, this operand size override on an instruction in a 16-bit segment indicates to the processor that the following instruction is using 32-bit operands rather than 16-bit operands.

VxD code runs in a single 32-bit segment, so operands default to 32 bits. Therefore, if the operand size override prefix precedes an instruction in a VxD, the operand size is assumed to be 16 bits. As an example, consider the assembly language instruction MOV AX,BX. The machine code for this instruction in real mode is 8B C3. The machine code for MOV EAX,EBX requires an operand-size override prefix. The machine code in real mode for this instruction is 66 8B C3—the 66 is the machine code for the operand-size override.

In a 32-bit code segment, such as in a VxD, the machine code for MOV EAX,EBX is 8B C3. This is the same machine code for the corresponding

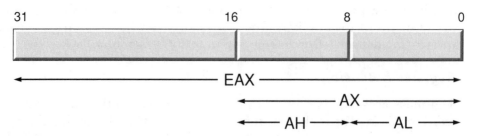

FIGURE 7-3 EAX Register

16-bit operation in real mode but, since the processor is executing out of a 32-bit code segment, the processor assumes 32-bit operands. As you may have guessed by now, the machine code for MOV AX,BX is 66 8B C3 when the system is running in a VxD.

While the actual code generated may seem unimportant, note that the override byte increases the size of the instruction by 50 percent in this example. In the VxD examples, you will often see instructions using all 32 bits of a register when only the lower 16 are important. The programmer has chosen the 32-bit form of the instructions to save a byte. Another, more subtle benefit of the 32-bit instruction is that the CPU does not have to fetch the occasional extra operand-size override.

32-Bit Addressing and Effective Address Calculation

In addition to being able to specify 32-bit operands in instructions, we can also specify 32-bit address offsets, also known as effective addresses. As with operand sizes, the assumed size of effective addresses in instructions is implied by the size of the code segment that the processor is currently executing in. Instead of an operand-size override, we have an address-size override whose value is 0x67. The default mode of the effective address sizes reverses in the same way it does in relation to operand sizes.

With the 8088 and 80286 processors, we can specify the effective address in an instruction by a few restricted methods. In the most complex form for these processors, we can specify an immediate 16-bit offset, adding BX and either DI or SI. When we are working with 32-bit offsets on the 386, we can specify a similar offset, using EBX and EDI or ESI instead. However, the 386 allows us a much more flexible way of specifying an effective address; we are not restricted to using EBX in combination with EDI and ESI only. When specifying a 32-bit effective address, we can use EAX, EBX, ECX, EDX, ESI, EDI, EBP, or ESP as a base and EAX, EBX, ECX, EDX, EBP, ESI, or EDI as an offset (note that ESP cannot be an offset).

To make things even easier for us, the processor allows a scaling factor of 1, 2, 4, or 8 to be combined with the offset. This last feature lets us remove old code that was used to multiply the offset by a fixed value before its use. As an example of the full power of this type of effective address calculation, consider this instruction:

```
LEA EAX,[ECX+4*EDX+123456h]
```

The instruction takes the contents of the EDX register, multiplies it by 4, adds the contents of the ECX register, adds 0x123456 to that result and places the final result in the EAX register. If you want to get really fancy, you can also effectively get a multiple of 3, 5, or 9 of any register. The following two instructions multiply the EAX register by 10 without modifying any other register:

```
ADD EAX,EAX         ; Multiply by 2
LEA EAX,[EAX+4*EAX] ; Then by 5
```

A particularly nice aspect of this type of effective addressing is that it allows us to examine stack variables directly without loading the EBP register. We can do this because we can specify ESP as a base register. Remember, though, that these capabilities are available only when we specify (or default to) 32-bit addressing.

Jump Instructions

The 386 conditional jump instructions are improved over their 16-bit counterparts in that they can now specify a NEAR offset instead of only a SHORT (8-bit relative). Note that, since in a 32-bit segment a NEAR offset spans 4 gigabytes, there is no longer a need to jump around another JMP instruction in order to achieve the same effect.

This additional capability provides a minor problem with the 3.0 DDK, however. MASM normally defaults to a NEAR jump when referencing a forward pointer and will generate a NEAR conditional jump when the target is a forward pointer. This can make an instruction that is normally two bytes long into one that is six bytes long. Because this can add up quite significantly over an entire system, I recommend that you become accustomed to putting a SHORT override on targets of conditional jump instructions until the MASM that is provided with the DDK provides the optimization capabilities introduced by version 6 of MASM.

Miscellaneous New Instructions

The 386 introduces a number of miscellaneous instructions that can improve performance of your driver if you become familiar with them. I will review some of the more interesting ones, but if you want specific details on these instructions, I recommend that you purchase one of the books listed in Appendix H that details 80386 assembly language programming.

If you are working with bitmaps, then you may be interested in the BSF and BSR instructions. These instructions scan an operand for a "1" bit, starting at either end of the operand. The result is a bit-index into the operand.

The BT instruction tests a single bit in an operand. You can achieve the same function using the TEST instruction, but the BT instruction allows you to specify an index rather than a mask. BTC complements a single bit; on the 8088 you might have used XOR with a mask. To set or reset a single bit, instead of using OR or AND, you can use BTS or BTR, specifying an index.

To facilitate moving values from 16-bit to 32-bit operands, the MOVSX instruction sign extends the 8- or 16-bit source into the 32-bit destination. The MOVZX instruction zero-extends the result.

The SHLD and SHRD instructions will shift bits out of a source operand into a destination operand, without affecting the source. These instructions extend the familiar SHL and SHR instructions by allowing the destination to be different from the source. SHLD and SHRD can be used in a bitblt where the bit offset of the source and destination are not the same.

There are a few other 386 instructions that are available to applications programs. If you have a 486 CPU, there is one final instruction that you may be interested in. The BSWAP instruction reverses the byte-order of a 32-bit register, exchanging the high- and low-order bytes and exchanging the middle-order bytes.

For a complete list of the 386 and 486 instructions, refer to one of the books listed in Appendix H.

The FLAT Memory Model

By now, you are probably intimately familiar with the various memory models supported by the various C compilers for DOS and Windows: TINY, SMALL, MEDIUM, COMPACT, and LARGE. For virtual drivers there is yet another model: FLAT. In the SMALL, MEDIUM, COMPACT, and LARGE models, there are always at least two segments: CODE and DATA. The TINY model consists of a single segment in which all code and data reside and in which pointers to code and data require only an offset. Any pointer can point to either code or data. Ironically, the FLAT model is most like the TINY model. Instead of a single 64K 16-bit segment, however, the FLAT model consists of a single 32-bit segment that (theoretically) may be as large as 4 gigabytes.

Unlike the TINY model, the segment registers in the FLAT model are not all the same. Since FLAT model code runs in protected mode, the CS register must refer to a memory descriptor that allows execution in its segment and disallows writing to the segment. The DS and SS registers refer to memory descriptors that allow reading and writing. Despite these differences, all registers contain the same linear base (namely 0x00000000) and limits, so that all pointers in the FLAT model consist of a single 32-bit offset.

Even if you have a clear understanding of Intel memory segmentation, you can forget most of it for understanding the FLAT model. If your background is in other operating systems, such as UNIX, or in other processors, such as Motorola's 68000 family, the idea of a FLAT model seems quite natural.

Unlike application environments, Windows FLAT model does not generally operate on a per-task or per-VM basis. The FLAT memory model that is seen by a virtual driver consists of all virtual memory in a Windows system. In other words, every single byte of the Windows kernel and every single byte of every VM is immediately visible by a VxD at all times and is addressable by a single 32-bit offset.

VM Memory

The linear memory space of VxDs does not allow the VxD to begin at linear address 0x00000000. This is because when running in V86 mode, the processor can only generate addresses from 0x00000000 to 0x0010FFEF. Therefore, memory in this range is reserved for the currently active VM.

In general, however, you should not rely on this fact to access memory in the current VM. Using the 386 paging mechanism, Windows keeps a copy of every VM in high memory in addition to the copy of the currently active VM in low memory. Thus, there are actually two copies of the currently active VM in memory: its low copy, and its high copy. This does not mean that the VM is actually using twice as much memory: the paging logic of the 386 processor allows multiple linear pages to be mapped to the same virtual memory. When your VxD accesses a VM's memory, it should always access the high copy, not the low one.

Program Memory

Since we are in a FLAT model, you may think that we no longer have program segments. While this is true for the most part, in terms of linking programs together, the concept of program segments is still significant. A VxD is still divided up into different sections or "objects," but these objects are not placed into different memory segments. They do retain their attributes, however, and a program segment marked DISCARDABLE will still be treated that way as an object in linear memory.

In the development of your VxD, you will not need most of the assembler directives related to program segmentation. Instead, you must rely on the macros that are provided with the DDK. The order, number, and names of the segments is fixed. Figure 7-4 lists the macros that bound the various segments in VxD source code.

The segments fall into two categories: initialization and permanent. The initialization segments are discarded after Windows has completed initialization. The permanent segments remain in memory throughout the Windows session. The exception to this is if the initialization code tells Windows not to load the driver. In this case, of course, all segments are discarded.

When reviewing the sample code, you will see references to the VxD_LOCKED_CODE_SEG macro. This macro is identical to the VxD_CODE_SEG macro. When reviewing the driver maps, you will also notice that one of the segment classes is always empty. This serves to separate code that remains physically locked in memory from code that is pageable. However, in the actual implementation there is currently no such distinction. In any case, the layout of your linker DEF file should match that of the sample VxDs in order to avoid confusing the VxD loader. You may wish to use the VxD_LOCKED... macros where appropriate if the separation is ever implemented by the enhanced mode kernel.

To emphasize the fact that the driver is in a FLAT model, you are not likely to find many (if any) ASSUME statements in the sample drivers. The segment-entry macros include an assume statement for their segment. In all but the real mode segment, the ASSUME statement indicates that all segment registers are assumed to refer to a pseudo-segment,

Macro Name	Segment / Class	Description
VxD_CODE_SEG VxD_CODE_ENDS	_LCODE / CODE	Permanent driver code
VxD_DATA_SEG VxD_DATA_ENDS	_LDATA / CODE	Permanent driver data
VxD_ICODE_SEG VxD_ICODE_ENDS	_ICODE / ICODE	Initialization code (discarded after initialization)
VxD_IDATA_SEG VxD_IDATA_ENDS	_IDATA / ICODE	Initialization data (discarded after initialization)
VxD_REAL_INIT_SEG VxD_REAL_INIT_ENDS	_RCODE / RCODE	Real mode initialization code and data (discarded after initialization)

FIGURE 7-4 Segment Definition Macros

namely FLAT. This segment is not defined anywhere in the code, but it is resolved at run time by the Windows VxD loader.

The Device Descriptor Block

A VxD exports only one address: that of its device descriptor block, or DDB. The DDB provides the links between the driver and the Windows kernel. This export is not a procedure, but rather an actual data structure in the device's permanent data segment. The DDB is defined by invoking the `Declare_Virtual_Device` macro.

The `Declare_Virtual_Device` macro takes up to nine parameters. The first parameter is the device name. The macro creates a public symbol using this name with `_DDB` appended. This symbol is the only symbol listed in the linker DEF file. Its ordinal must be 1.

The second and third parameters define the major and minor driver version numbers. The minor version number is treated as two decimal digits, so a driver for version 3.1, for example, would have the values 3 and 10.

The fourth parameter specifies the address of the VxD "control" entry point. This is the flat address of a routine that the Windows kernel calls to notify the driver of certain system events, such as the various stages of initialization and VM state changes (described later in this chapter).

The fifth parameter to `Declare_Virtual_Device` specifies the virtual device ID number. Your driver needs a device ID number if it provides services to the Windows kernel, to protect mode applications, to V86 mode applications, or if your driver is called back by V86 mode drivers or TSRs. If your device has no need for a device ID, you should specify the `Undefined_Device_ID` symbol for this parameter.

The sixth parameter indicates the order in which this driver should be initialized. Some VxDs may depend on the prior initialization of other VxDs. A lower number in this parameter indicates an earlier initialization. The order of the base VxDs is defined in the VMM.INC include file and you may use one of these values with an optional positive or negative bias to specify initialization before or after a particular base VxD. If your device is not dependent on initialization order, you should use the `Undefined_Init_Order` symbol for this parameter.

The seventh and eighth parameters to `Declare_Virtual_Device` specify the addresses of procedures that provide services to V86-mode and protect-mode programs, respectively. Applications access a FAR CALL entry point into these services by loading 0x1684 in the AX register, the VxD ID into the BX register, and invoking INT 2F. Then the application can call the entry point directly using an interface defined by the VxD.

Finally, the `Declare_Virtual_Device` macro creates a structure—not an explicit parameter—that declares services that the VxD provides to other VxDs. The Windows kernel uses this structure to allow the Windows kernel and other VxDs to call this VxD for various services using the `VxDcall` macro. Most VxDs provide at least one service which returns the VxD's version number in the AX register. Other VxDs use this version number service to test for the existence of a particular VxD. A driver defines a service table using the `Begin_Service_Table` and `End_Service_Table` macros, described in more detail later in this chapter.

All in all, although only one export is declared for a VxD, you can see that the DDB actually fans out into perhaps dozens of "logical" entry points into the VxD. I have already named four types of entry points into a VxD: event notification, V86 mode services, protected mode services, and services to other VxDs.

Usually, the first routine that Windows calls in a VxD is through the event notification, or control entry, point. Before that, however, a VxD may have initialization code that is to run in real mode, before Windows enters protected mode. This entry point is not explicitly exported, but is inferred by the VxD loader. Since a VxD can have only one 16-bit segment, Windows assumes that this segment contains the VxD's real mode initialization code and jumps to it during real mode initialization.

Before continuing further, you may wish to review a sample VxD to study its basic structure. The EBIOS VxD is a good one to start with because it is the simplest. This driver also provides an example of real mode initialization code.

Real Mode Initialization

Before running any other code or creating other VMs, the Windows kernel will allow a VxD to initialize itself in real mode. This allows the VxD to contain initialization code that is best run in real mode to test the environment to see if the VxD is able to or needs to load at all.

A virtual driver file contains only one 16-bit (USE16) segment. The kernel treats this segment as the VxD real mode initialization segment. It contains all code and data for real mode initialization. On entry CS, DS, and ES are the same and point to this segment. You may not assume, however, that the stack is also in this segment—that is, DS is not necessarily equal to SS. As with other drivers, the entry point to the initialization code is specified by the assembler END statement.

On entry to the real mode initialization code, Windows sets the CPU registers as follows:

AX The VMM Version Number (for example, 0x030Ah).

BX Bit flags:

   Bit 0: If set, this VxD has already been loaded.

   Bit 1: If set, this VxD is being loaded (again) by a request from a real mode program or driver that requested the VxD to be loaded in response to INT 2F function 1605h (described in Chapter 10).

   Bit 2: This VxD is being loaded by a request from a real mode program or driver that requested the VxD to be loaded in response to INT 2F function 1605h.

SI   The environment segment (containing environment variables).

EDX If BX bits 1 or 2 are set, this DWORD contains the reference information stored at offset 0Ah of the startup information structure returned in response to INT 2F function 1605h.

After completing real mode initialization, the VxD must exit using a NEAR return (RETN). On return, Windows expects the following in the CPU registers:

AX Return code:

   0   The VxD loader should continue loading this driver and Windows.

   1   The VxD loader should load Windows, but not this driver.

   2   Windows should abort loading entirely and return to real mode after displaying an error message identifying this VxD.

   8002h Windows should abort loading entirely and return to real mode without displaying any message.

BX An offset into the initialization segment that contains an array of pages that the Windows memory manager should not manage. The table consists of an array of 16-bit words in the range 0001h to 0019h. The table is terminated by a zero entry. The BX register should be zero if no table is to be specified.

SI   An offset into the initialization segment that contains an array of instance data items. Each item consists of three 16-bit words in the following format:

```
pData  DD  ?  ;  Segment:offset address of data item
sData  DW  ?  ;  Size, in bytes, of the item
```

The array is terminated by an entry containing all zeros. The SI register should be zero if no table is to be specified.

EDX   A DWORD of reference data to be passed to the VxD protected mode initialization code. If this instance of the driver is loaded by an INT 2F response, then this value will typically be the same value passed to the real mode initialization code.

Driver Event Notification

All events from Windows are passed to the VxD via the driver's "control" entry point, as defined in the `Declare_Virtual_Device` macro. Windows passes a function code in the EAX register on entry to this procedure. If your VxD is processing many different event messages, you can use the `Begin_Control_Dispatch`, `End_Control_Dispatch`, and `Control_Dispatch` macros to automatically build a jump table and dispatch code for your control entry point.

Events passed to the VxD's control entry point fall into four categories, as shown in Figure 7-5. The symbols shown in Figure 7-5 are defined in the VMM.INC include file.

Driver Initialization

Once Windows enters protected mode, a VxD is called in three stages to initialize itself. In each of the stages, the VxD may return from the control function with the carry flag set to indicate that the VxD should not be loaded.

In some of these initialization functions, the EBX register contains what is called the **VM handle**. This handle is simply a flat pointer to a structure: the **VM control block**. The VM control block contains instance-unique information for the specified VM. A VxD can allocate its own portion of the control block using VxD services described in Chapter 8.

Windows makes the first call, `Sys_Critical_Init`, to allow the VxD to initialize critical functions. Interrupts are disabled when this function is called, and the VxD must not enable interrupts here, even for a

Driver Initialization
Sys_Critical_Init Device_Init Init_Complete
Driver Termination
System_Exit Sys_Critical_Exit

VM Initialization
Create_VM VM_Critical_Init VM_Init Sys_VM_Init
VM Termination
Query_Destroy VM_Terminate Sys_VM_Terminate VM_Not_Executable Destroy_VM
VM Transitions
VM_Suspend VM_Resume Set_Device_Focus Begin_Message_Mode End_Message_Mode Reboot_Processor Begin_PM_App End_PM_App Debug_Query

FIGURE 7-5 VxD Control Functions

moment. In general, and unless otherwise specified, the VxD may not call other VxDs for services.

After system critical initialization, Windows calls Device_Init as the second stage of VxD initialization. When this function is called, Windows has already created the system VM and passes the address of its control block (its handle) in the EBX register. Windows will not call the Create_VM control when the system VM is created, so any instance data for the system VM should be initialized at Device_Init time. Interrupts are enabled when this control is called and the VxD can freely call on other VxDs for services. In particular, the VxD can call VxD services to allocate system VM instance and control block data, to hook interrupts and I/O ports, and to call real mode code using the `Simulate_Int` and `Exec_Int` services (described in Chapter 8).

Windows marks the last stage of VxD initialization by calling the `Init_Complete` control. This provides the VxD with a final opportunity to scan VM memory for various structures that may have been initialized by other VxDs.

After all stages of initialization are complete, Windows records a copy of the system VM (its "snapshot") and saves it. Windows uses this copy of the system VM to create subsequent VM instances.

Driver Termination

When Windows shuts down, either normally or abortively, it calls the VxD control procedure in stages similar to the stages of initialization.

First, Windows calls the `System_Exit` control. On entry, EBX contains the handle to the system VM. Although interrupts are enabled, the VxD may not call other VxDs for services. Although the system VM is no longer active, its memory is still available. In processing this control, the VxD may modify the system VM memory. Any such modifications made will remain in DOS after Windows exits completely.

Finally, Windows calls the `Sys_Critical_Exit` control. Interrupts are disabled for this call and must not be enabled. The VxD should put its hardware into a quiescent state or return its state to whatever is expected by DOS drivers or TSRs.

VM Initialization

Just as Windows generates control messages for the various stages of Windows initialization and termination, it generates similar messages for the initialization and termination of virtual machines. In all of these messages, the EBX register contains the address of the VM's control block. In general, the control function returns with the carry flag set to indicate failure, and the VM is not created.

Whenever Windows creates new VMs (except the system VM), it first calls the `Create_VM` control of every VxD. The VxD may call other VxDs to allocate resources and memory for the emerging VM. If the VxD has allocated control block space, the VxD should initialize that space here. The VxD should not call any VM code yet, since the VM is not fully initialized.

At the next stage of VM initialization, Windows calls the `VM_Critical_Init` control (again, except for the system VM). The VxD is still not able to call real mode code. This control can contain initialization code that does rely on calling real mode code.

The last stage of VM initialization is indicated by Windows calling the `VM_Init` control (or the `VM_Sys_Init` control for the system VM). At this point, the VxD may call real mode code to complete VxD initialization.

VM Termination

When a VM shuts down, as you might guess by now, Windows calls the control function for each VxD in stages. These controls are not called if Windows shuts down abnormally or crashes. For all of these calls, the EBX register contains the VM handle on entry to the control.

If a VM is terminating abnormally, Windows first calls the VxD's `Query_Destroy` control. This control returns with the carry flag set to indicate that the VxD cannot be gracefully terminated without sacrificing system integrity. The VM will not be destroyed, but the VxD should display a message explaining the reason for preventing VM termination (beware of internationalization issues). The remainder of the VM termination controls must return with the carry flag clear, as these calls cannot be failed.

The first stage of normal VM termination is marked by a call to the `VM_Terminate` control (or to the `Sys_VM_Terminate` control for the system VM). If a VM is shut down abnormally, this call is not made. In this control, the VxD should generally only perform shutdown activity that needs to be run in real mode.

The second stage of VM termination begins with a call to `VM_Not_Executable` (sic). Although this control may not call any real mode code, it is called even if a VM is shut down abnormally. Therefore, this control should be responsible for critical VM shutdown. Windows passes some flags in the EDX register that provide additional information about the VM shutdown:

Bit	Description
`VNE_Crashed`	The VM failed abnormally, probably by violating rules of system integrity.
`VNE_Nuked`	The VM was destroyed while active, typically by the user.
`VNE_CreateFail`	A VxD failed the `Create_VM` control.
`VNE_CrInitFail`	A VxD failed the `VM_Critical_Init` control.
`VNE_InitFail`	A VxD failed the `VM_Init` control.

The last call made to a VxD about a VM is `Destroy_VM`. This control differs from `VM_Not_Executable` in that the VM may still remain in memory and as a Window until `Destroy_VM` is called. Since a VM can be created without the "close on exit" attribute, the time delay between the call to `VM_Not_Executable` and this control may be considerable, since it is ultimately up to the user. This call indicates that the VxD may relinquish all resources related to the VM. Note that resources that are accessible to the VM only while it is running (such as I/O ports) can be relinquished during the call to `VM_Not_Executable`.

VM Transitions

In addition to making control calls to a VxD during VM creation and termination, Windows regularly calls VxDs whenever certain VM transitions occur. Windows always passes the VM handle in EBX for all of these controls.

Windows calls the `VM_Suspend` control when another VxD has requested that Windows suspend a VM. The VxD processing this control should relinquish exclusive access to any resources it owns. A VxD cannot cancel this function and must return with the carry flag cleared. When the VxD that suspended the VM is ready to resume it, Windows calls the `VM_Resume` control. If the VxD is not able to restore the VM to a runnable state (if, for example, it is unable to lock required resources), it may fail this call.

At any instance, only one VM has the focus or the immediate attention of the user. Windows calls each VxD whenever the focus changes between VMs using the `Set_Device_Focus` control. This call does not imply that the target VxD's focus is set to the current VM. The EDX register contains the VxD ID of the VxD that is to focus on the specified VM. If EDX is zero, then all VxDs should focus on the specified VM. If your VxD is told to focus on a specified VM, it should take extra steps to improve the performance of that VM.

The `Begin_Message_Mode` control puts the keyboard, mouse, and display VxDs in a special suspended mode that allows Windows to have more direct control over the keyboard and display. Specifically, when the user presses Alt+Tab, without releasing the Alt key, message mode begins. The user can press and release the Tab key, rotating through the various VMs and applications, without having the Tab keystrokes forwarded to the VMs. Finally, when the user releases the Alt key, Windows sends the `End_Message_Mode` control to all VxDs.

The `Reboot_Processor` is a special control that is handled by only one VxD. The first VxD that receives this control resets the entire system. This control is typically sent in response to the user pressing Ctrl+Alt+Del and handled by the virtual keyboard driver.

Windows issues the `Begin_PM_App` control whenever a VM starts a protected mode application, such as with the DPMI services. On entry to this control, if the low bit (bit 0) of EDX is set, the application is a 32-bit application. A VxD may fail this call by returning with the carry flag set, consequently preventing the application from loading. When the protected mode application terminates, Windows issues the `End_PM_App` control.

The remaining control to be discussed is not really a transition control, but is used by the WDEB386 debugger. It provides a way for you to invoke your VxD to display status information. If you enter a period (.) followed by the name of your VxD at the WDEB386 prompt, Windows calls your VxD's `Debug_Query` control.

Control Summary

As you may have inferred, there are a number of controls that most drivers will not be interested in processing. Since Windows calls only one entry point for all of these controls, it is easy enough for your VxD to ignore those that do not affect it. If you use the `Control_Dispatch` macros to dispatch your controls, you need only enumerate those controls that your VxD will process. The `End_Control_Dispatch` macro will automatically return with the carry flag cleared for any control not listed.

Driver-Specific Services

In addition to providing basic hardware virtualization for VMs, a VxD can also provide services to other VxDs and to VM applications. The `Declare_Virtual_Device` macro builds the table by which Windows transfers control to services provided by the VxD.

VxD Services

The VxD service table allows a VxD to provide support for other VxDs. You define the service table in your VxD using the `Begin_Service_Table` and `End_Service_Table` macros. If your device is named FOO and you set the symbol `Create_FOO_Service_Table` before invoking the `Begin_Service_Table` macro, it creates another macro that is based on the parameter passed to it. For example, if your device name is FOO, then the macro `FOO_Service` is created. You then use this macro to declare all of the VxD services that your VxD provides. If you do not set the

`Create_FOO_Service_Table` symbol before including VMM.INC, then symbols are defined that allow other VxDs to reference your services, provided they include one of your include files that contains the `FOO_Service` macros.

For example, you can have an include file, named FOO.INC, that contains the following:

```
Begin_Service_Table FOO
FOO_Service     FOO_Get_Version, LOCAL
End_Service_Table FOO
```

Your source code, FOO.ASM, for example, might contain these lines:

```
include vmm.inc
Create_FOO_Service_Table equ 1
include foo.inc
```

This will cause the service table to be created. Another program might include your definitions with the following code:

```
include vmm.inc
include foo.inc
```

This causes the macros to generate declarations without actually creating the table. Another VxD can then call your service with the following macro invocation:

```
VxDcall    FOO_Get_Version
```

The LOCAL parameter on the `FOO_Service` macro invocation indicates that the service function is declared in the same source module that contains the `Create_FOO_Service_Table` definition. The actual code for the service might look like this:

```
BeginProc FOO_Get_Version, SERVICE
    movzx eax,030Ah
    clc
    ret
EndProc FOO_Get_Version
```

Incidentally, note the use of the `BeginProc` and `EndProc` macros. The SERVICE parameter indicates that this function is a VxD service.

Other optional parameters might be `High_Freq` or `PUBLIC`. The `High_Freq` option simply aligns the entry point to a 32-bit boundary to speed up execution on entry. `PUBLIC` creates a public linker symbol.

VM Application Services

In addition to providing services to other VxDs, a VxD can provide services to VM applications. The seventh and eighth parameters to the `Declare_Virtual_Device` macro name the procedures in a VxD that will handle service requests from VM applications.

The entry points into the VxD for service requests are distinguished on the basis of the mode the VM caller runs in: V86 mode or protected mode. Requests may be generated from any VM, including the system VM. Since Windows applications are protected mode applications running in the system VM, requests from these applications will enter through the protected mode services entry point.

A VxD can also service requests from standard device drivers. These device drivers run in protected mode in the system VM so, like Windows applications, their requests enter through the protected mode services entry point.

Although requests from both traditional DOS applications and protected mode applications arrive at the device driver through different entry points, both types of applications use the same method to call a VxD. Although a VM application cannot call the VxD services entry point directly, Windows provides a way to transfer requests from a VM application to a VxD. INT 2F function 1684h returns the VM-mode address of the entry point into the services for a VxD. On entry to this function, the BX register contains the 16-bit ID for the desired VxD. The function returns the VM-mode address for the VxD services in ES:DI. The parameter-passing conventions for the VxD services are entirely up to the VxD, although the AX register generally contains a request identifier.

Note that the address return from this INT 2F function is different in V86 and protected modes. Therefore, if an application runs in both modes, it must obtain the VxD services address for each mode.

The following code illustrates how a VM application might request a version number service from a VxD:

```
xor di,di
mov es,di
mov ax,1684h
mov bx,FOO_Device_ID
int 2Fh
```

```
                mov ax,es
                or ax,ax
                jz skip
                mov WORD PTR [pFOOServices],DI
                mov WORD PTR [pFOOServices+2],ES
                mov ax,0; code for Get_Version_Number
                call pFOOServices
                .
                .
                .
        skip:
```

This same code can be used in a traditional DOS application, a protected mode DPMI application, a protected mode Windows application, or a Windows device driver (but not a VxD).

When a VM application makes such a request, Windows passes control from the VM application to the VxD. Remember, however, that the VxD is running at ring 0 and that VM applications run at outer rings (rings 1 and 3 in Windows version 3). Since Windows maintains a separate copy of the current register contents for each ring, the registers passed from the VM application are not reflected in the contents of the registers passed to the VxD when a VM calls the VxD's services entry point. Before calling the VxD services entry point, Windows pushes the contents of the outer ring registers onto the ring 0 stack and essentially passes the registers as parameters to the VxD services entry point.

The VxD services entry point accesses the VM application registers through offsets from the EBP register. The VMM.INC include file defines the offsets of the ring 0 stack where the contents of each of the VM registers are stored. The following code illustrates how a VxD might provide a single "get version" function:

```
BeginProc FOO_PM_API_Entry
  cmp [ebp.Client_AX],0            ; Get version?
  jne short api1                   ; No, skip
  mov [ebp.Client_AX],030Ah        ; Pass result to VM client
  and [ebp.Client_Flags],not 1     ; Indicate success
  jmp short api2
api1:  or  [ebp.Client_Flags],1    ; Set carry to indicate error
api2:
EndProc FOO_PM_API_Entry
```

CB_VM_Status	Various state flags describing the VM
CB_High_Linear	The flat linear address of the first byte of the VM's V86 memory
CB_Client_Pointer	The flat linear address of the VM's control block
CB_VMID	The VM ID

FIGURE 7-6   VM Control Block Variables

Note that the value returned to this function is also returned in the client register frame. Unlike higher-level language parameters, modifying the actual parameter here will also modify the client's registers.

Although code identical to that shown here could also be used for servicing V86 mode requests, be aware that addresses passed from a V86 application will be in segment:offset form and not in selector:offset form, which they would be if passed from protected mode applications. Resolving the actual address in this case, however, is trivial. For example, here a V86 application passes a pointer in ES:BX that the VxD will use to access the byte that it points to:

```
movzx    eax,[ebp.Client_ES]
shl      eax,4                 ; Multiply segment by 16
movzx    ecx,[ebp.Client_BX]   ; Get offset into segment
add      eax,ecx               ; Get V86 linear address
add      eax,[ebx.CB_High_Linear]; Add offset into VM
mov      al,[eax]              ; Access the byte
```

Note the use of the VM handle, EBX, in this example. Recall that the VM handle is also the address to the VM's control block, which contains the linear base address of the client VM. The VM control block also contains a number of other useful values, as listed in Figure 7-6.

Summary

The concept of a virtual machine distinguishes 386 enhanced mode from the other modes. VMs can be scheduled, allowing multitasking of applications. These additional capabilities result in more complex device drivers and allow for the concept of a virtual device driver.

The structure of a VxD is unlike anything else in Windows. Since it works only with 386 enhanced mode, we can take full advantage of the 386 instruction set and a FLAT memory model. Although it is similar to a DLL, a VxD exports only one symbol, which Windows uses to gain access to perhaps dozens of "logical" entry points or control services. A VxD can provide additional services for other DOS and Windows applications and for other VxDs.

So far, I have discussed only the static structure of a VxD and how it fits into Windows. In the next chapter, I will expand on how a VxD can do its work by taking advantage of the numerous services provided by Windows and other VxDs.

CHAPTER

8

Virtual Driver Services

A VxD is called by Windows during its various phases. In addition, it can be entered as the result of hardware interrupts or special VM activity, such as accessing I/O ports. Through the use of the Virtual Machine Manager (VMM) services, a VxD controls a VM's view of the outside world. A VxD can trap VM interrupts, trap I/O port accesses, change a VM's scheduler priorities, and control and query a full range of VM resources.

In this chapter, I will review some of the services provided to a VxD, both by other VxDs and the Windows kernel. While it is possible to replace one of the basic Windows VxDs with your own, you should generally expect that the services I describe here will be available in almost every Windows environment.

Services provided by a VxD can be viewed from two different perspectives. The first is from the point of view of the VxD's clients. Since the services I describe here are from the Windows kernel itself and from the fundamental Windows VxDs, I will describe the services from the point of view of the client. Later in this chapter, I will review some of the more variable VxDs from the point of view of the serving VxD, with the idea that you may be replacing such VxDs with your own.

There are two ways that a VxD can call the various services: these are with the VMMcall and the VxDcall macros. Like most Windows device driver interfaces, there is no consistent convention for the VMM services. Some services have parameters passed in registers, other services have parameters passed on the stack. Usually (but not always), services that take parameters on the stack have an underscore (_) prefixing the service name. Services that take parameters in registers have no such prefix.

Both macros have the identical format, but the VMM call macro is reserved for calling VMM services. Otherwise, the macros are the same. For functions that accept parameters on the stack, you can push the parameters yourself (in reverse order) or enumerate them in the macro invocation.

Appendix F lists detailed information about the interfaces to the VMM services. Because these interfaces are internal to Windows, they are likely to change from release to release. Although I will review the fundamental concepts here, the most timely information will come from the DDK itself.

Scheduler Services

In Chapter 7 I explained the basic structure of the Windows schedulers. A VxD can work with the primary scheduler to coordinate a VM's execution priority. A VxD may, for example, want to give a VM higher priority while it processes an interrupt. If a VxD wants exclusive access to a structure accessible to all VMs, it can tell the VMM to suspend any VM that attempts to obtain the critical section.

Figure 8-1 lists the services provided by the primary scheduler. Use the VMMcall macro for these services.

```
Adjust_Exec_Priority         Get_Crit_Section_Status
Begin_Critical_Section       No_Fail_Resume_VM
Call_When_Not_Critical       Release_Critical_Section
Claim_Critical_Section       Resume_VM
End_Crit_And_Suspend         Suspend_VM
End_Critical_Section
```

FIGURE 8-1 Primary Scheduler Services

A VxD can boost or lower its VM's execution priority by calling `Adjust_Exec_Priority`. If this call lowers the specified VM below the highest execution priority, the VM is suspended. If the call raises the specified VM above the current highest priority, Windows dispatches the VM immediately, at the expense of all others.

A VxD calls the `Begin_Critical_Section` and `End_Critical_Section` services to claim exclusive access to the critical section. If another VM attempts to claim the critical section while it is owned by another, Windows will suspend the second VM until the first VM releases the critical section. The critical section is an imaginary resource, but can represent a resource that is critical to the operation of all VMs. If a VxD needs to execute some code when no VxD is in the critical section, it can call `Call_When_Not_Critical`. This service causes Windows to call back to the VxD when the critical section is released.

The `Begin_Critical_Section` and `End_Critical_Section` services keep a count of the number of times the critical section is claimed. If the critical section is claimed five times, then it must be released five times to release fully the critical section for another VM. The `Claim_Critical_Section` and `Release_Critical_Section` services allow a VxD to specify a count on the number of claims and releases. The `Get_Crit_Section_Status` service queries the current critical section claim count. The `End_Crit_And_Suspend` service allows a VxD to end the critical section and immediately suspend the current VM in one automatic operation.

The `Suspend_VM` service suspends execution of the specified VM until `Resume_VM` is called (by another VM) to resume it. Recall that when a VM is suspended, Windows sends the `VM_Suspend` control to all VxDs. It sends the `VM_Resume` control to all VxDs when the VM is resumed. It is possible for a VxD to fail this control if, say, the VxD is unable to acquire sufficient resources (such as memory) to restore the VM. Therefore, it is possible for the `Resume_VM` service to fail. The `No_Fail_Resume_VM` service cannot fail, but will possibly display an error message to the user and will not return until the specified VM is able to resume.

In addition to primary scheduler services, Windows also provides control over the time slicer. Figure 8-2 lists the services provided by the time slicer. Use the `VMMcall` macro for these services, too.

Recall that the time slicer works with two priority values for each VM (the foreground priority and the background priority) and with various flags. The time slicer uses these values to determine how much execution time a VM will be allowed during its time slice. A VxD can determine which VM is in the foreground with the `Get_Execution_Focus` service, or it

```
Adjust_Execution_Time          Release_Time_Slice
Call_When_Idle                 Set_Execution_Focus
Get_Execution_Focus            Set_Time_Slice_Granularity
Get_Time_Slice_Granularity     Set_Time_Slice_Priority
Get_Time_Slice_Info            Wake_Up_VM
Get_Time_Slice_Priority
```

FIGURE 8-2 Time Slicer Services

can force the current VM or the system VM into the foreground by calling
`Set_Execution_Focus`.

The `Get_Time_Slice_Priority` service returns the current foreground and background priorities and the time slicer flags for a specified
VM. The `Set_Time_Slice_Priority` service lets a VxD change these
values. A VxD can override the time slice priority for a VM and specify the
amount of time, in milliseconds, to increase or reduce the VM's time slice
using the `Adjust_Execution_Time` service. This service works only with
relative values, but a VxD can determine the absolute size of a VM's time
slice by calling `Get_Time_Slice_Granularity`.

If a VxD determines that a VM is idle, it can release its time slice
entirely by calling `Release_Time_Slice`. In addition, if the VM is not in
the foreground, its background time slice priority is also reduced.

Memory Management Services

Most VxDs will be interested only in a few of the memory management services. A VxD gets some memory by virtue of its static data areas. This
memory is maintained on a global basis, and only one copy, or instance, is
available. A VxD can allocate memory on a per-VM basis or on a global
memory basis using the VMM services. Some VxDs will want to virtualize
memory itself, providing controlled access to memory mapped devices.

Small Structure Allocation

The VM handle is actually an address to a control block that is dedicated
to its VM. A VxD can extend the size of this control block and keep
VM-instance data in the control block for its own use with the

`Allocate_Device_CB_Area` service. This memory is maintained in system memory and is not accessible by the VM.

Some VxDs may want to keep instance data that is accessible to a VM in V86 memory. Normally, Windows maps some areas of V86 memory so that if one VM modifies the memory, then the changes appear in all VMs. A VxD can override this behavior for small areas using the `AddInstanceItem` service. A device driver might do this, for example, for certain structures in the BIOS data area that it wishes to maintain separately for each VM.

For memory that is not already assigned by DOS, but which a VxD needs to maintain in V86 memory, it can call `Allocate_Global_V86_Data_Area`. If the memory is only needed temporarily, such as during Windows initialization, the VxD can call `Allocate_Temp_V86_Data_Area`.

It is possible for a VxD to tell if a certain area of V86 memory is global or instanced by passing the address and length of the area to the `TestGlobalV86Mem` service. Some VxDs can use this service to optimize V86 memory access.

The most direct method for a VxD to allocate relatively small blocks of global memory is with the `HeapAllocate` service. This service allocates memory with a granularity of approximately 16 bytes and has an overhead of about 16 bytes per block. The memory can be re-allocated using `HeapReAllocate` or freed using `HeapFree`. The `HeapGetSize` service returns the current size of a specified block of memory. These services are comparable to the C run time memory allocation functions.

Linked List Management

Some small structures are best managed as a linked list. The Windows linked list services provide an easy mechanism to allocate small memory structures in linked lists and to manage the lists. Figure 8-3 lists the VMM services provided for linked list management.

The first call to these services, `List_Create`, creates a root structure that Windows uses to manage the list. Each element of the list must be of the same fixed size. This function returns a handle, which a VxD passes to all of the other list management functions. The `List_Destroy` function destroys the entire list.

The `List_Allocate` function allocates a single list element. The element is then added to the head of the list using `List_Attach`, to the tail using `List_Attach_Tail`, or at any arbitrary position in the list using `List_Insert`. You can remove an arbitrary list element by calling

```
List_Allocate                    List_Get_First
List_Attach                      List_Get_Next
List_Attach_Tail                 List_Insert
List_Create                      List_Remove
List_Deallocate                  List_Remove_First
List_Destroy
```

FIGURE 8-3 Linked List Services

List_Remove, or you can determine the element at the head of the list and remove it in a single operation by calling List_Remove_First. A list element is returned to the free list by calling List_Deallocate.

The list functions also facilitate traversing a linked list. List_Get_First returns the first element in a list. If you already have the address of an element in a list, you can get the next element in the list by calling List_Get_Next.

If your VxD manages multiple lists, these functions also let you move elements among them. A node taken from one list using List_Remove can be added to another list using List_Attach. The only restriction is that the elements have the same size. The element may have been allocated from either list.

Large Structure Allocation

If your VxD requires very large blocks of memory, it may be more efficient to use the page allocation services. The PageAllocate service allocates memory with a granularity of one page, or 4096 bytes. The pages can be allocated on a global basis or assigned to a particular VM. Memory assigned to a VM instance is not allocated for each VM, but rather for a specified VM.

You can use the PageAllocate service in its simplest form to allocate global system memory. In its fullest form, the PageAllocate service is quite complex, but very powerful and flexible. With it, you can allocate pages that are fixed at a physical address in memory or that are automatically paged in and out with most of the rest of Windows memory. You can allocate memory that is aligned to certain sizes, such as 128K. You might want to allocate memory on a 128K boundary, for example, if you expect to use the memory as the source or target for DMA reads or writes. The

`PageReAllocate` service works the way any heap-managed memory allocation does. `PageFree` frees allocated pages.

You can determine the largest amount of physical and virtual memory that can be allocated by calling `PageGetAllocInfo`. This service returns the largest number of physical and virtual pages that can be allocated in a single call to `PageAllocate` or `PageReallocate`.

After allocating memory, you can reserve V86 memory space by calling `Assign_Device_V86_Pages` and map the allocated pages into V86 memory by calling `MapIntoV86`. If you need to map memory that your VxD does not own, and if you do not have a handle to it, you can call `LinMapIntoV86` instead. For pages that you have assigned, but do not wish to map to any memory, call `MapIntoV86`, specifying a null memory handle, that you obtain by calling `GetNulPageHandle`.

Accessing Physical Memory

Many VxDs will need to access specific physical memory addresses. Some virtual display drivers, for example, need to access physical memory from addresses 0xA0000 to 0xBFFFF. Some device adapters have memory for a CPU on the adapter that is also shared by the main CPU. LAN cards typically have memory-mapped addresses for I/O buffers. In addition to devices that map addresses in the 0xA0000 to 0xFFFFF range, many devices are mapped above all physical RAM at physical addresses above 0xF00000.

The `MapPhysToLinear` service takes a physical memory address and returns a linear address, which the VxD can use to access the physical memory. To allow a V86 application to access particular areas of physical memory, the VxD instead calls `PhysIntoV86`.

Before calling `PhysIntoV86`, the VxD must first insure that the desired V86 memory pages are available by calling `Get_Device_V86_Pages_Array`. Next, a call to `Assign_Device_V86_Pages` reserves the desired pages for the VxD. Once the pages are assigned, the VxD calls `PhysIntoV86` to map the linear pages to physical memory. The virtual display driver (VDD) uses `PhysIntoV86` to map physical pages into a foreground full-screen VM. When the VM is in a Window or when it is in the background, it maps physical memory that it allocated with `PageAllocate` into the same locations. For VMs in a window, the VDD can periodically scan the background physical memory for changes and update the Window accordingly.

Instead of actually comparing changes in memory contents, the VDD takes advantage of the 386 paging hardware and some of the VMM paged-memory services. In the memory page table, the 386 sets a flag (the dirty flag) in a page entry whenever the page is written to. The Windows VDD periodically looks for pages with the dirty flag set using the `CopyPageTable` service. It then clears all of the dirty flags using the `ModifyPageBits` service.

Some memory-mapped devices can be used only if written to directly by the application; saving updates in a memory and then transferring the updates to the hardware does not work. Some video adapters work this way, because the video memory does not work in the same way that regular RAM does. For devices that work this way, a VxD can map the actual device to one VM and map invalid pages to other VMs that might attempt to access the device. These invalid pages are allocated with `PageAllocate`, but have a special attribute (`PG_HOOKED`) that indicates that a VxD routine should be called if the pages are accessed when there is no physical memory assigned to them. The VxD routine to call, the hook page fault handler, is specified by a call to `Hook_V86_Page`. When a "not present" page is accessed by the VM, the VxD may attempt to virtualize the hardware or may post a message and suspend the VM until the physical hardware is available. You can mark pages not present by calling `ModifyPageBits`. Pages are marked present by a call to `MapIntoV86` or `PhysIntoV86`. The VDD may wish to hook not-present pages, for example, to suspend a VM that attempts to access video memory. The VDD resumes the VM when it is brought into full screen mode.

Paged Memory Management

Usually when a VxD allocates pages of memory, it allocates pageable memory—that is, memory that can be saved to disk when physical memory is overcommitted and recalled when the page is next accessed. A VxD can coordinate with the Windows memory manager to optimize memory access to pages that the VxD uses.

The `PageLock` service locks a block of memory allocated by `PageAllocate`. Locking a block of memory insures that the pages are present and assigned to physical memory. Locked pages will not be swapped by the Windows memory manager. This service allows a VxD to maximize performance for a block of virtual memory that it will be working with or that is otherwise required to remain assigned to physical memory. If the VxD does not own the memory and does not have a handle to it, it can call `LinPageLock` to lock the memory. Pages can be subsequently unlocked using `PageUnlock` or `LinPageUnlock`. The unlock services can also indicate that the unlocked pages are to be marked "least recently used" so that they are the next pages to be paged to disk.

Normally, when V86 memory is mapped using `MapIntoV86`, the pages are locked. A VxD can unlock these pages using the `SetResetV86Pageable` service. This service differs from `PageLock`/`PageUnlock` in that it is specifically intended for V86 memory and takes a V86-mode linear address, rather than a memory handle.

When a VxD has allocated pages of memory and is no longer interested in their contents, such pages can be marked "discardable" by calling `PageDiscardPages`. This tells the Windows memory manager that these pages do not need to be saved to disk when physical memory is overcommited. Instead, the physical pages are immediately placed in the free pool.

VM Trapping Services

A VxD can tell Windows to call it under a variety of different events or circumstances. In the previous section I mentioned how a VxD might trap certain types of memory accesses. A common occurrence is that a VM attempts to access an I/O port that is managed by a VxD, but the VxD is also interested in a variety of other events, such as when a VM enables interrupts, when a VM executes certain privileged instructions, or even when a VM executes at a certain address.

I/O Port Events

The most common task of a VxD is to manage access to a physical device's I/O ports. By default, all VMs have unrestricted access to I/O ports. To manage access to an I/O port, a VxD first calls the `Install_IO_Handler` service. This service is available only during Windows initialization and should be called in response to the `Device_Init` control.

When a VxD calls `Install_IO_Handler`, it passes the address of a routine that Windows will call when the specified I/O port is accessed by any VM. Note that Windows does not call the handler if the I/O port is accessed by any VxDs, since VxDs run at ring 0. Most VxDs will want to manage access to a number of I/O ports. The `Install_Mult_IO_Handlers` service accepts the address of an array that specifies each I/O port to be hooked and the procedure to be called for each port.

Trapping for a particular port can be disabled and re-enabled by calling `Enable_Global_Trapping` and `Disable_Global_Trapping`, respectively. More typically, a VxD will want to disable port trapping for a VM that is using the I/O port heavily, but keep trapping enabled for other VMs. The `Disable_Local_Trapping` and `Enable_Local_Trapping` functions disable and enable port trapping on a per-VM basis.

Windows calls the hook routine for an I/O port whenever the port is accessed in any way, using any of the variety of 80x86 I/O instructions. The port can be accessed by an input instruction, an output instruction, a BYTE, WORD, or DWORD access, and might even be combined with a REP prefix for string I/O. Windows decodes the instruction and passes the various parameters to the hook routine in the ring 0 registers. The client DX register does not contain any useful information, since if it was specified as an immediate operand in the I/O instruction it does not reflect the I/O port, but you will need to examine or set the client AL (or AX or EAX) register.

You can use the decoded instruction information to optimize I/O port access, but most VxDs will be satisfied to assume the simplest case: single byte I/O. The `Simulate_IO` service makes this easier by repeatedly calling the I/O hook for each byte to be transferred to the I/O port. This service not only breaks up a repeated instruction, but also breaks down a WORD or DWORD instruction into its component byte I/O accesses. Your hook routine then only needs to distinguish between input and output.

The call to `Simulate_IO` can be made even simpler by using the `Emulate_Non_Byte_IO` or `Dispatch_Byte_IO` macros provided with the DDK. The `Emulate_Non_Byte_IO` macro jumps to `Simulate_IO` if the I/O instruction is not a byte I/O instruction. The `Dispatch_Byte_IO` macro takes two arguments; the first is the procedure to handle byte input, the second is the procedure to handle byte output. This macro also calls `Simulate_IO` to simplify the I/O instruction into single-byte accesses.

If you are optimizing instructions with a REP prefix yourself, the client CX (or ECX) register contains the repeat count and the client ES:(E)DI or DS:(E)SI registers contain the memory addresses for the INS and OUTS instructions, respectively.

Processor Traps and Exceptions

The CPU performs trap processing for certain instructions, such as INT, INTO, and BOUND. The CPU performs fault processing for exceptional conditions such as accessing a not-present page, loading an invalid selector, or a division overflow. The CPU performs interrupt processing as the result of an event external to the processor.

A VxD can hook traps (such as those resulting from execution of an INT, INTO, or BOUND instruction) for code executing in V86 mode by calling `Hook_V86_Int_Chain`. This service may be called only during VxD initialization. The `Set_V86_Int_Vector` will change the real mode interrupt vector table and can specify a routine only in the VM itself. A VxD can also hook traps for protected mode applications by calling `Set_PM_Int_Vector`. If `Set_V86_Int_Vector` or `Set_PM_Int_Vec-tor` is called before the system VM "snapshot" is taken during initialization, the changed vector appears in all subsequent VMs; otherwise, the call only affects the current VM. The `Get_V86_Int_Vector` and `Get_PM_Int_Vector` services return the current values for the specified vectors in the current VM.

There are several steps involved in hooking a V86 mode vector. Whenever a trap occurs in a VM, the CPU executes the code specified by the protected mode vector (the interrupt descriptor table, or IDT). Generally, Windows sets up the IDT entries so that they point to a small routine that simply simulates the vector in real mode. If a VxD needs to hook a V86 mode vector, it first hooks the protected mode vector by calling `Set_PM_Int_Vector`. This will cause the CPU to transfer control to the VxD when the trap is effected. After processing the trap itself, the VxD takes one of three actions. It can pass control on to the previous protected mode routine (obtained by a call to `Get_PM_Int_Vector`); it can simulate the INT call into real mode (as does the default Windows routine); or it can simulate an IRET instruction into the virtual machine by modifying the client registers, consequently returning to the next instruction in the V86 code after the instruction that generated the trap.

Instead of hooking the trap before any V86 mode processes it, a VxD may wish to process a trap after all V86 mode code has completed. In other words, the VxD may wish to hook itself at the end of the interrupt service chain, rather than at the beginning. A VxD does this by first calling `Hook_V86_Int_Chain` and, when called back for that trap, calling `Call_When_VM_Returns`. When the VM processes its IRET instruction (actual or simulated) to return from the trap, Windows calls the callback routine. This provides a way for a VxD to hook the tail end of a trap.

A VxD can hook processor faults for code executing in any and all system rings. The `Hook_V86_Fault` service hooks faults that occur when the CPU is in V86 mode (ring 3); `Hook_PM_Fault` hooks faults and traps that occur when the CPU is executing a protected mode VM application; and `Hook_VMM_Fault` hooks faults and traps that occur when the CPU is running at ring 0. All of these services return the address of the previous handler, and your handler can, at its own discretion, chain any fault or trap to the previous handler.

When a VxD processes a fault, it can make calls only to VMM services that are listed as asynchronous (see Appendix F). In order to make calls to other VMM services, the VxD must first call `Begin_Reentrant_Execution`. After all necessary calls are made, the VxD calls `End_Reentrant_Execution`. These services are provided for fault handling routines only. To call VMM services in response to an interrupt, see the Interrupt-Time Processing section later in this chapter.

If your VxD needs to hook a hardware interrupt, it should call one of the virtual programmable interrupt controller driver (VPICD) services described later in this chapter. The only exception to this is if the VxD needs to hook the nonmaskable interrupt (NMI). In this case, it should first call the `Get_NMI_Handler_Addr` service to get the current NMI handler address and `Set_NMI_Handler_Addr` to set the handler to its own routine.

An NMI handler cannot call any VMM services, so there is little it can do except set a flag in memory. If you need to perform more complex processing, you will also need to specify an NMI event handler by calling the `Hook_NMI_Event` service. This service tells Windows to call the VxD back as soon after an NMI as the VxD is able to call VMM services.

Note that all of these handlers and the event hook exit from their procedures using a NEAR return instruction (RETND instead of IRETD).

Miscellaneous Events

The `Install_V86_Break_Point` service tells Windows to call the VxD whenever a V86 application executes at a specific location. A VxD might use this service to breakpoint the entry point in an existing DOS driver and replace the DOS driver's functions with its own. The breakpoint may be temporary and can be removed with a call to `Remove_V86_Break_Point`.

The `Call_When_Task_Switched` service tells Windows to call the VxD each time Windows switches between executing VMs. The callback for this service is called very frequently and should perform only minimal tasks.

The `Call_When_Idle` service tells Windows to call the VxD when all VMs have indicated that they are idle, specifically when all VMs have released their time slice. A VxD can work what it considers a very low priority item in the callback routine. You may have observed disk activity in 386 enhanced mode when nothing seems to be running. This is the page-swap device writing aged dirty pages to disk to speed up response when the system is more active (and has less time to swap).

Interrupt-Time Processing

When a VxD processes a hardware interrupt, it is restricted by the number of VMM services it may call. Most of the VMM services are not re-entrant. Instead of performing all interrupt processing at interrupt time, a VxD can tell Windows to call it back when it is appropriate for the VxD to call VMM services. Of course, all of the services in this section may be called at interrupt time.

Usually, when Windows calls a VxD, it passes the VM handle in EBX. At interrupt time, however, the registers can contain anything. A VxD may be interesting in finding out what the handle for the current VM is or if a particular VM was active when the interrupt was received. A VxD can query the current VM by calling the `Get_Cur_VM_Handle` service; it can test to see if a specified VM is current by calling `Test_Cur_VM_Handle`; or it can test to see if the current VM is the system VM by calling `Test_Sys_VM_Handle`. The `Validate_VM_Handle` tests to see if a given handle is valid at all.

To allow complex processing of an interrupt, the `Schedule_Global_Event` service tells Windows to call back the VxD as soon as possible after processing the interrupt, without any other restrictions. When Windows calls the VxD back, the VxD is free to call any normal VMM service.

The `Schedule_VM_Event` service tells Windows to call back the VxD as soon as possible after the interrupt is processed and the specified VM is active. If the VM is currently active, the callback procedure is called before the return from `Schedule_VM_Event`.

A VxD may wish for a callback to be made only if the hardware interrupt occurs within a VM (and not within the VMM). The `Get_VMM_Reenter_Count` service indicates if the interrupt was received while the VMM was executing. The `Call_Global_Event` service tells Windows to call the specified callback immediately, provided that the current interrupt does not occur during execution in the VMM. If this is not the case, the callback is scheduled with `Schedule_Global_Event`. This condition can be further qualified to require that the interrupt occurs in a specific VM by calling `Call_VM_Event`. If the condition is not satisfied at the time of the call, the callback is scheduled with `Schedule_VM_Event`.

Frequently a VxD will want all of the following conditions to be satisfied before it is called back: (1) a particular VM is executing, (2) that VM's interrupts are enabled, and (3) no VM has requested critical priority scheduling.

The `Call_Priority_VM_Event` service tells Windows to call the VxD when any or all of the above conditions have been satisfied (as specified by the caller). In addition, this service contains an implicit call to `Adjust_Exec_Priority` so that the VxD can claim higher priority for the VM when it is called back.

The `Cancel_Global_Event`, `Cancel_Priority_VM_Event`, and `Cancel_VM_Event` services cancel any event that was scheduled by one of the aforementioned event services.

VM Control Services

Virtual Execution and CPU Control

In addition to being able to virtualize hardware accesses, a VxD can virtualize CPU activity within a VM. You already know how to change a VM's registers by modifying the client register structure passed to the VxD. A VxD can also simulate a number of instructions to be executed in a VM, and can actually call code within a VM.

In its simplest form, one way to simulate an instruction is to modify the client registers' contents. For example, the following code simulates a V86 LODSB instruction (assuming that the direction flag is clear):

```
movzx    eax,[ebp.Client_DS]
shl      eax,4                    ; Get segment linear base
movzx    ecx,[ebp.Client_SI]      ; Add index
add      eax,ecx                  ; Get V86 offset of byte
add      eax,[ebx.CB_High_Linear]; Add offset into VM
mov      al,[eax]                 ; Get the byte
mov      [ebp.Client_AL],al       ; Move to client register
inc      [ebp.Client_SI]          ; Increment the source pointer
```

If you were simply to return from a VxD or otherwise allow a VM to run, it would begin execution at the address specified by the client CS:(E)IP registers. In order to redirect a VM into other code, you need to change the CS:(E)IP registers and provide a way for the VM to return back to the VxD. Instead of modifying the client registers directly, however, you should call the `Simulate_Far_Jmp` service. This service changes the client registers and performs other housekeeping chores. Note that this function does not actually perform the jump; it only modifies the client registers so that the next time the VM starts, it will begin execution at an address that is different from that originally indicated by the client register.

A VxD can simply force a jump within a VM, but will more likely be interested in performing some VM code and then returning back to the VxD. When a VxD executes, the VM is suspended. Any changes made by the VxD are usually not seen by the VM until the VxD exits. One way to execute code in a VM is to set a breakpoint in a VM and return from the VxD, returning back to the VxD in a callback when the breakpoint is reached. Fortunately, Windows provides a number of services that make this process easy.

Before calling back into a VM, a VxD must save the registers of the VM, so that when the VxD ultimately returns to the VM, its registers will not have been altered by the intermediate code called in the VM. The `Save_Client_State` service saves the client registers in a buffer. You can also invoke the `Push_Client_State` macro, which saves the client registers on the VxD stack. The `Pop_Client_State` macro calls the `Restore_Client_State` service to pop the client registers back from the VxD Stack.

Before calling back into a VM, the VMM must also be prepared to be re-entered, in case the VM code requires any other VMM services. The `Begin_Nest_Exec` service returns after the VMM is in a state in which it can be re-entered. In addition, this service records the CS:(E)IP of the VM so that execution in the VM can resume where it left off. Once the VxD has completed all calls back into the VxD, it calls `End_Nest_Exec`.

To actually pass control to a VM, a VxD calls the `Resume_Exec` service. This service lets the VM run until it reaches the same instruction that it was at when `Begin_Nest_Exec` was called. This may seem pointless and, in fact, if we call `Begin_Nest_Exec`, followed by `Resume_Exec`, followed by `End_Nest_Exec`, nothing useful happens. However, there are times when this feature is useful.

The `Simulate_Far_Call` service, like the `Simulate_Far_Jmp` service, modifies the client CS:(E)IP. In addition, however, it first saves the previous client CS:(E)IP on the client stack. This has the same effect as the execution of a CALL instruction in the VM. Let's put these calls together in the following code fragment:

```
Push_Client_State            ; Save client regs
VMMcall Begin_Nest_Exec      ; Remember starting point
mov                          cx,[pV86Routine]
```

```
movzx   edx,[pV86Routine]   ; Specify VM CS:IP
VMMcall Simulate_Far_Call   ; Simulate the call
VMMcall Resume_Exec         ; Execute in the VM
VMMcall End_Nest_Exec       ; Done calling the VM
Pop_Client_State            ; Restore VM's registers
```

This example calls the code at the V86 VM address specified by pVMRoutine. The comments detail each step.

There are a number of other services to simulate VM instruction execution. The Simulate_Int service simulates an INT instruction. The Exec_Int service is a shorthand way of calling Simulate_Int immediately followed by Resume_Exec. The Simulate_Int service may not have the effect you desire, since when the VM runs, it immediately returns to protected mode to process the trap and also processes all VxD hooks associated with the interrupt. The Build_Int_Stack_Frame also simulates an INT instruction, but instead of using the address specified in the interrupt vector table, this service accepts a starting address as a parameter.

To facilitate calling various V86 VM services, the Exec_VxD_Int service is similar to Exec_Int, except that parameters are passed and returned in the VxD registers. You should use this service only for functions that do not return values in the ES or DS registers, since they will not be valid across modes. Use Exec_Int instead. The VxDint macro provides for more readable code when Exec_VxD_Int is called. You do not need to save and restore the client registers when using this service.

In addition to simulating call instructions in a VM, VMM services also simulate return instructions. Simulate_Far_Ret and Simulate_Far_Ret_N simulate the RET and RETN instructions. The Simulate_Iret service simulates an IRET instruction. It is easier to use these services than to modify the client registers and stack yourself, since they automatically account for the possibility that the VM may be running in a 32-bit protected mode segment, and make proper adjustments for how instructions behave in that mode.

Although most simulation services affect the client only, two services, Simulate_Push and Simulate_Pop, actually work between the VxD EAX register and the current client's stack. They provide 16- or 32-bit transfer, depending on the mode of the current VM.

All of the services mentioned apply to a VM running in either real or protected mode and will call back the VM in whatever mode it was in when the VxD was called. If you need to force a particular mode before calling the VM, you can call Set_PM_Exec_Mode or Set_V86_Exec_Mode first, to force protected or V86 mode, respectively. The `Begin_Nest_V86_Exec` service is similar to `Begin_Nest_Exec` combined with `Set_V86_Exec_Mode`, except that the final call to `End_Nest_Exec` will restore the VM to its original mode.

Miscellaneous Control Services

The `Nuke_VM` service destroys the specified VM. This call is normally reserved for the user shell. If a VxD needs to destroy a VM due to a catastrophe, it should call `Crash_Cur_VM`, but only in the most extreme circumstances.

Virtual Interrupt Services

Hardware interrupts from devices are managed in hardware by a device know as the programmable interrupt controller, or PIC. In Windows, the virtual PIC driver (VPICD) manages interrupts for virtual drivers. A VxD should never access the actual PIC directly, but instead should rely on VPICD services to manage interrupts.

The VPICD handles all interrupt request (IRQ) lines, each of which can be individually enabled (unmasked) or disabled (masked) by writing to PIC I/O ports. By default, the VPICD handles interrupts in two different ways, depending on whether or not they are enabled when the VPICD initializes. Those that are enabled when the VPICD initializes are treated as global IRQs, and those that are disabled are treated as local IRQs.

When an interrupt occurs on a global IRQ, the VPICD immediately reflects the interrupt into the current VM. This is based on the assumption that the interrupt code will be the same in each VM. In other words, the interrupt service routine will be in global VM memory.

Local IRQs are initially disabled, so no interrupts will be received on those lines. If a VM application enables a local IRQ, however, the interrupts may be received. The assumption here is that the code to handle the interrupt is valid only in the VM that enables the interrupt, and the VPICD only routes the interrupt request to that VM. The VM is said to own the particular local IRQ. If another VM attempts to enable a local IRQ that is owned by another VM, the VPICD will terminate the second VM, after displaying an error message to the user.

A VxD can modify this default behavior by virtualizing the IRQ itself. To do so, it first calls the `VPICD_Virtualize_IRQ` service. In the call to this service, the VxD passes a structure that contains various option indicators and the addresses of up to five callback routines. The VPICD returns a virtual IRQ handle in response.

Once a VxD has the handle to a virtual IRQ, it can assert an interrupt into a VM by calling `VPICD_Set_Int_Request`. Note that the following conditions must be satisfied before the interrupt is actually simulated:

- The interrupt must be enabled by the VM's virtual PIC.
- There is no higher priority IRQ being serviced.
- The VM's virtual interrupts are enabled.

Beyond these normal conditions, the VM may still be suspended, in which case the interrupt will not be simulated. When the interrupt is simulated, virtual interrupts are disabled and the flags are saved on the VM stack. Then the VM transfers control to the VM's interrupt routine specified in the VM's interrupt vector table or interrupt descriptor table (depending on the current VM mode). In addition, so that the VxD can synchronize with the actual time that an interrupt is processed by a VM, the VPICD calls the `VID_Virt_Int_Proc` callback in the VxD when the interrupt is virtualized.

Before enabling virtual interrupts (as a result of executing IRET), a VM first sends EOI to the interrupt device, typically by issuing some command to the VxD's virtual ports for the VM. Upon detecting EOI, the VxD calls the `VPICD_Clear_Int_Request` service to clear the interrupt. Finally, the VM issues EOI to the virtual PIC to de-assert the interrupt from the virtual PIC and executes an IRET instruction.

Let's review this sequence in a little more detail:

1. The actual PIC hardware interrupts the CPU, transferring control to the VPICD.
2. The VPICD calls the `VID_Hw_Int_Proc` callback in the VxD.
3. The VxD calls `VPICD_Set_Int_Request`, specifying the VM that owns the IRQ.
4. The VM services the interrupt, essentially sending EOI to the virtual device.
5. The VxD services the interrupt, essentially sending EOI to the actual device.
6. The VxD calls `VPICD_Clear_Int_Request` to release the virtual interrupt.

7. The VM issues EOI to the virtual PIC.

8. The VPICD calls the `VID_EOI_Proc` callback in the VxD.

9. The VxD issues EOI to the hardware by calling `VPICD_Phys_EOI`.

This sequence describes a "passthrough" virtualization of hardware. In practice, the accesses to and interrupts from hardware do not necessarily have to exist. An entirely virtual environment might process an interrupt as follows:

1. The VxD calls `VPICD_Set_Int_Request`.

2. The VM services the interrupt, essentially sending EOI to the virtual device.

3. The VxD calls `VPICD_Clear_Int_Request`.

4. The VM issues EOI to the virtual PIC.

With these four steps, a VxD can repeatedly send virtual interrupts to a VM without any corresponding hardware interrupts.

If a VxD repeatedly simulates interrupts into a VM without any delay, it must do so in a carefully prescribed manner. The most direct method might be simply to loop according to the four steps in the previous list. Under this method, however, the VM's stack can overflow. Consider the following code fragment:

```
in  al,dx       ; Send EOI to the device
mov al,20h
out 20h,al      ; Send EOI to the PIC
sti             ; Allow other interrupts at this level
```

As soon as the `sti` instruction is executed, the VPICD simulates another interrupt into the VM. Since the VM is already executing on the interrupt stack, the stack will again be used for the next interrupt. This type of code is common in DOS environments and does work effectively in nested stack use. In a virtual environment, however, the pending interrupts may cause the nesting to be deeper than it would be in a DOS environment, causing the stack to overflow.

Eventually, the VM relinquishes the interrupt stack when it finishes processing the interrupt. It does this when it executes the IRET into the interrupted code. Ideally, the VxD delays the assertion of the next interrupt until this stack is available again. It can do this by monitoring the VM execution of the final IRET instruction. The VPICD calls back the VxD on this event via the `VID_IRET_Proc`. Using this new information, we can reconstruct the steps needed to achieve repeated multiple interrupts into a VM:

1. The VxD calls `VPICD_Set_Int_Request`.
2. The VM services the interrupt, essentially sending EOI to the virtual device.
3. The VxD calls `VPICD_Clear_Int_Request`.
4. The VM issues EOI to the virtual PIC.
5. The VM enables interrupts.
6. The VM completes interrupt processing and performs an IRET.
7. The VPICD calls the `VID_IRET_Proc` callback.
8. The VxD proceeds with step 1.

At step 7, the stack is in the same position that it was in at interrupt time and the VxD is free to go ahead and interrupt the VM again, without the risk of overflowing the VM stack. There is a certain risk that the VPICD will not be able to detect when step 6 occurs. In this case, the VPICD calls back the `VID_IRET_Proc` after a prespecified timeout period.

One callback has not been mentioned. The VPICD calls the `VID_Mask_Change_Proc` whenever a VM modifies the interrupt mask for the interrupt controlled by the VxD. This callback might tell a VxD when an additional VM has requested the interrupt and provide opportunity for the VxD to arbitrate access to the virtual PIC.

A VxD can query the status of its physical IRQ at any time by calling `VPICD_Test_Phys_Request`. The `VPICD_Get_Status` service returns the virtual status of an IRQ and `VPICD_Get_Complete_Status` service returns both virtual and physical status information for any IRQ.

A VxD can alter the state of its physical IRQ mask by calling `VPICD_Physically_Mask` and `VPICD_Physically_Unmask`. The VxD can tell the VPICD to let the VMs decide the state of the mask by calling `VPICD_Set_Auto_Masking`. This enables the default state of the physical mask, which is to enable the physical mask only if at least one VM has enabled its corresponding virtual mask.

One final VPICD service needs mentioning. Normally, a VxD will want to be called back only when an interrupt occurs on its own specific

IRQ line. However, a VxD can request to be called back for any type of hardware interrupt by calling the VPICD_Call_When_Hw_Int service.

Virtual DMA Services

The virtual DMA device (VDMAD) has a number of memory addressing issues to resolve in order to virtualize the DMA device. A program running under Windows in 386 enhanced mode accesses memory in two stages in the CPU. The first stage converts the specified segment descriptor and address offset into a linear address. The second stage takes the linear address and converts it to a physical address. Memory in V86 mode is in the low one-megabyte of linear space. As occurs throughout Windows memory, these linear memory addresses do not correspond to the same physical address. The 386 paging hardware allows these linear addresses to map to anywhere in physical memory. The paging hardware even allows the linear addresses to map to nowhere, resulting in a CPU fault if a program attempts to access the memory.

The 386 paging hardware maps memory in units of pages of 4096 bytes each. Each page falls on a 4096-byte boundary. Consider a page in memory that is visible from an application. This memory page, for example, may be at linear address 0x00005000. The page at this address is sometimes referred to by its page number (0x00005) rather than its linear address. Windows can map this page to any physical page in memory, say at linear address 0x00060000. Windows might, instead, have written this page to disk, in which case the page is nowhere in physical memory. In addition to these CPU addressing issues, computers conforming to standard industry standard architecture (ISA) will not perform DMA across a 128K-byte physical memory boundary for word transfers, or across a 64K-byte physical memory boundary for byte transfers.

If the device that is performing DMA is not virtualized, the VDMAD will do all of the virtualization of the DMA hardware that is necessary to allow the DMA transfers to proceed. In this case, the actual device hardware coordinates its activity with the DMA device.

With normal hardware, a device sends signals over the system bus indicating to the DMA hardware when it should transfer data between the device and memory. In a virtual environment, however, it is the VxD that must communicate with the VDMAD in order to cause the transfer of information between the virtual device and the virtual DMA device.

To register itself with the VDMAD, a VxD first calls VDMAD_Virtualize_Channel. This call essentially disconnects a VM's virtual DMA device from the DMA hardware. The virtual DMA state is modified and maintained according to I/O instructions from the VM, but the VDMAD does not perform corresponding operations on the physical device.

Thus, when the VM programs the client VxD's device for DMA transfer and tells it to begin, the VxD need only call VDMAD_Get_Virt_State to determine what the virtual DMA transfer is supposed to do. From that point, it is up to the VxD actually to perform the transfer. The method used to transfer the data is entirely up to the VxD—the DMA hardware might not be involved at all.

If a VxD does decide to perform a DMA transfer, it has a number of options to choose from. First, consider the memory area where the DMA transfer will occur. If the memory is already locked (that is, not pageable), then the physical address can be determined with a call to CopyPageTable. The VxD must next determine whether the buffer is fully within a 64K or 128K boundary, as appropriate, and whether or not the physical pages are contiguous in physical memory.

If all these requirements are satisfied, the VxD can call the VDMAD_Set_Region_Info and VDMAD_Set_Phys_State services to program the DMA hardware to begin DMA transfer. The VxD may also need to call VDMAD_UnMask_Channel to enable DMA transfer on the specified channel. Normally with ISA hardware, DMA channels 1 through 3 are reserved for byte transfers, and channels 4 through 7 are reserved for 16-bit word transfers. On non-ISA hardware, these defaults can be changed, so to determine their actual values, your VxD should call the VDMAD_Get_EISA_Adr_Mode. This service indicates if the DMA channels are set up for 8-, 16-, or 32-bit transfers, and if the transfer count is in words or in bytes.

Rather than determining if the memory is locked and contiguous by reading the page table to determine the physical address and checking for DMA boundaries, a VxD can simply call the VDMAD_Lock_DMA_Region service. If all the conditions are satisfied, this service returns the physical address of the region. The VxD can then perform the DMA as described and then call VDMAD_Unlock_DMA_Region to unlock the memory.

If the lock fails, the VxD has a couple of possible solutions: either it can transfer the data in pieces, or it can copy the data to a buffer that is known to be valid for DMA transfer.

The VDMAD_Scatter_Lock service will lock a linear region, even if all of its physical pages are not contiguous, and will return the physical addresses of each valid region. After making this call, the VxD can then perform separate DMA transfers for each valid region. When the transfer is complete, the VxD calls the `VDMAD_Scatter_Unlock` service to unlock the memory.

Instead of performing the DMA in pieces, the VxD can copy the data to a memory buffer that is known to be valid for DMA transfer. To do this, the VxD first calls `VDMAD_Request_Buffer`. The size of the buffer is limited by the VDMAD, but the limit can be extended during `Sys_Critical_Init` control processing by calling `VDMAD_Reserve_Buffer_Space` during VxD initialization. For a DMA transfer from device to memory, the VxD first transfers the data to be written from its original location to the VDMAD buffer by calling `VDMAD_Copy_To_Buffer`. Once the DMA is complete and the transfer was from memory to device, the VxD calls `VDMAD_Copy_From_Buffer` to transfer the data to its ultimate destination. When the VxD is finished using the buffer, it calls `VDMAD_Release_Buffer` to free it.

A couple of other VDMAD services might be useful for more complex DMA transfers. The `VDMAD_Set_Virt_State` sets the virtual state of a DMA channel. The `VDMAD_Disable_Translation` service indicates to the VDMAD that all addresses are to be interpreted as physical addresses rather than linear addresses. The `VDMAD_Enable_Translation` service reverts back to assuming linear addresses.

User Shell Services

There are often limits to what we can program a VxD to do in order to manage virtualization of devices, and, from time to time, a VxD may have to ask the user what to do. The user shell services provide a way of posting messages to the user and getting responses.

The `SHELL_Message` service displays a Windows message box containing the specified text and response buttons. This service returns immediately after being called, and the VxD must return before Windows displays the message box. A VxD may specify a callback routine to service to which Windows will call back when the user responds to the message box.

The `SHELL_SYSMODAL_Message` service works in a similar fashion, but does not require allocating system memory, so is more likely to succeed. For simple contention resolution, the `SHELL_Resolve_Contention` service displays a standard system modal dialog box asking the user to assign the specified device to one of two contending VMs.

Debugging Services

When building a VxD, you should have conditional assembly statements that provide debug messages when Windows is running in debug
mode. You can display messages whether or not a debugger is installed. You can test for the presence of a debugger by calling the
`Test_Debug_Installed` service.

To debug your VxD, use the WDEB386 debugger as described in the
SDK documentation. There is a dot (.) command that is particularly useful
when you are debugging a VxD. The dot command specifies what VxD to
call. When the user enters the dot command and specifies your VxD, Windows issues the `Debug_Query` control to your VxD. This gives your VxD
an opportunity to display extended debugging information.

You can display a message on the debugging screen by invoking the
`Trace_Out` macro. This macro accepts two parameters. The first parameter is a delimited string. The second parameter, if present, indicates that
the debug string should not end with a carriage-return/line-feed combination. This macro can affect system performance, so there is another macro,
`Queue_Out`, which is much faster and puts the message into a memory
buffer instead of writing it to the screen. When debugging, you can enter
the .LQ command to the most recent contents of the debugging buffer.

You can stop your program and pass control to the debugger by
executing a single-step debug trap (INT 1). To display a message and then
trap, use the `Debug_Out` macro, which first calls `Trace_Out` before
trapping.

Miscellaneous Services

Windows provides a large number of other services that a VxD can call on
to obtain status information and perform miscellaneous tasks during initialization and regular operation. Most of these services do not fall into a
particular category, but there are a few interesting services that deserve
more than just a reference in the appendix.

When virtualizing a system, you often need to put hooks in many
places in order to simulate an environment in just the right way.
We have seen how to hook software interrupts, hardware interrupts, and
even I/O port accesses. It is even possible to hook other VxDs.
The `Hook_Device_Service` service allows a VxD to monitor service
messages sent to another VxD, and the `Hook_Device_V86_API` and

`Hook_Device_PM_API` services allow a VxD to hook the API service routines of another VxD. A VxD can even send system control messages to all VxDs, using the `System_Control` service.

Although the `Declare_Virtual_Device` macro provides entry points for API service for a VxD, a VxD may need to have a separate API entry point. The `Allocate_V86_Call_Back` and `Allocate_PM_Call_Back` services provide direct entry points into a VxD from VM V86 mode and protected mode clients, respectively. The V86 and protected mode services specified in the `Declare_Virtual_Device` macro perform these services implicitly, but this call is provided to allow a VxD to add additional service entry points. A VxD may use one of these services if it wishes to save the time spent dispatching to a subfunction from its standard service routine, or if it wishes to hook a V86 interrupt and process messages via the extended API entry point.

Summary

Windows 386 enhanced mode services not only allow a VxD to have thorough control over a particular VM or device virtualization; they also allow control over the entire operation of Windows itself. The performance of a VxD can have a direct impact on the overall operation of Windows, so it is critical that a VxD be written to be as efficient as possible. In addition to having a good understanding of the hardware that a VxD is emulating and of the PC hardware environment, the VxD developer must also have a good understanding of all of the services provided to a VxD.

Windows and other VxDs provide numerous services. These services are the tools of a VxD developer. Even if you do not understand the full capabilities and purposes of these tools, you should at this point have a general idea of what types of tools are available. It is futile to try to explain each of these tools fully—only experimentation will make you a master of their possibilities.

The services that Windows and some of the basic VxDs provide have been described from the point of view of a client of these services. The VPICD and VDMAD services are a case in point; they are VxDs that a developer is not likely to change, since their hardware components are fundamental to PC compatibility. We can also look at VxD services from the point of view of the VxD that provides the services.

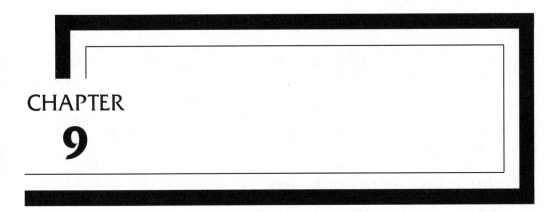

System Virtual Drivers

Only a few of the device drivers fundamental to the operation of Windows are likely to be changed to accommodate new hardware. This chapter reviews such drivers. These drivers not only emulate hardware, but also provide services that other VxDs and Windows itself rely on for proper operation. Therefore, keep in mind while you are customizing or developing a driver for your own use, that Windows requires some of the interfaces to remain intact, regardless of the underlying hardware.

This chapter discusses the virtual driver interfaces for three of the system drivers: the display driver, the keyboard driver, and the communication driver. The next chapter presents a more general discussion of custom drivers that are not integral to Windows.

Virtual Display Driver

As with the base display driver for Windows, the performance of the virtual display driver (VDD) is directly related to Windows' performance. The VDD is likely to be the most complex VxD for this and for other reasons. Closely coupled with the VDD is the display grabber, which is responsible for saving, restoring, and maintaining windowed and full-screen views of DOS–VM displays.

Like other virtual drivers, the VDD does not replace the basic display driver of the graphics device interface (GDI). Instead, it coordinates access to the video hardware between virtual machines (VMs), including the system VM where the GDI display driver runs. The 386 enhanced mode grabber, on the other hand, replaces the standard mode grabber and is tightly coupled with the VDD. In fact, both the VDD and the 386 grabber communicate directly with one another in supporting the 386 enhanced mode display.

Virtual Display Driver Functions

The primary purpose of the VDD is to coordinate VM access to the video hardware and to simulate video hardware access if the VM is not in full-screen mode. Ideally, for a VM that is not in full-screen mode, the VDD will allow it to run unhindered, even if the VM attempts to access what it thinks is the video hardware. When the VM is visible, the VDD can update the video hardware with the current state of the VM's virtual display. When the system VM (Windows) is in the foreground and the background VM is in a window, the VDD can work with the display grabber to display the virtual screen within a window. Like the base display driver, the VDD is the most complex virtual driver, and its performance is critical to the overall performance of Windows.

The VDD exports a number of miscellaneous services to Windows and to other VxDs, as listed in Figure 9-1. These services allow Windows and other VxDs to coordinate their activities with the VDD.

VDD_Get_GrabRtn	VDD_Msg_SetCursPos
VDD_GetModTime	VDD_Msg_TextOut
VDD_Get_Version	VDD_PIF_State
VDD_Hide_Cursor	VDD_Query_Access
VDD_Msg_BakColor	VDD_Set_HCurTrk
VDD_Msg_ClrScrn	VDD_Set_VMType
VDD_Msg_ForColor	

FIGURE 9-1 Miscellaneous VDD Services

```
VDD_Msg_BakColor
VDD_Msg_ClrScrn
VDD_Msg_ForColor
VDD_Msg_SetCursPos
VDD_Msg_TextOut
```

FIGURE 9-2 VDD Message Mode Services

Figure 9-2 lists services that allow other Windows VxDs to control the display directly. These message mode services can be called after the VDD receives the `Begin_Message_Mode` control. Generally, other VxDs do not call the VDD services, but instead are called by Windows itself.

In addition to these services, the VDD can also export protected mode program services to the enhanced mode video grabber (described in the next section).

The details of actually implementing a VDD are beyond the scope of this book. This is because most of the work in implementing a VDD has more to do with the specifics of the actual video hardware than with the Windows interface. The sample drivers that are provided with the DDK provide an excellent starting point if your video adapter is similar to an EGA, VGA, or 8514-A. Later releases of the DDK may provide even more samples.

386 Enhanced Mode Display Grabber

In DOS session displays, the most salient difference between standard and 386 enhanced mode is that the latter display can be shown in a window. By virtue of the VDD, the application need not access the video hardware directly in order to run, even though the application thinks that it does. One of the main functions of the standard mode grabber is to save and restore screen contents. In 386 enhanced mode, however, the VDD maintains the state of all virtual displays. Thus, the main function of the 386 enhanced mode grabber is different. Specifically, it converts the virtual display format into one that is appropriate for display in a window to the Windows display driver.

The format of the 386 enhanced mode grabber file is different from its standard mode counterpart. The 386 enhanced mode grabber runs in protected mode rather than in real mode. Its file is constructed as a conventional Windows DLL. Its entry points are exported and parameters to the functions are passed in PL/M form, with arguments on the stack and stack cleanup by the called function. The grabber initializes itself like any DLL, with a library initialization function specified by the module entry address. Figure 9-3 lists the primary grabber functions.

For a newly created session, the VDD first calls `CheckGRBVersion` to insure that the version of the VDD and the grabber are matched. Windows then calls `GetFontList` to get a list of the fonts the grabber will need to display the session in a Window. Normally, Windows does not call the grabber in full-screen mode until the session ends, when Windows calls `ScreenFree` to free all grabber resources associated with the DOS session. Windows will also call the grabber for a full-screen session if the user presses ALT+PRINT-SCREEN. In this case, once the VDD is finished grabbing the screen, it calls the grabber `GrabComplete` function. The `GrabEvent` function is intended for private communication between the VDD and the grabber, but is not used in most existing video grabbers.

Most of the grabber calls are made when the associated DOS session is displayed as a window. Also, most of these function calls accept a single parameter, the address of an extended paint structure, `EXTPAINTSTRUC`.

Windows frequently calls the grabber `GetDisplayUpd` function, even if there is no video activity in the DOS session. Perhaps, by communicating with the VDD, a later version of Windows will recognize when there is no screen activity in the session and will only call this function when needed. As it stands now, you should in most cases make your implementation of `GetDisplayUpd` as efficient as possible, because Windows calls it frequently. The call to `GetDisplayUpd` suspends the current session, preventing further screen changes. Soon after calling this function, Windows calls the `GrbUnlockApp` function to unlock the session. Consequently, Windows calls the `GrbUnlockApp` function frequently, so this function also should be optimized.

`CheckGRBVersion`	`GetFontList`	`Initialization`
`CursorOff`	`GrabComplete`	`PaintScreen`
`CursorOn`	`GrabEvent`	`ScreenFree`
`GetDisplayUpd`	`GrbGetTextColor`	`SetPaintFnt`
`CursorPosit`	`GrbUnlockApp`	`UpdateScreen`

FIGURE 9-3 386 Enhanced Mode Grabber Functions

When Windows does detect a change in the display, it calls the grabber to update the changes in the session's window. Before updating the display, however, Windows first calls the `SetPaintFnt` function, which returns the font dimensions (if the screen is in a text mode), the screen dimensions in pixels, and, if in text mode, the screen dimensions in character units.

To actually update the display, Windows calls either the `UpdateScreen` or the `PaintScreen` function. If a DOS application updates its virtual display, Windows calls the `UpdateScreen` function to update the Windows view of the screen. If the display is updated as a result of Windows activity (such as a `WM_PAINT` message), Windows calls the `PaintScreen` function to update the window. To actually paint the screen, the grabber calls normal Windows output functions, such as `TextOut` and `BitBlt`.

When a DOS session is not active, the grabber is responsible for turning off the cursor in the session's windows. The `CursorOff` function turns off the cursor, and the `CursorOn` function turns it back on. Windows tells the grabber the position of the cursor with the `CursorPosit` function.

Grabber Editing Functions

In addition to its primary function of displaying a DOS window, the 386 enhanced mode grabber also supports screen clipboard copy and other miscellaneous functions. Figure 9-4 lists the functions exported by the 386 enhanced mode grabber that support the Windows copy function.

There are a number of steps involved in performing a copy operation from a DOS screen. The selection and copy functions are supported by Windows only in 386 enhanced mode. The steps differ depending on whether the user is using the keyboard or a mouse. I will review the steps involved when the keyboard is used to select an area to be copied. The mouse method results in similar calls.

AdjustInitPoint	InvertSelection
BeginSelection	KeySelection
ConsSelRec	MakeSelctRect
EndSelection	RenderSelection

FIGURE 9-4 Grabber Editing Functions

First, the user presses ALT+SPACEBAR to bring up the session's system menu. If the session was previously a full screen, Windows changes the session to a windowed session. Next, the user selects the Mark command from the system menu of the window for the DOS session. This causes Windows to call the grabber's `BeginSelection` function, specifying the starting position of the mark operation, initially the upper left position on the screen. The `BeginSelection` function moves the cursor to this position. At this time, the selection area is a single character, starting and ending at the same screen position.

To select the actual desired starting position, the user moves the cursor with the cursor keys. These keystrokes cause Windows to call the grabber's `KeySelection` function, followed by calls to `EndSelection` and `BeginSelection` again. First these calls move the selection to subsequent single-character areas. The call to `KeySelection` tells the grabber to reposition the cursor, the call to `EndSelection` tells the grabber to cancel the previous (single-character) selection, and the call to `BeginSelection` specifies the beginning of the new (single-character) selection area.

Next, to expand the selection beyond one character, the user holds down the shift key while moving the ending position with the cursor keys. Again, each cursor keystroke causes Windows to call `KeySelection` to reposition the cursor but, since the starting position does not change, Windows also calls the `MakeSelctRect` function to specify the expanded (or reduced) selection area. Also, as each direction key is pressed and as the selection area changes, Windows calls the grabber's `InvertSelection` function to remove the previous selection. Then, after calling `MakeSelctRect`, Windows calls `InvertSelection` again to display the new selection rectangle. It is possible for the user to select the lower right corner of a rectangle first; thus, to normalize the selection area, Windows calls `ConsSelecRec` as the user changes the selection area.

Finally, when the user presses the Enter key (or the right mouse button), Windows uses the last selection area to call the grabber `RenderSelection` function to obtain the text or bitmap representing the area of the screen the user selected.

Virtual Keyboard Driver

At its lowest level, the virtual keyboard driver (VKD) is responsible for virtualizing the keyboard hardware. However, since the keyboard is so critical for Windows, this driver is also responsible for a number of higher-

```
VKD_Cancel_Hot_Key_State      VKD_Get_Version
VKD_Cancel_Paste              VKD_Local_Disable_Hot_Key
VKD_Define_Hot_Key            VKD_Local_Enable_Hot_Key
VKD_Define_Paste_Mode         VKD_Peek_Msg_Key
VKD_Flush_Msg_Key_Queue       VKD_Reflect_Hot_Key
VKD_Force_Keys                VKD_Remove_Hot_Key
VKD_Get_Kbd_Owner             VKD_Start_Paste
VKD_Get_Msg_Key
```

FIGURE 9-5 VKD Services

level functions. These higher-level functions include not only the services listed in Figure 9-5, but also coordination with the Windows time slicer to improve overall Windows performance.

Although the general driver model intends, at some level, to provide hardware independence, all interfaces to the keyboard driver assume PC-compatible hardware, at least with regard to the hardware ports simulated and the scan codes used. The listed services are provided by the VKD to other VxDs.

Clipboard Pasting

The most obvious capability provided by the VKD is the simulation of keystrokes into a VM. To the end-user, this is a "paste" operation: keystrokes are pasted from the Windows clipboard into a VM. The simplest way to simulate keystrokes into a VM is to enqueue the keystrokes into the BIOS buffer and let the application retrieve the keystrokes using BIOS INT 16. Many applications (including TSRs), however, do not access keys through the BIOS, but instead read keystrokes directly from the keyboard hardware, processing keyboard interrupts and reading scan codes from the keyboard I/O ports.

Normally, the VKD can automatically detect which method a DOS application is using in order to read keystrokes. If it cannot, another VxD can override this detection by calling VKD_Define_Paste_Mode. To actually paste keys into a VM, Windows calls the VKD_Start_Paste service. This service accepts a buffer of entries, each containing the OEM key code (as returned by the BIOS), the hardware scan code, and the desired shift state. The VKD is responsible for simulating shift key changes if the current virtual keyboard state doesn't match the pasted values. In addition, the VKD will simulate the keystrokes into the VM at a rate that is closer to the rate an actual typist uses, rather than sending all codes at once. Since a paste operation can take some time, relative to the CPU, it is possible to cancel a paste operation in midstride, by calling VKD_Cancel_ Paste. Windows calls this function if the user presses the Escape key, for example.

Another VxD can also force raw scan codes into a VM by calling VKD_Force_Keys. This is a very low-level method of simulating keystrokes into a VM, which even allows hot keys to be simulated. Generally, the VKD_Start_Paste service is more useful, though.

Hot Keys

In addition to pasting, the VKD is also responsible for managing hot key processing. To an end-user, a **hot key** is a keystroke that will cause an application to pop up. To other VxDs, a hot key is a keystroke that will cause the VKD to call back the VxD that registered the hot key.

The VKD_Define_Hot_Key service defines a hot key. The hot key is specified as a scan code and shift state. The shift state may be any combination of shift keys in conjunction with pressing the main hot key. When most keys on the keyboard are pressed, the keyboard hardware sends a scan code when the key is first pressed. Subsequent scan codes are set for each repeat. A release scan code is sent when the key is released. A parameter to VKD_Define_Hot_Key specifies under what conditions the VxD callback routine is called—the callback may be called for the down code only, the repeats only, or the up code only.

Some hot keys may be directed to a particular VM. The callback routine for a hot key can tell Windows to forward the hot key sequence to a VM by calling VKD_Reflect_Hot_Key. This allows a hot key to be pressed from any VM, but to be simulated into a particular VM.

A hot key can be disabled by calling VKD_Remove_Hot_Key. This removes the callback processing established by VKD_Define_Hot_Key. When VKD_Define_Hot_Key is first called, the hot key is active in all VMs. A VxD can selectively disable or enable hot keys in a specific VM by calling VKD_Local_Disable_Hot_Key or VKD_Local_Enable_Hot_ Key, respectively. This limits a hot key's activity to a particular VM or allows the hot key to be active in all but a particular VM.

Message Mode

The VKD is also responsible for providing keyboard access to other VxDs. A VxD can begin message mode in a VxD by calling the Windows `System_Control` function, specifying the target VM and the `Begin_Message_Mode` control. When Windows broadcasts the `Begin_Message_Mode` control to VxDs, the VKD puts itself into message mode. In this mode, the VKD does not simulate keystrokes into the VM. Instead, it is polled by a call to the `VKD_Get_Msg_Key` service. Another VxD can also perform a nondestructive read by calling `VKD_Peek_Msg_Key`. Both of the services return a scan code and shift state. A VxD can also flush the message mode buffer entirely by calling `VKD_Flush_Msg_Key_Queue`.

Virtual Communications Driver

Virtualization of the serial communications ports is actually shared by two virtual drivers: the virtual communications driver (VCD) and the virtual communications buffer (COMBUFF). The VCD is responsible for supporting the Windows serial port driver (COMM.DRV) and for virtualizing the serial port hardware. COMBUFF is responsible for buffering serial port data into a VM and providing transparent XON/XOFF support. The COMM.DRV driver runs in the system VM and communicates directly with the VCD.

Both COMBUFF and the normal communications driver expect a few services from the VCD that are listed in Figure 9-6. COMBUFF uses the `VCD_Virtualize_Port` service to hook itself to the VCD. Subsequent port activity is reflected to COMBUFF rather than processed directly by the VCD. The virtual mouse driver (VMD) uses the `VCD_Set_Port_Global` service to cause the mouse's serial port to be shared by all VMs,

```
VCD_Get_Version
VCD_Get_Focus
VCD_Set_Port_Global
VCD_Virtualize_Port
```

FIGURE 9-6 VCD VxD Services

```
VCD_PM_Acquire_Port
VCD_PM_Free_Port
VCD_PM_Get_Port_Array
VCD_PM_Get_Port_Behavior
VCD_PM_Get_Version
VCD_PM_Set_Port_Behavior
```

FIGURE 9-7 VCD Protected Mode Services

since the VMD will manage contention for the mouse, rather than letting the VCD handle contention at an inappropriately low level.

The VCD exports a number of services to protected mode code. These are listed in Figure 9-7. Currently, COMM.DRV only uses the first two services listed, VCD_PM_Acquire_Port and VCD_PM_Free_Port. The VCD_PM_Acquire_Port function assigns a port to a particular VM. Once a port is assigned, an attempt by another VM to use it should result in a message to the user requesting resolution of port ownership. The VCD_PM_Get_Port_Array service returns a bit-packed word indicating which ports are available to protected mode code. The VCD_PM_Get_Port_Behavior and VCD_PM_Set_Port_Behavior functions tell the VCD whether to handle contention for the specified port automatically.

Some of the specifics of the communications driver may be different for later releases of Windows, although the fundamental functions will remain the same. This means, however, that any detailed explanation of the current VCD will not be of much use.

Summary

Standard Windows VxDs are viewed from two perspectives: as clients of system services and as providers of system services. When modifying any of the existing VxDs (including those not described in this chapter), keep these two perspectives in mind to avoid incompatibilities with drivers that are not necessarily part of any standard Windows configuration. This restriction is removed for device drivers that are not part of the normal Windows repertoire of drivers. The next chapter describes some aspects of developing a nonstandard device driver.

CHAPTER

10

Nonstandard Device Drivers

Although up to this point I have discussed the implementation of existing drivers and types of drivers for Windows, many applications require device driver support for devices that are not necessarily part of mainstream Windows applications. Such drivers often provide interfaces for controlling and monitoring manufacturing or laboratory equipment, but any type of input or output device falls into this category. Two exceptions are digital pens and scanners, which are supported and specified with the Pen Windows and multimedia environment. Most other types of devices have no standard interface into Windows. The type of interface for these drivers is entirely up to the application developer.

There are no examples for nonstandard drivers in the DDK, so the task of developing your own nonstandard driver may be more difficult. Before developing the driver, you need first to define what the interface into the driver will be. Before you can do that, however, you must first understand what types of interfaces work best for Windows drivers and weigh the various considerations between standard and 386 enhanced modes.

Device Driver Packaging

As mentioned in Chapter 1, there is no fundamental model for Windows device drivers. Each application under Windows may have a different form of driver and a different type of interface. With the drivers that Windows relies upon, each type of driver has its own interface, but there are a few common aspects among the different types of drivers.

It is possible to write a driver using any of the following types of file formats and interfaces:

1. Standard DOS device driver
2. DOS TSR
3. Windows application
4. Windows dynamic link library
5. Virtual device driver

You can implement support for your device using one or more of these types. The method you choose will depend on the types of applications that will use your driver and the interfaces it expects.

DOS Device Drivers and TSRs

A conventional DOS device driver is installed in the usual way by specifying the name of the driver file with the DEVICE command in CONFIG.SYS. This type of driver provides access to DOS applications that use standard INT 21 function calls.

Windows applications can call this type of device driver too, also using INT 21 function calls. Although Windows runs in protected mode, when an application performs an INT 21 function, Windows switches to real or V86 mode and calls DOS to carry out the standard DOS function. If the function is for your standard driver, DOS in turn calls your driver to carry out the device function. This type of driver is easy to develop and will support DOS and Windows applications equally well, but it has some serious limitations.

The first limitation is that Windows must first change to DOS mode in order to pass control to the driver. For standard mode Windows running on a 286 processor, this means that the system must actually perform a CPU reset in order to switch to real mode. This is an extremely slow process, taking on the order of dozens of milliseconds. For many applications, this delay is unacceptable.

For interrupt-driven drivers, this delay is also imposed whenever the device driver processes an interrupt that occurs while Windows is in protected mode. Again, the system must change to real mode, and the interrupt must be passed to the driver. For many devices, this delay can cause loss of data.

A second limitation of the standard DOS device driver is that the parameters to the device driver must be translated when it is called from a protected mode application. When a protected mode application calls the INT 21 function, it passes pointers to data in selector:offset format. The interface to the device driver requires that pointers to data be presented in *segment*:offset format. Furthermore, it is likely that the protected mode application points to data at addresses above 1MB—segment:offset pointers can refer to data only at addresses below 1MB. In most cases, Windows provides the necessary translation. For write operations this usually means that the data must be copied to low memory buffers, called **translation buffers**, and the pointer must be redirected to the translation buffers before transferring control to DOS. For read operations, the reverse happens: the data is copied out of the translation buffers into the original application buffer after the call to DOS. In addition, the translation buffers are limited in size, so for transfers of larger blocks of data, Windows must convert the accesses to a series of calls, transferring the data a piece at a time. This can have undesirable effects for some device drivers.

A third limitation of DOS device drivers is that they consume potentially precious DOS memory. Furthermore, they consume memory in every DOS session under 386 enhanced mode. By default, this memory is shared among all VMs, but it is possible to force Windows to provide an instance of the driver in each VM through the use of the SYSTEM.INI local variable.

A final limitation of DOS device drivers is that they normally wait for data, delaying the return to the calling application until the data is ready. While this may be acceptable for DOS applications, Windows applications expect to be able to process Windows messages relatively quickly. A delay in a device driver suspends all activity on the Windows display until the driver returns. It might be possible to create a driver that does not wait, but this is not the norm.

Related to standard DOS drivers are drivers that are implemented as TSRs. These drivers are packaged as normal DOS .EXE files and are run after DOS has completed its bootstrap process. They typically do not provide normal INT 21 interfaces, the way standard DOS drivers do. Instead they have their own proprietary interfaces. A TSR that is to provide support for Windows applications only has the advantage that it cannot consume memory in all VMs, since it can be loaded in the system VM only by means of WINSTART.BAT. However, TSRs do not have the benefit of automatic translation of pointers and buffers between protected and real modes; they typically transfer only nonpointer parameters in CPU registers. TSRs can be assisted by protected mode drivers that perform the necessary translation, which is automatically provided to standard DOS drivers. A complete implementation with a TSR usually requires the assistance of a protected mode driver in standard mode or a VxD in 386 enhanced mode.

DOS Driver Support in Standard Mode

The only support beyond translation services that Windows provides DOS device drivers is to inform them when Windows starts and ends via an INT 2F callout. A driver's behavior depends on whether Windows is running and can release certain resources that allow Windows to run most efficiently. The driver can also tell Windows not to load if there are incompatibilities that the driver is aware of.

When Windows loads, it issues an INT 2F call with the following register values:

AX   0x1605

ES:BX   0:0 in standard mode Windows

DS:SI   0:0

CX   Normally zero; if this value is nonzero, the function should be ignored and the driver should immediately return from the callout

DX   Bit 0 is set for standard mode initialization or clear to indicate 386 enhanced mode initialization; the remaining bits are undefined

DI   Version number—for version 3.1, for example, the value of DI is 0x030A

When Windows issues the INT 2F call, the device driver must first enable interrupts and call the previous trap routine that was assigned to

INT 2F. If, after calling the previous function, the value of CX is nonzero, the previous driver has aborted the load and the driver should return immediately. Next, it performs any necessary functions in preparation for Windows and exits with CX set to zero. If the driver determines that Windows should not load, it returns with CX set to 1. In either case, all other registers are returned unmodified.

Windows performs INT 2F when Windows unloads, passing the following values:

AX   1606h

DX   Bit 0 is set for standard mode initialization or clear for 386 enhanced mode initialization; the remaining bits are undefined

This callout tells the DOS driver to return its state to what it was before the Windows load callout was issued. Note that this callout may be called immediately after the load callout if this or another DOS driver indicated that the Windows load was to be canceled.

The following code fragment shows how the callouts are used.

```
pPrevINT2F  DD  ?       ; Saved value of previous INT 2F
MyISR PROC FAR
   sti                  ; Enable interrupts
   pushf                ; Simulate an INT
   call  pPrevINT2F     ; Call the previous ISR
   cmp   ax,1605h
   je    LoadWin        ; Skip if Windows is loading
   cmp   ax,1606h
   jne   AllDone        ; Skip if not our callout
   pusha
   call  PrepareForUnload  ; Prepare for DOS mode again
   popa
   jmp   short AllDone
LoadWin:
   pusha                ; Save registers
   call  PrepareForLoad ; Prepare for Windows to load
   popa                 ; Restore registers
   jnc   AllDone        ; Skip if OK to run Windows
   mov   cx,1           ; Else, tell Windows to cancel
AllDone:
   iret
MyISR ENDP
```

DOS Driver Support in 386 Enhanced Mode

Windows provides a number of functions with INT 2F beyond the callout just described. These INT 2F callouts in turn provide additional capabilities when Windows starts in 386 enhanced mode. Specifically, a DOS driver can tell Windows to instance specified data areas and can tell Windows to load specific, named VxDs. Although the user can configure Windows to instance an entire device driver (via SYSTEM.INI), the callout return from INT 2F function 1605h can specify a smaller and more specific area to instance without requiring user configuration.

The DOS driver specifies areas to be instanced and VxDs to be loaded by adding entries to a linked list of initialization structures. The ES:BX values passed in the INT 2F callout actually point to the first entry of a list of instance structures. Each entry in the linked list has the following format:

```
InitStruct struc
is_Version    db 3,10  ; For version 3.10, for example
is_next       dd 0     ; Pointer to next entry in list
is_pVxDName   dd 0     ; Pointer to VxD name (ASCIIZ)
is_RefData    dd 0     ; Data to pass to VxD init
is_pInstData  dd 0     ; Pointer to InstData structure
InitStruct ends
```

To add your device's entry to the list, you store the passed value of BX into the is_next field, and load ES:BX with the address of your driver's entry. The is_pVxDName field points to a NUL-terminated (ASCIIZ) string that names the file containing the VxD to be loaded. Windows assumes that the VxD file is in the Windows SYSTEM directory. The is_RefData field contains the value that Windows passes to the VxD (in the EDX register) when it calls the VxD's real mode initialization code. The is_pInstData field contains a pointer to an InstData structure, which describes the area to be instanced as follows:

```
InstData struc          ; Declares area to be instanced
inst_pData  dd  ?       ; Address of the area
inst_sData  dw  ?       ; Size, in bytes, of the area
InstData ends
```

As happens in standard mode, the return from this callout returns with CX equal to zero to tell Windows to continue loading or with CX equal to 1 to indicate that the load should be aborted.

After Windows has completed the initialization of all VxDs, it issues INT 2F function 1608h to tell DOS mode drivers it has completed initialization. After a DOS mode driver has received this call, it is free to call on VxDs for their services.

When enhanced mode Windows terminates, it first calls INT 2F function 1609h. It does this before issuing the `Sys_VM_Terminate` control to VxDs, so VxD services are still available. The callout for unloading Windows, INT 2F function 1606h, is identical to the standard mode callout, except that bit 0 of DX is clear (zero).

In addition to the load and unload callouts, VxDs can call real mode drivers for information. The convention is for a VxD to call the real mode driver with INT 2F function 1607h. The value of BX is, by convention, the device ID of the calling VxD.

Windows in 386 enhanced mode not only calls DOS mode device drivers with commands and information but also provides the following INT 2F functions that DOS mode drivers can call.

INT 2F Function 1600h—Query 386 Enhanced Version. This function queries the version number of 386 enhanced mode Windows. If the AL register is less than three or greater than 127, then enhanced mode Windows is not running. Otherwise, the AL register contains the major version number and the AH register contains the minor version number. For version 3.10, for example, the AL register contains 3 and the AH register contains 10.

INT 2F Function 1680h—Yield VM. This function yields the current VM's time slice. A driver that polls a device for input, for example, might do this to indicate that the VM is idle until data is available. This prevents the VM from consuming time that may be more effectively spent in other VMs. Even if your driver does not directly support Windows applications, calling this function at appropriate times can improve Windows performance.

INT 2F Function 1681h—Enter Critical Section. This function tells Windows not to switch VMs. A driver may issue this function when it needs to insure that another VM will not execute. This may be particularly important to a driver that is instanced or has instanced areas. Such a driver may wish to insure that no other instances of itself execute within a particular section of code. The exception to this restriction is if a hardware interrupt is destined for another VM. In this case, the other VM is allowed to execute, but only to process the hardware interrupt.

INT 2F Function 1682h—Exit Critical Section. This function releases the critical section obtained by INT 2F function 1681h.

INT 2F Function 1683h—Query Current VM ID. This function returns the ID of the currently executing VM in the BX register. A DOS driver can use this ID internally to manage instance information about each VM. A DOS driver can determine the VM ID of the system VM by calling this function when Windows calls out INT 2F function 1608h.

INT 2F Function 1684h—Get VxD Entry Point. This function returns an address that the DOS mode driver can call to request services from a VxD. The DOS mode driver passes the device ID in the BX register. The function returns the address of the real mode entry point in the ES:DI register pair. If it returns NULL, the requested VxD does not provide real mode services.

INT 2F Function 1685h—Switch VMs and Call Back. Use this function if your driver must perform certain operations in a particular VM, such as the system VM, or if you want to call a driver that is loaded in a particular VM. The function tells Windows to change the context to the VM specified by the VM ID in the BX register. The other registers are specified as follows:

CX   Bit 0 is set to indicate that Windows must wait until interrupts are enabled before calling callback in the VM; bit 1 is set to indicate that Windows must wait until the critical section is unowned before calling the callback in the specified VM; the remaining bits must be clear (zero).

DX:SI   The 32-bit amount by which to boost the target VM's priority before changing contexts: DX contains the upper 16 bits and SI contains the lower 16 bits. This value is the same as the value passed to the VxD `Adjust_Exec_Priority` support function described in Appendix F.

ES:DI   The segment:offset address of the routine to call in the target VM.

DOS Drivers: Conclusion

Although the limitations of standard DOS and TSR drivers are serious and may be unacceptable for many applications, some applications will be able to provide full functionality through these drivers. In addition, you may be able to improve the performance of DOS mode drivers that are required for DOS operation by understanding the implications of running in a Windows VM and using the services that Windows provides in that environment. Often what is needed is a relatively simple Windows mode driver to complement an existing DOS mode driver. For Windows applications, the key is to understand the limitations of this type of driver and the possible advantages of writing a driver that is more fully integrated into the Windows environment.

Dynamic Link Library Drivers

The most obvious benefit of implementing a device driver as a Windows DLL is that the driver code (or portions of it) can reside in extended memory. This frees more of DOS memory for DOS applications. This is particularly beneficial if the driver is intended to support only Windows applications and no DOS applications.

Although driver code can be implemented as part of a normal Windows application, packaging the driver as a DLL provides other benefits. Clearly, such an implementation has the normal DLL benefits: isolation of code and ease of component distribution, but there are additional benefits that result from Windows' direct assistance in the implementation of device drivers as DLLs. Device support code provided as part of a normal Windows application image file (or .EXE file) is not treated in the same way as the same code packaged as part of a DLL.

Specifically, when a static segment in a DLL is marked FIXED, not only is the segment placed in a fixed location in linear memory, but the linear address of the segment is guaranteed to lie below the 1MB boundary. This allows a DLL to contain code that can execute in either protected mode or in real (or V86) mode. This characteristic of DLL FIXED segments is helpful, for example, with code that is accessed at interrupt time, when the interrupt may occur while the system is in either real or protected mode.

In 386 enhanced mode the way DLL FIXED segments are assigned has an additional characteristic: The memory is assigned to a fixed (and contiguous) physical memory region in addition to being assigned to a fixed linear memory region. This is helpful for a driver data segment that needs to guarantee that its data is never paged to disk, such as data that is accessed at interrupt time.

These characteristics of DLL FIXED segments apply not only to static segments assigned in the DLL's image, but also to any memory that the DLL allocates by calling `GlobalAlloc` with the `GMEM_FIXED` attribute.

Another advantage of implementing a driver in a DLL is that Windows does not need to change to DOS mode to access the device or to process an interrupt for the DLL. When it is called from a Windows application, the transfer goes directly into the DLL and is no more complex than a CALL instruction. For interrupt processing, the DLL can direct an interrupt vector to an internal interrupt service routine (ISR) simply by calling the DOS set vector function (function 0x25). When Windows is in standard mode, an interrupt causes a direct transfer to the ISR. These benefits, however, apply only if the system remains on the Windows screen and no DOS sessions are activated.

In standard mode, Windows maintains interrupt tables for both real and protected modes. If the system receives a hardware interrupt in real mode, Windows transfers control to the routine specified in the real mode interrupt vector table (IVT). If the interrupt occurs in protected mode, control is first transferred to the ISR specified in the protected mode interrupt descriptor table (IDT). Unless a protected mode application changes the protected mode vector, the protected mode ISR reflects the interrupt into real mode. However, if a DLL driver has assigned its own ISR, the interrupt is processed much more quickly, avoiding the need to change to real mode to process the interrupt.

Unfortunately, this means that if the interrupt is received while the system is in real mode, the real mode vector is used, and the ISR assigned by the DLL is not called. One solution to this problem is to assign separate ISRs for both modes. Although the DOS function called from the DLL can be used only to assign the protected mode IDT, Windows does provide a few functions, in the form of the DOS protected mode interface (DPMI), that assist in the solution. Specifically, a DLL can call DPMI function 0x0201, set real mode interrupt vector, to direct the real mode IVT to the DLL. If a DLL does this, the ISR must reside in a FIXED segment, so that it resides in memory below 1MB and is thus accessible from real mode. A clever implementation will allow the same ISR to be used in either real or protected mode.

This provides a good solution for a standard mode Windows ISR but is less than ideal for Windows in 386 enhanced mode. Windows 386 enhanced mode never changes the processor state to real mode, so there is no need for separate real and protected mode ISRs. Although this may simplify the solution in one regard, the complexity of multiple virtual machines increases the complexity of interrupt processing.

Consider the case of a user running a DOS application under 386 enhanced mode and an interrupt for the DLL device drivers occurs. In order to process the interrupt, Windows must suspend the current VM and change contexts so that the system VM can execute and pass control to the DLL's ISR. This context switching takes time and can result in lost interrupts and data overrun. Fortunately, there is another solution for 386 enhanced mode that will allow a faster response.

Virtual Device Drivers

Virtual device drivers (VxDs) are exclusive to 386 enhanced mode and provide a number of special benefits. The most obvious is that the driver executes in a single segment and provides flat addressability to all of Windows' linear memory. A VxD can access the memory of any VM through a single 32-bit offset pointer.

Another advantage of a VxD is that it is not dedicated to a single virtual machine. A driver that is packaged as a DLL runs in the system VM, and that VM must be executing in order for the DLL to run. A VxD, on the other hand, has global context across all VMs. Instead of having to change contexts to process an interrupt, an ISR in a VxD receives control at the lowest level and no context changes are necessary (other than potential ring transitions).

When code such as that of a DLL runs in a VM, it runs at a restricted ring (ring 1 in Windows 3.0). But a VxD always runs at the most privileged level, ring 0. A VxD has direct access to all I/O ports and the accesses cannot be virtualized. A VxD has full reign of the processor and the system environment, without any restrictions. The sole exception is that a VxD can be trapped if it attempts to access a virtual memory page that is not present in physical memory. In this case the Windows virtual memory manager will map in the physical page.

One disadvantage of a VxD is that there is no direct interface between a Windows application and a VxD. It is not difficult for a Windows application to gain access to a VxD through the use of assembly language instructions, but the interface is not as direct as that provided by a DLL. For this reason, it may be advantageous to provide a DLL along with a VxD, even if the environment is restricted to 386 enhanced mode Windows. The DLL can export normal high-level language interfaces to Windows applications and perform the machine-level translation in order to pass control to the VxD.

Another disadvantage of a VxD is that it requires the purchase of the Microsoft DDK. The tools that create VxDs, the flat model assembler, the linker, and a file-marking utility are available only from the DDK. With the recent release of OS/2 2.0, and with the flat model assemblers and linkers available, it may be possible to create a VxD without the DDK, but the only sure way, with the current version of Windows, is to buy the DDK.

When an existing DOS device driver, TSR, or DLL already provides support for standard mode Windows, the original driver also may be used in 386 enhanced mode Windows with some additional support from a VxD.

Typically a combination of a base driver and a VxD will provide complete application support.

API Mapping

When a protected mode application executes an INT instruction, the CPU first transfers control to the protected mode address specified by the protected mode IDT entry. Unless you have assigned a protected mode address to the interrupt number, Windows will switch to DOS mode (in the current VM for enhanced mode Windows) and will pass control to the real mode ISR. Except for certain system-reserved interrupts (such as DOS and BIOS interrupts), Windows will simply transfer control without providing any translation of addresses or pointers. The contents of nonsegment registers remain intact.

If you have a DOS TSR service that can be called from a protected mode application, then you are responsible for any translation that needs to be performed. If your TSR accepts and returns only nonpointer information in nonsegment registers, you may not have to change or write anything to call your TSR from a Windows application. If, however, you pass pointers to data, you will need to copy data from extended memory to the memory accessible to the TSR, and you will need to convert the pointers from selector:offset form to segment:offset form. This conversion of pointers and buffers is referred to as API mapping.

API Mapping in 386 Enhanced Mode

API mapping in 386 enhanced mode is normally performed by a VxD. Windows provides a handful of functions that make API mapping in enhanced mode relatively easy. Windows provides the following services to a VxD to facilitate API mapping:

```
V86MMGR_Allocate_Buffer          V86MMGR_Load_Client_Ptr
V86MMGR_Free_Buffer              V86MMGR_Map_Pages
V86MMGR_Free_Page_Map_Region     V86MMGR_Set_Mapping_Info
V86MMGR_Get_Mapping_Info
V86MMGR_Get_Xlat_Buff_State      V86MMGR_Set_Xlat_Buff_State
V86MMGR_Get_VM_Flat_Sel          V86MMGR_Xlat_API
```

The easiest translation function takes a real mode segment:offset pointer and creates a protected mode selector:offset pointer. This is useful when a DOS mode TSR returns the pointer to an object in real mode memory. The `V86MMGR_Load_Client_Ptr` service performs this function.

It is a more difficult task to take a protected mode pointer to data and convert it to a pointer that a DOS mode TSR expects as an input parameter. Clearly, if the memory is above 1MB, the first task is to copy the data source to low memory. For copying to take place, however, there must first be an available area in low memory. Windows maintains a translation buffer in each VM below 1MB. The size of this buffer is initially one page (4,096 bytes), but a VxD can increase this default size at initialization time by calling the `V86MMGR_Set_Mapping_Info` service. This service must be called during processing of the `Sys_Critical_Init` or `Device_Init` controls.

Before copying data into the translation buffer, the VxD must allocate some space from it by calling `V86MMGR_Allocate_Buffer`. This service can also copy data to the translation buffer. If the buffer data is being passed to the DOS API, the VxD copies the data into this buffer as the space is allocated.

For data transfer in the other direction—that is, from the DOS API to the protected mode program—the data must be copied from the translation buffer to extended memory. After allocating the buffer and calling the DOS mode API, the VxD copies the data from the translation buffer and finally deallocates the space in the translation buffer. The `V86MMGR_Free_Buffer` will free the space allocated by `V86MMGR_Allocate_Buffer` and will optionally copy data out of the buffer before releasing the space.

It is possible for the translation buffer to be filled. In this case, you can tell Windows temporarily to use a different translation buffer. You must have allocated the buffer yourself by some other means, such as through one of the VxD memory management services. Once the buffer is allocated, you tell Windows to use it by calling `V86MMGR_Set_Xlat_Buff_State`. After the translation of your API is performed, you need to return the original translation buffer. You can get information about the original translation buffer by calling `V86MMGR_Get_Xlat_Buff_State`. You can save the original information and, after performing your API translation, call `V86MMGR_Set_Xlat_Buff_State` to restore the original buffer.

Some drivers need to keep translation data in an area of memory that is accessible to all VMs. For example, a DOS driver that is interrupt-driven receives a request in one VM when a different VM is executing. Instead of waiting to reschedule the original VM, the driver can access the data in the current VM and process them immediately. A DOS driver can keep data that is global to all VMs, or a VxD can use a global translation buffer instead.

If your VxD needs a global translation buffer, it can specify the buffer's size during VxD initialization by calling `V86MMGR_Set_Mapping_Info`. A VxD can specify both the normal and global translation buffer sizes by this call. The actual sizes can be obtained after initialization by calling `V86MMGR_Get_Mapping_Info`.

Unlike the normal translation buffer, the global translation buffer is mapped as a number of pages, rather than bytes. When an API requires a global translation buffer, the VxD calls `V86MMGR_Map_Pages` to map high linear pages into the V86 memory space. After completing API translation, the VxD unmaps the pages by calling `V86MMGR_Free_Page_Map_Region`.

Automatic API Mapping

The remaining API mapping function, `V86MMGR_Xlat_API`, provides a method of performing certain types of API translation automatically. Unlike the other mapping APIs, which perform primitive mapping services, this function actually interprets a table of commands that describe an API. The commands consist of macros that generate the commands to the mapper function. They are as follows:

```
Xlat_API_ASCIIZ        Xlat_API_Jmp_To_Proc
Xlat_API_Calc_Len      Xlat_API_Return_Ptr
Xlat_API_Exec_Int      Xlat_API_Return_Seg
Xlat_API_Fixed_Len     Xlat_API_Var_Len
```

All of these macros are treated like instructions in a script. After performing the function specified by a macro, the mapping function advances to the next macro, unless the macro is `Xlat_API_Int` or `Xlat_API_Jmp_To_Proc`. These macros terminate the script and cause the mapper function to return to the calling VxD. Every script must end with one of these two macros.

The `Xlat_API_Exec_Int` macro accepts a single parameter, the interrupt number that is to be called in V86 mode. This macro tells the interpreter to simulate an INT instruction in the VM. Despite its name, the `Xlat_API_Jmp_To_Proc` macro does not jump to a procedure, but rather tells the interpreter to call the specified procedure. The single parameter to this macro specifies a procedure in the VxD. The target procedure must preserve all registers on return. The target procedure returns with the carry flag set to abort the translation script.

The `Xlat_API_Return_Seg` macro tells the interpreter to return a selector that maps to the corresponding segment register in V86 mode. This macro accepts one parameter, the name of the segment that is to be translated. For example, if the DOS driver returns a pointer whose segment is in the ES register, the macro returns a selector value in ES that maps to the same memory. A similar function, `Xlat_API_Return_Ptr`, accepts and converts two registers that specify a selector and an offset. For 16-bit protected mode clients, this macro performs the same function as `Xlat_API_Return_Seg` (the offset register is unmodified). For 32-bit clients, however, this function returns a selector that maps all of V86 memory and a 32-bit offset that points to the specified V86 memory.

The remaining translation macros copy data between V86 and protected mode memory. Before the terminating INT macro call, they transfer the specified data into V86 memory. After the macro call, they transfer the specified data back up into protected mode memory. All of the macros take a pointer to the data and a length of the data, which is provided either implicitly or explicitly as a parameter.

The `Xlat_API_Fixed_Len` macro accepts a pointer specified as a segment register and an offset register. The third parameter specifies a constant length. The `Xlat_API_Var_Len` macro is similar, except that the third parameter specifies a 16-bit register that contains the length. The `Xlat_API_Calc_Len` macro specifies a VxD procedure to call that will return the length of the data in the ECX register. The VxD procedure called must preserve all registers (except ECX). The `Xlat_API_ASCIIZ` macro accepts only two parameters, the segment and offset registers of the data to be copied. The length is implied, as suggested by its name, by the length of the NUL-terminated string that the segment and offset pointer refer to.

For a good example of a VxD that performs API mapping, see the BIOSXLAT VxD in the DDK. This VxD performs mapping for the BIOS functions that require pointer translation, such as the video BIOS palette and write string functions.

API Mapping in Standard Mode

The API mapping support that Windows provides in standard mode is much more primitive than that provided by 386 enhanced mode. The only functions provided are the DPMI functions that hook the DOS interrupts and provide transfer between protected and real modes.

To set the protected mode interrupt vector, your driver calls the normal DOS function to set the vector, INT 21h function 25h. Unlike its real mode counterpart which expects a segment and an offset, when called from protected mode this function expects to receive a selector and an offset. This function does not affect the real mode IVT, but changes the protected mode IDT.

When an application executes an INT instruction, your API mapper needs to perform manually whatever translation is necessary. Your driver may have previously allocated DOS memory, via `GlobalDosAlloc`, to use as a translation buffer. It can copy the data down to the DOS area, modify the real mode registers in the DPMI real mode register data structure, and call DPMI function 0x0300, simulate real mode interrupt, to call the DOS mode API.

On return, your mapper can copy the data from your own translation buffer back into protected mode memory and copy relevant registers from the real mode register data structure into the protected mode registers. If the calling function returns a pointer that was not passed as input, your mapper can create a pointer to return. Remember that Windows already has selectors available that point to various memory addresses, including all of the upper memory area; otherwise you may need to create your own selectors.

Clearly, API mapping in standard mode is much more difficult than in 386 enhanced mode. What makes matters worse is that a solution for standard mode will not work for 386 enhanced mode. If the standard mode solution is used in 386 enhanced mode, it will only provide mapping for Windows applications, since the code will only be active in the system VM. This solution will not work for protected mode applications (DPMI clients) in other VMs. If this restriction is acceptable, and you know that other VMs will not be invoking your DOS mode code, then this solution can be effective, since it will be appropriate for both environments.

DMA Transfer

DMA transfers under enhanced mode Windows require special care due to the virtualization provided by V86 mode and by the linear addressing used in 386 enhanced mode in general. DMA procedures for Windows standard mode do not suffer from the problems introduced by 386 enhanced mode. The virtual DMA services are described in Chapter 8; you may want to review that section before continuing.

By default, when a real mode DOS driver performs DMA transfers in V86 mode under Windows, the virtual DMA device driver (VDMAD) virtualizes the DMA hardware ports in the VM. Consider the case of a DOS driver that has direct access to the DMA hardware registers. The addresses specified in the DMA hardware must be physical addresses. These are the raw addresses that are to appear on the memory address lines on the system bus. A DOS application running in real mode can determine a physical address simply by multiplying the address segment by 16 and adding the address offset. In virtual 8086 mode with paging enabled, however, the resultant address is a linear address. The physical address is determined by the paging hardware within the 386 CPU and can map to anywhere in physical memory or, in the case of nonpresent pages, to nowhere at all. Even if a DOS application can determine the physical address of its linear pages, the physical addresses of V86 memory are transient and change whenever Windows dispatches control to a different DOS VM.

Despite the complexities, the VDMAD allows the DOS driver to program the virtual DMA hardware in the same way that it would program the real DMA hardware. The actual DMA transfer occurs in separate buffers maintained by the VDMAD, and the actual data is transferred between the V86 memory and the DMA buffers as needed. This virtualization, however, pays for this indirection, because the transfer of data between the VM memory and the VDMAD buffer memory adds to the overall transfer time.

If a DOS device driver is Windows aware, it can coordinate and cooperate with the VDMAD to optimize DMA performance. The DOS device driver communicates with the VDMAD through interrupt 4Bh. Before accessing the services provided via this interrupt, the DOS device driver should first examine bit 5 (0x20) of the byte at real-mode address 0x0040:007B. If the bit is set, then the INT 4B services are available. Otherwise, the driver may assume that linear addresses are equal to physical addresses and no special coordination is required.

Another reason a driver may need to coordinate with Windows for DMA activity is that the DMA to be performed may not be performed by the standard DMA hardware, for which the VDMAD is normally responsible. For example, a device that performs its own DMA rather than relying on the base DMA hardware is not virtualized by the VDMAD and can be programmed only with physical addresses—it has no way of performing the conversion between linear addresses and physical addresses. That information is maintained by the Windows paging subsystem.

The lock region service, function 0x8103, prepares for a DMA transfer. This service causes the specified memory region to be locked to physical memory addresses and the physical address to be returned. If necessary, this service will remap the memory paging to insure that the memory is contiguous and does not cross a 128K physical boundary. This service also allows compromises, and the caller can tell the service not to remap memory if the physical addresses do not already meet the requirements. Otherwise, the physical memory is locked—it cannot be paged to disk or relocated in physical memory.

Once the device driver has the physical address, it can program the DMA hardware to perform the transfer. Since the VDMAD does not need to virtualize the ports in this case and can specify physical addresses to the DMA hardware, the device driver can disable the VDMAD by calling the disable DMA translation service, function 0x810B. When disabled, interrupts in the VM should remain disabled to prevent other device drivers from interrupting and accessing the DMA hardware, expecting it to be virtualized. A device driver should disable the DMA translation, program the DMA hardware as required, and re-enable translation before re-enabling interrupts. DMA translation is enabled by calling the enable DMA translation service, function 0x810C.

The DMA buffers should not be locked while they are in use. For devices that perform DMA only occasionally, the DMA buffers should be unlocked between transfers. For devices that continuously perform DMA or do so for a period of time, keeping the buffers locked will provide better performance. The DMA buffers can be unlocked with the unlock DMA region service, function 0x8104.

For device drivers that are willing to compromise, the lock DMA region and unlock DMA region services will optionally manage DMA transfer buffers instead of locking the specified linear addresses. If the lock service allocates a buffer, it can optionally copy data from the original DMA transfer area into the buffer when called. The returned physical address then points to the allocated buffer and not the original DMA transfer area. When the lock service allocates a buffer, the unlock service will de-allocate the buffer, optionally copying its contents to the original DMA transfer area.

A device driver can choose to bypass the attempt to lock its original DMA transfer area and proceed to allocate a DMA transfer buffer directly by calling the request DMA buffer service, function 0x8107. This service allows for optional transfer of data into the allocated buffer. An allocated buffer can be released by calling the release DMA buffer service, function 0x8108. This service also allows for data to be transferred from the released buffer before de-allocation. Two more services, copy into DMA buffer and copy from DMA buffer, functions 0x8109 and 0x810A, respectively, simply copy data in and out of the specified DMA buffer that was allocated with the request DMA buffer or lock DMA buffer services.

Some of the newest high-performance hardware not only will perform DMA transfers without the assistance of the standard DMA hardware, but can also accommodate a DMA transfer that involves data that are scattered throughout physical memory. If this is the case, the operating system memory managment software needs only to insure that the memory is resident and locked; it does not need to insure that it is contiguous. The INT 4B scatter/gather lock region service will accept a linear address and size as input and will return the physical addresses of each region where the linear memory is mapped. This information can then be programmed into the external DMA hardware to perform the scattered DMA transfer. Once the DMA transfer is complete, the device driver calls the scatter/gather unlock region service to unlock the linear transfer area. Incidentally, the term scatter/gather comes from the idea that data read from the device are scattered throughout memory and data read from the memory are gathered together for transfer to the device.

Unfortunately, unless the DMA transfers are large, scatter/gather transfers may not perform any more effectively than the conventional approach of using a previously allocated transfer buffer and performing normal DMA transfers. You may want to experiment to determine the more effective method.

Summary

Although not specifically designed into Windows, you can develop non-standard device drivers and take full advantage of all of the services intended for the original, standard Windows drivers. These services include INT 2h function and callbacks, DMA services, DPMI services and, for virtual drivers, VxD services. With the exception of VxDs, all of these services are available to any application that can be developed with standard Windows SDK tools.

Some developers may restrict their Windows conversion to touching up existing DOS drivers to become Windows aware, and others may develop a full-blown Windows DLL driver with a virtual driver for 386 enhanced mode support. Once your driver is at least Windows aware, you might choose to make your installation program a Windows application, possibly allowing the end-user to avoid DOS entirely.

Driver Installation

Installing a driver under Windows can be as simple as copying the driver file onto the hard disk and changing a configuration file. You can write your own installation program to do this, or you can use one of the tools that Windows provides.

Before considering the tools, let's review the way the system is configured and how the configuration files are organized.

The Windows SYSTEM Directory and SYSTEM.INI

To start Windows, you run a small program, WIN.COM, that determines the mode in which Windows is to run. If the processor is a 286 or if the extended memory manager (typically HIMEM.SYS) reports that less than 1MB of extended memory is available, WIN.COM transfers control to DOSX.EXE which, in turn, transfers control to KRNL286.EXE (via DOSX.EXE). Otherwise, Windows runs KRNL386.EXE (via WIN386.EXE). These programs are not in the main Windows directory, but are in a subdirectory of the main directory, named SYSTEM.

While initializing, Windows refers to the SYSTEM.INI file, which is in the main Windows directory. The SYSINI.TXT, SYSINI2.TXT, and SYSINI3.TXT files, which are provided with Windows, explain the fields in this file. The [boot] section of this file contains the names of the basic drivers used with Windows in either mode (with the exception of the grabbers).

Basically, all that is needed to replace a standard mode driver under Windows is to change the appropriate field in the [boot] section of SYSTEM.INI to specify your driver and to copy the driver into the SYSTEM directory. Generally speaking, standard mode drivers also run in enhanced mode, but often with the cooperation of an enhanced mode virtual device driver. In enhanced mode, the standard mode drivers run in protected mode in the System VM. Thus, the entries in the [boot] section of SYSTEM.INI apply equally to standard and enhanced modes.

The [386Enh] section of SYSTEM.INI specifies drivers and flags that apply exclusively to 386 enhanced mode. Most of the driver fields refer to a driver contained with WIN386.EXE. The virtual keyboard driver, for example, is referred to as keyboard=*vkd. You can override this value, say, for your driver named "vkdxx" by changing this line to keyboard=vkdxx. You can add any virtual driver, even nonstandard ones, by adding a device= line to this section.

The flags contained in the [386Enh] section relate to various virtual drivers. This section is already cluttered with the flags from a number of drivers, so you may wish to add your own section to SYSTEM.INI to make your parameters easier to locate.

The SYSTEM.INI file is the way to install the base drivers for Windows, but some drivers are configured into Windows by making changes to WIN.INI.

The WIN.INI Configuration File

WIN.INI is the central configuration file for Windows. Not only is it used for many system configuration parameters; it is also used by many applications to store their own configuration information. The latter use is a carry-over from the API of Windows 2.x; today's applications in contrast can easily manage their own configuration files with the Windows 3 API. But because of this history, the WIN.INI file has become extremely cluttered with all sorts of configuration information. If you have more than a few configuration items for your driver and if Windows does not require them to be located in WIN.INI, you should probably consider using your own configuration file.

If your driver is normally associated with an active application only, then it can be treated like any DLL, loaded and unloaded only when an associated application needs it. If, on the other hand, you need the driver to be loaded when Windows starts, you can easily have Windows load it for you by including it on the `load=` or `run=` lines of WIN.INI. If you do this, your driver either must be a Windows program or, if a DLL, it must have a .EXE filename suffix. A DLL loaded in this manner will never be unloaded, so this is an excellent way to load a permanent driver into Windows.

Printer Drivers and WIN.INI

The default printer is specified by the `device=` field of the `[windows]` section of WIN.INI. This comma-separated field has three tokens. The first specifies a text description of the driver, the second specifies the name of the printer driver (without the .DLL suffix), and the third specifies the port that the device is attached to. This field is not normally modified by the installation procedure, but rather is modified by the Windows Control Panel or by applications that provide for printer configuration, such as the Windows Write accessory. These applications fill in these fields based on the contents of other fields in WIN.INI.

The `[PrinterPorts]` and `[devices]` sections list each printer driver installed. The `[devices]` section is provided for backward compatibility with Windows 2.x applications. You won't normally reference this section except to provide backward compatibility. The SYSINI.TXT and SYSINI2.TXT files describe the specifics of the contents of these WIN.INI sections.

The `[ports]` section lists all of the devices to which the user can output to directly. This list includes serial ports, parallel ports, and other miscellaneous output methods, all of which can be specified as output by a printer driver when it calls the `OpenJob` service.

Other printer-related sections in WIN.INI are left up to the printer device driver. Your driver might keep printer configuration information here, such as the printer model, the memory expansion options, or the default printer configuration, as specified by an application by means of the printer driver `ExtDeviceMode` function.

Printer Drivers and the Windows Control Panel

If you have developed a printer driver, Windows provides an easy and consistent method for installing it by means of the Windows Control Panel. To create an installation diskette for a printer driver, the minimum requirement is simply to put the driver file on the diskette. During installation, the control panel scans the installation diskette (or directory) specified for files that have valid executable file headers (that is, EXE and DLL files). The Control Panel then reads the description information from the file, which must have been specified in the linker DEF file for the driver.

The DESCRIPTION field for a printer driver must be in a specific format for this installation to work properly. For example, the description line for the PostScript driver is:

```
DESCRIPTION 'DDRV PostScript Printer:100,300,300'
```

The first five characters of the description must be "DDR V". The sixth character is ignored. Subsequent characters, up to a colon (:) character contain the text description of the driver; in this case PostScript Printer. This text cannot contain a comma, since commas are used in the [PrinterPorts] section of WIN.INI to separate the fields. The following three numbers are the aspect ratio, the horizontal pixels-per-inch resolution, and the vertical pixels-per-inch resolution, respectively. The aspect ratio is specified as a percentage of the horizontal resolution to the vertical resolution, 100 percent in this example. The control panel uses these values to install fonts that are appropriate for the printer.

If you have help files or other auxiliary files, you will need to specify them in a file named OEMSETUP.INF on the installation diskette. This file is similar to a Windows INI file. For example, if you have two printer drivers named FOOBAR1.DRV and FOOBAR2.DRV, with associated fonts and help files, the OEMSETUP.INF file might look something like this:

```
[Disk]
1 = . ,"Widget Inc. Printer Drivers"

[IO.Device]
1:FOOBAR1.DRV,"Widget Model 2143 Printer","DEVICESPECIFIC"
1:FOOBAR2.DRV,"Widget Model 2141-1 Printer [2141 Series]",
        "207,203,96]
1:FOOBAR2.DRV,"Widget Model 2141-2 Printer [2141 Series]",
        "104,203,196"
1:FOOBAR2.DRV,"Widget Model 2141-3 Printer [2141 Series]",
        "104,203,196","200,203,96"
```

```
[IO.Dependent]
FOOBAR1.DRV=1:FOOBAR1.HLP, FOOBAR1.INI
FOOBAR2.DRV=1:FOOBAR2.HLP
```

The [Disk] section simply identifies the diskettes that are involved in the installation. Normally, one diskette contains all of the information for a particular OEMSETUP.INF file. The [IO.Device] section enumerates the various printers supported by the drivers on the installation diskette. Note that FOOBAR2.DRV appears more than once, since it drives several printer models. Each item in this section contains three or more fields. The first field specifies the diskette (1) and filename of the driver file, the second field specifies the text associated with the printer model supported, the third and subsequent fields specify the font aspect ratios and densities supported by the driver and printer model.

The [IO.Dependent] section identifies files that are required along with the driver, but are not embedded within the driver DLL. Both drivers in this example have associated help files. The FOOBAR1.DRV driver has an additional file, FOOBAR1.INI, which is required for downloading to the printer before any printer output (the driver is responsible for copying the file to the printer, perhaps as part of the printer's setup function).

The SETUP Utility and OEMSETUP.INF

If you have written a replacement driver for Windows, you may be interested in using the Windows SETUP utility to install your driver. Printer drivers should be installed with the Control Panel. The SETUP utility is intended primarily for the more fundamental Windows drivers, such as for the keyboard or mouse. You may wish to review the SETUP utility by running it under Windows or in DOS mode.

The first option in the SETUP utility is the base system to be installed. This generally refers to the base PC-compatible system, such as a NEC system, a Toshiba system, or a 100% compatible PC clone. When this item is changed (or specified during initial Windows configuration) and the user presses the Enter key to proceed with setup, Windows copies the associated files for the configuration (including the files for the remaining options) and modifies the SYSTEM.INI file appropriately to reflect the new configuration.

If, however, the user does not change the basic system—only changing the keyboard type, for example—then SETUP only changes the SYSTEM.INI file, without copying the driver from the installation diskette. Apparently, SETUP assumes that the driver has already been copied into the Windows SYSTEM directory. Since it is so easy for a user to specify only the device change without having to specify the base system change, it is best not to rely on the SETUP utility to perform the installation of a custom driver.

Instead, you should take your knowledge of the SYSTEM.INI file and write your own installation program. Granted, this may not be so easy, since you might have to run the installation program without Windows running (since the system may require your driver's presence in order run). This means that you would have to provide your own version of `SetPrivateProfileString` and other functions.

Summary

Overall, the SETUP utility provided with Windows is not very useful for installing individual drivers. You will probably get better results if you use your knowledge of the SYSTEM.INI file to write your own installation program. Granted, this may not be so easy, since you might have to run the installation program without Windows running (since the system may require your driver's presence in order to run). If it is possible to run Windows without your driver, you may be able to use the SETUP program example (not to be confused with the Windows installation program of the same name) provided with the software development kit.

After learning all you need to know to write your device driver, you may be tempted to slack off on the installation program. Unfortunately, the installation program may be the only portion of your effort that the user recognizes as yours; if you are interested in making a good impression on the end user, the installation program may be your opportunity. Make the appearance of the installation program reflect the effort that you put into writing your device driver.

APPENDIX

A

GDI Structures

This appendix lists the GDI driver-specific structures for GDI drivers. The structures that are identical in normal Windows API and drivers are not included. Note, however, that definitions of these structures with the standard API often have `int` fields that will remain as 16-bit fields to GDI drivers, but are 32-bit fields with 32-bit Windows applications.

These descriptions do not usually indicate the type or size of each field in their structures. For these details, refer to the DDK include files.

BITMAP   Device-Dependent Bitmap

Synopsis   A physical bitmap in memory.

Contents

bmType   This value is zero to indicate a normal bitmap. Otherwise, the entire physical `BITMAP` structure is driver-defined.

`bmWidth,` `bmHeight,` `bmWidthBytes,` `bmPlanes,` `bmBitsPixel,` `bmBits`	These fields correspond to and have the same meaning as the same-named fields in the Windows API `BITMAP` structure.
`bmWidthPlanes`	Set equal to `bmWidthBytes*bmHeight`.
`bmlpDevice`	A FAR pointer to the corresponding `PDEVICE` structure for this bitmap.
`bmSegmentIndex`	This value specifies the selector increment value for a bitmap that is larger than 64K. It is identical to the `__AHINCR` index.
`bmScanSegment`	For bitmaps larger than 64K, this value represents the number of scan lines contained in each 64K segment. With bitmaps larger than 64K, scan lines do not span segments.
`bmFillBytes`	For bitmaps larger than 64K, this value represents the number of unused bytes remaining at the end of each segment. This value is 65,536—`bmScanSegment*bmWidthBytes`.

Description This structure describes the physical bitmap structure passed to GDI driver bitmap manipulation functions. Note that the first field indicates the validity of the remaining fields. The driver may choose to redefine all of these fields by changing the `bmType` field to a nonzero value.

GDIINFO   **GDI Driver Characteristics**

Synopsis   The characteristics of a particular "session" of a GDI driver.

Contents

`dpVersion`	The version of Windows with which the driver is compatible. For Windows 3.1, this value is 030Ah, but later versions of Windows will likely require a different value.
`dpTechnology`	The general class of the device. It indicates, for example, if the device is a plotter, a raster display, or a printer.

dpHorzSize, dpVertSize	The physical width and height of the display area, measured in millimeters.
dpHorzRes, dpVertRes	The physical width and height of the display, measured in the smallest discrete unit supported by the device in the configured mode.
dpBitsPixel	The number of bits per pixel in a *single plane* (see dpPlanes).
dpPlanes	The number of planes.
dpNumBrushes	The number of pattern brushes supported by the device.
dpNumPens	The number of line-pattern pens supported by the device.
dpNumFonts	The number of fonts supported by hardware.
dpNumColors	The number of colors supported by this device.
dpDEVICEsize	The size, in bytes, of the PDEVICE data structure for this device.
dpCurves	A bit-mapped indicator of the device's ability to create various curved figures.
dpLines	This bit-mapped value indicates whether or not the device can create various combined lines.
dpPolygonals	This bit-mapped value indicates whether or not the device can create various line figures.
dpText	This bit-mapped value indicates the various text-drawing capabilities of the device.
dpClip	This value indicates whether the device is capable of clipping output within a specified clipping rectangle.
dpRaster	This bit-mapped value indicates various raster-device capabilities.
dpAspectX, dpAspectY, dpAspectXY	The aspect ratio of the device.
dpStyleLen	The minimum length, in pixels times dpAspectX, of a line generated by a styled pen.
dpMLoWin, dpMLoVpt	The width and height of the window and viewport when in MM_LOMETRIC mapping mode.
dpMHiWin, dpMHiVpt	The width and height of the window and viewport when in MM_HIMETRIC mapping mode.

`dpELoWin,` `dpELoVpt`	The width and height of the window and viewport when in `MM_LOENGLISH` mapping mode.
`dpEHiWin,` `dpEHiVpt`	The width and height of the window and viewport when in `MM_HIENGLISH` mapping mode.
`dpTwpWin,` `dpTwpVpt`	The width and height of the window and viewport when in `MM_TWIPS` mapping mode.
`dpLogPixelsX,` `dpLogPixelsY`	The number of pixels per inch in the horizontal and vertical directions, respectively.
`dpDCManage`	This bit-mapped value specifies how multiple device contexts (DCs) for the same device are treated.
`dpPalColors`	The number of entries in the Windows 3.x system palette.
`dpPalReserved`	The number of reserved entries in the Windows 3.x system palette.
`dpPalResolution`	The actual simultaneous-color resolution of the device, in bits per pixel.

Description   A GDI device driver initializes this structure in response to a call to the driver's `Enable` function. Chapters 3 through 5 provide detailed descriptions of this function.

CURSORINFO   Cursor Movement Rate

Synopsis   The horizontal and vertical cursor motion rates for mouse movement.

Contents

`dpXRate`	The horizontal Mickeys per pixel ratio.
`dpYRate`	The vertical Mickeys per pixel ratio.

Description   This information is returned by the display driver in response to a call to the display driver's `Inquire` function.

CURSORSHAPE   Cursor Shape

Synopsis   Cursor size information.

Contents

csHotX, csHotY   The cursor hotspot location.

csWidth   The pixel-width of the cursor.

csHeight   The cursor height, in pixels.

csWidthBytes   The cursor width, in bytes.

csColor   Not used. Should be set to zero.

csBits   Two cursor-shape bitmaps. The first contains the value to be ANDed with the current display; the second contains the value to be XORed with the current display.

Description Windows passes this structure to a display driver in the driver's SetCursor call.

DRAWMODE   Raster Output Mode

Synopsis Output drawing mode parameters.

Contents

Rop2   The binary raster operation code. This is the value specified by a Windows application using the SetROP2 API function.

bkMode   For styled lines and brushes, this value specifies the color of the background portion of the style or pattern. If this value is TRANSPARENT, the color of the original background is used; otherwise, it is OPAQUE, indicating that the background color (bkColor) should be used.

bkColor   A PCOLOR structure indicating the color of the background.

TextColor   A PCOLOR structure indicating the color of foreground or text.

TBreakExtra   The total number of fill pixels that are to be inserted in a string that is output via ExtTextOut. This value corresponds to the *nBreakExtra* parameter to the SetTextJustification API.

BreakExtra	The number of fill pixels per character that are to be inserted in a string that is output via ExtTextOut. This value is calculated as the rounded quotient of TBreakExtra and BreakCount.
BreakErr	This value is cleared when an applications calls the SetTextJustification API with *nBreakExtra* set to zero.
BreakRem	The remainder of fill pixels to be distributed between characters in a justified line. This is the remainder from the division of TBreakExtra by BreakCount.
BreakCount	The number of character breaks that require fill pixel insertion. This value corresponds to the *nBreakCount* parameter of the SetTextJustification API.
CharExtra	The number of fill pixels to be output between characters by ExtTextOut. This value corresponds to the *nCharExtra* parameter specified in the SetTextCharacterExtra API.
LbkColor	The logical color of the background.
LTextColor	The logical color of the text.

Description   Windows passes this structure to the driver when calling various output functions such as ExtTextOut and LineTo. It contains supplemental information describing how the pixels in an output operation are to be combined with the target bitmap. It contains the binary raster operation code, the background and text colors, and various text-justification parameters.

PCOLOR   Device-Dependent Color

Synopsis   The device-driver-dependent representation of a physical color.

Contents   *Device-driver defined.*

Description   This structure must be 32-bits in size. The high bit (31) is reserved by GDI as an error indication and is normally zero. The remaining bits are device-driver specific. At the discretion of the device-driver developer, this structure may be a pointer that refers to a more detailed structure (provided the high-bit is ignored).

PBRUSH   Device-Dependent Brush

Synopsis   The device-driver-dependent representation of a physical brush.

Contents   *Device-driver defined.*

PDEVICE   Device-Dependent Device Status

Synopsis   The device-dependent structure containing GDI device state and mode.

Contents

fDevice   This 16-bit value indicates that the device is not a memory device for managing memory bitmaps.

Description   Except for the first 16-bits, the contents and size of this structure are entirely device dependent. The driver returns the size of this structure in the GDIINFO structure returned from the call to the `Enable` function when bit 0 of the *wStyle* parameter is 1.

PPEN   Device-Dependent Pen

Synopsis   The device-driver-dependent representation of a physical pen.

Contents   *Device-driver defined.*

RGB   Color Value

Synopsis   A color specified.

Contents

`red`	The intensity of the color red.
`green`	The intensity of the color green.
`blue`	The intensity of the color blue.
`flags`	Normally zero. It is nonzero when the RGB value specifies a palette RGB entry or a palette index.

Description   This structure provides a convenient way of storing color information for a single pixel or graphics item. This structure corresponds to the C-language RGB, RGBPALETTE, and RGBINDEX macros defined in the **WINDOWS.H** include file. The order of the colors in this structure is the reverse of the order of colors in the RGBQUAD structure.

GDI Driver Entry Points

`AdvancedSetupDialog/@93`   **Advanced Printer Setup**

Synopsis Display a dialog box to allow the user to specify advanced printer job characteristics beyond those provided by the `ExtDeviceMode` function.

C Prototype

```
WORD FAR PASCAL AdvancedSetupDialog(HWND hWnd, HANDLE
hDriver, LPDEVMODE lpDevModeIn, LPDEVMODE lpDevModeOut)
```

hWnd, hDriver	These parameters are identical to the *hWnd* and *hDriver* parameters of the Windows API `ExtDeviceMode` API.
lpDevModeIn	The input `DEVMODE` structure or `NULL` (see the description that follows). Normally, this structure contains the contents of the `DEVMODE` structure returned by a previous call to this function or to `ExtDeviceMode`.
lpDevModeOut	A copy of the input `DEVMODE` structure, modified as indicated by the user's responses to the dialog box.

Return Value   This function returns either IDOK (1) or IDCANCEL (2).

Description   This function expands on the ExtDeviceMode function, allowing the device driver to provide a more detailed configuration for a printer job, the details of which are at the discretion of the driver developer.

The common dialog printer setup dialog box calls this function when the user selects the More... button. If the setup dialog box calls this function without a pre-existing DEVMODE structure, it will pass NULL for *lpDevModeIn*. In this case, the driver should fill in *lpDevModeOut* with default values and immediately return IDOK without displaying a dialog box.

Otherwise, if *lpDevModeIn* is not NULL, the driver should first copy the DEVMODE structure from *lpDevModeIn* to *lpDevModeOut*. If the *lpDevModeIn* DEVMODE structure indicates that it was created by a pre-version-3.1 driver, as indicated by the dmSpecVersion field, the driver should return IDOK without displaying a dialog box. If the version is current, the driver should display the dialog box and make the appropriate changes to the output structure. The dialog box must present OK and Cancel buttons and must return either IDOK or IDCANCEL, depending on how the user exits the dialog box.

Applicable Drivers   Printer (optional).

BitBlt/@1   Transfer Graphic Image

Synopsis   Transfer a graphic image, performing specified logical operations with the source, destination, and brush.

C Prototype
```
VOID FAR PASCAL BitBlt(VOID FAR *lpDestDev, short
sDestXOrg, short sDestYOrg, VOID FAR *lpSrcDev, short
sSrcXOrg, short sSrcYOrg, WORD sXExt, WORD sYExt, LONG
lRop3, PBRUSH FAR *lpPBrush, DRAWMODE FAR *lpDrawMode)
```

lpDestDev   A pointer to a PDEVICE structure or, if the destination is memory, a BITMAP data structure. If the pointer is a PDEVICE structure, it refers to one that was created by this device driver.

sDestXOrg, sDestYOrg	The starting X and Y coordinates of the destination bitmap.
lpSrcDev	A pointer to a `PDEVICE` structure or, if the source is not needed for the operation specified in `lRop3`, a long `NULL` pointer. If the pointer is not `NULL`, it refers to a `PDEVICE` structure that was created by this device driver. Display drivers must allow both *lpSrcDev* and *lpDestDev* to refer to the device. Printer drivers may elect to fail if requested to transfer from the device.
sSrcXOrg, sSrcYOrg	The starting X and Y coordinates of the source bitmap. Note that the GDI may pass negative numbers for these parameters. If the values passed are negative, the driver must clip the image accordingly. The source and destination bitmaps may overlap. The driver must be careful about the direction of transfers and may need to create a temporary memory bitmap or be able to transfer data starting from the end of the bitmap.
sXExt, sYExt	The width and height in pixels, respectively, of the image to be transferred. Since no scaling is performed by `BitBlt`, these values apply to both the source and destination bitmaps. Note that *wDestXOrg+wXExt* and *wDestYOrg+wYExt* refer to the ending coordinates of the destination bitmap and *wSrcXOrg+wXExt* and *wSrcYOrg+wYExt* refer to the ending coordinates of the source bitmap.
lRop3	The type of operation to be performed. This value specifies a *ternary raster operation* that indicates how the source bitmap, the destination bitmap, and the specified brush are to be combined in order to modify the destination bitmap. This value is encoded. The high 16 bits of *lRop3* contain the *operation index*. The low 16 bits contain the *operation code*. See Chapter 3 for a thorough description of this parameter.
lpPBrush	A pointer to a `PBRUSH` structure previously realized by the driver in the `RealizeObject` function.

lpDrawMode   A pointer to a `DRAWMODE` structure. This parameter
                       is used only in operations that require a conversion
                       between monochrome and color. For example, if the
                       device supports colors, Windows may call `BitBlt` to
                       convert a monochrome bitmap to one that is compat-
                       ible with the device. Only the color fields of
                       lpDrawMode are used by `BitBlt`. All other fields are
                       ignored.

Return Value   *None.*

Description   `BitBlt` and `ExtTextOut` are the most primitive functions
that a raster device driver provides to Windows and both must be
implemented by all types of raster device drivers. If the device driver
"stubs" certain functions, Windows performs bitmap operations in memory
and calls this function to output the bitmap to the device. Windows uses
the information supplied in the `GDIINFO` structure in order to determine
what raster operations the driver is capable of handling. If the driver is
unable to perform certain raster operations, Windows will not pass such
operations to the driver, but instead will perform the operations itself and
pass simpler operations to the driver. An application also calls this function indirectly using the GDI application-level `BitBlt` function.

   If the source bitmap or the brush is in monochrome and the destination is in color, `BitBlt` must set black (0) bits to the color specified by the
`TextColor` field of *lpDrawMode* and white (1) bits to the color specified by
the `bkColor` field of *lpDrawMode*. If the destination bitmap is monochrome and the source bitmap or the brush are in color, `BitBlt` must convert pixels that match the color specified by the `bkColor` field of
lpDrawMode to white (0) and all other pixels to black (1).

   If the driver has indicated `C1_TRANSPARENT` capability, the driver
must check the `bkMode` field of *lpDrawMode*. If its value is `TRANSPAR-
ENT1`, destination bits that correspond to source bits of the color `bkColor`
are not modified.

Applicable Drivers

Display (required).

Printer (required for raster printers). This function is not meaningful for
plotter drivers, whose `dpRaster` field of the driver's `GDIINFO` structure
must be clear (0).

CheckCursor/@104   Timer Interrupt

Synopsis   Process timer interrupt.

C Prototype
VOID FAR PASCAL CheckCursor(VOID)

Return Value   *None.*

Description   CheckCursor is called on every timer interrupt. It is typically used to redraw a cursor that has been hidden, but may now be shown.

Applicable Drivers
Display (required).

ColorInfo/@2   Convert Color Format

Synopsis   Convert colors between the Windows RGBQUAD format and the physical format.

C Prototype
DWORD FAR PASCAL ColorInfo(PDEVICE *lpDestDev*, DWORD
dwColorIn, PCOLOR FAR *lpPCOLOR*)

lpDestDev	A pointer to a PDEVICE structure or a BITMAP data structure. If the pointer is a PDEVICE structure, it refers to one that was created by this device driver.
dwColorIn	The type and meaning of this parameter differs, depending on the value of *lpPCOLOR*. If *lpPCOLOR* is a valid pointer: *dwColorIn* contains an RGB color value that is to be converted to the physical form for the device. The RGB color value contains the 8-bit blue intensity in the low 8 bits (0–7), the green intensity in the next 8 bits (8–15), the red intensity in the next 8 bits (16–23), and zeros in the remaining bits (24–31). If the high 16 bits are FF00 hex, the low 16 bits specify a palette index. If *lpPCOLOR* is NULL *dwColorIn* contains a PCOLOR value that is to be converted to the closest corresponding color value.

Return Value   The return value contains the 8-bit blue intensity in the low 8 bits (0–7), the green intensity in the next 8 bits (8–15), the red intensity in the next 8 bits (16–23), and zeros in the remaining bits (24–31). This format is not compatible with the RGBQUAD data structure. The function may also return a palette index in the lower 16 bits, and FF00 hex in the upper 16 bits (see description).

Description   The function performed depends on the value of *lpCOLOR*. If *lpCOLOR* is a valid pointer, then the function converts from a logical color to a physical color. The function converts the given RGB value in *dwColorIn* to the physical color, stores the physical color in the memory pointed to by lpCOLOR, and returns the nearest matching RGB color as the function result. If the device is palette-capable and *dwColorIn* specifies a nonstatic color, the function returns a palette index in the low 16 bits and FF00 hex in the high 16. If the device is palette capable and *dwColorIn* specifies a palette index (the high 8 bits are FF), the function returns *dwColorIn* as the function result. The GDI uses this function to set text, background, and pixel colors using the Pixel function.

   If *lpCOLOR* is NULL, the function converts from a physical color to a logical color. The function converts the physical color specified in *dwColorIn* and returns an RGB color as an RGBQUAD type as the function result (note that the order of the colors in RGBQUAD is the reverse of the colors in *dwColorIn* when the convert-to-physical mode of this function is used).

Applicable Drivers
Display (required).

Printer (required).

Control/@3   Device Control

Synopsis   Send special control information to and receive special information from the device driver.

C Prototype
```
WORD FAR PASCAL Control(PDEVICE lpDestDev, WORD wFunction,
VOID FAR *lpInData, VOID FAR *lpOutData)
```

lpDestDev   A pointer to a PDEVICE structure.

wFunction   The function code, also referred to as the *escape*.

lpInData	A pointer to parameters that are sent to the device.
lpOutData	A pointer to a buffer that will receive results from the device.

Returns   The function returns a positive value to indicate success and zero or a negative value to indicate failure. Many of the printer device escapes return the following error codes:

Code	Description
SP_ERROR	General failure.
SP_APPABORT	The application abort procedure returned FALSE.
SP_USERABORT	The user aborted the job via the print manager.
SP_OUTOFDISK	There is not enough disk space for spooling.
SP_OUTOFMEMORY	There is not enough memory available.

Description   Windows calls this function to pass special control information to or to obtain special information from a device. The GDI calls this function to satisfy calls to the application-level Escape function.

This entry point is primarily intended for printer drivers, but both printer and display drivers must implement the QUERYESCSUPPORT function. If you are writing a display driver, you may also be interested in implementing the GETCOLORTABLE and SETCOLORTABLE functions.

Applicable Drivers   Display (required). A display driver must support the QUERYESCSUPPORT function. Many applications may be able to use the GETCOLORTABLE and SETCOLORTABLE functions. The remaining functions are optional.

Printer (required). All printer drivers must support the following escapes:

QUERYESCSUPPORT	NEWFRAME
SETABORTPROC	ENDDOC
STARTDOC	ABORTDOC

Most raster printer drivers will also support the BANDINFO and NEXTBAND escapes. If not, the GDI will simulate them for applications that issue these escapes.

DeviceBitmap/@16   Required Stub

Synopsis   This dummy stub is required for GDI drivers.

C Prototype

```
WORD FAR PASCAL DeviceBitmap(VOID FAR *, WORD, BITMAP
FAR *, BYTE FAR *)
```

Returns   This function must return zero.

Description   This function is not yet documented or needed and should perform no action, but it must be exported by GDI drivers.

Applicable Drivers

Display (required).

Printer (required).

DeviceBitmapBits/@19   Transfer DIB Bitmap

Synopsis   Transfer a bitmap between device-independent and device-dependent formats.

C Prototype

```
WORD FAR PASCAL DeviceBitmapBits(VOID FAR *lpDestDev,
WORD fGet, short iStartLine, short nScanLines, LPSTR lpDIBits,
LPBITMAPINFO lpBitsInfo, DRAWMODE FAR *lpDrawMode, VOID
FAR *lpConvInfo)
```

lpDestDev	A PDEVICE or BITMAP structure.
fGet	A flag indicating the mode of operation. If this flag is zero, then the transfer is from DIB format to device-specific format. Otherwise, the transfer is from device-specific to DIB format.
iStartLine	The starting scan line (the X offset) in the DIB.
nScanLines	The number of scan lines to transfer.
lpDIBits	The device-independent-bitmap data or, if a "get" operation, DIB data or NULL. If NULL then this function does not transfer bits, but only initializes the biSizeImage field of *lpBitsInfo*.
lpBitsInfo	A BITMAPINFO structure specifying the color format and dimensions of the DIB.
lpDrawMode	A DRAWMODE structure.
lpConvInfo	The color conversion translate table.

Return Value   This function returns the number of scanlines success-fully transferred. If there is an error in the input parameters or some other error occurs, the function returns zero. The function returns –1 if it is not capable of performing the specified transfer. If the function returns –1, then the GDI will simulate the operation.

Description   This function converts bitmaps between DIB and physical formats. The GDI calls this function to support the Windows API functions `GetDIBits` and `SetDIBits`.

Applicable Drivers   Display (optional). If a display driver is to provide support for device-independent bitmaps, bit 7 (0x0080) in the `dpRaster` field of `GDIINFO` must be set. If the bit is set, then this function is required. If the bit is not set, the GDI will simulate this function in monochrome.

DeviceMode/@13   Prompt User for Printer Configuration

Synopsis   Display a dialog box to allow the user to select a change in the current printing modes.

C Prototype

```
VOID FAR PASCAL DeviceMode(HWND hWnd, HANDLE hInstance,
LPSTR lpDestDevType, LPSTR lpOutputFile)
```

hWnd	A window handle to be passed to `DialogBox`.
hInstance	The instance handle of the calling application.
lpDestDevType	A pointer to a string that contains the type of the device, if the driver supports more than one type of device.
lpOutputFile	A pointer to a string that contains the name of the output file or device.

Returns   *None.*

Description   This function displays a dialog box for setting the current printing modes for the printer device and driver and changes the current printing modes as requested by the user. The dialog box should follow dia-log box conventions. It is important that it responds to depression of the ESC key by canceling the dialog box and returning. This can be facilitated by setting the control ID for the Cancel pushbutton to `IDCANCEL`.

Applicable Drivers Printer (optional). This function is required for device drivers that are capable of changing modes.

Disable/@4 Disable Device

Synopsis Stops all device activity.

C Prototype

VOID FAR PASCAL Disable(PDEVICE FAR *lpDestDev)

lpDestDev   A pointer to a PDEVICE structure.

Return Value *None.*

Description Windows calls Disable to disable the device. Windows may call this function if it is exiting to DOS or if a DOS application is to be run in real or standard mode.

Applicable Drivers

Display (required).

Printer (required).

Enable/@5 Start or Resume Device

Synopsis Start or resume device activity.

C Prototype

WORD FAR PASCAL Enable(VOID FAR *lpDestDev, WORD *wStyle*, LPSTR *lpDestDevType*, LPSTR *lpOutputFile*, VOID FAR *lpData*)

lpDestDev	This value depends on the value of *wStyle*. If the low bit (0) of *wStyle* is zero (0), it is a pointer to a PDEVICE structure. If the low bit (0) of *wStyle* is one (1), it is a pointer to a GDIINFO structure.
wStyle	The type of action to take. It may have one of the following values:
	0x0000 Initialize the device and the driver according to the information in PDEVICE.
	0x0001 Initialize and fill in the given GDIINFO structure.

	0x8000 Initialize and fill in the given PDEVICE structure.
	0x8000 Initialize and fill in the given GDIINFO structure.
lpDestDevType	For device drivers that are capable of driving more than one type of device, this points to an ASCIIZ string specifying the type of the device. For example, the Epson printer driver might accept the string "Epson 9 Pin" or "Epson 24 Pin." This parameter corresponds to the *lpDeviceName* parameter of the Windows API function CreateDC. This parameter may be NULL for drivers that support only one type of device.
lpOutputFile	The ASCIIZ name of the physical device. For example, for a printer driver that drives a printer on a serial port, this value could be COM1. This parameter corresponds to the *lpOutput* parameter of the Windows API function CreateDC. This parameter may be NULL for video display drivers.
lpData	A pointer to device-specific initialization information, or NULL if the application has no such initialization information. A Windows application may directly call the ExtDeviceMode entry point to obtain this information from the driver.

Return Value   If successful, this routine returns a nonzero value. If the function fails, it returns zero.

Description   For printer drivers, GDI calls this entry point when the application calls the Windows API function CreateDC. Windows calls this function with *wStyle* as 0x0001 to get the GDIINFO structure and to determine the length of the driver's PDEVICE structure before calling with *wStyle* as 0x0000. It is possible for the GDI to call other device entry points, particularly those that can modify a memory bitmap, before calling this function.

Applicable Drivers

Display (required).

Printer (required).

EnumDFonts/@6   **Enumerate Available Fonts**

Synopsis   Call the specified callback function for each font supported by the device.

C Prototype
```
WORD FAR PASCAL EnumDFonts(VOID FAR *lpDestDev,
VOID FAR *lpFaceName, FARPROC FAR *lpfnCallback,
VOID FAR *lpClientData)
```

lpDestDev	A `PDEVICE` or `BITMAP` structure.
lpFaceName	An `ASCIIZ` string containing the face name for which fonts are to be enumerated, or `NULL`. If *lpFaceName* is `NULL`, then all face names of the device are enumerated, by passing the information for a randomly selected font for each typeface.
lpfnCallback	A pointer to the callback function (or its instance thunk). *lpfnCallback* must point to a function with the following prototype:

```
WORD PASCAL CallBack(LPLOGFONT lpLogFont,
LPTEXTMETRIC lpTextMetrics, WORD wFontType,
VOID FAR *lpClientData)
```

lpClientData	User-defined data that is passed along to the callback function.
lpLogFont	A Windows API `LOGFONT` structure.
lpTextMetrics	A Windows API `TEXTMETRIC` structure.
wFontType	The font type. It may be either `RASTER_FONTTYPE` or `DEVICE_FONTYPE`.

Return Value   If no fonts are supported for the specified typeface, or if *lpFaceName* is `NULL` and no typefaces are supported, then this function returns 1. Otherwise, it returns the last value returned by the function.

Description   This function calls the callback function for each font or typeface that satisies the parameters. The call corresponds directly to the Windows API `EnumFonts` function. If the device is capable of text tranformations, only the base font will be passed to the callback function. The system can determine what other fonts the device can create from the transformation information in the `dpText` field of `GDIINFO`.

Applicable Drivers

Display (required).

Printer (required).

EnumObj/@7   **Enumerate Available Objects**

Synopsis   Call the specified callback function for each pen or each brush available on the device.

C Prototype

```
WORD FAR PASCAL EnumObj(VOID FAR *lpDestDev, WORD wStyle,
FARPROC lpfnCallback, VOID FAR *lpClientData)
```

lpDestDev	A PDEVICE or BITMAP structure.
wStyle	The type of object to be enumerated. It is OBJ_PEN for pens, or OBJ_BRUSH for brushes.
lpfnCallback	A pointer to the callback function (or its instance thunk). *lpfnCallback* points to a function with the following prototype:

```
WORD FAR PASCAL Callback (VOID FAR
*lpLogObj, VOID FAR *lpClientData)
```

lpClientData	User-defined data that is passed along to the callback function.
lpLogObj	A Windows API LOGPEN or LOGBRUSH structure.
lpClientData	The user-defined data supplied to EnumObj.

Return Value   If no objects of the specified type are available, then this function returns 1. Otherwise, it returns the last value returned by the callback function.

Description   This function directly corresponds to the Windows API EnumObjects function. When enumerating pens and brushes, EnumObj must first enumerate the following colors in this order:

R,G,B	Color
00,00,00	Black
FF,FF,FF	White
FF,00,00	Red
00,FF,00	Green

00,00,FF	Blue
FF,FF,00	Yellow
FF,00,FF	Magenta
00,FF,FF	Cyan

Some applications limit the choices that are presented to a user, so the EnumObj routine, after enumerating the preceding eight colors, should enumerate the remaining colors in order of decreasing desirability. EnumObj should not enumerate patterned or dithered brushes.

Applicable Drivers
Display (required).
Printer (required).

ExtDeviceMode/@90   Query or Set Configuration

Synopsis   Query or set the printer configuration, optionally with a dialog box.

C Prototype
```
int FAR PASCAL ExtDeviceMode (HWND hWnd, HANDLE hDriver,
DEVMODE FAR *lpDevModeOutput, LPSTR lpDeviceName, LPSTR
lpPort, DEVMODE FAR *lpDevModeInput, LPSTR lpProfile, WORD
wMode)
```

The parameters to this function are described in the Microsoft Software Development Kit (SDK).

Return Value   If successful, this function returns IDOK. If the user presses the Cancel button on the dialog box, this function returns IDCANCEL. If this function fails, this service returns a negative value.

Description   A Windows application calls this function directly, bypassing the GDI. An application loads the driver using the LoadLibrary function. An application uses this function to obtain and set printer settings that are specified or were previously specified by the user.

Applicable Drivers   Printer (required).

ExtTextOut/@14   **Write Text String**

Synopsis   Write a text string with the specified fonts and attributes to the device or bitmap.

C Prototype

```
POINT FAR PASCAL ExtTextOut(VOID FAR *lpDestDev, WORD
wDestXOrg, WORD wDestYOrg, LPRECT lpClipRect, LPSTR lpString,
short nCount, FONTINFO FAR *lpFontInfo, DRAWMODE FAR
*lpDrawMode, TEXTXFORM FAR *lpTextXForm, LPINT
lpCharWidths, LPRECT lpOpaqueRect, WORD wOptions)
```

lpDestDev	A PDEVICE or BITMAP structure.
wDestXOrg, wDestYOrg	The origin of the string.
lpClipRect	The clipping rectangle. The rectangular area described by this rectangle includes the pixels along the top and left borders, but excludes the pixels along the bottom and right borders. For example, for a clipping rectangle 8 pixels wide by 8 pixels high, the driver would only consider a 49-pixel area.
lpString	The string to be drawn.
nCount	If greater than zero, the number of characters in lpString. If *nCount* is less than zero, no text is drawn and the ExtTextOut function is to return the bounding rectangle of the string without regard to the clipping rectangle. The DRAWMODE structure is updated as if the text were drawn.
lpFontInfo	A FONTINFO structure describing the font to be used.
lpDrawMode	A DRAWMODE structure describing the character attributes and character spacing to be applied. This function should ignore the Rop2 field of this structure.
lpTextXForm	A TEXTXFORM structure describing additional font attributes that may override those specified by *lpFontInfo*.
lpCharWidths	An array of integers that specify the spacing between characters or NULL. If NULL, the spacing specified by the other parameters is used.

lpOpaqueRect   An opaquing rectangle or NULL. The *wOptions* parameter indicates the meaning of this rectangle.

wOptions   Drawing options. This value is bit-mapped. If the ETO_OPAQUE bit is set, then the clipping region is taken to be the intersection (AND) of the *lpOpaqueRect* and *lpClipRect* rectangles. If the ETO_CLIPPED bit is set, then the region described by the intersection of the *lpOpaqueRect* and *lpClipRect* rectangles is to be filled by the device driver, regardless of the opaque/transparent mode indicated in DRAWMODE.

Return Value   For *nCount* > 0, this function returns x==0 for success or x==0x8000 to indicate an error. The function should return a zero in the y field. For *nCount* ≤ 0, this function returns the size of the bounding rectangle as a POINT structure.

Description   This function draws the upper left corner of the first character at the point specified by *wDestXOrg* and *wDestYOrg*.

Applicable Drivers

Display (required).

Printer (required).

FastBorder/@17   Draw Bordered Rectangle

Synopsis   Draw a rectangle with a border.

C Prototype

```
POINT FAR PASCAL FastBorder(LPRECT lpRect, WORD
wHorizBorderThick, WORD wVertBorderThick, DWORD dwRasterOp,
LPSTR lpDestDev, VOID FAR *lpBrush, DRAWMODE FAR
*lpDrawMode, LPRECT lpClipRect)
```

lpRect   The rectangle to be drawn, specifying the upper left and lower right corners.

wHorizBorderThick   The thickness, in pixels, of the left and right borders.

wVertBorderThick   The thickness, in pixels, of the top and bottom borders.

dwRasterOp	A ROP3 raster operation, as defined and used by the BitBlt function, with the restriction that the operation will contain brush and destination operands only; operations that specify a source operand are not permitted.
lpDestDev	A PDEVICE structure.
lpBrush	A PBRUSH structure.
lpDrawMode	A DRAWMODE structure. This function needs to use only the bkColor field of this structure. The other fields may be ignored.
lpClipRect	The clipping rectangle.

Return Value   This function returns 0 for success, or 1 to indicate an error.

Description   This function draws a rectangle with the specified attributes.

Applicable Drivers   Display (required).

GetCharWidth/@15   Query Character Widths

Synopsis   Return the widths of a range of characters in the specified font.

C Prototype

```
WORD FAR PASCAL GetCharWidth(LPSTR lpDestDev, LPINT lpBuf-
fer, WORD wFirstChar, WORD wLastChar, FONTINFO FAR
*lpFontInfo, DRAWMODE FAR *lpDrawMode, TEXTXFORM FAR
*lpFontTrans )
```

lpDestDev	A PDEVICE structure (ignored by display drivers).
lpBuffer	The buffer that is to receive the character widths. The size of this buffer will be at least (*wLastChar* − *wFirstChar* + 1) * 2 bytes long.
wFirstChar, *wLastChar*	The range of characters to be queried.
lpFontInfo	A FONTINFO structure describing the font to be queried.
lpDrawMode	A DRAWMODE structure.

lpFontTrans   A TEXTXFORM structure describing the various text
                         transformations applied to the font.

Return Value   This function returns a nonzero value to indicate success.
It returns zero to indicate failure.

Description   This function directly corresponds to the Windows API
GetCharWidth function.

Applicable Drivers
Display (required).

Printer (recommended).

GetDriverResourceID/@450   Query Resource ID

Synopsis   Obtain the named resource ID.

C Prototype
```
WORD FAR PASCAL GetDriverResourceID(short iResID, LPSTR
lpResType)
```

iResID   The resource type to return, if none better in the cur-
                         rent mode is available.

lpResType   An ASCIIZ string specifying the name of the
                         resource type to return.

Return Value   The indicated resource ID.

Description   This function applies to drivers that are capable of supporting multiple modes and resolutions. The various default resources, such as
bitmaps and cursors, are different for each of the supported modes. If the
driver has a better resource (a higher-resolution bitmap, for example) than
the one specified, then it should be returned instead.

Applicable Drivers   Display (optional). This function applies only to display drivers that support multiple display modes.

GetPalette/@23   Query Color Palette

Synopsis   Query the color palette.

C Prototype

```
VOID FAR PASCAL GetPalette(short nStartIndex, short
nEntries, DWORD FAR *lpPalette)
```

nStartIndex	The index of the first palette entry to query.
nEntries	The number of palette entries to query.
lpPalette	A buffer into which the specified palette entries are returned.

Return Value   *None.*

Description   This function returns the values of the specified palette entries.

Applicable Drivers   Display (optional). If a display driver is to provide palette support, the RC_PALETTE bit in the dpRaster field of GDIINFO must be set. If the bit is set, then this function is required.

GetPalTrans/@25   Query Palette Logical Translation

Synopsis   Query the current palette logical translation.

C Prototype

```
VOID FAR PASCAL GetPalTrans(WORD FAR *lpTransTable)
```

lpTransTable	A buffer that will receive the array of WORDs specifying the current logical-to-physical translation.

Return Value   *None.*

Description   This function returns the current logical-to-physical color palette translation table.

Applicable Drivers   Display (optional). If a display driver is to provide palette support, the RC_PALETTE bit in the dpRaster field of GDIINFO must be set. If the bit is set, then this function is required.

Inquire/@101   Query Mickey/Pixel Ratio

Synopsis   Query the mickey-to-pixel ratio for the display.

C Prototype

WORD FAR PASCAL Inquire(CURSORINFO FAR *lpCursorInfo)

lpCursorInfo   A CURSORINFO structure. This structure is filled in by this function.

Return Value   This function returns 4 (the size of the CURSORINFO structure).

Description   This function returns the mickey-to-pixel ratio for a screen. Windows calls this function each time the device Enable function is called.

Applicable Drivers   Display (required).

MoveCursor/@103   Move the Pointer

Synopsis   Move the pointer to the specified position.

C Prototype

VOID FAR PASCAL MoveCursor(WORD *wAbsX*, WORD *wAbsY*)

wAbsX, wAbsY   The new "hot spot" location for the pointer.

Return Value   *None.*

Description   Since this function specifies the location of the hot spot, it is possible that part of the pointer extends beyond the edge of the display. In this case, the driver should clip the pointer appropriately. Windows will call this function even when the pointer is not visible, in which case the device driver should record the current pointer position for use when the pointer is next made visible.

   This function can be called at mouse interrupt time, which may occur within this function, resulting in indirect recursion.

   If displaying the pointer requires changing the hardware display bitmap, this function is responsible for saving and restoring any portion of the display that the pointer may overwrite.

Applicable Drivers   Display (required).

Output/@15   **Draw Shapes**

Synopsis   Draw shapes.

C Prototype
```
WORD FAR PASCAL Output(VOID FAR *lpDestDev, WORD wStyle,
WORD wCount, LPINT lpPoints, PPEN lpPPen, PBRUSH lpPBrush,
DRAWMODE FAR *lpDrawMode, LPRECT lpClipRect)
```

lpDestDev	A PDEVICE or BITMAP structure.
wStyle	The type of shape to be drawn.
wCount	The number of points in *lpPoints*.
lpPoints	An array of POINT structures that describe the corners or essential points (as with arcs) of the shape to be drawn.
lpPPen	A PPEN structure returned from a previous RealizeObject call.
lpPBrush	A PBRUSH structure returned from a previous RealizeObject call.
lpDrawMode	A DRAWMODE structure describing various drawing characteristics and raster operations.
lpClipRect	The clipping rectangle for the device or NULL if no clipping is desired. This rectangle may extend beyond the bounds of the device drawing area. If this value is NULL, the shape to be drawn may extend beyond the bounds of the device drawing area. If the dpClip field in the GDIINFO structure indicates no clipping, then this parameter may be ignored.

Return Value   This function returns 1 to indicate success. It returns 0 to indicate unrecoverable failure, or −1 to indicate that the driver cannot draw the specified shape and style. If the function returns −1, Windows GDI will simulate the shape drawing.

Description   This function draws various shapes. A GDI driver may choose to implement a subset of the possible shapes passed to this routine. The shapes that this function can draw are indicated in the GDIINFO structure. In general, a driver should support the functions that are implemented in the device's hardware to speed up processing. Other functions will be simulated by the Windows GDI by calling the driver with simpler request. If both a pen and a brush are specified, the drawing with the brush should precede the drawing with the pen. If *lpPPen* is NULL, then the driver must not draw a border. If *lpPBrush* is NULL, then the interior should not be filled.

Applicable Drivers
Display (required).

Printer (required).

Pixel/@9   Set or Query Pixel

Synopsis Set or query the specified pixel state.

C Prototype
DWORD FAR PASCAL Pixel(VOID FAR *lpDestDev, WORD *wX*, WORD *wY*, DWORD *dwPhysColor*, DRAWMODE FAR *lpDrawMode*)

lpDestDev	A PDEVICE or BITMAP structure.
wX, wY	The physical coordinates of the pixel to set or query.
dwPhysColor	A PCOLOR structure.
lpDrawMode	A DRAWMODE structure, or NULL if the pixel state is to be queried.

Return Value If the function fails either the query or the set operation, it returns 0x80000000. For a successful set operation, the function returns 0x00000001. For a successful query operation, the function returns a PCOLOR structure describing the color of the pixel.

Description The *lpDrawMode* parameter indicates whether the set or the query function is selected. If *lpDrawMode* is NULL, the function returns the current state of the specified pixel, otherwise the pixel is to be set according to the parameters.

Applicable Drivers
Display (required).

Printer (required).

QueryDeviceNames/@92   Query Supported Devices

Synopsis   Return an array of the supported driver model names.

C Prototype

short FAR PASCAL QueryDeviceNames(HANDLE *hDriver*, LPBYTE *lpaDeviceNames*)

hDriver	The module-instance handle of the driver.
lpaDeviceNames	A pointer to a return buffer or NULL. The return buffer is an array of 64-byte structures. This function copies the name of each supported model into each element of the array, unless *lpaDeviceNames* is NULL.

Return Value   The number of supported device models. This value is returned whether or not *lpaDeviceNames* is NULL, to allow the caller to determine the required size for the return buffer.

Description   This function helps standardize the standard printer dialog box. The normal printer DeviceMode function should not display a list of printer models but instead should return their names here.

Applicable Drivers

Display (required for multimodel displays).

Printer (required for multimodel printer drivers).

RealizeObject/@10   Create Device-Dependent Object

Synopsis   Create or destroy the structures necessary for using a pen, brush, or font on the physical device.

C Prototype

WORD FAR PASCAL RealizeObject(VOID FAR **lpDestDev*, short *iStyle*, VOID FAR **lpInObj*, VOID FAR **lpOutObj*, VOID FAR **lpTextXForm*)

lpDestDev	A PDEVICE or BITMAP structure.
iStyle	The indication to create or destroy an object. If *iStyle* is negative, the device driver is to destroy the object referred to by *lpOutObj*. Otherwise, *iStyle* may be

OBJ_PEN, OBJ_BRUSH, or OBJ_FONT to indicate that the device driver is to create a pen, brush, or font structure, respectively.

lpInObj A Windows API LOGPEN, LOGFONT, or *modified* LOGBRUSH structure (as indicated by *iStyle*). If *iStyle* is OBJ_BRUSH, the structure is similar to LOGBRUSH, but with an additional DWORD appended that indicates the physical color for the background of a hatched brush.

lpOutObj The device-dependent PPEN, PBRUSH, or FONTINFO structure to be created or destroyed. If it is a FONTINFO structure, the dfType through dfFace fields must be valid, with the dfDevice and dfFace fields containing FAR pointers to strings, rather than file offsets.

lpTextXForm Additional information about a font. This parameter is meaningful only if *iStyle* is OBJ_FONT.

Return Value   This function returns a nonzero value to indicate success. It returns zero if the driver cannot create specified object.

Description   When an object is created, this function initializes the physical structures associated with the object. The Windows GDI passes the addresses of these structures back to the driver through other entry points in order to draw text and shapes on the device. Although the physical structures will mostly contain driver-defined information, the structures have some common fields which GDI expects to be in a certain format. The remaining information in the driver is left up to you, the developer.

Applicable Drivers
Display (required).
Printer (required).

SaveScreenBitmap/@92   Save or Restore Display Bitmap

Synopsis   This function saves or restores a rectangular region of the video display.

C Prototype

```
WORD FAR PASCAL SaveScreenBitmap(LPRECT lpRect, WORD
wCommand)
```

lpRect   The rectangle, in device coordinates, to be saved.

wCommand   The function to be performed: 0 means save rectangle; 1 means restore and discard saved rectangle; 2 means discard previously saved rectangle.

Return Value   This function returns 1 to indicate success and 0 to indicate failure.

Description   When this function saves the bitmap, it must save it to memory that has already been allocated from the system at initialization time; it cannot make calls into the Windows kernel to allocate the memory. If Windows calls this function to save a rectangle when a rectangle is already being saved, or if this function is called to restore a rectangle when none has been saved, it should return an error indication.

Applicable Drivers   Display (required).

ScanLR/@12   Scan for Pixel

Synopsis   Scan physical bitmap for the specified pixel.

C Prototype

```
WORD FAR PASCAL ScanLR(VOID FAR *lpDestDev, WORD wX, WORD
wY, DWORD dwPhysColor, WORD iStyle)
```

lpDestDev   A PDEVICE or BITMAP structure.

wX, wY   Location at which to start the scan.

dwPhysColor   A PCOLOR structure.

wStyle   The scan direction and mode. Bit 0 of this word indicates the mode, and bit 1 indicates the direction. If bit 0 is set, it scans for nonmatch of *dwPhysColor*. If bit 0 is clear, it scans for match of *dwPhysColor*. If bit 1 is set, it scans right and if bit 1 is clear, it scans left.

Return Value   This function returns the X coordinate that satisfies the scan criteria or -1, if the scan fails. If wX or wY is out of range, this function returns 0x8000.

Description   The Windows GDI calls this function to perform flood fills.

Applicable Drivers
Display (required).
Printer (required).

SelectBitmap/@29   Select Bitmap

Synopsis   Select a physical bitmap.

C Prototype
```
WORD FAR PASCAL SelectBitmap(VOID FAR *lpDestDev,
LPBITMAP lpPrevBitmap, LPBITMAP lpBitmap, DWORD dwFlags)
```

lpDestDev	A PDEVICE structure.
lpPrevBitmap	The previously selected bitmap.
lpBitmap	The new bitmap to be selected.
dwFlags	This parameter must be zero for version 3.1.

Return Value   This function returns 1 to indicate success and 0 to indicate failure.

Description   This function allows a driver to select a bitmap that is not in main memory. Windows calls this function in response to an application call to the Windows API SelectObject function.

Applicable Drivers
Display (optional).

Printer (optional). This function must be exported if the RC_DEVBITS flag is set in the driver's GDIINFO structure.

SetAttribute/@18   Set Attribute

Synopsis   Microsoft has provided no information about this function.

C Prototype
```
WORD FAR PASCAL SetAttribute(VOID FAR*, WORD, WORD,
WORD)
```

Return Value   This function must return zero.

Description   This function is reserved for future use by Microsoft. It is required and may be called by the Windows GDI.

Applicable Drivers
Display (required).

Printer (required).

SetCursor/@102   **Set or Clear Pointer Bitmap**

Synopsis   Set or clear the display pointer bitmap.

C Prototype
VOID FAR PASCAL SetCursor(CURSORSHAPE FAR *lpCursorShape)

lpCursorShape   A CURSORSHAPE structure or NULL, if the bitmap is to be cleared.

Return Value   *None.*

Description   This function sets or clears the pointer bitmap. If the pointer is currently visible, it is removed from the display and replaced with the specified bitmap.

Applicable Drivers   Display (required).

SetDIBitsToDevice/@21   **Copy DIB to Device**

Synopsis   Copy a bitmap from device-independent format to the display.

C Prototype
WORD FAR PASCAL SetDIBitsToDevice(VOID FAR *lpDestDev,
WORD *wDestX*, WORD *wDestY*, short *iScanStart*, short
nScanLines, LPRECT *lpClipRect*, DRAWMODE FAR *lpDrawMode*,
LPSTR *lpDIBits*, LPBITMAPINFO *lpBitsInfo*, VOID FAR *lpConvInfo*)

lpDestDev   A PDEVICE structure. Unlike many other raster function calls, this function does not need to provide support for transfer to a memory bitmap.

wDestX, wDestY   The screen destination origin (top left).

iScanStart	The starting scan line (*Y* coordinate) in the DIB.
nScanLines	The number of scan lines in the DIB.
lpClipRect	A RECT structure, describing the clipping rectangle.
lpDrawMode	A DRAWMODE structure.
lpDIBits	The device-independent bitmap data or, if a get operation, DIB data or NULL. If NULL, then this function does not transfer bits, it only initializes the biSizeImage field of *lpBitsInfo*.
lpBitsInfo	A BITMAPINFO structure specifying the color format and dimensions of the DIB.
lpConvInfo	The color conversion translate table.

Return Value   This function returns the number of scanlines successfully transferred. If there is an error in the input parameters or some other error occurs, the function returns zero. The function returns −1 if it is not capable of performing the specified transfer. If the function returns −1, then the GDI will simulate the operation.

Description   This function converts a DIB to physical format directly to the display. It differs from DeviceBitmapBits in that it may be better implemented by copying the bitmap one pixel at a time. Windows offers this interface to allow for optimization of this common function. The sample DDK drivers are inconsistent with the name that they assign to this function, although the export ordinal is the same.

Applicable Drivers   Display (required). Bit 9 (0x0200) in the dpRaster field of GDIINFO must be set.

Printer (optional). Bit 9 (0x0200) in the dpRaster field of GDIINFO must be set.

SetPalette/@22   Set Color Palette

Synopsis   Set the color palette.

C Prototype

```
VOID FAR PASCAL SetPalette(short nStartIndex, short
nEntries, DWORD FAR *lpPalette)
```

nStartIndex	The index of the first palette entry to be set.
nEntries	The number of palette entries to be set.
lpPalette	The array of new palette entries.

Return Value   *None.*

Description   This function modifies the palette entries according to the specified parameters.

Applicable Drivers   Display (optional). If a display driver is to provide palette support, the RC_PALETTE bit in the dpRaster field of GDIINFO must be set. If the bit is set, then this function is required.

SetPalTrans/@24   Set Palette Logical Translation

Synopsis   Set the palette logical translation.

C Prototype
```
VOID FAR PASCAL SetPalTrans(WORD FAR *lpTransTable)
```
lpTransTable   An array of WORDs specifying the logical-to-physical translation, or NULL to disable translation.

Return Value   *None.*

Description   This function establishes a logical-to-physical color palette translation table to be used in subsequent memory-to screen-bitmap operations. This function should also construct a corresponding physical-to-logical table to be used in subsequent screen-to memory-bitmap operations.

Applicable Drivers   Display (optional). If a display driver is to provide palette support, the RC_PALETTE bit in the dpRaster field of GDIINFO must be set. If the bit is set, then this function is required.

StretchBlt/@27   Scale Bitmap

Synopsis   Scale bitmap between memory and device.

C Prototype
```
WORD FAR PASCAL StretchBlt(VOID FAR *lpDestDev, WORD
wDestX, WORD wDestY, WORD wDestXExt, WORD wDestYExt, VOID
```

FAR **lpSrcDev*, WORD *wSrcX*, WORD *wSrcY*, WORD *wSrcXExt*, WORD *wSrcYExt*, DWORD *lRop3*, PBRUSH FAR **lpPBrush*, DRAWMODE FAR **lpDrawMode*, LPRECT *lpClipRect*)

lpDestDev	A PDEVICE or BITMAP structure specifying the destination.
wDestX, wDestY, wDestXExt, wDestYExt	The destination rectangle origin and size.
lpSrcDev	If *lpDestDev* is a PDEVICE structure, then this parameter is the source BITMAP structure. If *lpDestDev* is a BITMAP structure, then this parameter is the source PDEVICE structure.
wSrcX, wSrcY, wSrcXExt, wSrcYExt	The source rectangle origin and size.
lRop3	The ternary raster operation code (See BitBlt).
lpPBrush	A PBRUSH structure.
lpDrawMode	A DRAWMODE structure.
lpClipRect	The clipping rectangle, in destination coordinates.

Return Value   This function returns 1 to indicate success or 0 to indicate an unrecoverable failure. This function returns −1 to indicate that the Windows GDI should simulate the operation.

Description   The Windows GDI will not call this function unless the RC_STRETCHBLT flag is set in GDIINFO. This function is similar to the Windows API StretchBlt function. The Windows GDI allows a driver to provide this entry point if the hardware is capable of performing this function. If the device is capable of limited stretching, the driver should provide this entry point, and return −1 if the device is not capable of providing the specific operation requested, so that the GDI may simulate it.

Applicable Drivers
Display (optional).

Printer (optional).

`StretchDIBits/@28`   **Transfer and Scale DIB**

Synopsis   Transfer and scale a bitmap between device-independent and device-dependent formats.

C Prototype

WORD FAR PASCAL StretchDIBits(VOID FAR *lpDestDev, WORD *fGet*, WORD *wDestX*, WORD *wDestY*, WORD *wDestXExt*, WORD *wDestYExt*, WORD *wSrcX*, WORD *wSrcY*, WORD *wSrcXExt*, WORD *wSrcYExt*, LPSTR *lpDIBits*, LPBITMAPINFO *lpBitsInfo*, VOID FAR *lpConvInfo*, DRAWMODE FAR *lpDrawMode*, LPRECT *lpClipRect*)

lpDestDev	A `PDEVICE` or `BITMAP` structure.
fGet	A flag indicating the mode of operation. If this flag is zero, then the transfer is from DIB format to device-specific format. Otherwise, the transfer is from device-specific to DIB format. In Windows 3.0, the GDI will call this function only when the parameter is set to zero, so the device-specific-to-DIB transfer need not be implemented for Windows 3.0 drivers.
wDestX, wDestY, wDestXExt, wDestYExt	The destination rectangle origin and extent.
wSrcX, wSrcY, wSrcXExt, wSrcYExt	The source rectangle origin and extent.
lpDIBits	The device-independent bitmap data or, if a "get" operation, DIB data or `NULL`. If `NULL`, then this function does not transfer bits, but only initializes the `biSizeImage` field of *lpBitsInfo*.
lpBitsInfo	A `BITMAPINFO` structure specifying the color format and dimensions of the DIB.
lpConvInfo	The color conversion translate table.
lRop3	A ternary raster operation code (see `BitBlt`).
lpBrush	A `PBRUSH` structure.
lpDrawMode	A `DRAWMODE` structure.
lpClipRect	A `RECT` structure, describing the clipping rectangle.

Return Value   This function returns the number of scanlines success-fully transferred. If there is an error in the input parameters or some other error occurs, the function returns zero. The function returns –1 if it is not capable of performing the specified transfer. If the function returns –1, then the GDI will simulate the operation.

Description   For Windows 3.0, this function converts a DIB to physical format, either to a memory bitmap or the actual display. The GDI calls this function to support the Windows API function StretchDIBits. Future versions of Windows may require support for transfer from physical format to DIB format.

Applicable Drivers   Display (optional). If a display driver is to provide DIB support, bit 7 (0x0080) in the dpRaster field of GDIINFO must be set. If the bit is set, then this function is required. If the bit is not set, the GDI will simulate this function in monochrome.

UpdateColors/@26   Update Colors in Display

Synopsis   Update the colors in the specified display rectangle.

C Prototype

```
VOID FAR PASCAL UpdateColors(WORD wStartX, WORD wStartY,
WORD wExtX, WORD wExtY, WORD FAR *lpTranslate)
```

wStartX, *wStartY*, *wExtX*, *wExtY*	The origin and extent, in device coordinates, of the display rectangle to be updated. The origin is the upper left corner of the rectangle.
lpTranslate	An array of WORDs that specifies the replacement color indexes. Each word contains a physical color index.

Return Value   *None.*

Description   This function modifies each pixel in the rectangle by read-ing its current color and performing a direct palette translation according to the array of indexes passed in *lpTranslate*.

Applicable Drivers   Display (optional). If a display driver is to provide palette support, the RC_PALETTE bit in the dpRaster field of GDIINFO must be set. If the bit is set, then this function is required.

`UserRepaintDisable/@500`   **Suspend or Resume Display Updates**

Synopsis   Suspend or resume display updates.

C Prototype
`VOID FAR PASCAL UserRepaintDisable(BYTE` *fSuspend* `)`

fSuspend   The operation indicator. If this byte is nonzero, then suspend display hardware updates until further notice. If this byte is zero, then resume display hardware updates.

Return Value   *None.*

Description   The GDI calls the function to tell the display driver to suspend calling Repaint.

Applicable Drivers   Display (optional). If a display driver is to provide palette support, the `RC_PALETTE` bit in the `dpRaster` field of `GDIINFO` must be set. If the bit is set, then this function is required.

`WEP/@17`   **Unload Driver**

Synopsis   Prepare the driver to be removed from memory.

C Prototype
`WORD FAR PASCAL WEP(BYTE` *bExitCode* `)`

bExitCode   Type of exit. This value is TRUE if Windows is being shut down (the Windows session is ending). It is FALSE otherwise.

Return Value   This function should always return 1.

Description   This function should relinquish all resources and set the device to a quiescent or self-controlled state in preparation for removing the driver from memory. A bug in earlier versions of Windows prevented this function from being useful (or safe), so it is always stubbed and does nothing at all.

Applicable Drivers   Printer (required).

APPENDIX

C

Device Driver Support Functions

This appendix lists functions that are exported by Windows libraries and that are accessible to any Windows application. A Windows device driver can call most of the functions that a regular application can make, but the functions that are listed here will be of particular interest to the device-driver developer.

With the exception of dmTranspose, the GDI driver brute functions are omitted from this appendix, since they mimic their corresponding driver entry point functions, which are described in Appendix B.

Many of these functions are highly version specific and may not be supported under future releases of Windows. Refer to the Windows DDK and SDK documentation for the most current information.

__AHINCR   **Huge Object Selector Distance**

Synopsis   The offset between huge object selectors.

C Prototype   *Not applicable.*

Return Value   *Not applicable.*

Description   This is not a function, but rather an externally declared ABS value that contains the offset between selectors of a huge object (a memory object that is larger than 64K bytes). Programs written in C can allocate huge objects using the C-runtime _halloc function. Any program can create such objects using GlobalAlloc, specifying a segment size greater than 64K. The C compiler automatically generates the correct code to use such pointers, but if you are programming in assembler you need to be familiar with how huge pointers are managed.

In real mode, huge objects are allocated in contiguous physical memory. To access memory in the second 64K, you only need to add 0x1000 to the segment of the base. In protected mode, however, selector arithmetic is not normally allowed but the selectors for a single huge object are numerically separated by a constant value. This value may be determined by examining __AHINCR. In real mode, this value is 0x1000, but in standard and enhanced modes, this value is different. By using this symbol, you can make your code mode-independent. In assembler, the value is referenced as follows:

```
EXTRN    __AHINCR:ABS
MOV AX,ES         ; Get selector to this seg
ADD AX,__AHINCR   ; Add huge offset
MOV ES,AX         ; Get selector to the next seg
```

AllocCStoDSAlias   Create Data Alias to Code

Synopsis   Allocate a new data selector that aliases an existing code selector.

C Prototype
WORD FAR PASCAL AllocCStoDSAlias(WORD *selCode*)
selCode   The input code selector.

Return Value   A copy of *selCode*, or zero if the function fails.

Description   This function allocates a new selector, which addresses the same memory as the specified code selector. This function differs from PrestoChangoSelector in that it allocates a new selector, instead of modifying an existing selector. This selector can be used by a device driver to modify its own code. If you do this in your driver, it will be effective only for FIXED segments, since changes to DISCARDABLE segments can be lost.

If this function is called by a driver that can be unloaded (such as a printer driver), then the driver must de-allocate the selector before unloading, using the `FreeSelector` function. This function is the converse of the `AllocDStoCSAlias` function.

AllocDStoCSAlias   Create Code Alias to Data

Synopsis   Allocate a new code selector that aliases an existing data selector.

C Prototype
```
WORD FAR PASCAL AllocDStoCSAlias(WORD selData)
```
selData   The input data selector.

Return Value   A copy of *selCode*, or zero if the function fails.

Description   This function allocates a new selector, which addresses the same memory as the specified code selector. This function differs from `PrestoChangoSelector` in that it allocates a new selector, instead of modifying an existing selector.

You may be particularly interested in this function if you are writing a GDI driver that implements the `BitBlt` function. Due to the many types of operations that can be requested via `BitBlt` it may prove to be more practical and efficient to generate code "on the fly" by generating machine instructions in memory. When running in protected mode, the hardware does not allow execution out of a data segment. This function allows the program to create a code selector that maps to the same data area.

If this function is called by a driver that may be unloaded (such as a printer driver), then the driver must de-allocate the selector before unloading, using the `FreeSelector` function.

This function is the converse of the `AllocCStoDSAlias` function.

AllocSelector   Allocate Selector

Synopsis   Allocate a selector for use by the device driver.

C Prototype

```
WORD FAR PASCAL AllocSelector(WORD *wSel)
```
wSel   The selector to be aliased, or 0x0000.

Return Value   If *wSel* is nonzero, this function returns a new selector, which has the same base, limit, and access rights as *wSel*. If *wSel* is zero, this function returns a new selector that is uninitialized.

Description   This function returns a selector index that may be used as is or initialized and used by the device driver. Although this function is documented in the SDK, it is included here because of its particular importance to device drivers. Since protected mode does not allow direct access to physical memory, a device driver must initialize a selector to point to the desired linear memory, such as with the `SelectorAccessRights`, `SetSelectorBase` and `SetSelectorLimit` functions.

If this function is called by a driver that can be unloaded (such as a printer driver), then the driver must de-allocate the selector before unloading, using the `FreeSelector` function.

The Windows kernel has a limited number of predefined selectors that map certain areas of physical memory. The Windows 3.0 kernel exports the selectors as ABS symbols. The kernel exports __0000H, __0040H, __A000H, __B000H, __B8000H, __C000H, __D000H, __E000H, and __F000H, which map areas of the lower 640K. You can refer to the __0040H selector, for example, as follows:

```
EXTRN   __0040H:ABS
MOV AX,__0040H
MOV ES,AX
```

You can refer to the same selector from a C program as follows:

```
extern _near _0040H ;
LPSTR pBIOSData = (LPSTR) MAKELONG(0,WORD(& _0040H)) ;
```

AllocSelectorArray   Allocate Huge Selector Array

Synopsis   Allocate an evenly spaced array of selectors.

C Prototype

```
WORD FAR PASCAL AllocSelectorArray(WORD nSelectors)
```
nSelectors   The number of selectors to be allocated.

Return Value   If successful, this function returns the value of the first selector in the array. Otherwise, it returns 0x0000.

Description   This function allocates an array of selectors that are evenly spaced apart. The spacing between the selectors is specified by __AHINCR. This allows the base selector to be used as the selector portion of a C-language _huge pointer. This function does not allocate any memory and is intended to map device memory, not normal Windows-managed memory. Before use, each selector in the array must be initialized using the `SetSelectorAccessRights`, `SetSelectorBase`, and `SetSelectorLimit` functions.

---

dmTranspose   Transpose Bitmap

Synopsis   Transpose the specified bitmap.

C Prototype
```
VOID FAR PASCAL dmTranspose(BYTE FAR *lpSource, BYTE FAR
*lpDest, SHORT nBytes)
```

lpSource	The source bitmap.
lpDest	The destination bitmap.
nBytes	The size of a scan line, in bytes. The size, in bytes, of the `lpSource` and `lpDest` buffers are 8 * *nBytes*. This value may be negative. If it is negative, its absolute value is the size, in bytes, of a scan line and the transposition will reverse the order of bits in the bytes transposed.

Return Value   *None.*

Description   This function transposes raw bitmap data. Unlike most bitmap functions, it does not reference a `BITMAP` structure. This function assumes a square bitmap. The bitmap is viewed as one bit per pixel, and the matrix is assumed to have dimensions of *nBytes* by *nBytes* pixels. Since some hardware assumes that the low-order bit is the leftmost bit, and other hardware assumes that the high-order bit is the leftmost bit, this function will perform the transposition either way. A negative value of *nBytes* indicates that the low-order bit of each byte is the leftmost and a positive value indicates that the high-order bit is the leftmost.

This GDI function is intended primarily for printer drivers. The GDI calls the display driver to perform the function.

CreatePQ   Create Priority Queue

Synopsis   Create a GDI priority queue.

C Prototype
HANDLE FAR PASCAL CreatePQ(short *iNumMax*)

iNumMax   The queue size. This number represents the maximum number of entries allowed at a time.

Return Value   The handle to the newly created queue or zero if the GDI cannot create the queue.

Description   This function creates a priority queue and assigns an initial size to the queue. You can change this initially assigned size as needed after creation, by calling SizePQ. Since this function allocates system resources, you must call DeletePQ when you are finished with the queue.
This function is in the GDI library and is intended for printer device drivers.

DeletePQ   Delete Priority Queue

Synopsis   Delete a GDI priority queue.

C Prototype
short FAR PASCAL CreatePQ(HANDLE *hPQueue*)

hPQueue   The queue handle. This is a handle returned from CreatePQ.

Return Value   This function returns a positive value to indicate success, or −1 to indicate an error.

Description   Delete a queue previously allocated by CreatePQ.
This function is in the GDI library and is intended for printer device drivers.

ExtractPQ   Remove Queue Entry

Synopsis   Remove the highest-priority entry from a GDI priority queue.

C Prototype
```
short FAR PASCAL ExtractPQ(HANDLE hPQueue)
```
hPQueue   The queue handle. This is a handle returned from
`CreatePQ`.

Return Value   The tag of the highest-priority entry in the queue, or −1 if
the queue is empty.

Description   This function removes the highest-priority entry from the
queue and returns the tag from the entry. Note that the highest-priority
entry is the one with the lowest numerical priority value.

     This function is in the GDI library and is intended for printer device
drivers

GetSelectorBase   Query Selector Linear Base Address

Synopsis   Query the linear base address of the specified selector.

C Prototype
```
DWORD FAR PASCAL GetSelectorBase(WORD wSel)
```
wSel   The selector to be queried.

Return Value   The linear base address of the specified selector.

Description   This function returns the Base field from the descriptor
table entry for the specified selector. This base address is the *linear*
address and may not be the physical address if Windows is running in 386
enhanced mode.

GetSelectorLimit   Query Selector Limit

Synopsis   Query the limit of the specified selector.

C Prototype
```
DWORD FAR PASCAL GetSelectorLimit(WORD wSel)
```
wSel   The selector to be queried.

Return Value   The limit of the specified selector. The G-bit of the selector access rights must be examined to determine if the units are pages or bytes.

Description   This function returns the Limit field from the descriptor table entry for the specified selector. Note that this limit is one less than the size (bytes or pages) of the segment and may range from 0 to 0xFFFFF. For a 32-bit segment, this limit might not be the size in bytes, but could be the number of 4K pages in the segment.

InsertPQ   Add Queue Entry

Synopsis   Add an entry to a GDI priority queue.

C Prototype

```
short FAR PASCAL InsertPQ(HANDLE hPQueue, short sTag,
short iPriority)
```

hPQueue	The queue handle. This is a handle returned from `CreatePQ`.
sTag	The tag for the queue entry.
iPriority	The priority. Lower numbers represent higher priorities. This value must not be –1 so that the end of the queue can be detected with `ExtractPQ` and `MinPQ`.

Return Value   This function returns a positive value to indicate success, or –1 to indicate an error.

Description   This function adds an entry to the specified queue. It is in the GDI library and is intended for printer device drivers.

MinPQ   Query Queue Entry

Synopsis   Query the highest-priority entry in a GDI priority queue.

C Prototype

```
short FAR PASCAL MinPQ(HANDLE hPQueue)
```

hPQueue	The queue handle. This is a handle returned from `CreatePQ`.

Return Value   The tag of the highest-priority entry in the queue, or –1 if the queue is empty.

Description   This function returns the tag from the highest-priority entry in the queue. Note that the highest-priority entry is the one with the lowest numerical priority value. This function is in the GDI library and is intended for printer device drivers.

`PrestoChangoSelector` [sic]   Create Selector Alias

Synopsis   Obtain an alias to a code or data selector.

C Prototype
```
WORD FAR PASCAL PrestoChangoSelector(WORD selInput, WORD
selOutput)
```

selInput	The input selector.
selOutput	An unused selector that will be initialized with the same base and limit as *selInput*, but with different access rights.

Return Value   A copy of *selCode*, or zero if the function fails.

Description   This function will create a data alias to a data selector or a code alias to a data selector. The value of *selInput* determines the function. This function creates a selector that may be loaded into the CS register, as with a `JMP` or `CALL` instruction. A device driver might use this function to access code that was generated at run time by the driver. A typical use for this function is by the display driver in order to generate, at run time, code that performs a specific `BitBlt` raster operation. A display driver that does this can generate highly efficient code for all possible situations, without requiring that the code be generated in advance.

   This function is identical to the Windows API `ChangeSelector` function, but with a more creative name and reversed parameter order. It differs from `AllocCStoDSAlias` and `AllocDStoCSAlias` in that it does not allocate a new selector, but instead modifies an existing one.

SelectorAccessRights   Query or Set Selector Attributes

Synopsis   Set the attributes of the specified selector.

C Prototype
```
WORD FAR PASCAL SelectorAccessRights(WORD wSel, WORD
fGet, WORD wRights)
```

wSel	The selector to be set or queried.
fGet	The operation indicator. It is nonzero to set the selector, or zero to query the selector.
wRights	If setting the selector, the new attributes to assign to the selector. Otherwise, this parameter is ignored. The attributes are bit-mapped as follows:

Bit	Description
0	Ignored.
1	For data segments, this bit indicates that writing is allowed to the segment. For code segments, this bit indicates that reading is allowed from the segment.
2	For data segments, this bit indicates an expand-down segment. For code segments, this bit indicates a conforming segment.
3	This bit is set for a code segment, or reset for a data segment.
4	This bit should normally be set. It is reset for constructing operating system segments (for example, call gates).
5–11	Ignored.
12	Programmer defined. You can use this bit as desired. It is normally zero.
13	Ignored.
14	For expand-down segments, this bit should match bit 15.
15	This bit indicates that the segment limit is measured in pages. Otherwise, the limit is measured in bytes.

Return Value   For the query operation, this function returns the current attributes, in the same format as that of the *wRights* parameter.

Description   This function sets or queries various attribute fields in the descriptor table entry for the specified selector. The details of these attributes are beyond the scope of this book. Figure 2-6 illustrates the layout of a segment descriptor.

SetSelectorBase   Set Selector Linear Base Address

Synopsis   Set the linear base address of the specified selector.

C Prototype

VOID FAR PASCAL SetSelectorBase(WORD *wSel*, DWORD *dwBase*)

wSel   The selector to be set.

dwBase   The new base for the segment.

Return Value   *None.*

Description   This function sets the Base field in the descriptor table entry for the specified selector. This base address is the *linear* address and may not be the physical address if Windows is running in 386 enhanced mode.

SetSelectorLimit   Set Selector Limit

Synopsis   Set the limit of the specified selector.

C Prototype

VOID FAR PASCAL SetSelectorLimit(WORD *wSel*, DWORD *dwLimit*)

wSel   The selector to be queried.

dwLimit   The new limit to be assigned to the selector.

Return Value   *None.*

Description   This function sets the Limit field in the descriptor table entry for the specified selector. Note that this limit is one less than the size (bytes or pages) of the segment and may range from 0 to 0xFFFFF. For a

32-bit segment with the descriptor G-bit set, this limit is not the size in bytes, but rather is the number of 4K pages in the segment.

SizePQ   Change Queue Size

Synopsis   Change the size of a GDI priority queue.

C Prototype

```
short FAR PASCAL SizePQ(HANDLE hPQueue, short sDeltaSize)
```

hPQueue   The queue handle. This is a handle returned from `CreatePQ`.

sDeltaSize   The change in queue size. If positive, this number indicates the number of empty queue entries to be made available. If negative, this number indicates the number of empty queue entries to be de-allocated.

Return Value   The maximum number of simultaneous entries allowed, or −1 if the GDI cannot satisfy the request.

Description   This function changes the size of the queue by a relative amount.

RepaintScreen   Repaint the Display

Synopsis   Tell the GDI to repaint the entire display.

C Prototype

```
VOID FAR PASCAL RepaintScreen(VOID)
```

Return Value   *None.*

Description   When OS/2 1.x is running and when a switch is made to the DOS compatibility box, the display driver calls this function to tell the GDI to repaint the entire display. The display driver may not call this function if the GDI has suspended updates by calling the driver's `UserRe-paintDisable` entry point.
NOTE: This function is in the Windows USER library, which is not accessible when the device driver is loaded. This means that you cannot link to an import library or specify this function in the IMPORTS section of the

driver's linker DEF file. Instead, this function address must be resolved at run time using the standard Windows functions `GetModuleHandle` (specifying USER) and `GetProcAddress` (specifying the ordinal value 275).

__WINFLAGS   Windows Environment Flags

Synopsis   The constant returned by `GetWinFlags`.

C Prototype

```
extern _near _WINFLAGS
```

Return Value   *Not applicable.*

Description   This is not a function, but rather an externally declared ABS value that contains the value normally returned by the standard `GetWinFlags` function. This value may be used instead of the function, however, in order to reduce the overhead required by the far call to `GetWinFlags`. In C, the value is referenced as follows:

```
WORD wFlags = (WORD)(&_WINFLAGS) ;
```

In assembler, the same value is referenced as follows:

```
EXTRN     __WINFLAGS:ABS
MOV wFlags,__WINFLAGS
```

Although this "variable" is treated like a constant, it is actually a special symbol that the Windows loader recognizes and "fixes up" when the segment that references it is loaded. The technique is valid since these values are fixed for a particular Windows session.

APPENDIX

D

Standard Mode Grabber Functions

This appendix lists the functions (or entry points, depending on your point of view) for the standard mode display grabber. The method that Windows uses to gain access to these entry points is described in Chapter 5.

Windows calls the display grabber only when the processor is in real mode. It assumes that the DS and CS registers are the same.

DisableSave   **Disable Context Switching**

Synopsis   Disables switching between Windows and DOS sessions.

Parameters   *None.*

Return Value   *None.*

Description   Windows calls this function to tell the grabber that it will not make any more calls to switch video contexts. This function is the inverse of `EnableSave`. If the grabber has swap file opened by `SaveScreen`, this function should close it.

EnableSave   Enable Context Switching

Synopsis   Enables switching between Windows and DOS sessions.

Parameters   *None.*

Return Value   *None.*

Description   Windows calls this function to enable screen context saves. The grabber typically installs hooks in the system to allow context switching. This function is the inverse of `DisableSave`.

GetBlock   Copy Screen Rectangle

Synopsis   Copies the specified rectangular portion of the screen to a buffer.

Parameters   ES:DI is the address of a `GRABREQUEST` structure. The fields used in this structure are as follows:

`lpData`	The address of a buffer into which the data is to be returned. If `NULL`, this function returns the required size of the destination buffer without copying the data.
`XOrg, YOrg`	The *X* and *Y* coordinates of the upper left corner of the rectangle. The upper leftmost point of the display is (0,0).
`Xext, Yext`	The width and height of the rectangle. If either `Xext` or `Yext` is zero, the entire width or height, respectively, is assumed.
`Style`	If `fFormat` is `FMT_NATIVE`, the text is transferred in raw form (for example, with attributes, if in text mode). If `fFormat` is `FMT_OTHER` the data is copied in the format specified by the `GRABST` structure.

Return Value   On success, this function returns with the carry flag clear and the size of the return buffer in the AX register. Otherwise, the carry flag is set and AX contains the error code.

GetInfo   Query Grabber Information

Synopsis   Query the grabber's GRABINFO structure.

Parameters   ES:DI is the address of the return buffer to receive a copy of the GRABINFO structure contents.

Return Value   This function returns 0 in the AX register to indicate that a call to GetBlock is valid in the current mode. Otherwise, it returns 1 in the AX register.

GetVersion   Query Grabber Version

Synopsis   Return the grabber version number.

Parameters   *None.*

Return Value   The grabber version number is returned in AX. For version 3.1, for example, 0x30A is returned.

InitScreen   Initialize Screen Mode

Synopsis   Initializes the screen to text mode.

Parameters   AX is the number of lines per screen. For example, for standard VGA hardware this value can be 25, 43, or 50. If an unsupported value is specified, the grabber should choose the next lower supported value. This value corresponds to the ScreenLines value in SYSTEM.INI.

Return Value   *None.*

Description   Windows calls this function both to initialize a DOS session's display and whenever the user exits the session, either by switching sessions or by terminating a session.

InquireGrab   Query Grab Buffer Size

Synopsis   Query the size of the text or graphics grab buffer.

Parameters   The value of AX is 1 to query the size of the text mode grab buffer, or 2 to query the size of the graphics mode grab buffer. Other values indicate extended functions (see description).

Return Value   DX:AX is the size of the indicated grab buffer.

Description   This function also dispatches control to extended functions, as specified in the AX register. See Chapter 5 for details. Windows calls this function or InquireSave before any other Windows function. Your grabber can use this opportunity to initialize the grabber.

InquireSave   Query Save Buffer Size

Synopsis   Query the size of the text or graphics save buffer.

Parameters   The value of AX is 1 to query the size of the text mode save buffer, or 2 to query the size of the graphics mode save buffer.

Return Value   DX:AX is the size of the indicated save buffer.

Description   Windows calls this function or InquireGrab before any other Windows function. Your grabber can use this opportunity to initialize the grabber.

RestoreScreen   Restore Display

Synopsis   Restore the state and contents of the display.

Parameters   AX is the size of the save area. ES:DI is the area containing the saved screen context. DI is guaranteed to be zero.

Return Value   This function returns with the carry clear to indicate success, or with the carry flag set to indicate failure.

Description   This function restores the display contents as they were saved by SaveScreen. This function closes the swap file.

SaveScreen   Save Display

Synopsis   Save the state and contents of the display.

Parameters   AX is the size of the save area. ES:DI is the area to receive the saved screen context. DI is guaranteed to be zero.

Return Value   This function returns with the carry clear to indicate success, or with the carry flag set to indicate failure.

Description   This function saves the display contents to be later restored by `RestoreScreen`. This function should open the swap file if it is not already open.

SetSwapDrive   Specify Swap Path

Synopsis   Specify the drive and path of the grabber swap file.

Parameters   BL is the ASCII character for the swap drive; 0x43 ("C"), for example. ES:DI is an ASCIIZ string specifying the drive and path of the swap directory. This value corresponds to the `SwapPath` value in SYSTEM.INI.

Return Value   *None.*

Description   This function tells the grabber the location of the swap files. The grabber should not open the swap file here, but should simply save the information. The swap file is normally opened on a call to `SaveScreen`.

System Driver Entry Points

This appendix describes the entry points to the various basic system device drivers, including those for the keyboard, the mouse, the communication and printer ports, and the network.

Mouse Driver Entry Points

Initialization **Driver Initialization**

Synopsis   Initialize the mouse device driver.

C Prototype   *None.*

Return Value   *None.*

Description   Although it is not an explicit driver entry point, this function represents the DLL initialization function. The standard mouse driver determines the hardware type with this function and performs any initialization that is required to support the mouse driver `Enable` function. The starting address of this function is defined by the assembler `END` statement. If you are writing in the C language, you can use the assembler stub provided in the SDK in order to support this function.

Disable/@3   Disable Mouse

Synopsis   Suspend interrupt callbacks from the mouse device.

C Prototype

```
void FAR PASCAL Disable(void)
```

Return Value   *None.*

Description   This function tells the mouse driver to stop calling the mouse event procedure that was specified in the call to `Enable`. When Windows calls this function, it does not mean that the driver will no longer be needed, but that the driver should temporarily suspend calling the event procedure. A subsequent call by Windows to `Enable` will likely restore the callback.

Enable/@2   Enable Mouse

Synopsis   Enable calls to the Windows mouse event procedure.

C Prototype

```
void FAR PASCAL Enable(FARPROC lpEventProc)
```

lpEventProc   The address of the Windows mouse event procedure. The interface to the procedure is described below.

Return Value   *None.*

Description   Windows calls this function to establish the address of the Windows mouse event procedure. After Windows calls `Enable`, the mouse driver should call the Windows mouse event procedure whenever the mouse is moved or a mouse button is pressed or released. The event procedure uses an assembly language interface and expects parameters to be passed in registers rather than on the stack.

AX	The event codes. This is a bit-packed value that describes the various events being reported.

Bit	Description
0	The mouse has moved.
1	The left button was pressed.
2	The left button was released.
3	The right button was pressed.
4	The right button was released.
5–14	Reserved
15	The position values in BX and CX are in absolute coordinates.

BX	Horizontal position.
CX	Vertical position.
DX	Number of buttons on the mouse (typically, 2).

Inquire/@1   Query Mouse Information

Synopsis   Query information about the mouse characteristics.

C Prototype

```
WORD FAR PASCAL Inquire(MOUSEINFO FAR*lpMouseInfo)
```

lpMouseInfo   The address of a MOUSEINFO structure that will receive the information.

Return Value   The returned value is the number of bytes in the MOUSEINFO structure that were filled in.

Description   This function returns static information that describes the characteristics of the mouse. The information is returned in a MOUSEINFO structure as follows:

```
typedef _MOUSEINFO struct
     {
     BYTE Exists ;        /* TRUE if mouse exists */
     BYTE Relative ;      /* TRUE if positions are reported
                             in relative coordinates */
     WORD NumButtons ;  /* Typically 2 */
     WORD Rate ;          /* Frequency of calls to the event
                             procedure */
```

```
WORD XThresh ;            /* Horizontal threshold before
                                acceleration */
WORD YThresh ;            /* Vertical threshold before
                                acceleration */
WORD XRes ;               /* Horizontal resolution */
WORD YRes ;               /* Vertical resolution */
} MOUSEINFO ;
```

This structure is also described in assembler form in the WINDEFS.INC file in the DDK.

`MouseGetIntVect/@4`   **Query Mouse Interrupt Level**

Synopsis   Query the interrupt level used by the mouse hardware.

C Prototype

```
int FAR PASCAL MouseGetIntVect(void)
```

Return Value   The interrupt level of the hardware, or −1 if there is no mouse for the current Windows session.

Description   This function returns the interrupt level used by the mouse hardware. A mouse on COM1, for example, would return a value of 4.

`WEP`   **Windows Exit Procedure**

Synopsis   Perform DLL unloading cleanup.

C Prototype

```
int FAR PASCAL WEP(int fSystemExit)
```

fSystemExit   For most DLLs, this parameter indicates whether the DLL is being unloaded at system exit. Since this driver remains during the entire Windows session, this value is always 1.

Return Value   The return value must be 1.

Description   Windows calls this function when the Windows session ends. The driver should remove any hardware hooks acquired during driver initialization.

Comm Driver Entry Points

CClrBrk/@14   Clear Break State

Synopsis   Clear the Comm line break state.

C Prototype

int FAR PASCAL CClrBrk(BYTE *bCID*)

bCID   The Comm port identifier.

Return Value   This function returns 0 to indicate success, or 0xFFFF to indicate an invalid Comm ID.

Description   This function directly corresponds to the Windows API ClearCommBreak function. This function applies only to serial ports and sets the data line to a marking, or idle, state and resumes character transmission. This function is called after CSetBrk to end a communications break sequence.

CEvt/@11   Get Comm Event Word Address

Synopsis   Return the address of the Comm event word.

C Prototype

USHORT FAR * FAR PASCAL CEvt(BYTE *bCID*, USHORT *usEvtMask*)

bCID   The Comm port identifier.

usEvtMask   A mask that indicates which events the Comm driver should update in the event word.

Return Value   This function returns the address of the Comm event word, maintained in the driver's data segment. The function returns a NULL pointer if the specified Comm ID is not valid.

Description   This function directly corresponds to the Windows API SetCommEventMask function. The Comm device driver should continuously update this word in real time. A Windows application may sample this word at any time without calling any Comm driver function.

Therefore, the Comm driver should update this word whenever a hardware interrupt occurs that can change its value.

CEvtGet/@12   Clear and Query Events

Synopsis   Clear and query specified events in the Comm event word.

C Prototype
```
USHORT FAR PASCAL CEvtGet(BYTE bCID, USHORT usEvtMask)
```
bCID   The Comm port identifier.

usEvtMask   A mask that indicates which events the Comm driver should clear in the event word.

Return Value   This function returns the current Comm event word, masked by *usEvtMask*. It returns 0x0000 if *bCID* is not valid.

Description   This function directly corresponds to the Windows API `GetCommEventMask` function. A Windows application (indirectly) calls this function in order to query and clear the event status word in a single atomic operation, thus guarding against the loss of an event due to a status change between querying and clearing the word. By setting the desired bits in *usEvtMask*, an application can query and clear any subset of the events contained in the Comm status word.

CExtFcn/@9   Perform Extended Function

Synopsis   Perform an extended driver function.

C Prototype
```
USHORT FAR PASCAL CExtFcn(BYTE bCID, USHORT usFunction)
```
bCID   The Comm port identifier.

usFunction   The extended function code. The values 0 through 127 are reserved for Microsoft definitions. The values 128 through 255 are reserved for OEM (that's you) functions. The values currently reserved by Microsoft are:

Value	Description
1	Tell the driver to act as if the XOFF character has been received.
2	Tell the driver to act as if the XON character has been received.
3	Assert (set) the RS-232 RTS signal.
4	Negate (reset) the RS-232 RTS signal.
5	Assert (set) the RS-232 DTR signal.
6	Negate (reset) the RS-232 DTR signal.
7	Reset the device port.

Return Value   If successful, this function returns the Comm error word. If the function fails, it returns a Comm error code.

Description   This function directly corresponds to the Windows API `EscapeCommFunction` function. This function provides a mechanism for a custom driver to provide extended control functions.

CFlush/@10   Discard I/O

Synopsis   Discard the contents of a receive or transmit buffer.

C Prototype
```
USHORT FAR PASCAL CFlush(BYTE bCID, BYTE bBuffer)
```
bCID   The Comm port identifier.

bBuffer   The buffer identifier. A value of 0 indicates the transmit buffer. A value of 1 indicates the receive buffer.

Return Value   This function returns the Comm error word.

Description   This function directly corresponds to the Windows API `FlushComm` function. This function discards any data that may be pending in either the receive or transmit queues and returns immediately.

CommWriteString/@19   Transmit Block

Synopsis   Transmit a block of data over the serial port.

C Prototype

```
int FAR PASCAL CommWriteString(BYTE bCID, LPSTR lpData,
WORD wCount)
```

bCID	The Comm port identifier.
lpData	The address of the data to be transmitted.
wCount	The number of bytes in *lpData*.

Return Value   This function returns the number of bytes successfully added to the transmit queue.

Description   This function corresponds to the Windows API `WriteComm` function. This function only places the specified data in the transmit queue and does not wait for the data to be sent. If the number of remaining bytes in the queue is less than *wCount*, this function fills the queue with as much data as possible from *lpData* and returns the number actually enqueued.

CSetBrk/@13   **Set Break State**

Synopsis   Initiate a Comm line break state.

C Prototype

```
int FAR PASCAL CSetBrk(BYTE bCID)
```

bCID	The Comm port identifier.

Return Value   This function returns 0 to indicate success or 0xFFFF to indicate an invalid Comm ID.

Description   This function directly corresponds to the Windows API `SetCommBreak` function. It applies only to serial ports and sets the data line to a spacing state and suspends character transmission. A break sequence is typically from 150 to 1,000 milliseconds, after which the line is returned to a marking state with the `CClrBrk` function.

CTx/@6   **Transmit Byte Immediately**

Synopsis   Transmit a single byte before all others in the transmit queue.

C Prototype

```
USHORT FAR PASCAL CTx(BYTE bCID, BYTE bChar)
```

bCID   The Comm port identifier.

bChar   The byte to send.

Return Value   If successful, this function returns 0. Otherwise, this function returns 0x8000 if *bCID* is invalid or 0x4000 if the character cannot be transmitted (for example, if a previous `CTx` character is pending).

Description   This function directly corresponds to the Windows API `TransmitCommChar` function. This function places the specified byte at the head of the queue. For serial ports, if the communication hardware is currently transmitting a character (undergoing parallel to serial conversion), the character will be completely transmitted before the character specified in this function is transmitted.

GetDCB/@15   Get Comm DCB Address

Synopsis   Return the address of the DCB structure for the specified port.

C Prototype

```
DCB FAR * FAR PASCAL GetDCB(BYTE bCID)
```

bCID   The Comm port identifier.

Return Value   If successful, this function returns the address of the specified DCB structure. If *bCID* is not valid, this function returns a NULL pointer.

Description   Windows calls this function to implement the Windows API `GetCommState` function.

IniCom/@1   Initialize Comm Port

Synopsis   Initialize the specified Comm port.

C Prototype

```
int FAR PASCAL IniCom(DCB FAR *lpDCB)
```

lpDCB   The address of a DCB structure that describes the desired initial state of the port.

Return Value   This function returns 0 to indicate success or a negative value to indicate failure.

Description Windows calls this function after calling the driver's SetQue function. This function enables the Comm port and initializes it with the specified DCB information. Note that this function is unlike normal device driver initialization, as it is called for each port that is opened via OpenComm. In addition, this function does not assign the port number that is to be used: the port number is assigned by Windows. Windows calls this function with the Comm ID already set in the Id field of the passed DCB structure. It is up to the device driver to validate all of the fields in the DCB structure (including the ID) before initializing the specified port.

This function validates the specified DCB structure and copies it for its own use. Once this function is called, the device driver should allow data to be received into the device's receive buffer.

`ReactivateOpenCommPorts/@18`   **Re-enable Comm Ports**

Synopsis Re-enable Comm ports disabled by SuspendOpenCommPorts.

C Prototype
```
VOID FAR PASCAL ReactivateOpenCommPorts(VOID)
```

Return Value *None.*

Description In standard mode or real mode, Windows calls this function when returning to the Windows session from a DOS session. It restores the state of the driver as it existed before the DOS session was started. This function restores what was saved by SuspendOpenCommPorts. Windows provides this function since programs in a DOS session in real or standard mode can access the Comm hardware directly, possibly changing interrupt usage and mode. This function gives the driver the opportunity to restore the hardware to its saved state.

`ReadCommString/@20`   **Read Block of Data**

Synopsis Read bytes from the Comm receive buffer.

C Prototype
```
int FAR PASCAL ReadCommString(BYTE bCID, LPSTR lpData,
WORD wCount)
```

bCID	The Comm port identifier.
lpData	The address of a buffer into which the received data is returned.
wCount	The size, in bytes, of the *lpData* buffer.

Return Value   This function returns the number of bytes placed in the *lpData* buffer.

Description   Windows calls this function to implement the Windows API `ReadComm` function. This function does not wait for the indicated number of bytes to be received; it only transfers data already received from the receive queue into the return buffer specified by *lpData*.

RecCom/@4 Read Byte

Synopsis   Read a byte from the Comm receive buffer.

C Prototype

```
int FAR PASCAL RecCom(BYTE bCID)
```

bCID	The Comm port identifier.

Return Value   If a character is available, this function returns the character. Otherwise, this function returns –2. If an error is detected, this function returns –1.

Description   Windows 3.0 calls this function to implement the Windows API `ReadComm` function. Later versions of Windows call the `ReadCommString` function instead. Note that `RecCom` function returns only one byte at a time.

SetCom/@2 Set Configuration

Synopsis   Set the device configuration and state.

C Prototype

```
int FAR PASCAL SetCom(DCB FAR *lpDCB)
```

lpDCB	The address of a DCB structure that describes the desired new state of the port.

Return Value   This function returns 0 for success or an error code to indicate an error.

Description   Windows calls this function to implement the Windows API `SetCommState` function. Although an application can use this function to change the state of such signals as DTR and RTS, the Windows API `EscapeCommFunction` will more likely be used, instead. This function does not affect the state of the input/output queues.

`SetQue/@3`   **Specify I/O Buffers**

Synopsis   Specify the memory input/output buffers.

C Prototype
`int FAR PASCAL SetQue(BYTE `*bCID*`, `**`QDB FAR`**` *`*lpQDB*`)`

bCID	The Comm port identifier.
lpQDB	The address of a queue definition block (described below).

Return Value   This function returns 0 for success, or an error code to indicate an error.

Description   Windows calls this function during processing of the Windows API `OpenComm` function. This function is called *before* `IniCom`, since `IniCom` enables data to be received immediately into the buffer (which must have been previously defined). The C-language description of a queue definition block is as follows:

```
typedef struct _QDB
    {
    LPBYTE lpRxQueue ;/* Address of the receive queue
                            buffer */
    WORD cbRxQueue ;  /* Size of the Rx queue, in bytes */
    LPBYTE lpTxQueue ;/* Address of the transmit queue
                            buffer */
    WORD cbTxQueue ;  /* Size of the Tx queue, in bytes */
    }QDB;
```

The `lpRxQueue` and `cbRxQueue` fields may be zero for devices that cannot receive (such as LPT).

SndCom/@5   Transmit Byte

Synopsis   Place a character in the transmit queue.

C Prototype
```
int FAR PASCAL SndCom(BYTE bCID, BYTE bChar)
```
bCID   The Comm port identifier.

bChar   The character to be transmitted.

Return Value   This function returns 0 for success or an error code to indicate an error.

Description   Windows 3.0 calls this function during processing of the Windows API `WriteComm` function, sending one byte at a time to the device driver. Later versions of Windows call the `CommWriteString` function instead.

StaCom/@8   Query Port Status

Synopsis   Query the hardware and buffer status of the specified port.

C Prototype
```
int FAR PASCAL StaCom(BYTE bCID, COMSTAT FAR *lpComStat)
```
bCID   The Comm port identifier.

lpComStat   The address of the returned `COMSTAT` buffer.

Return Value   This function returns 0 for success, or an error code to indicate an error.

Description   Windows calls this function during processing of the Windows API `GetCommError` function. The `COMSTAT` structure is described in the SDK.

SuspendOpenCommPorts/@17   Suspend Comm Activity

Synopsis   Temporarily disable all Comm port activity.

C Prototype
```
VOID FAR PASCAL SuspendOpenCommPorts(VOID)
```

Return Value   *None.*

Description   In standard mode or real mode, Windows calls this function when switching to a DOS session. It disables interrupt activity to all Comm ports and transmissions are suspended. When suspended, any received data is lost. When returning back from the DOS session, Windows calls `ReactivateOpenCommPorts` to restore the ports to their original state.

`TrmCom/@7`   **End Port Activity**

Synopsis   Close the specified port.

C Prototype
```
VOID FAR PASCAL TrmCom(BYTE bCID)
```
bCID   The Comm port identifier.

Return Value   This function returns 0 for success, or an error code to indicate an error.

Description   Windows calls this function to process the `CloseComm` function. Windows will not call this function when ending the Windows session, so it is up to applications to properly close all Comm ports. If there is any data in the transmit queue buffer when `TrmCom` is called, the function will wait for all data to be transmitted. If the buffer data cannot be transmitted within a driver-defined amount of time, the driver closes the port and returns an error indication.

Keyboard Driver Entry Points

This section lists only the keyboard driver functions that do not correspond directly to Windows API functions. In particular, the following entry points are omitted from this appendix:

```
AnsiToOem           MapVirtualKey

AnsiToOemBuff       OemToAnsi

GetKBCodePage       OemToAnsiBuff
```

```
GetKeyboardType    OemKeyScan
GetKeyNameText
```

Disable/@3   **Disable Keyboard Driver**

Synopsis   Suspend interrupt callbacks and remove hooks.

C Prototype

void FAR PASCAL Disable(void)

Return Value   *None.*

Description   This function tells the keyboard driver to stop calling the keyboard event procedure that was specified in the call to `Enable`. When Windows calls this function, it does not mean that the driver will no longer be needed, but that the driver should temporarily suspend calling the event procedure. A subsequent call by Windows to `Enable` will restore the callback (unless the Windows session is ending).

Enable/@2   **Enable Keyboard Events**

Synopsis   Enable calls to the Windows keyboard event procedure.

C Prototype

void FAR PASCAL Enable(FARPROC *lpEventProc*, LPSTR
lpKeyState)

lpEventProc	The address of the Windows keyboard event procedure. The interface to the procedure is described below.
lpKeyState	The address of a state table that the keyboard driver will maintain for Windows. This table corresponds to the table returned by the Windows API `GetKeyboardState` function.

Return Value   *None.*

Description   Windows calls this function to establish the address of the Windows keyboard event procedure. After Windows calls `Enable`, the keyboard driver should call the Windows keyboard event procedure whenever a key is pressed or released. The event procedure uses an assembly language interface and expects parameters to be passed in registers rather than on the stack as follows:

AH	0x80 to indicate a key release, or 0x00 to indicate a key press.
AL	The virtual keycode. This keycode corresponds to the keycode returned in the `wParam` of the `WM_KEYDOWN` message.
BH	Extended key indication. This value is 0 for normal keys, or 1 for extended keys. For example, the keys on the cursor pad on the IBM extended keyboard are indicated as extended keys (BH=1). The cursor keys on the numeric keypad are returned as normal keys (BH=0). This allows a Windows application to distinguish between the two types of keys. This value corresponds to bit 24 of the `lParam` in the `WM_KEYDOWN` message.
BL	The hardware scan code. This corresponds to bits 16 through 23 of the `lParam` in the `WM_KEYDOWN` message.

EnableKBSysReq/@136   Control SysRq Processing

Synopsis   Enable or disable SysRq key processing.

C Prototype

void FAR PASCAL EnableKBSysReq(WORD *fEnable*)

fEnable	This bit-field word indicates how the SysRq key is to be treated by the keyboard device driver as follows:

Bit	Description
0	Enable INT 2 processing. If SysRq is pressed, execute an INT 2 instruction.
1	Disable INT 2 processing.
2	Enable `CVWBreak` processing. If SysRq is pressed, transfer control to the system `CVWBreak` entry point.
3	Disable `CVWBreak` processing.

Return Value *None.*

Description This function is called by Windows debuggers to control how the SysRq key is to be processed.

GetBIOSKeyProc/@137   Query BIOS ISR

Synopsis Query the address of the BIOS interrupt service routine.

C Prototype
```
FARPROC FAR PASCAL GetBIOSKeyProc(void)
```

Return Value The address of the BIOS keyboard interrupt service routine.

Description This function returns the address of the INT 9 interrupt service routine to what it was before the keyboard driver installed its interrupt hook. The keyboard driver obtains this information during `Enable` processing by calling INT 21h service 35h, Get Interrupt Vector.

GetTableSeg/@126   Initialize Translation

Synopsis This is an internal function that has no external purpose.

C Prototype
```
void FAR PASCAL GetTableSeg(void)
```

Return Value *None.*

Description For curiosity's sake, the keyboard driver calls this function to initialize one of its internal variables. It probably does not need to be exported.

Inquire/@1   Query DBCS Ranges

Synopsis This function returns the keyboard configuration structure that contains the DBCS ranges.

C Prototype
```
void FAR PASCAL Inquire(KBINFO FAR *lpKbInfoRet)
```

lpKbInfoRet　　　　　　The address of a 6-byte structure into which the keyboard configuration structure is returned. The first two bytes of the structure specify a range of bytes that signal the beginning of a double-byte character sequence (DBCS). The second two bytes specify a second range of DBCS characters. The last two bytes of the structure form a word that indicates the number of bytes of state information that the ToAscii function returns. This count must never be larger than 4.

Return Value　　The size of the KBINFO structure: 6.

Description　　The DBCS ranges specified here indicate the DBCS ranges that the driver supports. The ToAscii state size information indicates the number of bytes that the ToAscii function can return in the *lpChar* buffer, which the SDK documentation indicates is a 32-bit value; thus the 4-byte limit.

NewTable/@127　　　　　　Load Translation Tables

Synopsis　　Load the keyboard translation tables.

C Prototype
```
void FAR PASCAL NewTable(void)
```

Return Value　*None.*

Description　　Windows calls this function to let the keyboard driver load the translation tables specified in SYSTEM.INI. This is specified as an entry point separate from driver initialization since it can be called by the Control Panel while Windows is running.

ScreenSwitchEnable/@100　　　OS/2 Screen Switching Control

Synopsis　　Enable or disable OS/2 screen switching.

C Prototype
```
void FAR PASCAL NewTable(void)
```

Return Value   *None.*

Description   Windows calls this function when in a critical section in the display driver so that, when running under OS/2, the display driver has exclusive access to the display hardware.

System Driver Entry Points

The system driver (SYSTEM.DRV) is a specific driver in Windows and is not to be confused with the other system drivers described in this appendix. SYSTEM.DRV is likely to be changed only by motherboard hardware OEMs and is omitted from the DDK documentation and samples. The entry points that may be of interest to developers of other drivers, however, are listed here.

CreateSystemTimer/@2   Allocate a System Timer

Synopsis   Allocate a system timer to be used by a device driver.

C Prototype
```
WORD FAR PASCAL CreateSystemTimer(WORD wFreq, FARPROC
lpCallback)
```

wFreq	The frequency of the callback, in milliseconds.
lpCallback	The address of a DLL procedure to call back at the specified frequency.

Return Value   If successful, the timer handle, otherwise zero.

Description   This function consumes a system timer as described by the Windows API `SetTimer` function. The system calls the callback function at the specified frequency. The callback function is entered by a FAR CALL with the timer handle passed in the AX register. In standard mode, the callback is not called when a DOS session is active. In 386 enhanced mode, the latency for being called back can be quite significant: use a VxD if the callback latency is critical to your application.

InquireSystem/@1   **Query System Configuration**

Synopsis   Query various system configuration parameters.

C Prototype

DWORD FAR PASCAL InquireSystem(WORD *wItem*, WORD *wSubItem*)

wItem, *wSubItem*   These two values specify the information to be queried:

wItem/ *** wSubItem***	**Returned Value**
0/0	The resolution of the timer, in milliseconds.
1/*n*	Information about drive *n* (Drive A:=0). A return value in AX of 0 or 1 indicates that this is a logical drive and DX contains the drive number (Drive A:=1) of the physical drive. If AX = 0 or 2, the drive is removable, otherwise it is fixed. Similar information can be obtained from the Windows API GetDriveType function.

Return Value   *Varies by specific request.*

Description   See the prototype, above.

KillSystemTimer/@3   **Free a System Timer**

Synopsis   Free a timer to be used by a device driver.

C Prototype

WORD FAR PASCAL KillSystemTimer(WORD *wTimerHandle*)

wTimerHandle   The timer handle returned from a previous call to CreateSystemTimer.

Return Value   If successful, zero, otherwise the timer handle. (Note that this value is the opposite of that returned by KillTimer.)

GetSystemMSecCount/@6   Query Elapsed Time

Synopsis   Query the amount of elapsed time.

C Prototype

```
DWORD FAR PASCAL GetSystemMSecCount(VOID)
```

Return Value   The number of milliseconds elapsed.

Description   This function returns a relative time that may be useful for time stamping messages. The elapsed time is not necessarily real time, but reflects the interrupt frequency of the driver. This can vary from real time in standard mode, since the timer is disabled while a DOS session executes and the timer interrupts can be delayed or skewed while running in the system VM in 386 enhanced mode.

APPENDIX
F

VxD Services

This appendix describes the various services that Virtual Device Drivers may call, listed in alphabetical order. These services use two types of calling interfaces: 32-bit C and register-passing. For the 32-bit C interfaces, the C prototypes are included here. All byte and word parameters are promoted to 32-bit double-words and the leftmost argument is pushed last. In addition, the assembly language name of the called procedure has an underscore ("_") that prefixes the call. For example, to call the `Allocate_Global_V86_Data_Area` service:

```
push   dwFlags
push   dwSize
VMMcall   _Allocate_Global_V86_Data_Area
```

You can also pass parameters as part of the macro:

```
VMMcall   _Allocate_Global_V86_Data_Area,wSize,dwFlags
```

A small number of the C-calling convention services return a `UNS64` type. This type returns a 64-bit value. On return from such a function the EDX register contains the upper 32 bits, and the EAX register contains the lower 32 bits.

All of the C-calling convention services may modify the EAX, ECX, and EDX registers and the processor flags. Their return values are indeterminate unless otherwise specified. The remaining registers are returned unmodified.

In addition to the two types of interfaces, there are two different macros used. The VMMcall macro is for calling VMM services, including all of the C-calling interface functions, and the VxDcall macro is for calling other services. The macro used and the calling convention are included in the description of each service. With the C-calling interface services, the unsigned type refers to an unsigned int, which is a 32-bit value.

For the register-passing interfaces, the services modify only the registers specifically noted in this appendix. The remaining registers are returned unmodified unless otherwise specified. For all of these services, you may assume that the processor flags are modified and indeterminate on return, unless otherwise specified.

AddInstanceItem

Synopsis   Identify instanced memory block in V86 memory.

C Prototype
unsigned AddInstanceItem(InstStruct FLAT *linInstStr,
unsigned *ulFlags*)

linInstStr   A FLAT pointer to an instance data structure. See the description below.

ulFlags   This parameter must be zero.

Return Value   If successful, this function returns a nonzero value. If this function fails, it returns zero.

Comments   This function identifies an area of VM-linear memory that is to be instanced for each VM. Modifying the specified area in one VM will not affect the same area in any other VM.

Windows keeps track of each area in a linked list and traverses the list whenever a context switch occurs. The memory is copied into a save area. To maximize performance, a VxD should attempt to minimize the number of instance areas that it uses. The layout of the instance data structure is as follows:

```
typedef struct _InstStruct
    {
    unsigned Reserved[2] ;    /* Used internally*/
    VOID FLAT *linBase ;      /* Base address of area */
    unsigned nBytes ;         /* Size of area*/
    unsigned ulFlags ;        /* Attributes*/
    } InstStruct ;
```

The linBase field is a VM-linear address.

The ulFlags field is a bit field which may not be zero and must have only one of two flags set. The ALWAYS_Field flag (bit 9) indicates that the instance data is to be current for a $\overline{VM}$ whenever the VM is active. The INDOS_Field flag (bit 8) indicates that the data needs to be current only if the internal INDOS flag is set.

This function may be called only during Device_Init control processing.

Adjust_Execution_Time

Synopsis   Modify a VM's time slice execution time.

Calling Convention

VMMcall   Adjust_Execution_Time

EAX   A signed integer indicating the number of milliseconds to increase (or decrease, if negative) the VM's execution time.

EBX   The VM handle.

Return Value   *None.*

Adjust_Exec_Priority

Synopsis   Adjust the primary scheduler priority of the specified VM.

Calling Convention

VMMcall   Adjust_Exec_Priority

EAX   Amount to boost the priority. Instead of specifying a number, use one of the equates defined in VMM.INC in the DDK:

Cur_Run_VM_Boost specifies running the VM for its full time slice. Low_Pri_Device_Boost specifies giving the VM moderate priority over other VMs. High_Pri_Device_Boost specifies giving the VM significant priority over other VMs. Time_Critical_Boost specifies giving the VM priority even over a VM that is in a critical section (as indicated by a call to Begin_Critical_Section).

EBX   The VM Handle.

Return Value   *None.*

Comments   By definition, the VM with the highest priority is the current VM. Compare this service with the Call_Priority_VM_Event service, which will adjust the priority of a VM on a specified event.

Allocate_Device_CB_Area

Synopsis   Allocate VM control block space.

C Prototype

unsigned Allocate_Device_CB_Area(unsigned *nBytes*, unsigned *ulFlags*)

nBytes   The number of bytes to allocate from the control block.

ulFlags   This parameter must be zero.

Return Value   If successful, this function returns the offset of the addition to the control block. Your VxD must add the VM handle to this value to access the control block memory. The returned offset is guaranteed to be DWORD-aligned. If this function fails, it returns zero.

Comments   This function expands the size of a VxD's control block. The control block information is instanced for each VM. You can use this function to store small data items that relate to the instance of the VM. If you have large data items, it is better to allocate instance memory and store the pointer only to the instance memory in the control block.

The returned value is the offset from the base of the VM's control block, which is addressed by the VM's handle, normally in the EBX register. The following code illustrates how to access a private control block variable:

```
      mov    edi,ebx            ; Get base of control block area
      add    edi,oMyCBArea      ; Add offset of our private area
      mov    al,MyCB_State[edi] ; Get current state
```

Allocate_GDT_Selector

Synopsis   Allocate a selector from the global descriptor table (GDT).

C Prototype
UNS64 Allocate_GDT_Selector(unsigned *ulDesc1*, unsigned *ulDesc2*, unsigned *ulFlags*)

ulDesc1   The value to which the high-order 4 bytes of the descriptor are set.

ulDesc2   The value to which the low-order 4 bytes of the descriptor are set.

ulFlags   This parameter must be zero.

Return Value   If successful, EAX is the allocated selector value, the low 16 bits of EDX contain the allocated descriptor value (with RPL=DPL), and the high 16 bits contain the number of global selectors currently allocated by the system. If this function fails it returns with EAX set to zero.

Comments   The BuildDescDWORDs service facilitates the creation of the *ulDesc1* and *ulDesc2* parameters. Use the SetDescriptor service to change an existing entry and the Free_GDT_Selector service to free an entry.

Allocate_Global_V86_Data_Area

Synopsis   Allocate memory visible to all VMs.

C Prototype
unsigned Allocate_Global_V86_Data_Area(unsigned *nBytes*, unsigned *ulFlags*)

nBytes   The number of bytes to allocate.

ulFlags   A bit-field parameter containing a combination of flags. GVDAWordAlign, GVDADWordAlign, GVDAPara-Align, and GVDAPageAlign each specify a desired alignment of 2, 4, 16, and 4096 bytes, respectively. These flags may not be combined. The passed *nBytes* parameter should be similarly aligned.

GVDAInstance indicates that the area is to be instanced for each VM. If this flag is omitted, the allocated memory is shared among all VMs.

The GVDAReclaim flag may be set only if GVDAPageAlign is specified and GVDAInstance is not. The GVDAReclaim flag indicates that the memory manager may map NUL pages into the linear space allocated—no physical memory is required.

GVDAZeroInit indicates that the memory is to be set to zero before being allocated. Otherwise, the initial value of the memory is indeterminate.

Return Value   If successful, this function returns the VM-linear address of the allocated memory. The VM base address must be added to this value to access the memory from a VxD. This returned value must be converted to segment:offset form if it is to be used in V86 mode. If this function fails, it returns zero.

Comments   This function allocates memory that is addressable from and has the same address in every VM. The memory may be shared or instanced.

If called before System VM initialization and the GVDAInstance flag is specified, the value of the memory as modified by the VxD is copied into each subsequently created VM.

If the GVDAReclaim flag is specified, the VxD may later map physical memory into the space by calling one of the MapIntoV86, PhysIntoV86, or LinMapIntoV86 services for each VM. One of these calls should be made during Create_VM control processing to provide a valid initial value for the VM.

If you need to assign specific V86 memory addresses to the allocated memory, use the Assign_Device_V86_Pages instead.

Allocate_LDT_Selector

Synopsis   Allocate one or more selectors from a local descriptor table (LDT).

C Prototype

UNS64 Allocate_LDT_Selector(unsigned *hVM*, unsigned *ulDesc1*, unsigned *ulDesc2*, unsigned *nSelectors*, unsigned *ulFlags*, unsigned *ulFlags*)

hVM	The VM handle.
ulDesc1	The value to which the high-order 4 bytes of the descriptor are set.
ulDesc2	The value to which the low-order 4 bytes of the descriptor are set.
nSelectors	The number of contiguous selectors to allocate.
ulFlags	This parameter must be zero.

Return Value If successful, EAX is the allocated selector value (or the first value if *nSelectors* is greater than 1), the low 16 bits of EDX contain the allocated descriptor value (with RPL=DPL), and the high 16 bits contain the number of local selectors currently allocated in the specified VM. If this function fails it returns with EAX set to zero.

Comments If *nSelectors* is greater than one, then contiguous descriptors are allocated whose selector values are separated by a numerical value of 8. This feature allocates a _huge pointer (see the description of __AHINCR in Appendix C). The BuildDescDWORDs service facilitates the creation of the *ulDesc1* and *ulDesc2* parameters. Use the SetDescriptor service to change an existing entry and the Free_LDT_Selector service to free an existing entry (one selector at a time).

Allocate_PM_Call_Back

Synopsis Allocate a protected mode callback address.

Calling Convention

VMMcall   Allocate_PM_Call_Back

EDX	Data to be passed to the VxD when the callback is called.
ESI	The FLAT address of the VxD procedure to call.

Return Value EAX contains the protected mode selector:offset address of the callback.

Modifies   EAX

Comments   This function creates a stub of code that when called in protected mode, transfers control to the VxD. The callback address may be called from a Windows application or DLL. On entry to the VxD, the EBX register contains the VM handle of the calling client, EBP refers to the client register structure, and the EDX register contains the value passed in EDX when the `Allocate_PM_Call_Back` service was called. The VxD can accept additional parameters from the protected mode client via the VM's client register structure.

To allocate a callback that may be called from V86 mode, see the `Allocate_V86_Call_Back` service.

Allocate_Temp_V86_Data_Area

Synopsis   Allocate V86 memory for initialization.

C Prototype

unsigned `Allocate_Temp_V86_Data_Area`(unsigned *nBytes*, unsigned *ulFlags*)

nBytes   The size of the area to allocate

ulFlags   This parameter must be zero.

Return Value   If successful, this function returns a paragraph-aligned VM-linear address of the allocated memory. The VM base address must be added to this value to access the memory from a VxD. This returned value must be converted to segment:offset form if it is to be used in V86 mode. If this function fails, it returns zero.

Comments   This function allocates a temporary area to be used by a VxD during initialization. There is only one temporary area for all VMs, so this function will fail if another VxD has allocated the temporary area without freeing it.

This function is provided so that a VxD can temporarily allocate memory during initialization, such as for a translation buffer for calling services in V86 mode. This function may be called only during `Device_Init` control processing.

Memory allocated with this service must be freed using the `Free_Temp_V86_Data_Area` service.

Allocate_V86_Call_Back

Synopsis   Allocate a V86 mode callback address.

Calling Convention

VMMcall   Allocate_V86_Call_Back

EDX   Data to be passed to the VxD when the callback is called.

ESI   The FLAT address of the VxD procedure to call.

Return Value   EAX contains the V86 mode segment:offset address of the callback.

Modifies   EAX

Comments   This function creates a stub of code that when called in V86 mode, transfers control to the VxD. On entry to the VxD, the EBX register contains the VM handle of the calling client, EBP refers to the client register structure, and the EDX register contains the value passed in EDX when the Allocate_V86_Call_Back service was called. The VxD can accept additional parameters from the protected mode client via the VM's client register structure.

   To allocate a callback that may be called from protected mode, such as from a Windows application or DLL, see the Allocate_PM_Call_Back service.

Assign_Device_V86_Pages

Synopsis   Assign V86 linear addresses to a VxD.

C Prototype

unsigned Assign_Device_V86_Pages(unsigned *linBase*,
unsigned *nPages*, unsigned *hVM*, unsigned *ulFlags*)

linBase   The VM-linear base address of the area to assign.

nPages   The number of 4K pages to assign.

hVM   The handle of the VM, or zero if the addresses are to be assigned globally, that is to all VMs.

ulFlags   This parameter must be zero.

Return Value If successful, this function returns nonzero. If this function fails, it returns zero.

Comments This function reserves the specified VM-linear addresses either in a specific VM or in all VMs. This function does not assign physical memory to the addresses: the VxD must do that separately.

If called during `Device_Init` processing, the *hVM* parameter must be zero: only global allocations are permitted.

The `Deassign_Device_V86_Pages` service deassigns addresses that are allocated by this function.

Begin_Critical_Section

Synopsis Suppress activity in other VMs.

Calling Convention
```
VMMcall  Begin_Critical_Section
```

Return Value *None.*

Comments This function increases the primary scheduler execution priority for the specified VM, so that no other VM may execute unless another VM is assigned time-critical priority. This function allows a VxD to modify critical structures without the risk of simultaneous access by other VMs.

The time that a VM is in critical section should be minimized. A VxD exits a critical section by calling the `End_Critical_Section` service.

To allow a VxD to call subroutines that may also need critical sections, a count of the number of times `Begin_Critical_Section` is called is maintained. This count is incremented for every call to this service and is decremented for every call to the `End_Critical_Section` service. When the count is nonzero, the VM is in the critical section; when it is zero, the VM's priority is restored.

Begin_Nest_Exec

Synopsis Prepare for nested execution in the current VM.

Calling Convention
```
VMMcall  Begin_Nest_Exec
```

Return Value   *None.*

Modifies   Client_CS, Client_IP

Comments   A VxD calls this service in preparation for calling code in the current VM and before calling the `Exec_Int` or `Resume_Exec` services. The client's CS and IP registers are modified to point to a special breakpoint used for passing control to the VM. This service does not save client registers.

After completing activity in the VM, call the `End_Nest_Exec` service to restore the original state of the VM.

To prepare for nested execution in V86 mode, regardless of the current mode, use the `Begin_Nest_V86_Exec` service.

Begin_Nest_V86_Exec

Synopsis   Prepare for nested execution in V86 mode in the current VM.

Calling Convention
```
VMMcall  Begin_Nest_V86_Exec
```

Return Value   The VM is forced into V86 mode.

Modifies   Client_CS, Client_IP

Comments   A VxD calls this service in preparation for calling V86 code in the current VM and before calling the `Exec_Int` or `Resume_Exec` services. The client's CS and IP registers are modified to point to a special breakpoint used for passing control to the VM.

After completing activity in the VM, call the `End_Nest_Exec` service to restore the original state of the VM.

Begin_Use_Locked_PM_Stack

Synopsis   Ensure a locked PM stack.

Calling Convention
```
VMMcall  Begin_Use_Locked_PM_Stack
```

Modifies   Client_SS, Client_ESP

Comments   This function may be called only when the VM is executing in protected mode, after a call to `Set_PM_Exec_Mode`. It ensures that the protected mode stack is locked in physical memory and will not be demand-paged.

When finished with the locked stack, the VxD must call the `End_Use_Locked_PM_Stack` service.

To allow a VxD to call subroutines that may also need locked PM stacks, a count of the number of times `Begin_Use_Locked_PM_Stack` is called is maintained. This count is incremented for every call to this service and is decremented for every call to the `End_Use_Locked_PM_Stack` service. When the count is nonzero, the PM stack is locked; when it is zero, the VM's original stack is restored.

BuildDescDWORDs

Synopsis   Build parameters for the selector allocation services.

C Prototype

`UNS64 BuildDescDWORDs(unsigned` *ulBase,* `unsigned` *ulLimit,* `unsigned` *bType,* `unsigned` *ulSize,* `unsigned` *ulFlags)*

ulBase	The linear base address to assign to the memory segment.
ulLimit	The limit of the segment. This value is the size of the segment minus one. This limit is specified in bytes or pages, depending on the granularity bit in *ulType*.
bType	The access-rights byte of the descriptor.
ulSize	The linear base address to assign to the memory segment.
ulFlags	If this parameter is `BDDExplicitDPL`, the DPL value specified in *bType* is used for the descriptor. If this parameter is zero, the DPL of Windows protected mode applications is used. This parameter must be zero if the selector will be used by Windows application or DLL or by a DPMI client running in a VM in protected mode.

Return Value   EDX contains the *ulDesc1* parameter and EAX contains the *ulDesc2* parameter that is to be passed to the `Allocate_LDT_Selector` or `Allocate_GDT_Selector` services.

Comments   This service facilitates the construction of the *ulDesc1* and *ulDesc2* parameters of the selector allocation service functions.

Build_Int_Stack_Frame

Synopsis   Simulate an INT instruction.

Calling Convention

```
VMMcall   Build_Int_Stack_Frame
CX              Code segment of VM code to which control is transferred.
EDX             Offset of VM code to which control is transferred.
```

Return Value   *None.*

Modifies   Client_CS, Client_EIP, Client_ESP, Client_Flags

Comments   This function is similar to `Simulate_Int`, except that the target interrupt service routine need not have an interrupt vector assigned. Instead of accepting an interrupt vector number, this service accepts the address of the VM routine.

One of the `Begin_Nest_Exec` or `Begin_Nest_V86_Exec` services must be called before calling this service.

This function modifies only the client registers and the client stack. It does not actually call the function. To pass control to the VM, call the `Resume_Exec` service.

Call_Priority_VM_Event

Synopsis   Call the VxD under complex event conditions.

Calling Convention

```
VMMcall   Call_Priority_VM_Event
```

EAX   The amount to change the priority when called back. The value specified here corresponds to the values specified in the call to `Adjust_Exec_Priority`. In addition to the values specified there, this parameter may also be `Critical_Section_Boost` to claim the critical section flag for the VM (no count is maintained as with `Begin_Critical_Section`).

EBX   The handle of the VM of interest.

ECX   Flags specifying various options and event conditions. `PEF_Wait_For_STI` specifies that VM interrupts must be enabled. `PEF_Wait_Not_Crit` specifies that no VM may be in a critical section. `PEF_Dont_Unboost` specifies that Windows will not restore the VM priority on return from the callback. `PEF_Always_Sched` specifies that the event procedure will not be called if all of the conditions are not currently satisfied, but only when the conditions return to the specified states.

EDX   Reference data passed to be passed the callback subroutine.

ESI   The FLAT address of the VxD subroutine to call back.

Return Value   If the callback was called immediately, ESI is zero. Otherwise, ESI contains the event handle that may be passed to the `Cancel_Priority_PM_Event` service.

Comments   This service may be called from a ring 0 interrupt service routine. To cancel a pending callback, call the `Cancel_Priority_PM_Event` service.

When called back, the callback subroutine is given the VM handle of the current VM in EBX, the reference data in EDX, and a pointer to the client register structure in EBP. The callback routine need preserve only EBP and the stack and segment registers; all other registers need not be preserved.

Call_When_Idle

Synopsis   Call back the VxD when all VMs are idle.

Calling Convention
```
VMMcall   Call_When_Idle
```
ESI   The FLAT address of the VxD subroutine to call back.

Return Value   If successful, this function returns with the carry flag clear (0). Otherwise, the carry flag is set, and the callback subroutine will not be called.

Comments   Windows determines that all VMs are idle when they have all released their time slice before consuming it. A number of callbacks among VxDs may be registered, although each VxD should not register more than one call back. This service may be called from a ring 0 interrupt service routine.

When called back, the callback subroutine is given the VM handle of the system VM in EBX, with EBP referring to the client register structure. The callback routine may prevent the callback routines of other VxDs from being called by returning with the carry flag cleared (0). Otherwise, the VxD should return with the carry flag set (1).

Call_When_Not_Critical

Synopsis   Call back the VxD when the critical section is released.

Calling Convention

```
VMMcall   Call_When_Not_Critical
```

EDX   Reference data passed to be passed the callback subroutine.

ESI   The FLAT address of the VxD subroutine to call back.

Return Value   *None.*

Comments   A VxD calls this function when the current VM is in a critical section. Windows calls callback function when the critical section is released and before any other VM has the opportunity to execute (except time-critical VMs). This service may be called from a ring 0 interrupt service routine.

Compare this service with the `Call_Priority_VM_Event` service.

When called back, the callback subroutine is given the VM handle of the current VM in EBX, the reference data in EDX, and a pointer to the client register structure in EBP. The callback routine need preserve only EBP and the stack and segment registers; all other registers need not be preserved.

Call_When_Task_Switched

Synopsis   Call back the VxD whenever the active VM changes.

Calling Convention

```
VMMcall   Call_When_Task_Switched
```

ESI   The FLAT address of the VxD subroutine to call back.

Return Value *None.*

Comments This function tells Windows to call the VxD on each task switch. Since this callback will be called extremely frequently, it should perform a minimum of steps and return as quickly as possible. A VxD calls this service after a task switch, and immediately before passing control to the newly current VM. This service may be called from a ring 0 interrupt service routine.

When called back, the callback subroutine is given the VM handle of the current (new) VM in EBX, and the VM handle of the prior active VM in EAX. The callback routine need preserve only EBP and the stack and segment registers; all other registers need not be preserved.

Call_When_VM_Ints_Enabled

Synopsis Call back the VxD when the VM enables interrupts.

Calling Convention

VMMcall	Call_When_VM_Ints_Enabled
EDX	Reference data to be passed the callback subroutine.
ESI	The FLAT address of the VxD subroutine to call back.

Return Value *None.*

Modifies Client_Flags

Comments This service tells Windows to call the VxD when the current VM enables interrupts. If this service is called while VM interrupts are already enabled, Windows calls the callback routine immediately. This service may be called from a ring 0 interrupt service routine.

Compare this service with the Call_Priority_VM_Event service, which may be more convenient, but may not be fast enough for some VxDs.

In some versions of Windows, a VM may be permitted to disable physical interrupts to improve execution performance in the VM. In such versions, calling this service will cause Windows to lower IOPL in order to virtualize access to the interrupt flag. This will cause certain instructions, such as POPF, to be simulated by Windows, possibly resulting in degraded performance.

When called back, the callback subroutine is given the VM handle of the current VM in EBX, the reference data in EDX, and a pointer to the client register structure in EBP. The callback routine need preserve only EBP and the stack and segment registers; all other registers need not be preserved.

Call_When_VM_Returns

Synopsis   Call back the VxD when the current VM returns from the current interrupt.

Calling Convention

VMMcall   Call_When_VM_Returns

EAX	The number of milliseconds to wait before timing out, or zero if no timeout is desired. If this value is negative, the absolute value is used for the timeout, and Windows calls the callback on the return event *and* on the timeout.
EDX	Reference data to be passed the callback subroutine.
ESI	The FLAT address of the VxD subroutine to call back.

Return Value   *None.*

Modifies   Client_CS, Client_EIP

Comments   This service may be called only when the VM has entered ring 0 interrupt service, but before a client IRET frame has been constructed.

A VxD can call this service in order to be called after all client processing of the interrupt has completed. For example, a VxD may need to keep track of the results of a BIOS or DOS service that it is virtualizing.

When called back, the callback subroutine is given the VM handle of the current VM in EBX, the reference data in EDX, and a pointer to the client register structure in EBP. If the carry flag is set on entry to the callback, the service has timed out before the client processed the IRET frame. Otherwise, if the zero flag is set, the callback is being called back after timing out and after the client has processed the IRET frame. If the carry flag is clear on entry to the callback, the service did not time out and the client has processed the IRET frame. The callback routine need preserve only EBP and the stack and segment registers; all other registers need not be preserved.

Cancel_Priority_VM_Event

Synopsis   Cancel a callback registered by `Call_Priority_VM_Event`.

Calling Convention

VMMcall   Cancel_Priority_VM_Event

ESI   Priority event handle obtained from the call to `Call_Priority_VM_Event`.

Return Value   *None.*

Modifies   ESI

Comments   This function cancels the callback registered by a call to the `Call_Priority_VM_Event` service.

Cancel_Time_Out

Synopsis   Cancel a timeout callback.

Calling Convention

VMMcall   Cancel_Time_Out

ESI   Timeout event handle obtained from a call to `Set_VM_Time_Out` or `Set_Global_Time_Out`.

Return Value   *None.*

Comments   *None.*

Cancel_VM_Event

Synopsis   Cancel a VM event callback.

Calling Convention

VMMcall   Cancel_VM_Event

EBX   The VM specified in the prior call to `Schedule_VM_Event`.

ESI   VM event handle obtained from a prior call to Sched-
                    ule_VM_Event.

Return Value *None.*

Comments *None.*

Claim_Critical_Section

Synopsis Enter critical section and increase critical section count.

Calling Convention

VMMcall   Claim_Critical_Section

ECX   The number of times to increment the critical section
                    count. This value may not be negative.

Return Value *None.*

Comments This service has the same function as calling the
Begin_Critical_Section, except that instead of incrementing the
count by only one, the claim count is incremented by the specified amount.
Calling this function once with the specified count is faster than calling
Begin_Critical_Section the specified number of times.

Convert_Boolean_String

Synopsis Convert a string to a binary zero (0) or one (1).

Calling Convention

VMMcall   Convert_Boolean_String

EDX   A FLAT pointer to an ASCIIZ string.

Return Value If successful, this service returns with the carry flag clear
and EAX set to zero (0) to indicate True, or set to –1 (0xFFFFFFFF) to indicate False.

Comments This function may be called only during Sys_Crit_Init
control processing. A VxD typically calls this function after obtaining the
string from the Get_Profile_String service. A VxD may combine the
two services by calling Get_Profile_Boolean.

Convert_Decimal_String

Synopsis   Convert a decimal string to binary.

Calling Convention

VMMcall   Convert_Decimal_String

EDX   A FLAT pointer to an ASCIIZ string.

Return Value   This function returns with the binary result in EAX and a FLAT pointer to the first nondecimal character in the string in EDX.

Comments   This function may be called only during Sys_Crit_Init control processing. A VxD typically calls this function after obtaining the string from the Get_Profile_String service. A VxD may combine the two services by calling Get_Profile_Decimal_Int.

Convert_Fixed_Point_String

Synopsis   Convert a fixed-point decimal string to binary.

Calling Convention

VMMcall   Convert_Fixed_Point_String

ECX   The number of decimal places.

EDX   A FLAT pointer to an ASCIIZ string.

Return Value   This function returns with the binary result in EAX and a FLAT pointer to the first nondecimal fixed-point character in the string in EDX. The result in EAX is scaled by the number of decimal places. In other words, if x is the value of the string, the contents of EAX are $x*10ECX$.

Comments   This function may be called only during Sys_Crit_Init control processing. A VxD typically calls this function after obtaining the string from the Get_Profile_String service. A VxD may combine the two services by calling Get_Profile_Fixed_Point.

Convert_Hex_String

Synopsis   Convert a hexadecimal string to binary.

Calling Convention

```
VMMcall   Convert_Hex_String
```

EDX   A FLAT pointer to an ASCIIZ string.

Return Value   This function returns with the binary result in EAX and a FLAT pointer to the first nonhexadecimal character in the string in EDX. If the hexadecimal value ends with an "H" or "h" character, EDX points to the character after the "h."

Comments   This function may be called only during `Sys_Crit_Init` control processing. A VxD typically calls this function after obtaining the string from the `Get_Profile_String` service. A VxD may combine the two services by calling `Get_Profile_Hex_Int`.

CopyPageTable

Synopsis   Obtain a copy of specified CPU page table entries.

C Prototype

```
unsigned CopyPageTable(unsigned iPage, unsigned nPages,
BYTE FLAT *linPageBuf, unsigned ulFlags)
```

iPage   The starting page table entry to copy. This value is the linear address shifted left by 12 bits.

nPages   The number of page table entries to copy.

linPageBuf   A FLAT pointer to a buffer that will receive a copy of the page table entries. This buffer must be at least 4*nPages long, since each page table entry is 4 bytes long.

ulFlags   This parameter must be zero.

Return Value   This service returns a zero value if all of the indicated pages are mapped to physical pages. If any page in the specified range is not mapped to a physical page, the service returns a nonzero value.

Comments   The service obtains a copy of the 386 CPU page table entries. A VxD that needs to know the current linear-to-physical mapping of memory may use this service.

Unless your VxD has locked the specified pages, the information about them is volatile and may change once the VxD returns to Windows or if the VxD attempts to access the contents of one of the pages.

Deassign_Device_V86_Pages

Synopsis   Deassign memory allocated by `Assign_Device_V86_Pages`.

C Prototype
unsigned `Deassign_Device_V86_Pages`(unsigned *linBase*,
unsigned *nPages*, unsigned *hVM*, unsigned *ulFlags*)

linBase   The VM-linear base address of the area to deassign.

nPages   The number of 4K pages to deassign.

hVM   The handle of the VM , or zero if the addresses are to be
                   deassigned globally, that is from all VMs.

ulFlags   This parameter must be zero.

Return Value   If successful, this function returns nonzero. If this function fails, it returns zero.

Comments   This service may be called only after (and not during)
`Device_Init` control processing.

Crash_Cur_VM

Synopsis   Immediately terminate the current VM.

Calling Convention
VMMcall   Crash_Cur_VM

Return Value   *None.*

Comments   This service immediately terminates the current VM. If not
the system VM, the shell may notify the user of the catastrophe. If the system VM is the current VM, this service immediately exits Windows without performing VM shutdown on any other VM.

Disable_Global_Trapping

Synopsis   Disable port trapping on the specified port in all VMs.

Calling Convention
VMMcall   Disable_Global_Trapping

EDX   I/O port address.

Return Value *None.*

Comments A VxD calls this service to temporarily disable port trapping that was established by a call to the `Install_IO_Handler` service. A VxD may do this for an active VM if the device does not need to be virtualized, but only to be managed for contention with other VMs. I/O port access is significantly faster with port trapping disabled.

Disable_Local_Trapping

Synopsis Disable port trapping on the specified port in the specified VM.

Calling Convention
```
VMMcall   Disable_Local_Trapping
```
EBX   The VM handle.

EDX   I/O port address.

Return Value *None.*

Comments A VxD calls this service to temporarily disable port trapping that was established by a call to the `Install_IO_Handler` service. A VxD may do this for an active VM if the device does not need to be virtualized, but only to be managed for contention with other VMs. I/O port access is significantly faster with port trapping disabled.

Disable_VM_Ints

Synopsis Disable interrupts in the current VM.

Calling Convention
```
VMMcall   Disable_VM_Ints
```

Return Value *None.*

Comments Calling this service has the same behavior as the current VM client executing a CLI instruction.

Enable_Global_Trapping

Synopsis   Re-enable port trapping on the specified port in all VMs.

Calling Convention

VMMcall   Enable_Global_Trapping

EDX   I/O port address.

Return Value   *None.*

Comments   A VxD calls this service to re-enable port trapping that was suspended by a call to Disable_Global_Trapping.

Enable_Local_Trapping

Synopsis   Re-enable port trapping on the specified port in the specified VM.

Calling Convention

VMMcall   Enable_Local_Trapping

EBX   The VM handle.

EDX   I/O port address.

Return Value   *None.*

Comments   A VxD calls this service to re-enable port trapping that was suspended by a call to Disable_Local_Trapping.

Enable_VM_Ints

Synopsis   Enable interrupts in the current VM.

Calling Convention

VMMcall   Enable_VM_Ints

Return Value   *None.*

Comments   Calling this service has the same behavior as the current VM client executing a STI instruction. Callback procedures that trigger on this event will not be called immediately, but rather when the VM is re-scheduled for execution.

End_Crit_And_Suspend

Synopsis   End critical section and suspend VM.

Calling Convention

VMMcall   End_Crit_And_Suspend

Return Value   If successful, this service returns with the carry flag clear. If the service fails because the critical section count was not 1 or because it could not suspend the VM, this service returns with the carry flag set.

Comments   This service is similar to calling End_Critical_Section and Suspend_VM. This service does not return until the VM has been resumed by a call to Resume_VM. It is useful only if Begin_Critical_Section has been called only once.

End_Critical_Section

Synopsis   Decrement the critical section count by one.

Calling Convention

VMMcall   End_Critical_Section

Return Value   *None.*

Comments   This service decrements the critical section count that is incremented by a call to Begin_Critical_Section or Claim_Critical_Section. If the count is decremented to zero by this service, the critical section is released and the VM's primary scheduler priority is restored, possibly causing the active VM to change.

End_Nest_Exec

Synopsis   Restore VM state after nested execution.

Calling Convention

VMMcall   End_Nest_Exec

Modifies   Client_CS, Client_EIP

Comments   This service removes only the breakpoint patch installed by the call to `Begin_Nest_Exec`. It does not restore client registers (other than CS and EIP).

End_Use_Locked_PM_Stack

Synopsis   Decrement locked protected mode stack use count.

Calling Convention

`VMMcall   End_Use_Locked_PM_Stack`

Comments   This service decrements the use count incremented by the `Begin_Use_Locked_PM_Stack` service. If the count is decremented to zero, Windows restores the original protected mode stack.

Exec_Int

Synopsis   Simulate a VM interrupt and resume VM execution.

Calling Convention

`VMMcall   Exec_Int`

`EAX`   Interrupt number to execute.

Return Value   Possibly VM client registers.

Modifies   Possibly VM client registers.

Comments   This service puts an IRET frame on the client stack and resumes execution in the VM. This service returns when the IRET frame is processed by the VM.

Before calling this service, a VxD first must have prepared for nested execution by calling `Begin_Nest_Exec` or `Begin_Nest_V86_Exec`. If a VxD needs to access DOS or BIOS services in a VM, it can call the `Exec_VxD_Int` service, which will automatically perform the API mapping of registers and buffers between the VM client and the VxD.

Exec_VxD_Int

Synopsis   Call a VM service from a VxD.

Calling Convention

```
push        dword ptr intnum
```
other registers as needed
```
VMMcall     Exec_VxD_Int
```

Return Value   Varies by VM service.

Modifies   Varies by VM service.

Comments   *Notice the extremely unconventional calling convention!* The interrupt number to execute is pushed as a 32-bit value on the stack, like a parameter in a higher level language. Parameters to the VM service, however, are passed in the VxD registers. This service maps VxD registers and buffers to BIOS and DOS services, so the return values vary according to the various services.

This service performs API mapping in a similar fashion as API mapping for protected mode applications, except that protected mode hooks will not be called. Do not modify ES or DS when calling services that normally expect selector in ES or DS. Instead, pass the 32-bit offset in the 32-bit register corresponding to the 16-bit register of the original service. For example, if a service expects a pointer in DS:DX, do not modify DS, but instead pass the FLAT linear address in EDX.

This service may not be used to call VM services that return values in selector registers.

A VxD may call this service only during and after (but not before) Init_Complete control processing.

The DDK VxDint macro can be used to call this service.

Fatal_Error_Handler

Synopsis   Exit Windows immediately.

Calling Convention

```
VMMjmp      Fatal_Error_Handler
```
EAX	If bit zero is set, Windows does not return to DOS, but hangs the system, instead. All other bits must be zero.
ESI	The FLAT address of an ASCIIZ string to display on exit.

Return Value   This service does not return. Note the use of the VMMjmp macro.

Comments Windows will call all devices that have processed the `Sys_Critical_Init` control with the `Sys_Critical_Exit` control before exiting.

You may use the DDK `Fatal_Error` macro to call this service.

Fatal_Memory_Handler

Synopsis Exit Windows immediately with a message.

Calling Convention

VMMjmp   Fatal_Memory_Handler

Return Value This service does not return. Note the use of the VMMjmp macro.

Comments Calling this service is identical to calling `Fatal_Error_Handler` with message indicating that there is insufficient memory to run 386 enhanced mode Windows. Use this service instead of `Fatal_Error_Handler` to avoid internationalization issues.

This service should be called only during `Sys_Critical_Init` processing.

Free_GDT_Selector

Synopsis Free a selector previously allocated by `Allocate_GDT_Selector`.

C Prototype

unsigned Free_GDT_Selector(unsigned *ulSel*, unsigned *ulFlags*)

ulSel The selector allocated from a prior call to `Allocate_GDT_Selector`.

ulFlags This parameter must be zero.

Return Value If successful, this service returns a nonzero value. If this service fails, it returns zero.

Comments Do not attempt to free a selector that your VxD did not allocate.

Free_LDT_Selector

Synopsis   Free a selector previously allocated by `Allocate_LDT_Selector`.

C Prototype
`unsigned Free_LDT_Selector(unsigned` *ulSel*`, unsigned` *ulFlags*`)`

ulSel   The selector allocated from a prior call to `Allocate_LDT_Selector`.

ulFlags   This parameter must be zero.

Return Value   If successful, this service returns a nonzero value. If it fails, it returns zero.

Comments   Do not attempt to free a selector that your VxD did not allocate.

Free_Temp_V86_Data_Area

Synopsis   Free V86 memory that was used for initialization.

C Prototype
`unsigned Free_Temp_V86_Data_Area(void)`

Return Value   If successful, this function returns a nonzero value. Otherwise, it returns zero.

Comments   This function deallocates memory allocated by the `Allocate_Temp_V86_Data_Area` service.

GetAppFlatDSAlias

Synopsis   Return an application useable selector to system memory.

C Prototype
`unsigned GetAppFlatDSAlias(void)`

Return Value   An application-ring selector that a protected mode application can use to access system linear memory.

Comments   The returned selector allows read-only access to the data. This service allows a protected mode application to use the same FLAT pointers that a VxD uses to address memory. The returned selector is a GDT selector and may be used by all VMs.

GetDescriptor

Synopsis   Query the contents of the specified descriptor.

C Prototype
```
UNS64 GetDescriptor(WORD wSel, unsigned hVM, unsigned
ulFlags)
```

wSel   A selector specifying the descriptor entry to be queried. The selector may specify a GDT or an LDT descriptor.

hVM   The handle of the VM, if *ulSel* specifies an LDT descriptor. This parameter is required for LDT descriptors and is ignored if a GDT descriptor is being queried.

ulFlags   This parameter must be zero.

Return Value   If successful, EAX contains the first four bytes of the descriptor and EDX contains the second four bytes of the descriptor. If this service fails, it returns zero in EAX and EDX.

GetFirstV86Page

Synopsis   Query the page number of the VM's first application page.

C Prototype
```
unsigned GetFirstV86Page(void)
```

Return Value   The page number (linear address divided by 4096) of the first VM-linear page of memory.

Comments   This value changes after device initialization. Call this service to get the current value.

GetFreePageCount

Synopsis   Query the number of available memory pages.

C Prototype

```
UNS64 GetFreePageCount(unsigned ulFlags)
```

ulFlags   This parameter must be zero.

Return Value   This service returns the number of 4K pages available to be allocated by the `PageAllocate` service in the EAX register. The EDX register contains the number of pages that may be allocated and locked.

Comments   A VxD calls this service to determine how much linear memory space is available. Although it is possible to allocate a number of pages without committing or locking them, doing so consumes page table entries. Therefore, although linear space is not as expensive as physical memory space, it is still important for a VxD to be conservative in its consumption of linear space.

GetNulPageHandle

Synopsis   Return the memory handle of the system NUL page.

C Prototype

```
unsigned GetNulPageHandle(void)
```

Return Value   The memory handle of the system NUL page.

Comments   This service allows a VxD to map "don't care" pages to linear memory that it has assigned. Accessing the NUL page has no effect, causes no traps, and its contents are indeterminate.

GetSysPageCount

Synopsis   Return the number of system pages allocated.

C Prototype

```
unsigned GetSysPageCount(unsigned ulFlags)
```

ulFlags   This parameter must be zero.

Return Value   The number of pages in the system that are allocated as system pages.

Comments   System pages are those with the `PG_SYS` attribute set. See the `PageAllocate` service for more information.

GetV86PageableArray

Synopsis   Query list of a VM's pages with modified lock behavior.

C Prototype
```
unsigned GetV86PageableArray(unsigned hVM, unsigned
linBuffRet, unsigned ulFlags)
```

hVM   The handle to the VM being queried.

linBuffRet   A FLAT pointer to a buffer that will receive a bitmap indicating which pages have nondefault lock/unlock behavior. The buffer must be 32 bytes (256 bits) long. A set bit indicates a page whose lock/unlock behavior is modified.

ulFlags   This parameter must be zero.

Return Value   If this service succeeds it returns a nonzero value. If it fails, it returns zero.

Comments   This service returns a bitmap that identifies which pages in a VM have had their normal lock/unlock behavior modified. It does not indicate which pages are actually locked or unlocked.

GetVMPgCount

Synopsis   Query the number of pages allocated to a specific VM.

C Prototype
```
UNS64 GetVMPgCount(unsigned hVM, unsigned ulFlags)
```

hVM   The handle of the VM to be queried.

ulFlags   This parameter must be zero.

Return Value   If successful, this service returns in EAX the total number of nonsystem pages allocated to the specified VM, and in EDX returns the total number of nonsystem pages that are allocated to the VM, but are not mapped into the VM's V86 linear address space. If this function fails (due to a bad VM handle), this service returns zero in EAX and EDX.

Get_Crit_Section_Status

Synopsis Query the owner and count of the critical section priority.

Calling Convention
VMMcall Get_Crit_Section_Status

Return Value If the critical section is owned, the carry flag is set, the ECX register contains the use count, and EBX contains the VM handle of the critical section owner. A value of zero in EBX indicates the current VM. If the critical section is not owned, the carry flag is clear and ECX is zero.

Get_Cur_VM_Handle

Synopsis Query the handle of the current VM.

Calling Convention
VMMcall Get_Cur_VM_Handle

Return Value The EBX register contains the handle to the current VM.

Comments Since the EBX register normally contains the handle of the current VM whenever Windows passes control to a VxD, this service is necessary only for interrupt service routines.

Get_Device_V86_Pages_Array

Synopsis Query the list of a VM's assigned V86 pages.

C Prototype
unsigned Get_Device_V86_Pages_Array(unsigned *hVM*, BYTE FLAT **linBuffRet*, unsigned *ulFlags*)

hVM The VM to be queried or zero if global assignment status is desired.

linBuffRet A FLAT pointer to a buffer that will receive a bitmap indicating which V86 pages are assigned. The size of the buffer must be at least 36 bytes (288 bits). Each bit represents a page in V86 memory. If the bit is set, the page is assigned. Otherwise, the page is unassigned and is available for assignment. If global assignment information is queried (hVM = 0), a set bit indicates that the page is assigned in at least one VM and is unavailable for global assignment.

ulFlags   This parameter must be zero.

Return Value   If successful, this service returns a nonzero value. If this service fails due to an invalid VM handle, it returns zero.

Comments   A VxD may use this service to determine which V86 pages are available to be assigned to a device. A VxD can assign a VM's pages to a device with the `Assign_Device_V86_Pages` service.

Although the bitmap for a particular VM may indicate that a page is available for assignment, it does not necessarily mean that the same page is available in all VMs. To determine if a page is available in all VMs, pass zero as the *hVM* parameter to obtain the global assignment status.

Get_Environment_String

Synopsis   Query the value of a DOS environment variable.

Calling Convention

VMMcall   Get_Environment_String

ESI   A FLAT pointer to an ASCIIZ string containing the environment variable name.

Return Value   If the environment variable is found, then the carry flag is clear and EDX contains a FLAT pointer to the ASCIIZ string value of the variable. Otherwise, the carry flag is set.

Comments   This service may be called only during `Sys_Critical_Init` control processing.

This service is intended to provide back-level support to existing drivers. Do not define new environment variables for your virtual driver. Instead, use Windows initialization files and the `Get_Profile_String` service.

Get_Execution_Focus

Synopsis   Query the handle of the VM that has the input focus.

Calling Convention

```
VMMcall   Get_Execution_Focus
```

Return Value   The EBX register contains the handle of the VM with the input focus.

Comments   The VM with the input focus is not the same as the current VM. Due to multitasking, a foreground VM will have the focus, but a background VM could be executing in its own time slice.
   This service may be called from a ring-0 interrupt service routine.

Get_Exec_Path

Synopsis   Query the location of Windows system files.

Calling Convention

```
VMMcall   Get_Exec_Path
```

Return Value   The EDX register contains a FLAT pointer to an ASCIIZ string containing the fully qualified (including drive and directory path) file specification of WIN386.EXE. The ECX register contains the offset in the string of the last backslash character.

Comments   A VxD can use the returned string to determine the location of the Windows SYSTEM directory. A VxD can copy the string into its own data area and use the returned ECX register to store the filename of a file in the SYSTEM directory that it needs to open.

Get_Fault_Hook_Addrs

Synopsis   Query the addresses of active fault service routines.

Calling Convention

```
VMMcall   Get_Fault_Hook_Addrs
EAX             Interrupt number
```

Return Value   If the specified interrupt number is valid, the carry flag is clear, the EDX register contains the segment:offset of the V86 mode handler, the ESI register contains the selector:offset of the protected mode handler, and the EDI register contains the FLAT address of the ring-0 fault handler. If the specified interrupt number is invalid, the carry flag is set.

Comments   The interrupt number specified in this service may not be 2 (NMI). To query that fault handler, use the `Get_NMI_Handler_Addr` service.

Get_Last_Updated_System_Time

Synopsis   Query the current system time.

Calling Convention

VMMcall   Get_Last_Updated_System_Time

Return Value   This value returns the last updated system time in the EAX register.

Comments   Unlike the `Get_System_Time` service, this service may be called at interrupt time. The returned system time is guaranteed to be monotonically increasing. VxDs may use this service to place time stamps on device events.

Get_Last_Updated_VM_Exec_Time

Synopsis   Query the current VM execution time.

Calling Convention

VMMcall   Get_Last_Updated_VM_Exec_Time

Return Value   This value returns the last updated VM execution time in the EAX register.

Comments   Unlike the `Get_VM_Exec_Time` service, this service may be called at interrupt time. The returned system time is guaranteed to be monotonically increasing. VxDs may use this service to place time stamps on device events. See the description of the `Get_VM_Exec_Time` service for the meaning of VM execution time.

Get_Machine_Info

Synopsis   Query various configuration information.

Calling Convention

```
VMMcall  Get_Machine_Info
```

Return Value   AH and AL contain the DOS major and minor version numbers, respectively; BH contains the OEM serial number; BL contains the machine model byte contained at ROM location F000:FFFE; EDX contains the equipment flags returned by the BIOS INT 11h service; if the system has an extended BIOS data area, ECX contains the ring-0 linear address of the system configuration parameters as returned by the BIOS INT 15h, function 0C0h service; if the system does not have an extended BIOS data area, ECX is zero.

The high-16 bits of EBX contain various flags. Bit 16 set indicates that the system is an 80486, bit 17 set indicates that the system is an XT with a 386 or 486 accelerator card, bit 18 set indicates that the system has Micro Channel hardware, and bit 19 set indicates that the system has EISA hardware.

Comments   Note that the values returned in AH and AL are reversed from their values as returned by DOS INT 21h function 30h.

Get_Next_Profile_String

Synopsis   Query subsequent initialization file section entries.

Calling Convention

```
VMMcall  Get_Next_Profile_String
```

EDX	Value returned from a prior call to `Get_Profile_String` or `Get_Next_Profile_String`.
EDI	A FLAT address to an ASCIIZ string of the name of the initialization file section to enumerate.

Return Value   If successful, this service returns with the carry flag clear and the FLAT address to an ASCIIZ string of the subsequent item in the specified section. If there are no more strings, this service returns with the carry flag set.

Comments   A VxD must call the `Get_Profile_String` service before calling this service in order to initialize the passed parameter in EDX.

Get_Next_VM_Handle

Synopsis   Query the next VM handle in the system list.

Calling Convention

```
VMMcall   Get_Next_VM_Handle
EBX              A VM handle.
```

Return Value   EBX contains the next VM handle in the list.

Comments   The system maintains a circular linked list of all VM handles. A VxD can start with any VM and traverse the list with this service, making sure to stop when reaching the original VM handle.
   This service may be called from a ring-0 interrupt service list.

Get_NMI_Handler_Addr

Synopsis   Query the address of the current NMI service routine.

Calling Convention

```
VMMcall   Get_NMI_Handler_Addr
```

Return Value   ESI contains the FLAT address of the current NMI service routine.

Comments   A VxD calls this service to query the current address of the NMI handler so that it may hook the interrupt with `Set_NMI_Handler_Addr` and chain to the previous handler on a nonmaskable interrupt.

Get_PM_Int_Vector

Synopsis   Query the contents of a protected mode interrupt descriptor.

Calling Convention

```
VMMcall   Get_PM_Int_Vector
EAX              The number of the interrupt to query.
```

Return Value   The CX register contains the segment of the interrupt service routine, and the EDX contains its offset. If the interrupt descriptor refers to the default interrupt reflection code (which reflects the interrupt to real mode), the zero flag is set. Otherwise, if a protected mode application or DLL has hooked the interrupt, the zero flag is clear.

Comments This service does not report whether or not the interrupt service routine is in a USE16 or USE32 segment. Use the `GetDescriptor` service on the returned selector to obtain this information.

Get_Profile_Boolean

Synopsis Query initialization file Boolean field.

Calling Convention

VMMcall   Get_Profile_Boolean

EAX   The default return value.

ESI   The FLAT address of an ASCIIZ string containing the name of the section to query, or zero to query the [386Enh] section.

EDI   The FLAT address of an ASCIIZ string containing the name of the field to query.

Return Value If the entry is found and is valid, the carry and zero flags are clear and EAX contains the 0 to indicate False and 0xFFFFFFFF to indicate True. If the value is an empty string, the zero flag is set and EAX is returned unmodified. If the field is not found or its value is not a valid Boolean value, the carry flag is set and EAX is returned unmodified.

Comments For the U.S. version of Windows, valid values for False are "No," "N," "False," "Off," and "0" (zero). Valid values for True are "Yes," "Y," "True," "On," and "1" (one).

To query the Boolean value of a string that is obtained from other than the SYSTEM.INI file, see the `Convert_Boolean_String` service.

This service may be called only during `Sys_Critical_Init` processing.

Get_Profile_Decimal_Int

Synopsis Query initialization file decimal field.

Calling Convention

VMMcall   Get_Profile_Decimal_Int

EAX   The default return value.

ESI   The FLAT address of an ASCIIZ string containing the name of the section to query, or zero to query the [386Enh] section.

EDI   The FLAT address of an ASCIIZ string containing the name of the field to query.

Return Value   If the entry is found and nonnull, the carry and zero flags are clear and EAX contains the decimal value of the entry. If the value is an empty string, the zero flag is set and EAX is returned unmodified. If the field is not found, the carry flag is set and EAX is returned unmodified.

Comments   The decimal number specified in the field may be preceded by a plus sign (+) or a minus sign (−).

To query the decimal value of a string that is obtained from other than the SYSTEM.INI file, see the Convert_Decimal_String service.

This service may be called only during Sys_Critical_Init processing.

Get_Profile_Fixed_Point

Synopsis   Query initialization file fixed-point field.

Calling Convention

VMMcall   Get_Profile_Fixed_Point

EAX   The default return value.

ECX   The number of fixed decimal places.

ESI   The FLAT address of an ASCIIZ string containing the name of the section to query, or zero to query the [386Enh] section.

EDI   The FLAT address of an ASCIIZ string containing the name of the field to query.

Return Value   If the entry is found and nonnull, the carry and zero flags are clear and EAX contains the value of the entry scaled by ECX. If the value is an empty string, the zero flag is set and EAX is returned unmodified. If the field is not found, the carry flag is set and EAX is returned unmodified.

The result in EAX is scaled by the number of decimal places. In other words, if x is the value of the string, the contents of EAX are $x*10^{ECX}$.

Comments   The number specified in the field may be preceded by a plus sign (+) or a minus sign (−).

To query the value of a string that is obtained from other than the SYSTEM.INI file, see the `Convert_Fixed_Point_String` service.

This service may be called only during `Sys_Critical_Init` processing.

Get_Profile_Hex_Int

Synopsis   Query initialization file hexadecimal field.

Calling Convention

VMMcall	Get_Profile_Hex_Int
EAX	The default return value.
ESI	The FLAT address of an ASCIIZ string containing the name of the section to query, or zero to query the [386Enh] section.
EDI	The FLAT address of an ASCIIZ string containing the name of the field to query.

Return Value   If the entry is found and nonnull, the carry and zero flags are clear and EAX contains the hexadecimal value of the entry. If the value is an empty string, the zero flag is set and EAX is returned unmodified. If the field is not found, the carry flag is set and EAX is returned unmodified.

Comments   The hexadecimal number specified in the field may be followed by an optional "H" or "h," which is ignored.

To query the hexadecimal value of a string that is obtained from other than the SYSTEM.INI file, see the `Convert_Hex_String` service.

This service may be called only during `Sys_Critical_Init` processing.

Get_Profile_String

Synopsis   Query initialization file string.

Calling Convention

VMMcall   Get_Profile_String

EDX   A FLAT pointer to an ASCIIZ string containing the default return value.

ESI   The FLAT address of an ASCIIZ string containing the name of the section to query, or zero to query the [386Enh] section.

EDI   The FLAT address of an ASCIIZ string containing the name of the field to query.

Return Value   If the entry is found, the carry flag is clear and EDX contains a pointer to the system copy of the ASCIIZ value of the string. If the field is not found, the carry flag is set and EDX is returned unmodified.

Comments   This service returns the address of the system copy of the string. You must not modify the system copy; copy it to your VxD's data area if you need to modify it.

The returned string may be NUL; that is, EDX may point to a zero byte.

This service may be called only during Sys_Critical_Init processing.

Get_PSP_Segment

Synopsis   Query the segment address of the Windows session PSP.

Calling Convention

VMMcall   Get_PSP_Segment

Return Value   The AX register contains the V86 segment of the PSP. The high 16 bits of EAX are zero.

Comments   The PSP, or program segment prefix, contains information that may be useful to a device driver. Do not use this service to query DOS environment variables or the path of the Windows session: use the Get_Environment_String and Get_Exec_Path services instead.

It is trivial to convert the returned segment to a linear address simply by shifting it left by 4 bits.

This service may be called only during `Sys_Critical_Init` processing.

Get_System_Time

Synopsis   Query the current system time.

Calling Convention

VMMcall   Get_System_Time

Return Value   EAX contains the current system time, in milliseconds.

Comments   The system time is the time elapsed since Windows was started. VxDs may use this service to place time stamps on device events.

This service may not be called during a ring-0 interrupt: use the `Get_Last_Updated_System_Time` service, instead.

Get_Sys_VM_Handle

Synopsis   Query the handle of the system VM.

Calling Convention

VMMcall   Get_Sys_VM_Handle

Return Value   The EBX register contains the handle of the system VM.

Get_Time_Slice_Granularity

Synopsis   Query the time-slice allocation unit.

Calling Convention

VMMcall   Get_Time_Slice_Granularity

Return Value   The EAX register contains the time-slice allocation unit, in milliseconds.

Comments   VM time slices are an integral multiple of the value returned by this function. This returned value is also the minimum time-slice value.

Get_Time_Slice_Info

Synopsis   Query time-slicer status.

Calling Convention

```
VMMcall  Get_Time_Slice_Info
```

Return Value   The EAX register contains the number VMs scheduled, EBX contains the handle of the current VM, and ECX contains the number of idle VMs.

Comments   This service may be called during ring-0 interrupt service.

Get_Time_Slice_Priority

Synopsis   Query VM time-slice parameters.

Calling Convention

```
VMMcall  Get_Time_Slice_Priority
EBX             The handle of the VM to be queried.
```

Return Value   The EAX register contains the CB_VM_Status flags from the VM's control block, ECX contains the foreground time-slice priority, EDX contains the background time-slice priority, and ESI contains the percentage of CPU time assigned to the VM.

Comments   The control block status flags specify the Exclusive, Background, and High-priority background flags for the VM.

The percentage of time assigned to a VM may be less than the actual percentage used by a VM, since other VMs may release their time slices, if idle.

Get_V86_Int_Vector

Synopsis   Query the V86 interrupt vector for the current VM.

Calling Convention

```
VMMcall  Get_V86_Int_Vector
EAX             The interrupt number to query.
```

Return Value   The CX register contains the segment of the interrupt service routine (ISR), and DX contains the offset of the ISR.

Comments   The value returned is the 32-bits at the VM-linear address [EAX*4].

Get_VMM_Version

Synopsis   Return the version number of the virtual machine manager (VMM).

Calling Convention
```
VMMcall   Get_VMM_Version
```

Return Value   The AH register contains the major version number and the AL register contains the minor version number. For version 3.10, for example, AH contains 03h, and AL contains 0Ah.

Get_VM_Exec_Time

Synopsis   Query the current VM execution time.

Calling Convention
```
VMMcall   Get_VM_Exec_Time
```

Return Value   EAX contains the current VM execution time, in milliseconds.

Comments   The VM execution time is the amount of time that the VM has executed. This does not include time that the VM is suspended or when other VMs execute. This is a "virtual time" for the virtual machine. VxDs may use this service to place time stamps on device events.

   This service may not be called during a ring-0 interrupt: use the `Get_Last_Updated_VM_Exec_Time` service, instead.

HeapAllocate

Synopsis   Allocate a small block of memory from the VMM heap.

C Prototype

```
unsigned HeapAllocate(unsigned nBytes, unsigned ulFlags)
```

nBytes	The number of bytes to allocate.
ulFlags	Bit 0 (`HeapZeroInit`) is set to indicate that the memory should be zeroed. If not set, the contents of the allocated block are indeterminate. All other bits must be zero.

Return Value   If successful, this service returns the FLAT address of the newly allocated block of memory. If this service fails, it returns zero.

Comments   The returned pointer is guaranteed to be 32-bit aligned. A VxD calls this service to allocate relatively small memory blocks. A VxD calls this service instead of the page allocation services when allocation units of 4096 bytes are too large for the intended use.

HeapFree

Synopsis   De-allocate previously allocated heap memory.

C Prototype

```
unsigned HeapFree(unsigned linBlock, unsigned ulFlags)
```

linBlock	The FLAT memory address of a block of memory previously allocated by the `HeapAllocate` or `HeapReallocate` service.
ulFlags	This parameter must be zero.

Return Value   If successful, this service returns a nonzero value. Otherwise, this service returns zero.

HeapGetSize

Synopsis   Query the size of a block allocated from the heap.

C Prototype

```
unsigned HeapGetSize(unsigned linBlock, unsigned ulFlags)
```

linBlock	A FLAT pointer to a block of memory previously allocated by the `HeapAllocate` or `HeapReallocate` service.
ulFlags	This parameter must be zero.

Return Value If successful, this service returns the size, in bytes, of the allocated block. If this service fails, it returns zero.

HeapReallocate

Synopsis Re-allocate a previously allocated block of memory.

C Prototype
```
unsigned HeapReallocate(unsigned linBlock, unsigned
nBytes, unsigned ulFlags)
```

linBlock	The FLAT address of a block of memory previously allocated by the `HeapAllocate` service.
nBytes	The nonzero size, in bytes, of the new block of memory.
ulFlags	Only one of three flag bits may be set. If no bit is set, Windows copies the previous contents of the block of memory to the new block. If the new size of the block is larger than the old size, the contents of the expanded area are indeterminate. The other bits are defined as follows:

Bit	Description
0	If the size of the block of memory is increasing, this bit indicates that Windows should initialize the expanded area with zeros.
1	Indicates that Windows should initialize the entire new block of memory including the amount up to the old size (if increasing in size) to zero.
2	Indicates that Windows should not copy the contents of the old block of memory to the newly allocated block.

Return Value If successful, this service returns the FLAT address of the newly allocated block of memory. If this service fails, it returns zero.

Comments The returned address is not related to the passed *linBlock* address. The previous location of the block of memory, specified by *linBlock*, is not valid after a successful return from this service.

Hook_Device_PM_API

Synopsis   Hook the protected mode services entry point of another VxD.

Calling Convention

VMMcall   Hook_Device_PM_API

EAX   The device ID of the VxD to hook.

ESI   The FLAT address of the new handler for the other VxD's
                       service.

Return Value   If successful, this service returns with the carry flag clear
and the previous service routine address in ESI. If this service fails, due to
the absence of the specified VxD or the absence of a protected mode entry
point therein, this service returns with the carry flag set.

Comments   The new service routine specified is called whenever any
protected mode program requests a service from the specified VxD. Normally, the replacement routine will filter certain requests and pass others
on to the previous API service routine.

Hook_Device_Service

Synopsis   Hook another VxD's service or a VMM service entry point.

Calling Convention

VMMcall   Hook_Device_Service

EAX   The high 16 bits of EAX contains the device ID of the VxD
                       whose service is to be hooked. If a VMM service is to be
                       hooked, the upper 16 bits of EAX contain 0x0001. The low
                       16 bits of EAX contain the service ID of the service to
                       hook.

ESI   The FLAT address of the new handler for the other VxD's
                       service.

Return Value   If successful, this service returns with the carry flag clear
and the address of the previous service routine in ESI. If this service fails,
due to the absence of the specified VxD or the absence of the specified service, the carry flag is set.

Comments   All of the VxD service equates defined in the DDK are absolute numbers—not actual linker external references to the code. The low 16 bits of EAX contain the value of the service equate. For example, the following code hooks the `Get_VMM_Version` service:

```
mov      eax,1*10000h+Get_VMM_Version
mov      esi,OFFSET32 Fake_VMM_VerHook
VMMcall  Hook_Device_Service
```

Hook_Device_V86_API

Synopsis   Hook the V86 mode services entry point of another VxD.

Calling Convention

```
VMMcall  Hook_Device_V86_API
```

EAX   The device ID of the VxD to hook.

ESI   The FLAT address of the new handler for the other VxD's service.

Return Value   If successful, this service returns with the carry flag clear and the previous service routine address in ESI. If this service fails, due to the absence of the specified VxD or the absence of a V86 mode entry point therein, this service returns with the carry flag set.

Comments   The new service routine specified is called whenever any V86 mode program requests a service from the specified VxD. Normally, the replacement routine will filter certain requests and pass others on to the previous API service routine.

Hook_NMI_Event

Synopsis   Establish a nonmaskable interrupt callback.

Calling Convention

```
VMMcall  Hook_NMI_Event
```

ESI   The FLAT address of the callback routine.

Return Value   *None.*

Comments   A VxD is not allowed to call any VxD services when processing an NMI. This service allows a VxD to establish a callback that Windows calls after an NMI but when the VxD *is* permitted to call VxD services.

Since the callback routine is called after the NMI has been processed, the callback is not a normal interrupt service routine and cannot sense or acknowledge the interrupt if its own device caused the NMI. Therefore, the VxD must also hook into the actual NMI interrupt service chain with the Set_NMI_Handler_Addr service in order to acknowledge (send EOI to) its own device and set a flag for the callback to examine.

Hook_PM_Fault

Synopsis   Register a fault handler for the specified protected mode fault.

Calling Convention

VMMcall   Hook_PM_Fault

EAX   The interrupt number of the protected mode fault to hook. This value should correspond to one of the processor faults represented by interrupt numbers 00h, 01h, and 03h through 1Fh.

ESI   The FLAT address of the fault service routine. The callback is entered with interrupts disabled, EBX contains the current VM handle, and EBP points to the client register frame. The fault service routine does not perform an IRET to exit, but instead performs a RET instruction. If the callback chains to the previous service routine, it must preserve the contents of all registers.

Return Value   If successful, this service returns with the carry flag cleared and the address of the previous fault service routine in ESI, or zero if none was previously registered. If it fails, the carry flag is set.

Comments   This service is intended to allow a VxD to hook VM protected mode processor faults. To hook interrupt vectors in order to perform API mapping, use the Set_PM_Int_Vector service.

Hook_V86_Fault

Synopsis Register a fault handler for the specified V86 mode fault.

Calling Convention

VMMcall   Hook_V86_Fault

EAX   The interrupt number of the V86 mode fault to hook. This value should correspond to one of the processor faults represented by interrupt numbers 00h, 01h, and 03h through 1Fh.

ESI   The FLAT address of the fault service routine. The callback is entered with interrupts disabled, EBX contains the current VM handle, and EBP points to the client register frame. The fault service routine does not perform an IRET to exit, but instead performs a RET instruction. If the callback chains to the previous service routine, it must preserve the contents of all registers.

Return Value If successful, this service returns with the carry flag cleared and the address of the previous V86 mode fault service routine in ESI, or zero if none was previously registered. If it fails, the carry flag is set.

Comments This service is intended to allow a VxD to hook V86 mode processor faults. To hook V86 mode interrupt vectors, use the Hook_V86_Int_Chain service.

Hook_V86_Int_Chain

Synopsis Register a service routine for a V86 mode interrupt.

Calling Convention

VMMcall   Hook_V86_Int_Chain

EAX   The interrupt number to hook.

EBX   The FLAT address of the callback routine in the VxD. The callback indicates that it processed the interrupt by returning with the carry flag clear. Otherwise, if the carry flag is set, Windows passes control to the next callback in the interrupt service chain.

Return Value   If successful, this service returns with the carry flag clear. Otherwise, if the interrupt number is invalid, the carry flag is set.

Comments   This service allows VxD code to service a V86 mode interrupt. This is faster than creating a callback in the VM and hooking the interrupt with `Set_V86_Int_Vector`, since the latter method requires an extra ring transition to return to V86 mode to simulate the V86-mode interrupt.

Hook_V86_Page

Synopsis   Register page-fault handler for V86-mode pages.

Calling Convention

VMMcall   Hook_V86_Page

EAX	The page number of the page for which page faults are to be handled. This value may range from 0A0h to 0FFh, the upper memory area.
ESI	The FLAT address of a callback that Windows will call on the page fault. When Windows calls the callback routine the EAX register contains the faulting page number, EBX contains the current VM handle. Note that EBP does *not* refer to the client register structure. The callback routine need preserve only EBP and the stack and segment registers; all other registers need not be preserved

Return Value   If successful, this service returns with the carry flag clear. Otherwise, if the page number is invalid or the page is already hooked, the carry flag is set.

Comments   A VxD uses this service to virtualize a memory-mapped device, such as a display adapter. When the callback routine returns, the faulting instruction is re-executed. This allows the VxD to assign the page to a valid physical memory address using the one of the `MapIntoV86`, `PhysIntoV86`, or `LinMapIntoV86` services.

Hook_VMM_Fault

Synopsis   Register a fault handler for the specified ring-0 fault.

Calling Convention

```
VMMcall    Hook_VMM_Fault
```

EAX   The interrupt number of the ring-0 fault to hook. This value should correspond to one of the processor faults represented by interrupt numbers 00h, 01h, and 03h through 1Fh.

ESI   The FLAT address of the fault service routine. The callback is entered with interrupts disabled, EBX contains the current VM handle. The callback may call only asynchronous services: those that are callable from a ring-0 interrupt. The fault service routine does not perform an IRET to exit, but instead performs a RET instruction. If the callback chains to the previous service routine, it must preserve the contents of all registers.

Return Value   If successful, this service returns with the carry flag cleared and the address of the previous ring-0 fault service routine in ESI, or zero if none was previously registered. If it fails, the carry flag is set.

Comments   This service is intended to allow a VxD to hook ring-0 processor faults before the VMM services them. In order to do this, the VxD must call this service during or after `Device_Init` control processing. If called during `Sys_Critical_Init` processing, the VMM will service the fault before passing control the VxD's service routine.

To hook hardware interrupts, use the `VPICD_Call_When_Hw_Int` service. To hook the nonmaskable interrupt, use the `Hook_NMI_Event` and `Set_NMI_Handler_Addr` services.

Install_IO_Handler

Synopsis   Register a callback routine for I/O port virtualization.

Calling Convention

```
VMMcall    Install_IO_Handler
```

EDX   The I/O port address of the port to virtualize.

ESI   The FLAT address of the callback procedure. See the description of the `Simulate_IO` service for callback entry and exit parameters.

Return Value   If successful, this service returns with the carry flag cleared. If unable to hook the I/O port, then the carry flag is set.

Comments   This service may be called only during `Device_Init` control processing.

   To hook multiple ports, call the `Install_Mult_IO_Handlers` service.

Install_Mult_IO_Handlers

Synopsis   Register multiple callback routines for I/O port virtualization.

Calling Convention

VMMcall   Install_Mult_IO_Handlers

EDI   The FLAT address of a table created with the `Begin_Vxd_IO_Table`, `Vxd_IO`, and `End_Vxd_IO_Table` macros.

Return Value   If successful, this service exits with the carry flag cleared. Otherwise, this service exits with the carry flag set and the EDX register set to the I/O port address corresponding to the failing hook.

Comments   The following illustrates how to initialize a table that hooks two ports:

```
Begin_Vxd_IO_Table TableName
    Vxd_IO      wPort1, linCallback1
    Vxd_IO      wPort2, linCallback2
End_Vxd_IO_Table   TableName
```

The *wPort1* and *wPort2* parameters specify the ports to hook and the *linCallback1* and *linCallback2* parameters specify the callback routines for each port. The callback parameters may all refer to the same callback routine. See the description of the `Simulate_IO` service for details on the callback routine.

List_Allocate

Synopsis   Allocate a new list element.

Calling Convention

```
VMMcall   List_Allocate
ESI             A list handle obtained from a prior call to List_Create.
```

Return Value   If successful, this service returns with the carry flag cleared and with the FLAT address of the new element in EAX. If this service fails, its return depends on the list creation flags.

Comments   The returned address of the element may be used to store VxD related information. The number of bytes available for use is specified when List_Create is called. See the description of the List_Create service for a general discussion of the list management services.

List_Attach

Synopsis   Insert a list element at the head of an existing list.

Calling Convention

```
VMMcall   List_Attach
EAX             The element to insert.
ESI             A list handle obtained from a prior call to List_Create.
```

Return Value   *None.*

Comments   See the description of the List_Create service for a general discussion of the list management services.

List_Attach_Tail

Synopsis   Insert a list element at the tail of an existing list.

Calling Convention

```
VMMcall   List_Attach_Tail
EAX             The element to insert.
ESI             A list handle obtained from a prior call to List_Create.
```

Return Value   *None.*

Comments See the description of the `List_Create` service for a general discussion of the list management services.

List_Create

Synopsis Create a linked list.

Calling Convention

```
VMMcall  List_Create
```

EAX   List attribute flags, as follow:

   LF_Use_Heap   Allocate each element from the system heap. This flag cannot be combined with `LF_Async`.

   LF_Async   Allow the list manipulation services to be called from a ring-0 interrupt service routine. If this flag is set, all calls to the list manipulation services must be made with interrupt disabled, even if the caller is not processing an interrupt. This flag cannot be combined with `LF_Use_Heap`.

   LF_Alloc_Error   If clear, this flag indicates that a failure to allocate a list element with the `List_Allocate` service will crash the current VM and not return to the calling VxD. Otherwise, an allocation failure will cause `List_Allocate` to return with the carry flag set.

ECX   The size, in bytes, of each list element.

Return Value If successful, this service returns with the carry flag clear and the list handle in ESI. If the service is unable to create a list, it returns with the carry flag set.

Comments This service does not allocate any list elements, but only the initial structures required to maintain a list. To allocate a list element, use the `List_Allocate` service.

Unless the `LF_Use_Heap` flag is set, list elements are allocated from a private memory pool. If the size of each element is relatively large, set the `LF_Use_Heap` flag so that elements are allocated from the system heap.

List_Deallocate

Synopsis   De-allocate a list element.

Calling Convention

VMMcall   List_Deallocate

EAX   The element to de-allocate. It must not be in any list.

ESI   A list handle obtained from a prior call to List_Create.

Return Value   *None.*

Modifies   EAX

Comments   An element may not be referenced after it is de-allocated.

List_Destroy

Synopsis   Destroy a list.

Calling Convention

VMMcall   List_Destroy

ESI   A list handle obtained from a prior call to List_Create.

Return Value   *None.*

Modifies   ESI

Comments   This service automatically de-allocates any elements that are on the list.

List_Get_First

Synopsis   Obtain the first element from a list.

Calling Convention

VMMcall   List_Get_First

ESI   A list handle obtained from a prior call to List_Create.

Return Value   If the list is not empty, EAX contains the address of the first element. If the list is empty, EAX is zero.

Comments   This service only returns the address of the element: it does not remove the element from the list. The `List_Remove_First` service removes the first element from a list and returns a reference to it.

There is no service to obtain the last element of a list.

List_Get_Next

Synopsis   Get the next element of a list.

Calling Convention

```
VMMcall   List_Get_Next
```

EAX   The address of a list element.

ESI   A list handle obtained from a prior call to `List_Create`.

Return Value   If the given element is not the tail of the list, EAX contains the address of its following element. Otherwise, EAX is zero.

Comments   A VxD uses this service to traverse a list; it obtains the first element by calling the `List_Get_First` service.

There is no service to traverse the list in reverse order.

This service only returns the address of the element: it does not remove the element from the list. the `List_Remove` service removes an arbitrary element from a list and returns a reference to it.

List_Insert

Synopsis   Insert a list element after a specified element in an existing list.

Calling Convention

```
VMMcall   List_Insert
```

EAX   The element to insert.

ECX   The element after which the new element is to be inserted.

ESI   A list handle obtained from a prior call to `List_Create`.

Return Value *None.*

Comments See the description of the List_Create service for a general discussion of the list management services.

List_Remove

Synopsis Remove a list element from a list.

Calling Convention
```
VMMcall   List_Remove
EAX              The element to remove.
ESI              A list handle obtained from a prior call to List_Create.
```

Return Value *None.*

Comments After removing an element from a list, the VxD should deallocate the element with List_Deallocate, insert it back into the same list or insert it into another list with elements of the same size. See the description of the List_Create service for a general discussion of the list management services.

List_Remove_First

Synopsis Remove the last list element from a list.

Calling Convention
```
VMMcall   List_Remove_First
EAX              The element to remove.
ESI              A list handle obtained from a prior call to List_Create.
```

Return Value *None.*

Comments After removing an element from a list, the VxD should deallocate the element with List_Deallocate, insert it back into the same list, or insert it into another list with elements of the same size. See the description of the List_Create service for a general discussion of the list management services.

MapIntoV86

Synopsis   Map memory into a VM's V86 memory space.

C Prototype
unsigned MapIntoV86(unsigned *hMem*, unsigned *hVM*, unsigned *ulFirstPageVM*, unsigned *nPages*, unsigned *ulFirst-Page*, unsigned *ulFlags*)

hMem	A memory block handle returned from a call to PageAllocate or PageReallocate or the handle to the system NUL page returned from a call to GetNulPageHandle.
hVM	The handle of the VM to have its V86 memory remapped.
ulFirstPageVM	The page number of the first page in V86 memory to be remapped. This value must range from 10h to 10Fh and must have been previously assigned by a call to Allocate_Global_V86_Data_Area with the GVDAPageAlign attribute.
nPages	The number of pages to map.
ulFirstPage	The page offset into the memory block specified by *hMem*.
ulFlags	Under the debugging version of Windows, if the PageDEBUGNulFault flag (bit 16) is set and if *hMem* is the handle to the system NUL page, an access to the mapped region will cause a debugger exception. Otherwise, accesses to the memory are ignored.

Return Value   If successful, this service returns a nonzero value. If this service fails, it returns zero.

Comments   the P_USER, P_PRES and P_WRITE attributes are set and the P_DIRTY and P_ACC attributes are cleared for mapped pages. The PG_TYPE flag is copied from the source memory block. See the description of the PageAllocate service for the meaning of these flags.

Depending on the type of the Windows page-swap device, the memory block mapped into V86 address space may become page-locked when the specified VM is dispatched.

Memory that belongs to one VM may be mapped into another VM, but results are unpredictable if the owning VM terminates before the termination of the VM into which the pages are mapped. If your VxD maps pages between VMs, be sure to remap the pages to valid values when the owning VM terminates.

If you need to map VxD memory into a VM for API mapping, use the `V86MMGR_Map_Pages` service.

MapPhysToLinear

Synopsis Query the linear address of specific physical memory.

C Prototype
```
unsigned MapPhysToLinear(unsigned physMemory, unsigned
nBytes, unsigned ulFlags)
```

physMemory   The 32-bit physical memory address to query.

nBytes   The size of the physical memory area.

ulFlags   This parameter must be zero.

Return Value If successful, this service returns the linear address of the physical memory. If it fails, it returns 0xFFFFFFFF.

Comments The linear address returned by this service is assigned the first time this service is called, does not change for a particular memory address, and is valid throughout the Windows session.

To map physical memory into V86-addressable memory, use the `Allocate_Global_V86_Data_Area` or `Assign_Device_V86_Pages` service to assign the V86 memory and the `PhysIntoV86` service to map the physical memory into V86 memory.

Map_Flat

Synopsis Query the linear mapping of a V86 or protected mode VM address.

Calling Convention
```
VMMcall  Map_Flat
```

AH   The offset in the client register structure of the segment register containing the segment or selector of the address.

AL   The offset in the client register structure of the offset register containing the offset of the address.

Return Value   This service returns the linear value of the address in the specified client registers.

Comments   This service accounts for the possibility that the client may be running in V86 mode, in a 16-bit protected mode code segment, or in a 32-bit protected mode code segment.

ModifyPageBits

Synopsis   Modify memory page attributes.

C Prototype

unsigned ModifyPageBits(unsigned *hVM*, unsigned *ulFirstPageVM*, unsigned *nPages*, unsigned *ulBitsOff*, unsigned *ulBitsOn*, unsigned *ulType*, unsigned *ulFlags*)

hVM	The handle of the VM that is to have its page attribute modified.
ulFirstPageVM	The page number of the first page in the VM's V86 memory to have its attributes modified.
nPages	The number of pages to be modified. The specified range of pages must lie within the first VM-specific page and page 10Fh.
ulBitsOff	Zero-bits in this parameter correspond to page attribute bits that will be reset (set to zero). One-bits in this parameter correspond to page attribute bits that will not be reset by this service. Any combination of the P_PRES, P_WRITE, or P_USER attributes may be specified (in negated form) in this parameter.
ulBitsOn	One-bits in this parameter correspond to page attribute bits that will be set (set to one). Zero-bits in this parameter correspond to page attribute bits that will not be set by this service. Any combination of the P_WRITE, or P_USER attributes may be specified in this parameter. The P_PRES attribute may *not* be specified here.
ulType	This parameter must be either PG_HOOKED (0x7) to enable page hooks for the specified range of pages, or PG_IGNORE (0xFFFFFFFF) to leave the page-hook attribute of the pages unchanged (hooked or not).

ulFlags   This parameter must be zero.

Return Value   If successful, this service returns a nonzero value. If this service fails, it returns zero.

Comments   If the same attribute bit is specified in *ulBitsOff* and *ulBitsOn*, the results are unpredictable.

The P_PRES bit indicates that the specified page is mapped to physical memory. An attempt to access the page when this bit is reset causes a page fault and causes the page hook callback to be called if the page has the PG_HOOKED attribute. A VxD cannot use this service to set this bit but must instead map the page to some physical memory to set it. A VxD resets this bit when it needs to detect its access by a program running in a VM. Typically, the callback routine will perform the appropriate mapping to ensure proper virtualization or contingency management.

The P_USER bit indicates that the specified page is accessible from nonring-0 code. If this bit is reset, the page is accessible only from ring-0 code. If this bit is set, an attempt to access the page from nonring-0 code causes a page fault.

The P_WRITE bit indicates that the specified page may not be overwritten. If this bit is set, an attempt to modify the contents of the page causes a page fault.

The MapIntoV86 service also has the side-effect of modifying page attribute bits.

No_Fail_Resume_VM

Synopsis   Resume a suspended VM.

Calling Convention

VMMcall   No_Fail_Resume_VM
EBX   The handle of the VM to resume.

Return Value   *None.*

Comments   If the VM cannot be resumed (because of insufficient physical memory), this service will notify the user and Windows will resume the VM when it is possible. To suppress resuming the VM in the case of error, use the Resume_VM service.

OpenFile

Synopsis   Open a Windows initialization file.

Calling Convention

```
VMMcall   OpenFile
```

EDX   A FLAT pointer to an ASCIIZ string that contains the file specification of the file to open. If the specification includes a drive letter or directory specifications, this service performs no path searching. Otherwise, the first matching file in one of the following directories (in the following order) is opened:
  1) The Windows directory.
  2) The Windows SYSTEM directory.
  3) The directory that Windows was started from.
  4) The directories in the current PATH environment variable.

EDI   The address of a buffer into which the matching file specification of the opened file is returned. This is not necessarily the fully qualified path, but rather the string formed by stepping through the above list of directories and attempting to open the file.

Return Value   If successful, this service returns with the carry flag clear and the file handle in AX.

Comments   This service may be called only during `Device_Init` control processing. The file may be accessed using the normal INT 21h services for reading only (see the description of the `Exec_VxD_Int` service). The file must be closed before returning from `Device_Init` control processing.

PageAllocate

Synopsis   Allocate and conditionally map linear memory.

C Prototype

```
UNS64 PageAllocate(unsigned nPages, unsigned ulType,
unsigned hVM, unsigned ulAlignMask, unsigned physLo,
unsigned physHi, unsigned physMemory, unsigned ulFlags)
```

nPages   The number of pages to allocate.

ulType	The type of pages to allocate. It may be one of either `PG_VM`, `PG_SYS`, or `PG_HOOKED`. `PG_VM` memory is assigned exclusive to a single VM's address space. `PG_SYS` memory is globally owned and may be assigned to any VM. `PG_HOOKED` memory is memory that is typically used to virtualize memory mapped hardware. Invalid accesses to `PG_HOOKED` memory cause Windows to call a callback routine established by the `Hook_V86_Page` service.
hVM	The handle of the VM to which the memory is to be assigned or zero if `PG_SYS` memory is being allocated.
ulAlignMask	If the `PageUseAlign` flag (see *ulFlags*, following) is set, this parameter specifies additional alignment requirements. The returned physical memory page number ANDed with this value is guaranteed to be zero. For example, to guarantee 128K-byte (32-page) alignment, this parameter is 0x1F (= 32 − 1). The alignment must be a power of 2 number of pages (4K, 8K, 16K, 32K, 64K, or 128K bytes, for example).
physLo	If the `PageUseAlign` flag (see *ulFlags*, following) is set, this parameter specifies the minimum acceptable physical memory page number to map to the allocated linear memory. If there is no minimum limit, specify zero for this parameter.
physHi	If the `PageUseAlign` flag (see *ulFlags*, following) is set, this parameter specifies the maximum acceptable physical memory page number *plus one* to map to the allocated linear memory. If there is no maximum limit, specify 0xFFFFFFFF for this parameter.
linPhysRet	If the `PageUseAlign` flag (see *ulFlags*, following) is set, this parameter specifies the address of a 32-bit buffer into which the page number of the first physical page is returned. Unless the `PageContig` flag of the *ulFlags* parameter is set, the physical page number of any subsequent pages cannot be determined from this parameter (use the `CopyPageTable` service).
ulFlags	This parameter specifies various allocation flags:

The `PageZeroInit` flag indicates that the newly allocated memory is to be zeroed. If not set, the contents of initially mapped memory pages are indeterminate.

The `PageUseAlign` flag indicates that the service is to respect the *ulAlignMask*, *physLo*, *physHi*, and *linPhysRet* parameters. When this flag is set, the `PageFixed` flag must also be set. This flag may be set only during `Device_Init` control processing. If this flag is not set, the related parameters are ignored.

If the `PageUseAlign` flag is set, the `PageContig` flag indicates that the allocated physical memory pages must be physically contiguous. If this flag is not set, the allocated physical pages may be scattered throughout physical memory.

The `PageFixed` flag indicates that the allocated pages must be permanently assigned to physical pages. Fixed pages may never be unlocked, such as by `PageReallocate`. This flag must be set if the `PageUseAlign` flag is set. If this flag is not set, the physical memory assigned to the linear memory may change if `PageReallocate` is called.

The `PageLocked` flag indicates that physical memory should be assigned to the allocated linear pages. The memory can be unlocked with the `PageUnlock` service. If this flag is not set, only linear space is allocated—physical memory is not assigned until the linear memory is accessed. This flag may not be combined with `PageFixed` or `PageLockedIfDP`.

The `PageLockedIfDP` flag has the same function as `PageLocked` but only if the swap device accesses the disk through V86 mode code such as DOS or the BIOS. If the swap device accesses the hardware directly, without executing V86 mode code, this parameter has no effect. This flag may not be combined with `PageFixed` or `PageLocked`. This flag may not be set in calls to this service during `Sys_Critical_Init` or `Device_Init` control processing.

Return Value   If successful, this service returns with the handle to the memory block in EAX and the ring-0 FLAT address in EDX. Note also the return buffer specified by the *linPhysRet* parameter. If this service fails, it returns zero in EAX and EDX.

PageDiscardPages

Synopsis   Discard or page-out demand-loadable pages.

C Prototype

unsigned PageDiscardPages(unsigned *ulFirstPage*, unsigned
hVM, unsigned *nPages*, unsigned *ulFlags*)

ulFirstPage	The number of the first linear page to be flagged.
hVM	If *ulFirstPage* is less than 0x0110 or refers to a V86 page in high linear memory, *hVM* specifies the VM to which the *ulFirstPage* parameter applies. Otherwise, *hVM* must be zero.
nPages	The number of pages, starting at *ulFirstPage*, to flag.
ulFlags	The PageDiscard flag indicates that the specified pages do not need to be paged out to disk: their contents are no longer needed. If this flag is not set, the page is paged-out to disk at the next opportunity. If PageDiscard is set, the PageZeroInit flag indicates that the next time that any of the pages are accessed, they are to be initialized with zeros before the access is satisfied. If PageDiscard is set and PageZeroInit is not set, the next read from any of the pages will return indeterminate data.

Return Value   If successful, this service returns a nonzero value. If this service fails, it returns zero.

Comments   Despite its name, this service will also accelerate the paging-out of a page to disk, without discarding it. To tell Windows that the contents of the page are no longer needed, set the PageDiscard flag.

PageFree

Synopsis   De-allocate memory pages.

C Prototype

unsigned PageFree(unsigned *hMem*, unsigned *ulFlags*)

hMem	A memory handle returned from a prior call to PageAllocate or PageReallocate.
ulFlags	This parameter must be zero.

Return Value   If successful, this service returns a nonzero value. If this service fails, it returns zero.

Comments   Windows will not automatically free pages assigned to a VM when the VM terminates.

PageGetAllocInfo

Synopsis   Query the amount of free linear and physical memory.

C Prototype
```
UNS64 PageGetAllocInfo(unsigned ulFlags)
```
ulFlags   The parameter must be zero.

Return Value   On return, EAX contains the largest linear space in pages that can be allocated with a *single* `PageAllocate` call without specifying `PageLocked` or `PageFixed`. EDX contains the number of physical pages available to be locked.

Comments   Compare this service with the `GetFreePageCount` service. The former service returns the largest contiguous linear area, while the latter service returns the total number of unallocated pages.

PageGetSizeAddr

Synopsis   Query the size of an allocated memory block.

C Prototype
```
UNS64 PageGetSizeAddr(unsigned hMem, unsigned ulFlags)
```
hMem   A memory handle obtained from a prior call to `PageAllocate` or `PageReallocate`.

ulFlags   This parameter must be zero.

Return Value   If successful, this service returns the number of 4K pages in the block in EAX and the linear address of the block in EDX. If this service fails, both EAX and EDX are zero.

PageLock

Synopsis   Increment page lock count.

C Prototype
unsigned PageLock(unsigned *hMem*, unsigned *nPages*,
unsigned *ulFirstPage*, unsigned *ulFlags*)

hMem	A memory handle obtained from a prior call to PageAllocate or PageReallocate.
nPages	The number of pages to lock.
ulFirstPage	The page number of the first page to lock, relative to the first page specified by *hMem*.
ulFlags	PageLockedIfDP may be set (see the PageAllocate description).

Return Value   If successful, this service returns a nonzero value. If this service fails, it returns zero.

Comments   If the previous lock count was zero, this service assigns physical pages to the specified memory range. If the pages have been previously accessed, their contents are paged in from disk into the assigned physical memory.

The calling VxD should be prepared for an error return from this service, which will occur if there is insufficient physical memory to satisfy the request.

Calling this service consumes available physical memory, an extremely precious resource. Unlock the memory as soon as possible.

PageReallocate

Synopsis   Re-allocate a block of memory.

C Prototype
UNS64 PageReallocate(unsigned *hMem*, unsigned *nPages*,
unsigned *ulFlags*)

hMem	A memory handle obtained from a prior call to PageAllocate or PageReallocate.
nPages	The new size of the memory block, in 4K-byte pages.
ulFlags	Various initialization flags:

If the size of the block is increasing, the `PageZeroInit` flag indicates that the additional pages are to be initialized to zero. This flag may not be combined with `PageZeroReInit` or `PageNoCopy`.

The `PageZeroReInit` flag indicates that the new block of memory is to be entirely initialized with zeroes, discarding the previous contents of the memory. This flag may not be combined with `PageZeroInit` or `PageNoCopy`.

The `PageNoCopy` flag indicates that the contents of the previous memory block do not need to be copied to the new memory block. This flag may not be combined with `PageZeroInit` or `PageZeroReInit`.

If none of the above three flags is set, the previous contents of the memory block are copied to the new block, up to the size of the smaller block. If the new block is larger than the original block, the contents of the expanded area are indeterminate.

Either the `PageLocked` or `PageLockedIfDP` flags may also be set. See the description of the `PageAllocate` service for details.

Return Value   If successful, this service returns with the handle to the memory block in EAX and the ring-0 FLAT address in EDX. If this service fails, it returns zero in EAX and EDX.

Comments   This service cannot re-allocate memory that is currently locked (`PageLocked`) or that was originally allocated as fixed (`PageFixed`). Note that memory that has been mapped into a V86 context with the `MapIntoV86` service is normally locked and cannot be re-allocated.

The returned memory handle and linear address are not necessarily related to the values passed in. If this service succeeds, you may assume that the old handle (*hMem*) and base linear address are invalid.

PageUnlock

Synopsis   Decrement page lock count.

C Prototype
```
unsigned PageUnlock(unsigned hMem, unsigned nPages,
unsigned ulFirstPage, unsigned ulFlags)
```

hMem   A memory handle obtained from a prior call to `PageAllocate` or `PageReallocate`.

nPages   The number of pages that are to have their lock counts decremented.

ulFirstPage   The page number of the first page to have its lock count decremented, relative to the first page specified by *hMem*.

ulFlags   `PageLockedIfDP` may be set (see the `PageAllocate` description). The `PageMarkPageOut` flag indicates that if the pages are unlocked, then the contents of the specified pages are to be paged out to disk at the earliest opportunity.

Return Value   If successful, this service returns a nonzero value. If this service fails, it returns zero.

Comments   If the previous lock count was 1, this service marks the specified pages as pageable. This service has no effect on pages that were allocated with the `PageFixed` flag.

PhysIntoV86

Synopsis   Map physical memory into a VM's V86 memory space.

C Prototype
```
unsigned PhysIntoV86(unsigned ulFirstPhysPage, unsigned
hVM, unsigned ulFirstV86Page, unsigned nPages, unsigned
ulFlags)
```

ulFirstPhysPage   The page number of the first physical page to map into the V86 memory space.

hVM   The handle of the VM into which the physical memory is to be mapped.

ulFirstV86Page   The first page of V86 memory where the physical memory is to be mapped.

nPages   The number of pages to be mapped. The range of pages specified by this parameter and *ulFirstV86Page* must be between page 0x0010 and 0x010F, inclusive.

ulFlags   This parameter must be zero.

Return Value   If successful, this service returns a nonzero value. If this service fails, it returns zero.

Comments   This call is provided to allow a VxD to map a memory-mapped device into V86 memory. In a typical situation, one VM will have access to the device memory, while other VMs will have physical memory mapped to the same locations (mapped with the `MapIntoV86` service) or will have not-present pages mapped to the location (mapped with the `ModifyPageBits` service). Access to the not-present pages causes the VxD's page hook callback to be called so that the VxD can decide which VM will have access to the physical device.

Release_Critical_Section

Synopsis   Decrement the critical section count.

Calling Convention

VMMcall   Release_Critical_Section

ECX   The amount by which to decrement the critical section count.

Return Value   *None.*

Comments   If the critical section count is decremented to zero, the critical section is released. This service is similar to the `End_Critical_Section` service, except that it allows a count to be specified.

Release_Time_Slice

Synopsis   Immediately end the current VM's time slice.

Calling Convention

VMMcall   Release_Time_Slice

Return Value   *None.*

Comments   When a VxD has determined that the VM is not doing any useful work (such as looping while polling the keyboard queue), it calls this service to allow other VMs to execute. The time slicer may temporarily adjust the VM's relative time slice priority as a side effect of calling this service.

Restore_Client_State

Synopsis   Restore saved client registers.

Calling Convention

VMMcall   Restore_Client_State

ESI   The FLAT address of a copy of a client register structure to be restored.

Return Value   *None.*

Comments   This service may be more conveniently used by invoking the Pop_Client_State service macro, which restores the state saved by a previous invocation of the Push_Client_State macro.

The client register structure contains not only the general purpose registers, but all processor state registers, including the interrupt state and processor mode.

Resume_Exec

Synopsis   Resume nested execution of a VM.

Calling Convention

VMMcall   Resume_Exec

Return Value   *None.*

Comments   Before calling this service, the Begin_Nest_Exec or Begin_Nest_V86_Exec service must be called to establish a breakpoint in the VM. Normally, the client instruction pointer is changed (such as with a call to Simulate_Int) before calling Resume_Exec. This service transfers control to the VM and returns when the VM executes the breakpoint.

When this service is called any outstanding events are processed before passing control to the VM. Therefore, it may be useful to call Resume_Exec immediately after calling Begin_Nest_Exec without adjusting the client instruction pointer.

Resume_VM

Synopsis   Decrement a VM's suspend count by 1.

Calling Convention

VMMcall   Resume_VM

EBX   The handle of the VM that is to have its suspend count
               decremented.

Return Value   On success, this service returns with the carry flag
cleared. If the suspend count is 1, and the specified VM is not runable (due
to insufficient physical memory), this service returns with the carry flag
set and does not decrement the count.

Comments   Except in the case just mentioned in the *Return Value,* when
the count is decremented to zero, this service restores the specified VM's
primary scheduler priority. A VxD can suspend a VM and increment its
suspend count by calling the Suspend_VM service.

Save_Client_State

Synopsis   Save client register contents.

Calling Convention

VMMcall   Save_Client_State

ESI   The FLAT address of a buffer of the size of the client reg-
               ister structure that will receive a copy of the current cli-
               ent register structure.

Return Value   *None.*

Comments   This service may be more conveniently used by invoking the
Push_Client_State service macro. See the description of the Re-
store_Client_State service for how to restore the client registers.
      The client register structure not only contains the general purpose
registers, but all processor state registers, including the interrupt state
and processor mode. A VxD cannot simply copy the client register structure
itself and copy it back later: it must use the Save_Client_State and
Restore_Client_State services.

Schedule_Global_Event

Synopsis   Establish a global event callback.

Calling Convention

VMMcall   Schedule_Global_Event

EDX   Reference data to be passed to the callback routine.

ESI   The FLAT address of a callback routine that Windows will call before returning control to any VM. When Windows calls the callback routine, EBX contains the current VM handle, EDX contains the reference data passed to this service, and EBP refers to the current VM's client register structure.

Return Value   On return, ESI contains a handle that may be passed to Cancel_Global_Event.

Comments   This service is intended to schedule events that are not VM specific. This service may be called from a ring-0 interrupt service routine. An interrupt service routine may call this service when it needs to access nonasynchronous VMM services. It establishes the callback, returns from the interrupt, and completes its processing when called back.

Schedule_VM_Event

Synopsis   Establish a VM-specific event callback.

Calling Convention

VMMcall   Schedule_Global_Event

EBX   The handle of the VM for which the event is to be scheduled.

EDX   Reference data to be passed to the callback routine.

ESI   The FLAT address of a callback routine that Windows will call before returning control to the specified VM. When Windows calls the callback routine, EBX contains the specified VM handle, EDX contains the reference data passed to this service, and EBP refers to the current VM's client register structure.

Return Value   On return, ESI contains a handle that may be passed to `Cancel_VM_Event`.

Comments   This service may be called from a ring-0 interrupt service routine. An interrupt service routine may call this service when it needs to access nonasynchronous VMM services in order to take special action before the specified VM executes. It establishes the callback, returns from the interrupt, and completes its processing for the specified VM when called back.

SetDescriptor

Synopsis   Change the contents of a memory descriptor.

C Prototype

unsigned SetDescriptor(WORD *wSel*, unsigned *hVM*, unsigned *ulDesc1*, unsigned *ulDesc2*, unsigned *ulFlags*)

wSel	A selector identifying the descriptor to be changed. If this selector specifies the local descriptor table (LDT), then the *hVM* parameter must be valid.
hVM	If *wSel* specifies the local descriptor table (LDT), this parameter specifies the handle of the VM that is to have its LDT modified. If *wSel* specifies the global descriptor table (GDT), the *hVM* parameter is ignored.
ulDesc1	The value to which the high-order 4 bytes of the descriptor are to be set.
ulDesc2	The value to which the low-order 4 bytes of the descriptor are to be set.
ulFlags	This parameter must be zero.

Return Value   If successful, this service returns a nonzero value. If this service fails, it returns zero.

Comments   Calling the `BuildDescriptorDWORDs` service is a convenient way to create the values for the *ulDesc1* and *ulDesc2* parameters.

SetResetV86Pageable

Synopsis   Modify V86 memory paging characteristics.

C Prototype
```
unsigned SetResetV86Pageable(unsigned hVM, unsigned
ulFirstV86Page, unsigned nPages, unsigned ulFlags)
```

hVM	The handle of the VM that is to have its V86 pages modified.
ulFirstPage	The page number of the first page to be modified.
nPages	The number of pages to be modified. The range of pages specified by *ulFirstPage* and *nPages* must lie below 0x0100 and at or above the page number returned by the GetFirstV86Page service.
ulFlags	The PageSetV86Pageable flag indicates that the specified pages are allowed to be paged in and out. The PageClearV86Pageable flag indicates the normal state of V86 memory pages; the specified pages must not be paged in and out: they are to be locked. Only one flag may be specified.

Return Value   If successful, this service returns a nonzero value. If this service fails, it returns zero.

Comments   If a VxD can guarantee that a range of V86 pages will not be needed at interrupt time and will not be accessed by the page swapper device, then it can improve Windows performance by marking the pages as pageable. The default Windows behavior is to lock all V86 memory pages, since Windows does not know which areas of memory will be required at interrupt time.

A VxD can query the current state of V86 pages by calling the GetV86PageableArray service.

Set_Global_Time_Out

Synopsis   Establish a timeout callback.

Calling Convention
```
VMMcall   Set_Global_Time_Out
```

EAX	The amount of time, in milliseconds, to delay before calling the callback.
EDX	Reference data to be passed to the callback routine.
ESI	The FLAT address of a callback routine that Windows will call after the specified amount of time. When Windows calls the callback routine EBX contains the specified VM handle, EDX contains the reference data passed to this service, and EBP refers to the current VM's client register structure. The ECX register contains the amount of latency, in milliseconds, between the timeout and the call back.

Return Value   If successful, this service returns with the timeout handle in ESI. If this service fails, it returns with ESI set to zero.

Comments   A VxD can cancel a registered callback with the Cancel_Global_Time_Out service.

Although this service works in real time, there may be a delay between the time the specified amount of time passes and the callback is called. The ECX register as passed to the callback contains the relative delay, in milliseconds.

A VxD can establish a timeout in VM-relative time by calling the Set_VM_Time_Out service.

Set_NMI_Handler_Addr

Synopsis   Establish a nonmaskable interrupt (NMI) service routine.

Calling Convention

VMMcall	Set_NMI_Handler_Addr
ESI	A FLAT pointer to the entry point of the NMI service routine. The service routine must be in the VxD's locked code segment. The service routine may not make *any* calls to VMM services (even those normally accessible from a ring-0 interrupt service routine), but instead may only access data in a previously locked data segment. The callback may exit only by JMPing to the previously registered callback service routine. The callback is responsible for preserving all CPU registers and flags.

Return Value   *None.*

Comments   Before calling this service, a VxD must obtain the address of the previous NMI handler by calling the `Get_NMI_Handler` service.

A typical use of this service is for a VxD to determine if its physical device caused the interrupt and, if so, acknowledge its device and set a flag. The flag may then be examined by a callback that was established by a prior call to the `Hook_NMI_Event` service.

Set_PM_Exec_Mode

Synopsis   Force the current VM into protected mode.

Calling Convention

```
VMMcall   Set_PM_Exec_Mode
```

Return Value   *None.*

Comments   If the current VM is in V86 mode, this service puts the VM into protected mode. The segment registers are restored to their protected mode selector values and the protected mode stack and instruction pointers are restored.

If a VxD needs to call protected mode code, it should normally use the `Begin_Nest_Exec` service first, to prepare for nested execution.

Set_PM_Int_Vector

Synopsis   Register a protected mode interrupt service routine (ISR) in the current VM.

Calling Convention

```
VMMcall   Set_PM_Int_Vector
```

EAX	The interrupt number.
CX	The selector of the segment of the ISR.
EDX	The offset of the ISR.

Return Value   *None.*

Comments   Note that the interrupt service routine may be in either a 16-bit or 32-bit code segment. The descriptor referred to by CX determines the segment type.

Although this service affects only the current VM, if called during `Sys_VM_Init` control processing, the interrupt vector value will be copied to each new VM as it is created, and thus be installed in each VM.

A VxD can provide API mapping by creating a protected mode callback with `Allocate_PM_Callback` and setting the protected interrupt vector to the callback with the `Set_PM_Int_Vector` service. When a protected mode application executes the specified interrupt instruction, the VxD is entered via the callback.

A VxD may query the address of a protected mode ISR by calling the `Get_PM_Int_Vector` service.

Set_Time_Slice_Granularity

Synopsis   Set the allocation unit of a time slice.

Calling Convention

VMMcall   Set_Time_Slice_Granularity

EAX   The new allocation unit, in milliseconds.

Return Value   *None.*

Comments   The length of a VM's assigned time slice is a multiple of the value set by this service. A VxD can query the current value by calling the `Get_Time_Slice_Granularity` service.

Set_Time_Slice_Priority

Synopsis   Set the time slice parameters for a VM.

Calling Convention

VMMcall   Set_Time_Slice_Priority

EAX   Time slice flags parameter. The flags may be any combination of the following:

　　　　　　　　VM_Stat_Exclusive—No other VMs may execute while this VM is in the foreground.

                `VM_Stat_Background`—This VM may execute while in the background.

                `VM_High_Pri_Back`—This VM may execute in the background even if the foreground VM has its `VM_Stat_Exclusive` flag set.

EBX	The handle of the VM that is to have its time slice parameters changed.
ECX	The new foreground priority of the VM.
EDX	The new background priority of the VM.

Return Value If successful, this service returns with the carry flag cleared. Otherwise, this service returns with the carry flag set.

Comments The current time slice parameter values can be queried by calling the `Get_Time_Slice_Priority` service.

    The time slice parameters advise Windows on how to distribute execution time among the VMs. It is only advisory and a VxD cannot conclude what the actual effect will be on any VM. To obtain assured temporary exclusive execution within a VM, use the primary scheduler services, such as `Begin_Critical_Section` and `End_Critical_Section`.

Set_V86_Exec_Mode

Synopsis Force the current VM into V86 mode.

Calling Convention

```
VMMcall   Set_V86_Exec_Mode
```

Return Value *None.*

Comments If the current VM is in protected mode, this service puts the VM into V86 mode. The segment registers are restored to their V86 mode values and the V86 mode stack and instruction pointers are restored.

    If a VxD needs to call V86 mode code, it should normally use the `Begin_Nest_V86_Exec` service to prepare for nested execution in V86 mode.

Set_V86_Int_Vector

Synopsis   Register a V86 mode interrupt service routine (ISR) in the current VM.

Calling Convention

VMMcall   Set_V86_Int_Vector

EAX	The interrupt number.
CX	The segment of the ISR. This is a real mode segment value.
DX	The offset of the ISR.

Return Value   *None.*

Comments   Although this service affects only the current VM, if called during Sys_VM_Init control processing, the interrupt vector value will be copied to each new VM as it is created, and thus be installed in each VM.

A VxD can provide API virtualization by creating a V86 mode callback with Allocate_V86_Callback and setting the V86 mode interrupt vector to the callback with the Set_V86_Int_Vector service. When a V86 mode application executes the specified interrupt instruction, the VxD is entered via the callback.

A VxD may query the address of a V86 mode ISR by calling the Get_V86_Int_Vector service.

Set_VM_Time_Out

Synopsis   Establish a VM-time timeout callback.

Calling Convention

VMMcall   Set_VM_Time_Out

EAX	The amount of VM time, in milliseconds, to delay before calling the callback.
EDX	Reference data to be passed to the callback routine.
ESI	The FLAT address of a callback routine that Windows will call after the specified amount of VM time. When Windows calls the callback routine, EBX contains the specified VM handle, EDX contains the reference data passed to this service, and EBP refers to the current VM's client

register structure. The ECX register contains the amount of VM latency, in milliseconds, between the timeout and the call back.

Return Value   If successful, this service returns with the timeout handle in ESI. If this service fails, it returns with ESI set to zero.

Comments   VM time differs from real time in that it represents elapsed time while the VM is running. While a VM is suspended, for example, VM time does not elapse. When a VM has the critical section, VM time elapses in real time.

A VxD can cancel a registered callback with the Cancel_VM_Time_Out service.

There may be a delay between when the specified amount of VM time passes and the callback is called. The ECX register as passed to the callback contains the relative delay, in milliseconds, of VM time.

A VxD can establish a timeout in real time by calling the Set_Global_Time_Out service.

SHELL_Message

Synopsis   Display a Windows message box.

Calling Convention

VMMcall   SHELL_Message

EAX	Message box flags. These flags are identical to the flag values passed to the Windows API MessageBox function. See the Software Development Kit (SDK) for more information about this function.
EBX	The handle of the VM associated with the message event (not necessarily the system VM).
ECX	A FLAT pointer to an ASCIIZ string containing the message text.
EDX	Reference data to be passed to the callback, if ESI is non-zero.
ESI	Either zero to indicate that no callback is desired, or the FLAT address of a callback routine that Windows will call after the user responds to the message box. When Windows calls the callback routine, EAX contains the response from the message box (as in MessageBox), and

EDX contains the reference data passed to this service. The contents of EBP and EBX are indeterminate.

EDI   A FLAT pointer to an ASCIIZ string containing the text for the message box caption. If EDI is zero, (0x00000000) the message box will have a standard caption.

Return Value   If successful, this service returns with the carry flag cleared. If this service fails, it returns with the carry flag set. In either case, the contents of EAX are destroyed.

Comments   This service provides the same functionality as the Windows API MessageBox function.

If this service fails, it may be as the result of insufficient Windows heap memory. If so, a VxD may try to post the message using the SHELL_SYSMODAL_Message service, which relies on pre-allocated structures.

SHELL_Resolve_Contention

Synopsis   Query user to resolve device contention.

Calling Convention

VMMcall   SHELL_Resolve_Contention

EAX   The handle of the VM that currently owns the device.

EBX   The handle of the current VM.

ESI   The FLAT address of an 8-byte ASCII buffer containing the name of the device. This buffer must be padded on the right with spaces.

Return Value   If the user indicated one VM over the other, this service returns with the carry flag cleared. If the user was unable to resolve the contention, this service returns with the carry flag set.

Comments   This service displays a Windows dialog box presenting arbitration options to the user.

A VxD calls this service when it is unable to resolve the conflict of two VMs attempting to access the same device. Some VxDs virtualize the hardware in such a manner that this is not a problem. Others, however, can allow only one VM to have access to the hardware at a time.

The current VM must be one of the VMs that is contending for the device.

SHELL_SYSMODAL_Message

Synopsis   Display a system-modal message box.

Calling Convention

VMMcall   SHELL_SYSMODAL_Message

EAX	Message box flags. The MB_SYSTEMMODAL flag must be set. These flags are identical to the flag values passed to the Windows API MessageBox function. See the Software Development Kit (SDK) for more information about this function.
EBX	The handle of the VM associated with the message event (not necessarily the system VM).
ECX	A FLAT pointer to an ASCIIZ string containing the message text.
EDI	A FLAT pointer to an ASCIIZ string containing the text for the message box caption. If EDI is zero, (0x00000000) the message box will have a standard caption.

Return Value   This service returns the response from the message box (as in MessageBox).

Comments   This service may be used when there is not enough memory in the Windows USER heap for the SHELL_Message service to succeed.

Simulate_Far_Call

Synopsis   Simulate a FAR CALL instruction execution in a VM.

Calling Convention

VMMcall   Simulate_Far_Call

CX	The segment of the target procedure. If the VM is in V86 mode, this must be a real mode segment value. Otherwise, this must be a valid selector.
EDX	The offset of the target procedure. If the target segment is a 32-bit segment, this must be a 32-bit offset.

Return Value   *None.*

Comments   This service accounts for the processor mode (protected versus V86) and the code segment size (USE16 versus USE32).

Note that if the VM is in protected mode and the target procedure is in a 16-bit segment and the current code segment (before the simulated CALL instruction) is a 32-bit segment, the instruction offset (EIP) in the segment must be less than 64K so that the 16-bit routine can successfully return using a 16:16 FAR return address. In other words, the RET frame pushed onto the stack is of the form of the called code segment, not the calling code segment.

Simulate_Far_Jmp

Synopsis   Simulate a FAR JMP instruction execution in a VM.

Calling Convention

VMMcall   Simulate_Far_Jmp

CX	The segment of the target to jump to. If the VM is in V86 mode, this must be a real mode segment value. Otherwise, this must be a valid selector.
EDX	The offset of the target code. If the target segment is a 32-bit segment, this must be a 32-bit offset.

Return Value   *None.*

Comments   This service accounts for the processor mode (protected versus V86) and the code segment size (USE16 versus USE32).

Simulate_Far_Ret

Synopsis   Simulate a FAR RET instruction execution in a VM.

Calling Convention

VMMcall   Simulate_Far_Ret

Return Value   *None.*

Comments   This service accounts for the processor mode (protected versus V86) and the code segment size (USE16 versus USE32) to determine if the RET frame is 16:16 or 16:32.

Simulate_Far_Ret_N

Synopsis   Simulate a FAR RET *n* instruction execution in a VM.

Calling Convention

```
VMMcall    Simulate_Far_Ret_N
```

EAX   The number of bytes to pop after simulating the RET instruction.

Return Value   *None.*

Comments   This service accounts for the processor mode (protected versus V86) and the code segment size (USE16 versus USE32) to determine if the RET frame is 16:16 or 16:32.

Simulate_Int

Synopsis   Simulate an INT instruction execution in a VM.

Calling Convention

```
VMMcall    Simulate_Int
```

EAX   The interrupt number of the interrupt instruction to simulate.

Return Value   *None.*

Comments   If a VxD needs to map an API from a protected mode interrupts to real mode, it should use the Exec_Int service. If a VxD needs to access a real mode API itself, it should use the Exec_VxD_Int service.

   If the VM is in protected mode when this service is called, and there is no protected mode ISR for the specified interrupt, this service changes the VM to V86 mode and simulates a V86 mode INT instruction execution.

Simulate_IO

Synopsis   Decode a VM I/O instruction.

Calling Convention

VMMjmp   Simulate_IO

EAX   If single output instruction, this register contains the value to be output.

EBX   The handle to the current VM.

ECX   The type of I/O operation. The upper 16 bits contain the segment register for a string I/O operation. The lower 16 bits specify instruction-type flags. If all bits are off, the operation is an 8-bit input operation. Otherwise, the 8 bits are defined as follows:

Bit(s)	Description
0–1	*Reserved.*
2	An output operation.
3	A 16-bit operation
4	A 32-bit operation
5	A string I/O operation.
6	A repeated (REPNZ) operation.
7	A 32-bit address-size string operation.
8	The string operation direction is reversed.

Return Value   *This service does not return.* Note the use of the VMMjmp macro.

Comments   This service decomposes complex I/O instructions into single byte-input and byte-output operations. The input parameters to this function are identical to the parameters for the callback established by the Install_IO_Hook service. In fact, a call to this service should be the first thing that a VxD does in an I/O hook callback, after determining that the I/O instruction is more complex than a simple byte-input or byte-output instruction. The decomposition can be made even simpler by using the Dispatch_Byte_IO macro.

Most VxDs will not be interested in the parameters to this service or to the I/O hook callback, but will simply allow this service to decompose the operation into simple byte or word operations. Some VxDs, however, may be able to improve performance by interpreting these parameters on their own.

This service does not return, but instead re-enters the I/O hook callback with simpler parameters, specifically indicating that the I/O operation is single-byte input or output.

Simulate_Iret

Synopsis Simulate an IRET instruction execution in a VM.

Calling Convention
VMMcall Simulate_Iret

Return Value *None.*

Comments This service accounts for the processor mode (protected versus V86) and the current code segment size (USE16 versus USE32) to determine if the IRET frame is 16:16 or 16:32.

Simulate_Pop

Synopsis Simulate a POP instruction execution in a VM.

Calling Convention
VMMcall Simulate_Pop

Return Value The EAX register contains the value popped from the client stack. If the client is executing in a 16-bit segment, the upper 16 bits of EAX are zero.

Comments This service accounts for the processor mode (protected versus V86) and the current code segment size (USE16 versus USE32) to determine if the popped operand is 16 bits (AX) or 32 bits (EAX).

Simulate_Push

Synopsis Simulate a PUSH instruction execution in a VM.

Calling Convention
VMMcall Simulate_Push

EAX   Value to push. If the client code segment is 16 bits, this
                             service pushes 16 bits on the stack (AX). Otherwise, this
                             service pushes 32 bits on the stack (EAX).

Return Value   *None.*

Comments   This service accounts for the processor mode (protected versus V86) and the current code segment size (USE16 versus USE32) to determine if the pushed operand is 16 bits (AX) or 32 bits (EAX).

Suspend_VM

Synopsis   Increment a VM's suspend count.

Calling Convention

VMMcall   Suspend_VM

EBX   The handle of the VM that is to have its suspend count
                             incremented. This handle cannot refer to the system VM.

Return Value   If successful, this service returns with the carry flag clear. If this service fails, it returns with the carry flag set.

Comments   If on entry to this service, the VM's suspend count is zero, the VM is suspended and the suspend count is incremented to 1. All VxDs are sent the VM_Suspend control message indicating that the VM is being suspended.

TestGlobalV86Mem

Synopsis   Query locality of V86 memory.

C Prototype

unsigned TestGlobalV86Mem(unsigned *linV86Memory*, unsigned *nBytes*, unsigned *ulFlags*)

linV86Memory   The low linear address of the V86 memory block to query.

nBytes   The size of the memory block to query.

ulFlags   This parameter must be zero.

Return Value If the entire specified area is global, this service returns 1. If none of the range is global, this service returns zero (0). If the range contains both global and local areas, 2 is returned. If the entire range has global pages, but the range contains one or more instance areas, 3 is returned.

Comments A VxD can use this information in order to optimize certain services. For example, if a request for is issued in one VM, but the interrupt indicating that the data is available occurs while another VM is active, the VxD can complete the data transfer without waiting for the original VM to resume execution.

Test_Cur_VM_Handle

Synopsis Test if the specified handle is for the current VM.

Calling Convention

VMMcall   Test_Cur_VM_Handle

EBX   The handle to query.

Return Value If the specified handle is for the current VM, this service returns with the zero flag set. Otherwise, the zero flag is cleared.

Comments This service may be called during processing of a ring-0 interrupt.

Test_Debug_Installed

Synopsis Test if the system debugger is running.

Calling Convention

VMMcall   Test_Debug_Installed

Return Value If the system debugger is running, this service returns with the zero flag cleared (nonzero). Otherwise, the zero flag is cleared.

Comments This service may be called during processing of a ring-0 interrupt.

Test_Sys_VM_Handle

Synopsis   Test if the specified handle is for the system VM.

Calling Convention

VMMcall   Test_Sys_VM_Handle

EBX   The handle to query.

Return Value   If the specified handle is for the system VM, this service returns with the zero flag set. Otherwise, the zero flag is cleared.

Comments   This service may be called during processing of a ring-0 interrupt.

V86MMGR_Allocate_Buffer

Synopsis   Allocate a portion of the current VM's API mapper translation buffer.

Calling Convention

VxDcall   V86MMGR_Allocate_Buffer

EBX   The handle of the current VM.

EBP   The address of the current client register structure.

ECX   The number of bytes to allocate.

FS:ESI   If the carry flag is set on entry to this service, this is a 16:32 pointer to data that will be copied to the newly allocated translation buffer area.

Carry Flag   If set, copy the data pointed to by FS:ESI to the newly allocated translation buffer. If clear, the contents of the newly allocated buffer are indeterminate.

Return Value   If successful, ECX contains the actual number of bytes allocated and EDI contains the segment:offset address of the allocated area. If this service fails, it returns with the carry flag set.

Comments   This service is intended to be used by a VxD that is mapping an API from a protected mode client to a V86 mode server. On entry to this service, the client must be in protected mode.

Note that this service may indicate success even if the full number of requested bytes were not allocated. After performing API mapping the area should be de-allocated with the `V86MMGR_Free_Buffer` service.

In instances where it is not practical to copy memory, a memory area may be mapped into a V86 address space with the `V86MMGR_Map_Pages` service.

V86MMGR_Free_Buffer

Synopsis   De-allocate a portion of the current VM's API mapper translation buffer.

Calling Convention

VxDcall   V86MMGR_Free_Buffer

EBX	The handle of the current VM.
EBP	The address of the current client register structure.
ECX	The number of bytes to free. This is the value that was returned from a prior call to `V86MMGR_Allocate_Buffer`.
FS:ESI	If the carry flag is set on entry to this service, this is a 16:32 pointer to a buffer that will receive a copy of the contents of the translation buffer area that is being freed.
Carry Flag	If set, copy the data in the allocated translation buffer area to the buffer pointed to by FS:ESI before freeing the area. If clear, the contents of the translation buffer area are discarded.

Return Value   *None.*

Comments   This service is intended to be used by a VxD that is mapping an API from a protected mode client to a V86 mode server. On entry to this service, the client must be in protected mode.

Since the `V86MMGR_Allocate_Buffer` service may not allocate the requested number of bytes, the call to the `V86MMGR_Free_Buffer` service should specify the number of bytes actually allocated, not the number requested.

V86MMGR_Free_Page_Map_Region

Synopsis   Unmap previously mapped pages.

Calling Convention

VxDcall   V86MMGR_Free_Page_Map_Region

ESI   The handle of a map returned by a prior call to V86MMGR_Map_Pages.

Return Value   The contents of ESI are destroyed.

Comments   The unmapped pages are mapped to the system NUL page.

V86MMGR_Get_Mapping_Info

Synopsis   Query API page-mapping parameters.

Calling Convention

VxDcall   V86MMGR_Get_Mapping_Info

Return Value   This service returns the number of pages reserved for global page mapping in the CH register, and the number of pages available for global page mapping in CL.

V86MMGR_Get_VM_Flat_Sel

Synopsis   Obtain an application selector that maps a VM's entire V86 address space.

Calling Convention

VxDcall   V86MMGR_Get_VM_Flat_Sel

EBX   The handle of the VM for which the selector is to be obtained.

Return Value   This service returns a 32-bit data selector that maps all of the VM's V86 memory in AX. The upper 16 bits of EAX are zero.

Comments   The returned selector has a data privilege level (DPL) of VM applications, so a VxD may pass this selector to a protected mode VM application that may use it to access V86 memory.

V86MMGR_Get_Xlat_Buff_State

Synopsis   Query the status of a VM's API translation buffer.

Calling Convention

VxDcall   V86MMGR_Get_Xlat_Buff_State

EBX   The handle of the VM of the translation buffer to query.

Return Value   If the specified VM handle is valid, this service returns the segment of the translation buffer in EAX, the number of available bytes in ECX, and the total size of the buffer in EDX. If the VM handle is not valid, the return value is indeterminate.

Comments   A VxD calls this service to save the current translation buffer information before changing it with the V86MMGR_Set_Xlat_Buff_State service.

   If you are unsure of the validity of the VM handle, validate it with the Validate_VM_Handle service before passing it to this service.

V86MMGR_Load_Client_Ptr

Synopsis   Obtain a ring-0 pointer equivalent to a protected mode client pointer of the current VM.

Calling Convention

VxDcall   V86MMGR_Load_Client_Ptr

AH   The client register structure offset of the segment regis-
                   ter. For example, this value could be Client_ES.

AL   The client register structure offset of the segment regis-
                   ter. For example, this value could be Client_DI.

EBX   The handle of the current VM.

EBP   The FLAT address of the current VM's client register
                   structure.

Return Value   This service returns a 16:32 pointer equivalent in FS:ESI.

Comments   This service is intended to be used by a VxD that is mapping an API from a protected mode client to a V86 mode server. On entry to this service, the client must be in protected mode.

This service converts a client's pointer into a form that a VxD can use. Since a VxD can use client pointers directly, this service primary creates a 16:32 pointer if the client is in 16-bit mode. For a 32-bit client, this service is unnecessary, but this service makes it unnecessary for the VxD to distinguish between the two types of clients.

The register offsets have the same values, but different meanings depending on the mode of the client. If the client is a 32-bit client, and the offset value is `Client_DI`, for example, the EDI client register is used, and not only DI.

V86MMGR_Map_Pages

Synopsis Map the specified buffer into the V86 address space of every VM.

Calling Convention

VxDcall	V86MMGR_Map_Pages
ESI	The ring-0 linear address of the memory area to map.
ECX	The number of bytes to map.

Return Value If successful, this service returns with the carry flag clear. If this service fails, it returns with the carry flag set.

Comments This service is provided to allow a VxD to temporarily map pages into low memory to assist in the translation of an API call. For more long-term mapping of memory into one or more VM's, see the description of the `MapIntoV86` service.

Although a number of bytes are specified in the call to this service, the mapping unit is a 4K page.

The number of pages that may be mapped into the V86 address space is limited. The `V86MMGR_Get_Mapping` info returns the total and available number of pages for mapping.

This service maps the same memory into the same address space of all VMs. If one VM changes the contents of such memory, the change is immediately reflected in all VMs.

This service is relatively slow. If your VxD needs to perform API translation and the V86 service needs a buffer that was created by a protected mode application, the `V86MMGR_Allocate_Buffer` and `V86MMGR_Free_Buffer` services will provide better performance in general than this service.

V86MMGR_Set_Xlat_Buff_State

Synopsis   Specify an alternate API mapping translation buffer.

Calling Convention

VxDcall   V86MMGR_Set_Xlat_Buff_State

EAX	The V86 segment address of the new translation buffer. The upper 16 bits must be zero.
EBX	The handle of the VM that is to have its translation buffer changed.
ECX	The number of bytes not in use by the buffer.
EDX	The total size of the buffer. This value must be less than 10000h.

Return Value   *None.*

Comments   A VxD uses this service to temporarily change the current API translation buffer. Before calling this service, obtain the previous translation buffer parameters with the V86MMGR_Get_Xlat_Buff_State service. A VxD must restore the original translation buffer after mapping the API call.

V86MMGR_Xlat_API

Synopsis   Execute API translation script.

Calling Convention

VxDcall   V86MMGR_Xlat_API

EBX	The handle of the current VM.
EDX	The FLAT address of the script to execute. See the *Comments* below.
EBP	The FLAT address of the client register structure.

Return Value   If successful, this service returns with the carry flag cleared. If this service fails, it returns with the carry flag set. In any case, the contents of the EDX register are destroyed.

Comments   This service is provided to simplify API mapping. Chapter 10 contains a description of this service.

Some of the macros accept registers as parameters. Although the assembler register names are provided, they generally refer to their corresponding client registers. For example, an invocation of the `Xlat_API_Return_Seg` macro may look like this:

```
Xlat_API_Return_Seg   es  ; Convert ES on return
```

The macros provided for the translation script are:

`Xlat_API_Exec_Int`   *intnum*
Perform an INT instruction in the current VM and return from the `V86MMGR_Xlat_API` service.

`Xlat_API_Fixed_Len`   *segreg, offreg, length*
Take the buffer of length *length*, pointed to by the protected mode client *segreg* and *offreg* registers and copy it to the translation buffer. Modify the V86 mode client *segreg* and *offreg* registers to point to the translation buffer.

`Xlat_API_Var_Len`   *segreg, offreg, length_reg*
Take the buffer of the length specified in the protected mode client *length_reg* register, pointed to by the protected mode client *segreg* and *offreg* registers and copy it to the translation buffer. Modify the V86 mode client *segreg* and *offreg* registers to point to the translation buffer and the V86 mode client *length_reg* register to contain the length.

`Xlat_API_Calc_Len`   *segreg, offreg, linfnCalc*
Load FS:ESI with the address specified in the protected mode client *segreg* and *offreg* registers and call the VxD procedure pointed to by *linfnCalc* that will return the length of the buffer in the ring-0 ECX register. Take the buffer of this length and pointed to by the protected mode client *segreg* and *offreg* registers and copy it to the translation buffer. Modify the V86 mode client *segreg* and *offreg* registers to point to the translation buffer. The procedure pointed to by *linfnCalc* will preserve all registers except ECX.

`Xlat_API_ASCIIZ`   *segreg, offreg*
Take the ASCIIZ string pointed to by the protected mode client *segreg* and *offreg* registers and copy it to the translation buffer. Modify the V86 mode client *segreg* and *offreg* registers to point to the translation buffer.

`Xlat_API_Jmp_To_Proc` *linfnProc*
Terminate the script and jump to the procedure specified by *linfnProc*. When this macro is used, the call to the `V86MMGR_Xlat_API` service

will not return. Do not, however, use the `VxDjmp` macro to call this service, since another script entry may fail and return before this entry is reached.

`Xlat_API_Return_Ptr`   *segreg, offreg*

Modify the behavior of the `Exec_Int` macro execution so that after it returns from the VxD interrupt, it maps the protected mode client *segreg* and *offreg* registers so that they point to the same address referred to by the V86 mode client *segreg* and *offreg* registers. The protected mode client *offreg* value may be different from the V86 mode client *offreg* value. A VxD uses this macro to map a returned pointer from a V86 mode service to a protected mode client.

`Xlat_API_Return_Seg`   *segreg, offreg*

Modify the behavior of the `Exec_Int` macro execution so that after it returns from the VxD interrupt, it maps the protected mode client *segreg* register so that it points to the same address referred to by the corresponding V86 mode client register. A VxD uses this macro to map a returned segment register from a V86 mode service to a protected mode client.

Validate_VM_Handle

Synopsis   Test if a value is a valid VM handle.

Calling Convention

```
VMMcall   Validate_VM_Handle
EBX              The value to test.
```

Return Value   If the specified value is a valid VM handle, this service returns with the carry flag clear. Otherwise, this service returns with the carry flag set.

Comments   This service may be called during the processing of a ring-0 interrupt.

VDMAD_Default_Handler

Synopsis   Default callback routine for DMA virtualization.

Calling Convention

VxDjmp   VDMAD_Default_Handler

EAX   A DMA handle.

EBX   A VM handle.

Return Value *This service does not return.* Note the use of the VxDjmp macro.

Comments A DMA virtualization callback (see VDMAD_Virtualize_Channel) jumps to this service if it determines that the default DMA virtualization logic is satisfactory.

VDMAD_Copy_From_Buffer

Synopsis Copy data from a physical DMA buffer into a linear region.

Calling Convention

VxDcall   VDMAD_Copy_From_Buffer

EBX   A buffer ID returned from a prior call to VDMAD_Request_Buffer or VDMAD_Get_Region_Info.

ESI   The FLAT ring-0 destination address of the copy.

EDI   The source offset within the physical DMA buffer.

ECX   The number of bytes to copy.

Return Value If successful, this service returns with the carry flag cleared. Otherwise, the carry flag is set and AL contains 0Ah to indicate that the buffer ID is invalid, or 0Bh to indicate that the requested copy exceeds the limits of the specified DMA buffer.

Comments A VxD typically calls this service after performing a read-from-device/write-to-memory transfer. This service and its error return codes correspond to the V86 mode virtual DMA services function 810Ah

---

VDMAD_Copy_To_Buffer

Synopsis Copy data from a linear region into a physical DMA buffer.

Calling Convention

VxDcall   VDMAD_Copy_From_Buffer

EBX   A buffer ID returned from a prior call to VDMAD_Re-
                       quest_Buffer or VDMAD_Get_Region_Info.

ESI   The FLAT ring-0 destination address of the copy.

EDI   The source offset within the DMA buffer.

ECX   The number of bytes to copy.

Return Value   If successful, this service returns with the carry flag
cleared. Otherwise, the carry flag is set and AL contains 0Ah to indicate
that the buffer ID is invalid, or 0Bh to indicate that the requested copy
exceeds the limits of the specified DMA buffer.

Comments   A VxD calls this service before performing a read-from-mem-
ory/write-to-device transfer. This service and its error return codes correspond to the V86 mode virtual DMA services function 8109h.

VDMAD_Disable_Translation

Synopsis   Increment disable-translation count for the specified DMA
channel.

Calling Convention

VxDcall   VDMAD_Disable_Translation

EAX   The handle of the DMA channel as returned from a prior
                       call to VDMAD_Virtualize_Channel.

EBX   The handle of the VM that is to have its DMA channel dis-
                       able-translation count incremented.

Return Value   If successful, this service returns with the carry flag clear.
If this service fails (because the disable-count overflowed) it returns with
the carry flag set.

Comments   Some clients will expect to program physical addresses into
the DMA hardware. If so, DMA address translation must be disabled first.
When the disable-count is nonzero, DMA translation is disabled. To decrement the count, call the VDMAD_Enable_Translation service.
    This service and its return values correspond to the V86 mode virtual
DMA services function 810Bh.

VDMAD_Enable_Translation

Synopsis   Decrement the disable-translation count for a DMA channel.

Calling Convention

VxDcall   VDMAD_Enable_Translation

EAX   The handle of the DMA channel as returned from a prior call to VDMAD_Virtualize_Channel.

EBX   The handle of the VM that is to have its DMA channel disable-translation count decremented.

Return Value   If successful, this service returns with the carry flag clear and, if the count is decremented to zero, the zero flag is clear (nonzero indication). When the count is decremented to zero, DMA translation is re-enabled for the VM. If this service fails (because translation is already enabled) it returns with the carry flag set.

Comments   To increment the disable-translation count, call the VDMAD_Disable_Translation service.

This service and its return values correspond to the V86 mode virtual DMA services function 810Ch.

VDMAD_Get_EISA_Adr_Mode

Synopsis   Query the EISA DMA mode for a specified channel.

Calling Convention

VxDcall   VDMAD_Get_EISA_Adr_Mode

EAX   The DMA channel number or the DMA handle as returned from a prior call to VDMAD_Virtualize_Channel.

Return Value   The indication for the channel is returned in the CL register (the remaining bits of ECX are destroyed):

Value	Transfer Width	Transfer Count	Transfer Address
0	8 bits	Bytes	Byte offset
1	16 bits	Words	Word offset
2	32 bits	Bytes	Byte offset
3	16 bits	Bytes	Byte offset

Comments With normal standard industry standard architecture (ISA) hardware, DMA channels 1 through 3 are for 8-bit DMA transfers and DMA channels 4 through 7 are for 16-bit transfers (channel 0 is unavailable). The transfer width can be changed on a per-channel basis for EISA hardware with the `Set_EISA_Adr_Mode` service. If the values were never changed from a VxD, this service returns the configuration as reported by the `EISADMA` switch in the Windows SYSTEM.INI initialization file. It is the user's responsibility for the value in SYSTEM.INI to correspond to the actual hardware configuration.

VDMAD_Get_Region_Info

Synopsis Query DMA buffer parameters.

Calling Convention

VxDcall	VDMAD_Get_Region_Info
EAX	The handle of the DMA channel to query as returned from a prior call to VDMAD_Virtualize_Channel.

Return Value If the DMA handle is valid, BL contains the buffer ID; BH is zero if the pages are not locked, or nonzero if locked; ESI is a FLAG ring-0 pointer to the buffer_s linear region; and ECX is the size, in bytes of the buffer. If the DMA handle is not valid, the results are indeterminate.

VDMAD_Get_Virt_State

Synopsis Query the current state of a virtual DMA channel.

Calling Convention

VxDcall	VDMAD_Get_Virt_State
EAX	The handle of the DMA channel to query as returned from a prior call to VDMAD_Virtualize_Channel.
EBX	The handle of the VM that is to have its virtual DMA channel queried.

Return Value If translation is enabled for the specified channel, this service returns the high-linear address of the transfer buffer in ESI. If translation is disabled, the physical address of the transfer is returned in ESI.

Regardless of the translation mode, this service returns the number of bytes to transfer in ECX, the DMA mode in DL and, if Micro Channel hardware, the extended DMA mode in DH.

If the DMA handle is invalid, the return value from this service is indeterminate.

Comments   The returned information reflects the current state of the specified virtual DMA channel.

VDMAD_Lock_DMA_Region

Synopsis   Lock the specified linear memory region to contiguous physical memory.

Calling Convention

VxDcall   VDMAD_Lock_DMA_Region

ECX   The size, in bytes, of the region to lock.

DL   Zero (0) if no physical alignment is required, one (1) if to verify 64K-byte alignment of physical memory, or two (2) if to verify 128K-byte alignment.

ESI   The linear base address of the region to lock.

Return Value   If successful, this service returns with the carry flag cleared and the physical base address of the region in EDX. If this service fails, it returns with the carry flag set, the number of bytes that are lockable in ECX, and an error code in AL. AL is 1 if the specified region is not physically contiguous, 2 if the region crosses a physical-alignment boundary, or 3 if the individual pages could not be locked.

Comments   Memory locked by this service is unlocked by the VDMAD_Unlock_DMA_Region service.

If the physical memory does not need to be contiguous, use the VDMAD_Scatter_Lock service.

This service and its return values correspond to the V86 mode virtual DMA services function 8103h.

VDMAD_Mask_Channel

Synopsis   Suspend DMA activity on the specified DMA channel.

Calling Convention

`VxDcall    VDMAD_Mask_Channel`

EAX   The handle of the DMA channel to suspend as returned from a prior call to `VDMAD_Virtualize_Channel`.

Return Value   *None.* If the DMA channel handle is invalid, the results are indeterminate.

Comments   A DMA channel is unmasked by a call to the `VDMAD_Un-Mask_Channel` service.

VDMAD_Release_Buffer

Synopsis   De-allocate a DMA buffer.

Calling Convention

`VxDcall      VDMAD_Release_Buffer`

EBX   A buffer ID returned from a prior call to `VDMAD_Request_Buffer`.

Return Value   If successful, this service returns with the carry flag clear. If this service fails (due to an invalid buffer ID), it returns with the carry flag set.

Comments   To optimize overall system performance, a VxD should de-allocate a DMA buffer as soon as the DMA activity for the channel is complete.

   This service and its return values correspond to the V86 mode virtual DMA services function 8108h.

VDMAD_Request_Buffer

Synopsis   Allocate a DMA buffer.

Calling Convention

`VxDcall    VDMAD_Request_Buffer`

ECX   The size of the DMA region.

ESI   The linear address of the DMA region.

Return Value   If successful, this service returns with the carry flag clear, the buffer ID in EBX, and the physical address of the DMA buffer in EDX. If it fails, this service returns with the carry flag set and AL contains 05h to indicate that the size of the requested buffer is too large or 06h to indicate that there is no DMA buffer available.

Comments   This is the first call that a VxD makes when virtualizing DMA service. When the DMA activity is complete, the VxD should call the `VDMAD_Release_Buffer` service to release the buffer.

This service and its return values correspond to the V86 mode virtual DMA services function 8108h.

VDMAD_Reserve_Buffer_Space

Synopsis   Specify DMA buffer requirements during system initialization.

Calling Convention

VxDcall	VDMAD_Reserve_Buffer_Space
EAX	The number of 4K pages required.
ECX	The maximum physical address of a DMA transfer. If there is no maximum, this register should be zero.

Return Value   *None.*

Comments   This service is available only during `Sys_Critical_Init` control processing. The default values are specified by the `DMABufferIn1MB` and `DMABufferSize` variables in the Windows SYSTEM.INI initialization file.

VDMAD_Scatter_Lock

Synopsis   Lock the specified linear memory region to noncontiguous physical memory.

Calling Convention

VxDcall	VDMAD_Scatter_Lock
AL	The locking action and type of information to be returned:

Value	Description
0	Page in and lock the memory and fill the returned buffer with the starting physical address of each contiguous region and the size of each region.
1	Page in and lock the memory and fill the returned buffer with page table entries.
3	Same as (1), but do not page in not-present pages.

EBX   The handle of the VM to which the linear addresses correspond.

EDI   The extended DMA Descriptor Structure (DDS) (see below). The DDS is used to pass parameters and to accept the returned results. Before calling this service, the VxD must initialize the `dds_nBytes`, `dds_segBase`, `dds_offBase`, and `dds_numAvail` fields.

Return Value If successful, this service exits with the carry flag clear and the zero flag set. If only a portion of the region was successfully locked, this service exits with the both the carry flag and the zero flag clear.

The EDX register contains the number of page table entries required, the `dds_nBytes` field (see below) indicates the size, in bytes, of the locked region, the `dds_numUsed` field indicates the number of contiguous physical memory regions, and the extended DDS fields are updated.

If this service fails, it returns with the carry flag set.

Comments Note that the carry flag is returned clear if only a partial lock is performed. Memory locked by this service is unlocked by the `VDMAD_Scatter_Unlock` service.

If the physical memory needs to be contiguous, use the `VDMAD_Lock_DMA_Region` service.

The DDS has the following layout:

```
DDStruct  STRUC    ; DMA region descriptor
dds_nBytes     dd  ?   ; Size, in bytes
dds_offBase    dd  ?   ; Base offset
dds_segBase    dw  ?   ; V86 segment or prot-mode selector
dds_bufferID   dw  ?   ; Buffer ID
dds_physBase   dw  ?   ; Physical base address of the region
dds_Extension  dd  ?   ; Beginning of extension area
DDStruct  ENDS
```

```
dds_numAvail   equ (word ptr dds_physBase)
        ; The number of extended entries avail
dds_numUsed    equ (word ptr dds_physBase+2)
        ; The number of extended entries used
```

The format of the extension depends on the type of information requested. If the physical addresses and sizes are returned (AL=0), then the extension consists of a number of structures of the following form:

```
DDXStruct STRUC        ; Extended DMA region descriptor
ddx_physBase  dd  ?    ; Physical base
ddx_nBytes    dd  ?    ; Size, in bytes
DDXStruct ENDS
```

If page table entries are returned, the extension area consists of an array of 4-byte page table entries in hardware page table format.

A virtual driver uses this service to lock linear memory to prepare for a scatter-gather DMA transfer, available with adapters that have their own scatter-gather DMA hardware.

This service and its return values correspond to the V86 mode virtual DMA services function 8105h.

VDMAD_Scatter_Unlock

Synopsis   Decrement lock counts of previously locked linear memory region.

Calling Convention

VxDcall   VDMAD_Scatter_Unlock

EBX   The VM handle passed to the corresponding VDMAD_Scatter_Lock call.

EDI   The DMA Descriptor Structure (DDS) returned from the corresponding VDMAD_Scatter_Lock call. The extended entries are not needed.

Return Value   If successful, this service returns with the carry flag clear. If this service fails (no corresponding lock), it returns with the carry flag set.

Comments   This service decrements the lock count of memory that was locked by a prior call to the VDMAD_Scatter_Lock service. See the description of that service for the layout of the DDS.

This service and its return values correspond to the V86 mode virtual DMA services function 8106h.

VDMAD_Set_EISA_Adr_Mode

Synopsis Set the EISA DMA mode for a specified channel.

Calling Convention

VxDcall   VDMAD_Set_EISA_Adr_Mode

EAX   The DMA channel number or the DMA handle as returned from a prior call to VDMAD_Virtualize_Channel.

CL   The new DMA mode. See the description of the return values from the VDMAD_Get_EISA_Adr_Mode service for valid values.

Return Value *None.*

Comments This service is supported for extended industry-standard (EISA) hardware only.

With normal standard industry standard architecture (ISA) hardware, DMA channels 1 through 3 are for 8-bit DMA transfers and DMA channels 4 through 7 are for 16-bit transfers (channel 0 is unavailable). The current parameters can be queried by calling the Get_EISA_Adr_Mode service.

VDMAD_Set_Phys_State

Synopsis Program the mode of physical DMA hardware for the specified channel.

Calling Convention

VxDcall   VDMAD_Set_Phys_State

EAX   The handle of the DMA channel to program as returned from a prior call to VDMAD_Virtualize_Channel.

DL   The DMA mode.

DH   The extended DMA mode.

Return Value *None.*

Comments This service programs only the DMA hardware mode. The physical base address and length are set by a *prior* call to the VDMAD_Set_Region_Info service.

VDMAD_Set_Region_Info

Synopsis Program the base and limit of physical DMA hardware for the specified channel.

Calling Convention

VxDcall   VDMAD_Set_Region_Info

EAX	The handle of the DMA channel to program as returned from a prior call to VDMAD_Virtualize_Channel.
BL	A buffer ID returned from a prior call to VDMAD_Request_Buffer.
BH	A flag indicating if the pages are locked. If this value is zero, the pages are not locked. If this value is nonzero, the pages are to be locked.
ESI	The ring-0 linear address of the region. This is a high-linear address if the region is in V86 memory.
ECX	The size, in bytes, of the region.
EDX	The physical address to program for the transfer.

Return Value *None.*

Comments Note the inconsistent parameter passed in BL (the buffer ID is normally passed in a 32-bit register).

VDMAD_Set_Virt_State

Synopsis Set the current state of a virtual DMA channel.

Calling Convention

VxDcall   VDMAD_Set_Virt_State

EAX	The handle of the DMA channel to query as returned from a prior call to VDMAD_Virtualize_Channel.
EBX	The handle of the VM that is to have its virtual DMA channel set.

ECX	The transfer size, in bytes.
DL	The DMA mode. The meaning of the channel number bits are changed. DMA_masked indicates that the channel is to be masked. DMA_requested indicates that a DMA operation has been requested.
DH	Extended DMA mode (not for ISA hardware).
ESI	If DMA address translation is enabled, this is the high-linear address of the transfer region. If address translation is disabled, this is the physical address of the transfer region.

Return Value   If translation is enabled for the specified channel, this service returns the high-linear address of the transfer buffer in ESI. If translation is disabled, the physical address of the transfer is returned in ESI.

Regardless of the translation mode, this service returns the number of bytes to transfer in ECX, the DMA mode in DL, and, if Micro Channel hardware, the extended DMA mode in DH.

If the DMA handle is invalid, the return value from this service is indeterminate.

Comments   The returned information reflects the current state of the specified virtual DMA channel.

VDMAD_Unlock_Region

Synopsis   Unlock a DMA transfer region.

Calling Convention

VxDcall	VDMAD_Unlock_Region
ECX	The size, in bytes, of the region.
ESI	The ring-0 linear address of the base of the region to be unlocked.

Return Value   If successful, this service returns with the carry flag clear. If this service fails, it returns with the carry flag set.

Comments   This service unlocks a region that was locked by a prior call to VDMAD_Lock_Region. It is typically called after a DMA transfer has completed and the channel has been masked.

VDMAD_UnMask_Channel

Synopsis   Enable DMA activity on the specified DMA channel.

Calling Convention

VxDcall   VDMAD_UnMask_Channel

EAX   The handle of the DMA channel to enable as returned
                   from a prior call to VDMAD_Virtualize_Channel.

Return Value   *None.* If the DMA channel handle is invalid, the results
are indeterminate.

Comments   A DMA channel is masked by calling the VDMAD_Mask_
Channel service.

VDMAD_Virtualize_Channel

Synopsis   Disable default DMA channel virtualization.

Calling Convention

VxDcall   VDMAD_Virtualize_Channel

EAX   The DMA channel for which default virtualization is to be
                   changed.

ESI   The FLAT address of a callback routine that Windows will
                   call whenever a VM changes the state of a virtual DMA
                   channel. When Windows calls the callback routine, EAX
                   contains the DMA handle and EBX contains the handle of
                   the VM. If this parameter is zero, no callback is registered
                   and the DMA channel is disabled. The callback routine
                   need only preserve EBP and the stack and segment regis-
                   ters; all other registers need not be preserved.

Return Value   If successful, this service returns with the carry flag clear
and the DMA handle in EAX. If this service fails, it returns with the carry
flag set.

Comments   A VxD claims ownership of a DMA channel by calling this
service. If this service is not called, the virtual DMA device (VDMAD) will
virtualize DMA transfers for all channels. A VxD calls this service when it

can improve on performance and capabilities of its virtual device by virtualizing the DMA channel, too.

The callback procedure need not perform all of the steps required for virtualization. If it determines that the default handling of DMA virtualization is satisfactory for a specific DMA transfer, the callback can jump to the default virtualization callback service, `VDMAD_Default_Handler`.

VPICD_Call_When_Hw_Int

Synopsis Call the specified routine when any hardware interrupt occurs.

Calling Convention

```
VxDcall   VPICD_Call_When_Hw_Int
```
Interrupts must be disabled when calling this service.

ESI   The FLAT address of a callback routine that Windows will call on every hardware interrupt. When Windows calls the callback routine, EAX contains the IRQ handle of the interrupt and EBX contains the current VM handle. The callback does not exit, but jumps to the previously installed callback. Since the callback is called for *every* hardware interrupt it should be optimized for speed. The callback is called during interrupt processing, and is limited to the VxD services that it may call.

Return Value On return, ESI contains the address of the previously installed callback.

Comments Only one global interrupt callback may be installed at a time, so this service is responsible for chaining to the previously installed callback.

Interrupts must be disabled when calling this service and remain disabled until the returned callback address is available to the new callback routine.

The services that the callback may call are limited. When called back, the callback may wish to register another callback as with `Schedule_Call_Global_Event` in order to request more complicated services.

VPICD_Clear_Int_Request

Synopsis   Decrement virtual interrupt request count.

Calling Convention

VxDcall   VPICD_Clear_Int_Request

EAX   An IRQ handle obtained from a prior call to VPICD_Vir-
                   tualize_IRQ.

EBX   The handle to the VM for which the count is to be
                   decremented.

Return Value   *None.*

Comments   When the count is decremented to zero, the interrupt signal
is removed. With ISA hardware, the maximum count is one (1). With Micro
Channel and EISA hardware, however, the count may be greater since
these systems allow shared interrupts.
   This service may be called during ring-0 interrupt processing.

VPICD_Convert_Handle_To_IRQ

Synopsis   Query the interrupt request (IRQ) number for a given handle.

Calling Convention

VxDcall   VPICD_Convert_Handle_To_IRQ

EAX   An IRQ handle obtained from a prior call to VPICD_Vir-
                   tualize_IRQ.

Return Value   This service returns the IRQ number in the ESI register.
The results are indeterminate if the value passed in EAX is not a valid IRQ
handle.
   This service may be called during ring-0 interrupt processing.

VPICD_Convert_Int_To_IRQ

Synopsis   Query the IRQ number, if any, mapped to a given interrupt
vector.

Calling Convention

```
VxDcall    VPICD_Convert_Int_To_IRQ
EAX              An interrupt vector number.
```

Return Value   If the given interrupt vector has an IRQ mapped to it, this service returns with the carry flag clear and the IRQ number in the EAX register. Otherwise, this service returns with the carry flag set.

Comments   After a system reset, the system BIOS typically maps IRQ0 through IRQ7 to interrupts 08h through 0Fh. A VM can change this mapping by programming the programmable interrupt controller (PIC). The return from this service returns the current mapping.

This service may be called during ring-0 interrupt processing.

VPICD_Convert_IRQ_To_Int

Synopsis   Query the interrupt number mapped by a given IRQ.

Calling Convention

```
VxDcall    VPICD_Convert_IRQ_To_Int
EAX              An IRQ number (0 through 15).
EBX              The handle to the VM for which the interrupt number is
                 to be queried.
```

Return Value   This service returns the associated interrupt number in the EAX register.

Comments   After a system reset, the system BIOS typically maps IRQ0 through IRQ7 to interrupts 08h through 0Fh. A VM can change this mapping by programming the programmable interrupt controller (PIC). The return from this service returns the current mapping.

This service may be called during ring-0 interrupt processing.

VPICD_Get_Complete_Status

Synopsis   Query the state of a virtual interrupt level.

Calling Convention

```
VxDcall    VPICD_Get_Complete_Status
```

EAX	An IRQ handle obtained from a prior call to VPICD_Virtualize_IRQ.
EBX	The handle to the VM for which the interrupt status is to be queried.

Return Value This service returns status flags in the ECX register (the contents of unspecified bits are indeterminate):

Bit	Description
0	The interrupt has been simulated into the VM, and the VM has cleared the interrupt request, but the VM has not yet returned from servicing the interrupt (typically with an IRET instruction).
1	The virtual IRQ is currently in service.
2	The associated physical IRQ is masked (disabled).
3	The associated physical IRQ is currently in service.
4	The virtual IRQ is masked (disabled).
5	The virtual IRQ is currently asserted into the VM (as with VPICD_Set_Int_Request). It may not be in service, however, if, for example, the interrupt level is masked.
6	The associated physical IRQ is currently asserted.
7	The calling VxD is responsible for having asserted the virtual IRQ.

Comments An interrupt level may be asserted but not in service if, for example, the interrupt is masked at the PIC or if interrupts are disabled in the associated VM.

The VPICD_Get_Status service is faster than this service, but only returns bits 0 and 1 of the status.

VPICD_Get_IRQ_Complete_Status

Synopsis Query virtualization status of a given interrupt level.

Calling Convention

VxDcall	VPICD_Get_IRQ_Complete_Status
EAX	An IRQ number. This value must be from 0 to 15.

Return Value If the interrupt has not been virtualized, this service returns with the carry flag cleared. Otherwise, this service returns with the carry flag set.

In any case, this service returns with the interrupt status flags in the ECX register in the same form as returned by the `VPICD_Get_Complete_Status` service.

Comments A VxD may call this service to determine if another VxD has virtualized an interrupt. On a system that does not support interrupt sharing, only one VxD can virtualize a particular interrupt.

VPICD_Get_Status

Synopsis Query the virtual interrupt state of a virtual interrupt level.

Calling Convention

VxDcall   VPICD_Get_Status

EAX   An IRQ handle obtained from a prior call to `VPICD_Virtualize_IRQ`.

EBX   The handle to the VM for which the interrupt state is to be queried.

Return Value This service returns status flags in the ECX register (the contents of unspecified bits are indeterminate):

Bit	Description
0	The interrupt has been simulated into the VM, and the VM has cleared the interrupt request, but the VM has not yet returned from servicing the interrupt (typically with an IRET instruction).
1	The VM is currently processing the interrupt.

Comments The `VPICD_Get_Complete_Status` service returns the same information that this service does, but is significantly slower. That service returns additional interrupt information.

This service may be called during ring-0 interrupt processing.

VPICD_Get_Version

Synopsis   Query interrupt hardware capabilities.

Calling Convention

VxDcall   VPICD_Get_Version

Return Value

AH   The major version number of the virtual programmable interrupt device (VPICD).

AL   The minor version number of the VPICD.

EBX   Capability flags (the content of unspecified bits is indeterminate):

	Bit	Description
	0	If clear, there is a single PIC with interrupt levels 0 through 7 (XT-style). If set, there are cascaded PICs, with the slave PIC fed into IRQ2 of the master PIC (AT-style).

ECX   The maximum IRQ level supported (typically 07h or 0Fh).

VPICD_Phys_EOI

Synopsis   Acknowledge an interrupt at the physical programmable interrupt controller (PIC).

Calling Convention

VxDcall   VPICD_Phys_EOI

EAX   An IRQ handle obtained from a prior call to VPICD_Virtualize_IRQ.

Return Value   *None.*

Comments   This service issues the PIC EOI command for the specified level. This re-arms a latch in the physical PIC that allows it to recognize subsequent interrupts at that level.

This service takes the interrupt "out of physical service."

This service may be called during ring-0 interrupt processing.

VPICD_Physically_Mask

Synopsis   Disable auto-masking and suppress processing of the specified physical hardware interrupt.

Calling Convention

VxDcall   VPICD_Physically_Mask

EAX   An IRQ handle obtained from a prior call to VPICD_Virtualize_IRQ.

Return Value   *None.*

Comments   This service masks the specified interrupt at the physical PIC. Although the IRQ may be asserted, the PIC will not interrupt the CPU.

   The interrupt may be unmasked by calling the VPICD_Physically_Unmask service, or by the VM if auto-masking (see VPICD_Set_Auto_Masking) is re-enabled.

   This service may be called during ring-0 interrupt processing.

VPICD_Physically_Unmask

Synopsis   Disable auto-masking and enable processing of the specified physical hardware interrupt.

Calling Convention

VxDcall   VPICD_Physically_Unmask

EAX   An IRQ handle obtained from a prior call to VPICD_Virtualize_IRQ.

Return Value   *None.*

Comments   This service unmasks the specified interrupt at the physical PIC. If an IRQ is asserted, the PIC will interrupt the CPU.

   The interrupt may be masked by calling the VPICD_Physically_Mask service, or by the VM if auto-masking (see VPICD_Set_Auto_Masking) is re-enabled.

   This service may be called during ring-0 interrupt processing.

VPICD_Set_Auto_Masking

Synopsis   Allow VMs to control the masking of an associated physical interrupt.

Calling Convention

VxDcall   VPICD_Set_Auto_Masking

EAX   An IRQ handle obtained from a prior call to VPICD_Virtualize_IRQ.

Return Value   *None.*

Comments   The auto-masking capability provides that if any VM unmasks a virtual interrupt, the associated physical interrupt is unmasked. Otherwise, if the interrupt is masked in all VMs, the associated physical interrupt is masked.

This is the initial default state for each IRQ.

This service may be called during ring-0 interrupt processing.

VPICD_Set_Int_Request

Synopsis   Assert the specified virtual interrupt request.

Calling Convention

VxDcall   VPICD_Set_Int_Request

EAX   An IRQ handle obtained from a prior call to VPICD_Virtualize_IRQ.

EBX   The handle of the VM into which the interrupt is to be virtualized.

Return Value

EAX   An IRQ handle obtained from a prior call to VPICD_Virtualize_IRQ.

EBX   The VM handle of the VM for which the interrupt request is to be asserted.

Comments   This service asserts the virtual IRQ signal for the specified VM. This does not mean, however, that the interrupt is "in service." For an interrupt to be in service, the virtual interrupt level must be unmasked in the VM and VM interrupts must be enabled.

If conditions indicate, this service will process VPICD events in the VM before returning. Any callbacks associated with the specified VM may be called before this service returns to the caller.

This service may be called during ring-0 interrupt processing.

VPICD_Test_Phys_Request

Synopsis   Query the physical state of the specified interrupt request level.

Calling Convention

```
VxDcall   VPICD_Test_Phys_Request
```

EAX   An IRQ handle obtained from a prior call to VPICD_Virtualize_IRQ.

Return Value   If the specified interrupt request level is asserted, this service returns with the carry flag set. Otherwise, this service returns with the carry flag clear.

Comments   This service may be called during ring-0 interrupt processing.

VPICD_Virtualize_IRQ

Synopsis   Disable default PIC hardware virtualization.

Calling Convention

```
VxDcall   VPICD_Virtualize_IRQ
```

EDI   The address of an IRQ descriptor (see the following *Comments*).

Return Value   If successful, this service returns with the carry flag clear and the IRQ handle in EAX. If this service fails, it returns with the carry flag set.

Comments   If a VxD does not assume responsibility for an interrupt, the default behavior is determined by the virtual programmable interrupt controller device (VPICD). If an interrupt request level (IRQ) is unmasked when Windows starts, any physical interrupt will be simulated into the current VM. This behavior assumes that the interrupt service routine (ISR) is installed before Windows runs and is global to all VMs. If an IRQ is masked when Windows starts and a VM unmasks it, the VM owns the

IRQ. If a physical IRQ is asserted, it is asserted into the owning VM and is simulated when the VM is dispatched while its virtual interrupts are enabled.

The IRQ descriptor is a structure of the following format:

```
VPICD_IRQ_Descriptor   STRUC
VID_IRQ_Number         dw   ?   ; Typically 0 ... 0Fh
VID_Options            dw   0   ; Or VPICD_Opt_Can_Share
VID_Hw_Int_Proc        dd   ?   ; H/W int callback (reqd)
VID_Virt_Int_Proc      dd   0   ; Virt int callback (opt)
VID_EOI_Proc           dd   0   ; Virt EOI callback (opt)
VID_Mask_Change_Proc   dd   0   ; Mask change callback (opt)
VID_IRET_Proc          dd   0   ; IRET callback (opt)
VID_IRET_Time_Out      dd  500  ; Timeout value (nonzero)
VPICD_IRQ_Descriptor   ENDS
```

The `VID_Options VPICD_Opt_Can_Share` flag indicates that the VxD can share the interrupt. The `VID_IRET_Time_Out` field specifies the amount of time, in milliseconds, that VPICD will wait after simulating an interrupt into a VM before the VM returns from the interrupt. After the specified amount of time, VPICD will assume that the VM has returned from the interrupt, even if the corresponding IRET was not detected.

The remaining fields specify callback procedures. The callback procedures are all entered with physical interrupts disabled, but the callback procedure is free to re-enable them. On entry to the callback, the EAX register contains the IRQ handle and the EBX register contains the handle of the current VM. The callback procedures all return with a RET instruction (not IRET) and must preserve all registers except EAX, EBX, ECX, EDX, ESI, and the flags.

The `Hw_Int_Proc` is the only required callback procedure. The remaining callbacks are optional and their corresponding IRQ descriptor fields may contain zeros. VPICD calls the `Hw_Int_Proc` callback whenever the associated hardware interrupt occurs. This callback is called at ring-0 interrupt time and is limited to the VxD services that it can call. It may call the `Schedule_Global_Event` service if it needs to call more sophisticated VxD service.

VPICD calls the `Virt_Int_Proc` when it simulates the interrupt into a virtual machine. This does not necessarily occur when the interrupt is requested, but occurs when it is dispatched with interrupts enabled and the interrupt unmasked. A VxD may use this callback to boost the time slice or primary scheduler priority of the VM and restore the priority when the VM returns from the interrupt and VPICD calls the `IRET_Proc`.

VPICD calls the `EOI_Proc` when a virtual interrupt is cleared. A VxD may use this callback to delay issuing physical EOI for an interrupt until the owning VM issues the virtual EOI.

VPICD calls the `Mask_Change_Proc` whenever the virtual interrupt is masked or unmasked. On entry to this callback, the ECX register contains 0 if the interrupt is being unmasked (enabled) or nonzero if the interrupt is being masked.

This service may *not* be called during ring-0 interrupt processing.

VSD_Bell

Synopsis   Generate a warning sound.

Calling Convention
```
VxDcall    VSD_Bell
```

Return Value   *None.*

Comments   With the default Windows sound driver, this service returns immediately and begins sounding the warning beep.

VTD_Begin_Min_Int_Period

Synopsis   Specify a minimum timer interrupt period.

Calling Convention
```
VxDcall    VTD_Begin_Min_Int_Period
EAX                The minimum interrupt period, in milliseconds.
EBX                Description
```

Return Value   If successful, this service returns with the carry flag cleared. If the minimum period cannot be achieved, this service returns with the carry flag set.

Comments   Specifying a longer period that the current timer interrupt period has no effect. The normal default timer interrupt period is set to provide optimal performance for Windows. Decreasing this period can have a significant negative impact on Windows performance. The decreased period should be effective for a relatively short amount of time; the original period is restored by a call to `VTD_End_Min_Int_Period`.

VTD_Disable_Trapping

Synopsis Increment the timer I/O port trapping disable count for the specified VM.

Calling Convention

VxDcall   VTD_Disable_Trapping

EBX   The handle of the VM for which the count is to be incremented.

Return Value *None.*

Comments When the count changes from zero to one, the port virtualization is removed and VMs have direct access to the physical I/O ports.

A VxD calls this service when it determines that a VM client is frequently accessing the timer ports for read-only access. Since port virtualization is costly, calling this service can improve system performance. Trapping is re-enabled by calling the VTD_Enable_Trapping service.

VTD_Enable_Trapping

Synopsis Decrement the timer I/O port trapping disable count for the specified VM.

Calling Convention

VxDcall   VTD_Enable_Trapping

EBX   The handle of the VM for which the count is to be decremented.

Return Value *None.*

Comments When the count reaches zero, timer port access is virtualized. The count is incremented by a call to VTD_Disable_Trapping.

VTD_End_Min_Int_Period

Synopsis   Cancel a reduced minimum timer interrupt period.

Calling Convention

VxDcall   VTD_End_Min_Int_Period

EAX   The same minimum interrupt period specified in a prior call to VTD_Begin_Min_Int_Period.

Return Value   If successful, this service returns with the carry flag cleared. If the minimum period could not be achieved, this service returns with the carry flag set.

Comments   This service cancels a previous request to decrease the minimum timer interrupt period as specified by a call to VTD_Begin_Min_Int_Period.

VTD_Get_Interrupt_Rate

Synopsis   Query the current timer interrupt period (*not the rate*).

Calling Convention

VxDcall   VTD_Get_Interrupt_Rate

Return Value   This service returns the timer interrupt period, in milliseconds, in the EAX register.

VTD_Get_Version

Synopsis   Query the range of timer interrupt periods allowed.

Calling Convention

VxDcall   VTD_Get_Version

Return Value   This service returns the major version number of VTD in AH, the minor version number in AL, the smallest allowed interrupt period, in milliseconds, in the EBX register and the largest allowed interrupt period, in milliseconds, in the ECX register.

Wake_Up_VM

Synopsis   Restore a VM's time slice priority.

Calling Convention

VxDcall   Wake_Up_VM

EBX   The handle of the VM that is to have its time slice priority
                    restored.

Return Value   *None.*

Comments   This service restores the time slice priority of a VM that was
given deferred priority as a result of a call to the Release_Time_Slice
service.

APPENDIX

G

Japanese Printer Escapes

This appendix lists the printer escapes that apply to the Japanese version of Windows, also known as Kanji Windows. If you are developing a printer driver that will support Gaiji characters, then you will want to support these escapes. Providing all of the information required to support Kanji Windows is beyond the scope of this book, but this appendix is provided for reference.

I should warn you that these interfaces are extremely unconventional, so read the definitions carefully. In particular, note that the use of the *lpInputData* parameter to the `Control` function is not used as a pointer, but contains the value of the parameter (or parameters) itself.

Some of these escapes are highly version specific and may not be supported under future releases of Windows. Refer to the Windows DDK documentation or Microsoft Japan for the most current information.

GAIJIAREASIZE/#2577

Synopsis   Return the number of Gaiji areas that may be simultaneously allocated.

Parameters

lpInData   *Not used.*
lpOutData   *Not used.*

Return Value   *None.*

Description   This escape returns the number of Gaiji areas that may be simultaneously allocated.

GAIJIFONTSIZE/#2576

Synopsis   Return the size of a character in the standard Kanji font.

Parameters

lpInData   *Not used.*

lpOutData   A **POINT** structure that contains the dimensions specified in device coordinates.

Return Value   *None.*

Description   This escape returns the dimensions of a character in the standard Kanji font for the device. The dimensions are specified in device coordinates. Typical values are 16×16 and 24×24.

GAIJILOCALCLOSE/#2582

Synopsis   De-allocate a local Gaiji area.

Parameters

lpInData   Unlike most other escapes in Windows, this is *not* a pointer, but is a 32-bit value. The low 16 bits may be ignored. The high 16 bits contain the handle that was returned from the **GAIJILOCALOPEN** escape.

lpOutData   *Not used.*

Return Value   This function returns nonzero for success, and zero for failure.

Description   This escape de-allocates a Gaiji area previously allocated by a GAIJILOCALOPEN escape.

GAIJILOCALOPEN/#2581

Synopsis   Allocate a local Gaiji area.

Parameters

lpInData   *Not used.*
lpOutData   *Not used.*

Return Value   This function returns a nonzero handle to indicate success, or zero to indicate failure.

Description   This escape allocates a local Gaiji area and returns a handle to the newly allocated area.

GAIJILOCALRESTORE/#2585

Synopsis   Restore the saved copy of a local Gaiji area.

Parameters

lpInData   Unlike most other escapes in Windows, this is *not* a pointer, but is a 32-bit value. The low 16 bits contain the memory handle that was returned by the GAIJILOCALSAVE escape. The high 16 bits contain the handle returned from the GAIJILOCALOPEN escape.

lpOutData   *Not used.*

Return Value   The number of free Gaiji areas, plus one.

Description   This function restores a Gaiji area that was saved by a previous GAIJILOCALSAVE escape.

GAIJILOCALSAVE/#2584

Synopsis   Save a copy of a local Gaiji area.

Parameters

lpInData   Unlike most other escapes in Windows, this is *not* a
                          pointer, but is a 32-bit value. The low 16 bits contain
                          the memory allocation flags, as expected by the Win-
                          dows API `GlobalAlloc` function. The high 16 bits
                          contain the handle returned from the GAIJILOCAL-
                          OPEN escape.

lpOutData   *Not used.*

Return Value   The global memory handle that refers to the save area.

Description   This function allocates global memory, using the flags
passed in *lpInData*, and copies the specified local Gaiji area into the newly
allocated memory. The data stored in the save area are device specific.

GAIJILOCALSETFONT/#2583

Synopsis   Set the Gaiji area and return its Shifted-JIS code.

Parameters

lpInData   Unlike most other escapes in Windows, this is *not* a
                          pointer, but is a 32-bit value. The low 16 bits contain
                          a handle to the monochrome bitmap (`HBITMAP`) that
                          contains the Gaiji image. The high 16 bits contain
                          the handle returned from the GAIJILOCALOPEN
                          escape.

lpOutData   The address of a buffer that will receive the Shifted-
                          JIS code.

Return Value   *None.*

Description   This function sets the image for a local Gaiji character and
returns its Shifted-JIS code. The bitmap has the same dimensions
returned from the GAIJIFONTSIZE escape.

GAIJISYSTEMGETFONT/#2578

Synopsis   Return the image from a system Gaiji area and its Shifted-JIS code.

Parameters

lpInData   Unlike most other escapes in Windows, this is *not* a pointer, but is a 32-bit value. The low 16 bits contain a handle to the monochrome bitmap (HBITMAP) that will receive the Gaiji font pattern. The image data area pointer must be valid and must be large enough to receive the bitmap data. The high 16 bits of *lpInData* contain the handle returned from the GAIJILOCALOPEN escape.

lpOutData   The address of a buffer that will receive the Shifted-JIS code.

Return Value   *None.*

Description   This function retrieves the image for a system Gaiji area and its Shifted-JIS code. The bitmap has the same dimensions returned from the GAIJIFONTSIZE escape.

GAIJISYSTEMSETFONT/#2579

Synopsis   Set the image for a system Gaiji area and return its Shifted-JIS code.

Parameters

lpInData   Unlike most other escapes in Windows, this is *not* a pointer, but is a 32-bit value. The low 16 bits contain a handle to the monochrome bitmap (HBITMAP) that contains the image for the Gaiji character. The high 16 bits contain the handle returned from the GAIJILOCALOPEN escape.

lpOutData   The address of a buffer that will receive the Shifted-JIS code.

Return Value   *None.*

Description   This function sets the image for a system Gaiji area and returns its Shifted-JIS code. The bitmap has the same dimensions returned from the GAIJIFONTSIZE escape.

GAIJITOCODE/#2580

Synopsis   Return the Shifted-JIS code for the specified Gaiji area.

Parameters

lpInData	Unlike most other escapes in Windows, this is *not* a pointer, but is a 32-bit value. The low 16 bits are not used. The high 16 bits contain the handle returned from the GAIJILOCALOPEN escape.
lpOutData	The address of a buffer that will receive the Shifted-JIS code.

Return Value   This function returns a nonzero handle to indicate success, or zero to indicate failure.

Description   This function returns the Shifted-JIS code for the specified Gaiji area.

TTYMODE / #2560

Synopsis   Use the default font of the printer.

Parameters

lpInData	*Not used.*
lpOutData	*Not used.*

Return Value   *None.*

Description   This escape signals the device driver that the FONTINFO information passed to the driver routines should be ignored. Instead, the driver should use the hardware's internal Kanji font. The application assumes that the width of Romaji characters are half the width of Kanji characters.

   You should be aware that older applications may issue escape #15 instead of #2560 to perform this function. You should not, however, process escape #15, since the Windows GDI will translate this escape for you.

APPENDIX

H

Recommended Reading

To help with your device-driver development efforts, you may want to refer to some of the following books. For more timely information, you can also contact many experts in the field through one of the popular electronic information services, such as BIX or CompuServe.

Adobe Systems Inc. *PostScript Language Reference Manual,* 2d ed. Reading, Mass.: Addison-Wesley Publishing Company, 1990.
> *The standard for the PostScript language.*

Brown, Ralph, and Kyle, Jim. *PC Interrupts: A Programmer's Reference to BIOS, DOS, and Third-Party Calls.* Reading, Mass.: Addison-Wesley Publishing Company, 1990.
> *Undoubtedly the most comprehensive list of interrupt services ever compiled, this list has at its roots a similar list that has been circulated and expanded on the Usenet for years.*

Foley, James, van Dam, Andries, Feiner, Steven, *et al. Computer Graphics: Principles and Practices,* 2d ed. Reading, Mass.: Addison-Wesley Publishing Company, 1990.
> *This book is a necessity for any developer of graphic display devices or drivers. It provides much of the underlying theory for graphics displays and drivers.*

Intel Corp. *386 DX Programmer's Reference Manual.* 1990.

> *Although this book is "just the facts," it is an essential reference for those working with the 386 instruction set in general, and virtual 8086 mode in particular.*

Intel Corp. *486 Microprocessor Programmer's Reference Manual.* 1990.

> *Although the differences between the 386 and 486 instruction sets are small, simply understanding and using the 486* BSWAP *instruction when appropriate can mean a big difference in performance in bitmapped graphics functions.*

Petzold, Charles. *Programming in Windows: The Microsoft Guide to Writing Applications for Windows 3,* 2d ed. Redmond, Wash.: Microsoft Press, 1990.

> *In its own words, "the essential reference." There is probably no better way to learn Windows programming than by going through this book chapter by chapter and working through the examples. Charles Petzold has also had a regular column in* PC Magazine *on Windows programming for years. Back issues of this magazine can be invaluable. You can speak to Charles directly on CompuServe in the Ziff-Net "Programming" forum.*

Richter, Jeffrey. *Windows 3: A Developer's Guide.* Redwood City, Calif.: M&T Books, 1991.

> *This book is for the Windows programmer who wants to go beyond the basic aspects of Windows programming. The chapters on printer setup and message hooks will be of particular interest to device-driver developers.*

Rubenstein, Richard. *Digital Typography: An Introduction to Type and Composition for Computer System Design.* Reading, Mass.: Addison-Wesley Publishing Company, 1988.

> *A must-read if you intend to create your own fonts for general use or for your display or printer driver. Otherwise, an excellent reference on document layout.*

Schulman, Andrew, *et al. Undocumented DOS: A Programmer's Guide to Reserved MS-DOS Functions and Data Structures.* Reading, Mass.: Addison-Wesley Publishing Company, 1990.

> *Unfortunately, much of the information that we need in order to write device drivers for Windows and DOS remains undocumented. This book helps fill many gaps and is the most complete collection of otherwise undocumented DOS functions that I have seen.*

Schulman, Andrew, and Maxey, David. *Undocumented Windows: A Programmer's Guide to the Reserved Microsoft Windows API Functions.* Reading, Mass.: Addison-Wesley Publishing Company, 1990.

> *Forthcoming from Addison-Wesley in Spring 1992.*

Smith, Ross. *Learning PostScript: A Visual Approach.* Berkeley, Calif.: Peachpit Press, 1990.

> *This book, along with a display PostScript interpreter such as LaserGo's GoScript, provides an ideal way to learn the basics of the language.*

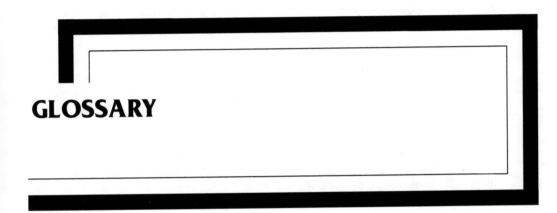

GLOSSARY

386 enhanced mode The protected mode of Windows that supports the 80386 and 80486 processors, virtual machines, and memory paging, but does not work with the 80286 processor or a system that has less than 2MB of available memory. This mode is specified on the command line by "win /3."

Address line 20 (A20) The twenty-first address line on the memory bus of an IBM PC/AT compatible system. The address lines on such a system are designated as A0 though A23. A PC/XT compatible system has only twenty address lines, designated A0 through A19.

Address line 20 mode (A20 mode) A special hardware mode of a PC/AT compatible system that indicates whether A20 reflects the actual address generated by the CPU (enabled) or if it is forced by external hardware to always appear as zero (disabled). A20 mode indicates if memory at the 1M boundary wraps to location zero when the CPU is running in real mode. A20 must be enabled in order for the CPU to execute in protected mode, but is often disabled in real mode to provide 8086 compatiblity.

Alias A selector to a memory segment that already has a different selector that references the same memory. A program can create a code alias to a data segment in order to execute code in a data segment. Due to memory discarding, it is not normally advisable to create a data alias to a code segment.

Application mode See **User mode**.

Band A logical portion of a print page that is separated by the order in which an application prints it. Bands may be separated by their physical location on a page, or by the type of information contained in a band, such as graphic or text information.

Brute functions The Windows GDI driver support functions that may use slow and unsophisticated methods to perform their operation. They are implemented by the GDI display driver and are accessible to printer drivers by the GDI support functions whose names begin with "dm."

Callback A procedure registered via an API that can be called back at a later time. Examples of callbacks are event procedures, event service routines, and post routines. Virtual device drivers often use callbacks to notify them when certain system events occur.

Current privilege level (CPL) The current privilege level of the CPU. The CPL is equivalent to the DPL of the code segment in which the CPU is currently executing.

Data privilege level (DPL) The privilege level of a memory segment. For a memory access to succeed, the DPL must be greater than or equal to the requested privilege level (RPL) specified by an accessing selector.

Dead key A keyboard key normally found on non-U.S. keyboards that specifies a diacritic mark to modify the following keystroke. Since it normally produces no immediate output, the key has the appearance of being inactive.

Descriptor table A table maintained by the Windows kernel that describes which areas of memory are directly accessible to the processor. A program accesses memory by specifying a selector and an offset; the selector specifies which descriptor table describes the target memory object.

Device descriptor block (DDB) A structure in a virtual device driver that describes the interface to the VxD. The DDB is the only label exported from a VxD.

Device driver A distinct program module that is integrated with an operating system to provide a standard interface between an application program and an external device.

Dispatch Transfer control to a 386 enhanced mode Windows VM. The primary scheduler and the time slicer determine which VM is to be dispatched. The dispatcher actually transfers control to the VM.

Display grabber A separately loaded portion of a display driver that is responsible for saving and restoring the video hardware context when the Windows session changes from foreground to background. The 386 enhanced mode display grabber has the additional responsiblity of capturing user-specified areas of a VM display, when it appears as a window in the Windows graphical session.

Event procedure A Windows-internal procedure that is called when certain specific system events occur. The keyboard driver calls an event procedure for each scan code received from the keyboard. The mouse driver calls an event procedure whenever the mouse moves or a button is pressed.

Event service routine A procedure that the Novell IPX software calls when it receives a response to an outstanding request (see also Post routine).

Execution priority A priority level assigned to a VM that the primary scheduler uses to determine which VM will execute next.

Expanded memory Special banked memory that is addressed below 1M and usually above 640K. Expanded memory allows a real mode application to access more than 1M of memory by banking expanded memory into its assigned addresses.

Extended memory All physical memory above 1M, including the high memory area. Except for the HMA, extended memory is not accessible when the processor is executing in real mode.

FLAT memory model A manner of organizing program memory so that there are no segments, all memory is addressed with a single 32-bit number, and the distance between objects is obtained by a simple arithmetic calculation.

Frame see **Page frame.**

Global descriptor table A descriptor table of which there is normally only one active copy in the system, and which is normally accessible to all applications (provided that they have sufficient ring-privilege).

Global heap A portion of memory the Windows kernel uses to allocate memory objects from.

Graphics device interface (GDI) The Windows application programming interface that provides a device-independent graphical interface to applications. Also, the portion of the Windows environment that supports that interface. The device independence is achieved by cooperation between the GDI portion of Windows and a GDI driver.

High memory area (HMA) The range of memory from 1M to 1M+64K–17, inclusive, which is accesible from real mode when address line 20 is enabled.

Hot key A keystroke sequence that causes special system action. Windows hot keys are typically combined with the Ctrl and Alt keys.

Interrupt descriptor table (IDT) A table in physical memory that specifies where the CPU is to transfer control when a hardware interrupt or instruction trap is detected when the processor is running in protected mode. The processor's IDT register indicates the actual physical location of the IDT. Entries in the IDT can specify call gates or interrupt service routines.

Interrupt service routine (ISR) A routine that services an interrupt or processor trap and is normally registered in the processor's interrupt vector table or interrupt descriptor table. An ISR is often referred to as an interrupt handler.

Interrupt vector table (IVT) A table in the first 1024 bytes of physical memory that specifies where the CPU is to transfer control when a hardware interrupt or instruction trap is detected when the processor is running in real mode. Each entry in the table specifies a segment:offset address of the beginning of the service routine for that vector.

I/O privilege level (IOPL) The maximum privilege level from which a program can access I/O ports without restriction. The IOPL is ignored when the processor runs in virtual 8086 mode and I/O port access is restricted by the I/O privilege bitmap (IOPM).

Large-frame mode see **Page frame**.

Limit The 20-bit field in a descriptor that specifies the size of the corresponding memory segment. The value of this field indicates the number of bytes or pages in the segment, minus one. For example, a segment that is 64K bytes long will have a byte limit of 0x0FFFF.

Linear address A 32-bit address that the protected mode CPU memory segmentation logic provides to the CPU memory paging logic. The linear address does not necessarily correspond to a physical memory address, which is determined by the paging logic.

Local descriptor table A descriptor table of which there is normally one copy per task. Windows 3, however, uses one local descriptor table, which is shared among all tasks, allowing any task to freely access (and corrupt) the memory of any other task.

Memory compaction A process performed by the Windows kernel when the system needs more memory than is immediately available. Compaction can take movable memory objects and make them contiguous, providing a larger contiguous free area, and compaction can discard discardable memory objects, directly freeing the memory.

Memory paging See **Paging**.

Offset The lower 16 bits of a 32-bit memory address specified in segment:offset form, which specifies the offset from the base of a memory segment.

Page A fixed-size unit of memory. For the 80386 processor paging hardware, a page is 4096 bytes.

Page fault A processor trap that occurs when the page table entry of a linear address is not present or indicates that there is no corresponding physical memory address. This does not necessarily indicate an error, but can occur normally as a result of paging.

Page frame A fixed-size unit of memory used for expanded memory support. An expanded memory page frame is typically 16K bytes (small-frame mode) but can be larger (large-frame mode).

Page table A CPU structure that indicates the physical memory address of a given linear address.

Paging In one sense, the automatic exchange of fixed-size pages between physical memory and disk providing an application virtual access to more memory than is physically available. This is distinguished from segment swapping, which transfers variable-sized blocks of memory. This term is used in another sense to describe the process of converting a linear address into a physical memory address.

Physical memory Actual random-access memory that is installed and directly addressable by the CPU. The limit of possible physical memory varies by processor. For the 8086 and 80186 processors, the limit is 2^{20} bytes. For the 80286 and 80386SX processors, the limit is 2^{24} bytes. For the 80386DX and 80486 processors, the limit is 2^{32} bytes.

Post routine A procedure that is called by the NETBIOS when a response is received to an outstanding NETBIOS request (see also Event service routine.)

Postfix A method of representing an algebraic operation which, when read from left to right, provides operands before the operator associated with the operands.

For example, the infix notation of (7+3)×5 is represented in postfix notation as 7,3,+,5,×.

Primary scheduler A portion of the 386 enhanced mode Windows kernel that is responsible for establishing which VMs are eligible to run based on their execution priorities. Once a VM is determined to be eligible to run, the time slicer determines how long the VM will run.

Printer driver A device driver that provides the interface between Windows GDI and a serial or parallel communications port. The printer driver converts high-level graphics and text commands into a data stream that is compatible with the specific type of printer it supports.

Privilege rings Levels of CPU system privilege. There are four 386 CPU rings, of which Windows uses two. They are referred to as rings since more privileged levels protect system objects from (and provide the interface to) outer rings.

Protected mode An operating mode of the Intel 80286, 80386, and 80486 CPUs that allows memory protection through the use of memory selectors and descriptors. For the 80386 and 80486, protected mode is required in order to enable the additional memory paging and virtual 8086 mode features of these CPUs.

Raster operation code The portion of a Windows ternary operation code that describes the operation in an encoded form.

Raster operation index The portion of a Windows ternary operation code that describes the operation as an index into a table.

Real mode In one sense, a mode of the processor that does not provide protected addressing or addressing of extended memory. In another sense, a mode of Windows 3.0 and earlier that runs in the real mode of the processor.

Requested privilege level (RPL) The privilege level specified by a memory selector. Before the CPU can load a selector into a segment register, the RPL must be less than or equal to the data privilege level (DPL) specified in the corresponding descriptor entry and the RPL of the selector must be greater than or equal to the current privilege level (CPL). In other words, DPL ≥ RPL ≥ CPL. The RPL of a selector is specified in the two most low-order bits of the selector.

Segment In one sense, a segment is the upper 16 bits of a 32-bit real mode address specified in segment:offset form, which specifies the beginning paragraph of a portion of memory. The term often refers to a portion of memory that is accessible without changing the upper 16 bits of a real or protected mode address. In this latter sense, the sizes of segments are 64K in real mode, but are likely to be smaller in protected mode.

Selector The upper 16 bits of a protected mode address. The selector specifies a descriptor table and index within the table that describes the segment of memory to which the address refers.

Small-frame mode See **Page frame**.

Standard mode The protected mode of Windows that can operate on the 80286, 80386, or 8046 processors, but does not support virtual machines or memory paging. This mode is specified on the command line by "win /s."

Supervisor mode The most privileged level of the CPU. This is often referred to as system mode and corresponds to ring zero.

System drivers In one sense, a system driver is a Windows device driver that provides an interface to standard system hardware components, such as the keyboard and the mouse. In a more specific sense, the Windows system driver provides the interface to even more fundamental system hardware components such as the system timer, the real time clock, and the floating point coprocessor.

System virtual machine The first virtual machine created in Windows 386 enhanced mode and the one in which the Windows graphical environment software executes.

Ternary operation code Generally, a code representing an algorithmic operation that has three input operands. In Windows, a ternary operation code specifies a graphical operation that has three operands consisting of a source bitmap, a pattern, and a destination bitmap.

Time slicer A portion of the 386 enhanced mode Windows kernel that determines how long a VM is to run. It determines this based on the VM's user-visible and user-settable VM time slicer priority in relation to the time slicer priority of other VMs.

Type The field in a memory descriptor that indicates the type of segment it refers to. Among other attributes, the type can indicate whether or not the segment is for code or for data.

User mode Any privilege level other than supervisor mode. Windows uses ring 3 for user mode.

Virtual device driver (VxD) A specific type of Windows device driver that assists 386 enhanced mode Windows in supporting virtual machines. A VxD can simulate external hardware or it can simulate a programming interface accessed by privileged instructions, such as through INT 21h.

Virtual display driver (VDD) A specific type of virtual device driver that virtualizes access to the display device. It cooperates with the Windows display driver operating in the system VM to display VMs in Windows.

Virtual DOS machine See **Virtual machine**.

Virtual machine (VM) A system environment that simulates an IBM PC or PC/AT running in real mode and allows DOS applications and TSRs to execute. This simulation requires the cooperation of an Intel CPU running in virtual 8086 (V86) mode, a system executive to manage low-level CPU virtualization, and virtual device drivers (VxDs) to simulate external hardware.

Virtual 8086 (V86) mode A special mode of the processor that simulates real mode, primarily by changing the addressing mode so that when a segment register is loaded, the segment register refers to the linear address that corresponds to the loaded value times sixteen. Other aspects of V86 mode enable an operating system to create a virtual machine environment.

VM control block A structure associated with each VM that contains VM-specific information about the VM and the state of its VxDs.

VM handle A 32-bit identifier that uniquely identifies a virtual machine. The handle is also the FLAT base address of the corresponding VM control block.

INDEX

Samples available on diskette

To obtain a diskette copy of sample programs, include files, and other useful code, please copy and mail the following order form with a check for $19.95 plus $4.00 to cover Priority Mail™ postage. Include New Jersey or Pennsylvania sales tax, if applicable.

Samples Diskette Order Form

Listings Diskette:	$ 19.95
NJ or PA Sales Tax, if applicable:	
Priority Mail™ Postage & Handling:	4.00
Total:	$

Name: _____

Company: _____

Address: _____

_____

City: _____

State/Province: _____

Zip/Postal Code: _____

Phone: _____

Mail to:

Cherry Hill Software
Meetinghouse Square, Suite 215
Hainesport-Mt. Laurel Road
Marlton NJ 08053

Phone: (609) 983-1414
Fax: (609) 983-4188
E-Mail: 76050.2204@CompuServe.COM